Flash® and PHP Bible

Flash® and PHP Bible

Matthew Keefe

Wiley Publishing, Inc.

Flash® and PHP Bible

Published by
Wiley Publishing, Inc.
10475 Crosspoint Boulevard
Indianapolis, IN 46256
www.wiley.com

Copyright © 2008 by Wiley Publishing, Inc., Indianapolis, Indiana

Published by Wiley Publishing, Inc., Indianapolis, Indiana

Published simultaneously in Canada

ISBN: 978-0-470-25824-8

Manufactured in the United States of America

10 9 8 7 6 5 4 3 2 1

No part of this publication may be reproduced, stored in a retrieval system or transmitted in any form or by any means, electronic, mechanical, photocopying, recording, scanning or otherwise, except as permitted under Sections 107 or 108 of the 1976 United States Copyright Act, without either the prior written permission of the Publisher, or authorization through payment of the appropriate per-copy fee to the Copyright Clearance Center, 222 Rosewood Drive, Danvers, MA 01923, (978) 750-8400, fax (978) 646-8600. Requests to the Publisher for permission should be addressed to the Legal Department, Wiley Publishing, Inc., 10475 Crosspoint Blvd., Indianapolis, IN 46256, (317) 572-3447, fax (317) 572-4355, or online at http://www.wiley.com/go/permissions.

LIMIT OF LIABILITY/DISCLAIMER OF WARRANTY: THE PUBLISHER AND THE AUTHOR MAKE NO REPRESENTATIONS OR WARRANTIES WITH RESPECT TO THE ACCURACY OR COMPLETENESS OF THE CONTENTS OF THIS WORK AND SPECIFICALLY DISCLAIM ALL WARRANTIES, INCLUDING WITHOUT LIMITATION WARRANTIES OF FITNESS FOR A PARTICULAR PURPOSE. NO WARRANTY MAY BE CREATED OR EXTENDED BY SALES OR PROMOTIONAL MATERIALS. THE ADVICE AND STRATEGIES CONTAINED HEREIN MAY NOT BE SUITABLE FOR EVERY SITUATION. THIS WORK IS SOLD WITH THE UNDERSTANDING THAT THE PUBLISHER IS NOT ENGAGED IN RENDERING LEGAL, ACCOUNTING, OR OTHER PROFESSIONAL SERVICES. IF PROFESSIONAL ASSISTANCE IS REQUIRED, THE SERVICES OF A COMPETENT PROFESSIONAL PERSON SHOULD BE SOUGHT. NEITHER THE PUBLISHER NOR THE AUTHOR SHALL BE LIABLE FOR DAMAGES ARISING HEREFROM. THE FACT THAT AN ORGANIZATION OR WEBSITE IS REFERRED TO IN THIS WORK AS A CITATION AND/OR A POTENTIAL SOURCE OF FURTHER INFORMATION DOES NOT MEAN THAT THE AUTHOR OR THE PUBLISHER ENDORSES THE INFORMATION THE ORGANIZATION OR WEBSITE MAY PROVIDE OR RECOMMENDATIONS IT MAY MAKE. FURTHER, READERS SHOULD BE AWARE THAT INTERNET WEBSITES LISTED IN THIS WORK MAY HAVE CHANGED OR DISAPPEARED BETWEEN WHEN THIS WORK WAS WRITTEN AND WHEN IT IS READ.

For general information on our other products and services or to obtain technical support, please contact our Customer Care Department within the U.S. at (800) 762-2974, outside the U.S. at (317) 572-3993 or fax (317) 572-4002.

Library of Congress Control Number: 2008925780

Trademarks: Wiley, and the Wiley logo, and related trade dress are trademarks or registered trademarks of John Wiley & Sons, Inc. and/or its affiliates, in the United States and other countries, and may not be used without written permission. Flash is a registered trademark of Adobe Systems Incorporated in the United States and/or other countries. All other trademarks are the property of their respective owners. Wiley Publishing, Inc., is not associated with any product or vendor mentioned in this book.

Wiley also publishes its books in a variety of electronic formats. Some content that appears in print may not be available in electronic books.

About the Author

Matthew Keefe is a new-media designer and developer, with a strong background in application development for the Web and offline. Originally a full-time graphic artist, he found that much of the programming associated with his design work was being outsourced. Matt quickly learned programming for the web and uncovered a valuable but little-known skill set in this industry, that skill being the ability to build a site and also the ability to powerfully design it. This was preferred by clients because they could do the entire project with one studio.

Matt has worked with companies such as Delphi, PhotoshopCafe, Kineticz Interactive, and Organi Studios to name a few. His work has been published in *How To Wow with Flash* (Peachpit Press) for which he was a contributing author and technical editor. Matt has also recently finished up work as the technical editor for *Essential ActionScript 3* (Adobe Dev Library).

Examples of his work can be found in his personal portfolio at mkeefe.com.

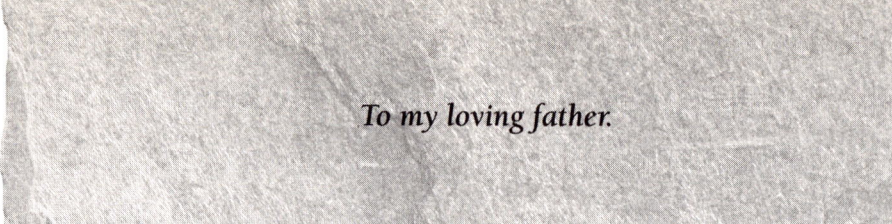

To my loving father.

Credits

Senior Acquisitions Editor
Stephanie McComb

Project Editor
Beth Taylor

Technical Editor
Navid Mitchell

Copy Editor
Kim Heusel

Editorial Manager
Robyn Siesky

Business Manager
Amy Knies

Sr. Marketing Manager
Sandy Smith

Vice President and Executive Group Publisher
Richard Swadley

Vice President and Executive Publisher
Bob Ipsen

Vice President and Publisher
Barry Pruett

Project Coordinator
Erin Smith

Graphics and Production Specialists
Claudia Bell
Jennifer Mayberry
Ronald Terry

Quality Control Technician
Susan Moritz

Media Development Project Manager
Laura Moss-Hollister

Media Development Coordinator
Jenny Swisher

Associate Producer
Shawn Patrick

Proofreading
Christine Sabooni

Indexing
Broccoli Information Management

Foreword

Macromedia . . . errr Adobe Flash is hands down one of the most impressive and powerful tools for any designer when it comes to bringing an experience to a user. And as Flash continues to evolve not just web, for which it got popular, but also offline users with platform developments such as Adobe AIR and the wide range of third-party tools that can be used.

But to a hardcore developer Flash has had a bad rap. Mainly due to the fact that AS 1.0 was an awkward, gawky, and immature language. Compared to other languages popular when AS 1.0 was introduced, it wasn't something to be taken seriously in a developer's eye and rightfully so. But then if Flash is so hindering, why am I even reading a foreword for a book on the subject?

Things have changed, drastically changed. AS 3.0 is here and it is one of the best languages around when understood. AS 2.0 was a step in the right direction, but AS 3.0 has surpassed every Flash developer's dreams. Small file sizes, very solid performance, and even some data handling that rivals Java, so really there isn't a developer who can say it is no longer a concrete language.

And with AS 3.0 a new era of data handling is introduced into Flash. And not only with Flash, but when you start mixing in PHP5, MySQL 5, ASP, AMFPHP, and other methods of handling data, the possibilities open up into a new realm. Data is up for grabs in AS 3.0, and it's only a matter of reading a book like this to apply it. Sockets, xml, web services, and other external data sources allow a Flash developer to get really dirty in a data source and update the content without touching the Flash files again. The benefit is allowing more time to develop an engaging user experience without worrying about repeat edits, a client's future budget, etc. It actually allows a serious Flash developer to continue to work with data sources as they are developed and concentrate on the benefits of finessing the content itself, rather than what the content is at the time of development that can change on a client's whim later on.

Gone are the days that you would build a client's website, have a ton of large swfs, only for them to constantly need updates for photos, copy, catalog items, etc. In this book you will read how to utilize the methods mentioned to broaden your understanding of taking out the last restriction to knowing powerful Flash, updating without ever republishing, opening up an FLA, or worrying if the client sent you the right copy, image, or other asset.

Get rid of the idea that a Flash project is now plagued with an ever-so-changing fla file and embrace the idea of run-time content generation.

Michael Minor
Director of Interactive Media
invertedCreative.com

Acknowledgments

I would like to thank Laura Sinise for helping me to get started. This book would not have been possible without the following people: Senior Acquisitions Editor, Stephanie McComb; Project Editor, Beth Taylor; Copy Editor, Kim Heusel; Technical Editor, Navid Mitchell; and Mary Keefe. I would also like to thank my friends Colin, Philip, Brooke, Frank, Jimmy, and Daz and my cousin Teisha for their huge amount of support. And lastly, I would like to thank my family for their understanding and patience while I was locked away in my office during all hours of the night.

Contents at a Glance

About the Author v
Foreword vii
Acknowledgments ix
Introduction xix

Part I: Understanding the Basics 1
Chapter 1: Getting Started with Flash and PHP 3
Chapter 2: Exploring Flash and PHP 37
Chapter 3: Getting Connected 63
Chapter 4: Working with Data 85
Chapter 5: Interacting with the User 99
Chapter 6: Working with Cookies 113

Part II: Developing Interactive Content 125
Chapter 7: Maintaining Security while Working with User Input 127
Chapter 8: Using Sockets 153

Part III: Extending Flash and PHP 189
Chapter 9: Working with Third-Party Libraries 191
Chapter 10: Using Object-Oriented Programming 219

Part IV: Developing Applications 237
Chapter 11: Developing Basic Applications 239
Chapter 12: Developing Real-World Applications 289
Chapter 13: Using Advanced Real-World Applications 335
Chapter 14: Debugging Applications 381

Part V: Server, Application, and Database Maintenance 393
Chapter 15: Maintaining an Application 395
Chapter 16: Maintaining a Scalable and More Efficient Server 405
Chapter 17: Building Complete Advanced Applications 429

Index 487

Contents

About the Author v

Foreword vii

Acknowledgments ix

Introduction xix

Part I: Understanding the Basics   1

Chapter 1: Getting Started with Flash and PHP 3

Adding Apache to a Web Server 3
    Installing Apache for Windows...4
    Installing Apache for UNIX..9
    Modifying Apache for Windows and UNIX 13
Installing MySQL 14
    Installing MySQL for Windows..14
    Installing MySQL for UNIX 25
    Protecting MySQL 26
Setting up PHP on the Web Server 27
    Installing PHP for Windows 27
    Installing PHP for UNIX 33
Summary 35

Chapter 2: Exploring Flash and PHP 37

Introduction to the Web Server 37
    Working with .htaccess files 37
    Protecting your content 38
    Gathering information about Apache 40
    Using custom error documents...42
Exploring the Basics of PHP 47
    Understanding variables 47
    Working with functions 49
    Understanding control structures 51
    Using type checking in PHP 56

Contents

Exploring the Basics of MySQL 57
    Using statements 57
    Conditions 58
Exploring Flash 59
    Flash IDE 59
    Alternative editors 61
    Flash-enabled devices 62
    Moving forward 62
Summary 62

Chapter 3: Getting Connected 63

Understanding Communications in Flash..63
    Determining the status of PHP 64
    Working with various connection types 65
Connecting Flash to PHP 69
Connecting PHP to MySQL 73
    Determining the status of MySQL 73
    Connecting to MySQL 74
    Bringing it all together 77
Summary 84

Chapter 4: Working with Data 85

Loading Data in Flash..85
    Understanding the classes used to load data 86
    Putting it all together 87
Handling Loaded Data 88
    One-way loading 88
    Two-way loading 88
Loading XML in Flash 89
Working with XML in PHP..92
    Loading XML 92
    Sending XML 93
Loading Images Using PHP 95
    Setting up the image loader 96
Summary 98

Chapter 5: Interacting with the User 99

Form Development Using Flash 99
Creating a Contact Form 101
    Calling the PHP 103
    Contact form event handlers..103
    Mailing in PHP 105
Login Module in Flash 106
    Code skeleton..106
    Login event handlers..107
    Server integration for login module 110
Summary 111

Contents

Chapter 6: Working with Cookies 113
Loading Cookies..113
    Using cookies with PHP 114
    Using cookies in Flash 118
    Discovering the benefits of using PHP cookies 122
Summary 124

Part II: Developing Interactive Content   125

Chapter 7: Maintaining Security while Working with User Input 127
Using Caution with User Input..127
    Safely handling file uploads 128
    Checking for valid input..131
Cleaning User Data...132
    Sanitizing the data 133
    Properly cleaning HTML data 136
Storing Data 136
    Securely writing to a file 137
    Creating and storing a safe password using PHP...................................141
Returning Data 143
    Securely returning data..143
    Using a more secure approach for returning data 144
Understanding the Flash Security Sandbox 145
    Setting the sandbox type..145
    Using the sandboxType property 145
    Determining the active sandbox 147
    Ensuring an application cannot be shared 151
Summary 152

Chapter 8: Using Sockets 153
Understanding Sockets...153
    Security in sockets 154
    Implementing a socket server 154
    Understanding the socket connection...154
Working with Sockets in PHP..154
    Looking for command-line version of PHP..155
    Building a socket server 156
    Testing the socket server...158
    Creating a persistent socket server 160
Working with Sockets in Flash 161
    Initializing a socket connection...161
    Event handlers 162
    Remote socket connections...163
    Using a class for socket connections 164

Contents

Building a Chat Client with Sockets Using Flash and PHP 167
    PHP socket server for the chat client 167
    Connecting to the socket server 175
    Building the Flash client 177
Summary 188

Part III: Extending Flash and PHP   189

Chapter 9: Working with Third-Party Libraries 191

Going over Third-Party Libraries 191
    Other types of third-party libraries 192
    Libraries in PHP 193
Installing Third-Party Libraries 193
    Installing libraries in Flash CS3 193
    Installing libraries in PHP 195
Using Third-Party Libraries 196
    Working with libraries in Flash CS3 196
    Working with Libraries in PHP 197
Glancing at AMFPHP 198
    AMFPHP for AS3 and PHP Developers 198
    Testing AMFPHP with a custom service 201
    Using AMFPHP in Flash 205
Building a Real-World Application Using AMFPHP 210
    AMFPHP services 210
    ActionScript for AMFPHP integration 216
Summary 218

Chapter 10: Using Object-Oriented Programming 219

Understanding OOP 219
    Overview of OOP practices 220
Using Classes in PHP 225
    Importing classes in PHP 226
    Instantiation 226
    Multiple classes 228
Using Classes in Flash 229
    Importing 229
    Document class 229
    Library classes 230
Using Flash and PHP to Build Custom Classes 231
Summary 235

Contents

Part IV: Developing Applications — 237

Chapter 11: Developing Basic Applications — 239

Understanding Elements of an Application — 239
    Understanding application design — 240
    Finalizing the planning stage — 242
Developing a Chat Client — 242
    The Flash portion — 242
    PHP for chat application — 252
Using PHP to Develop a Photo Gallery — 260
    Developing the ActionScript — 261
    Photo gallery navigation — 266
    PHP for the photo gallery — 270
Using PHP to Develop an RSS Reader — 274
    Importing classes — 275
    Loading the PHP — 275
Using PHP, Flash, and MySQL to Develop a Dynamic Banner Ad — 279
    Opening a browser window — 281
    Developing the PHP — 283
    Random selection — 283
Using PHP to Develop a Hit Counter — 285
    Hit counter logic — 285
    Developing the Flash hit counter — 286
Summary — 287

Chapter 12: Developing Real-World Applications — 289

Understanding Real-World Applications — 289
Using PayPal in Flash — 290
    Using POST data — 293
    Using sendToURL — 294
    Setting up PayPal communication — 294
Using Flash and PHP to Build a Cart — 295
    Designing the shopping cart — 296
    Building the PHP — 306
Using PHP and Flash to Build an Amazon Search Application — 317
    Using the Amazon Web Service — 317
    Simplifying the XML response — 319
Developing a Photo Gallery Using flickr — 326
    Interfacing with the Web service — 331
    Building the custom XML document — 332
Summary — 333

Contents

Chapter 13: Using Advanced Real-World Applications **335**

Building a Drawing Application in Flash 335
    Drawing API in Flash 336
Using GD Library in PHP 341
    Generating an image in the GD library 343
    Gathering the pixel data in Flash 345
Using Flash to Develop a Site Monitor 347
    Developing the PHP for the site monitor 347
    Using PHP to e-mail the administrator 349
    Developing the ActionScript for the site monitor 351
Using Flash to Develop a Video Player 359
Developing a Poll Application 364
    Building the PHP and MySQL 364
    Developing the ActionScript for the poll 368
Building a Simple File Editor 373
Summary 380

Chapter 14: Debugging Applications **381**

Using Error Reporting in PHP 381
    Displaying errors for debugging 383
    Understanding the error levels 383
Debugging in Flash 385
Using an Alternative Trace 389
Summary 392

Part V: Server, Application, and Database Maintenance   393

Chapter 15: Maintaining an Application **395**

Commenting Code 395
    Understanding styles for commenting code 396
    Removing comments and debug helpers 399
Managing a ChangeLog 399
    Bug tracking 399
    Additional uses 400
    Dynamic creation of changes 400
Managing Multiple Versions 401
    Version control applications 401
    Version control support in CS3 401
    Setting up version control 402
Using Custom Libraries 403
    Using custom libraries with version control 403
    Publishing an SWC 404
Summary 404

Contents

Chapter 16: Maintaining a Scalable and More Efficient Server 405

Running an Updated Server 405
- Using automatic updates 406
- Zend Platform..406

Working with Development Installs 406
- Building another version of Apache on the same system 406
- Working with bleeding-edge technology..407
- Dependencies 407

Caching and Optimizing 408
- Optimizing PHP 408
- Optimizing Apache..412
- Optimizing MySQL 413
- Caching 416
- Installing memcached on Linux 416
- Installing memcached on Windows 418
- Wrapping up installation for Linux and Windows 418
- Managing servers 420

Handling Backups 421
- File management 421
- Backup management 421
- Using PHP to back up databases..424

Summary 427

Chapter 17: Building Complete Advanced Applications 429

Building a Basic Video Player 429

Building a Video Player in Flash and PHP 432
- Getting started 432
- Remoting integration 437
- Advanced video player development 446
- Building the VideoListItem class...456

Working with Video Tracking..461
- Updating the video class...462
- updateVideoTracking method 463

Building a User Login Component in Flash 465
- Developing the LoginWindow class 466
- Testing the login component..473
- Building the PHP login manager class...476
- Adding remoting to the login component 478

Finalizing the Video Player 481
- Using an external library 482
- Adding the login component 482

Summary 486

Index 487

xvii

This book is a multipart exploration into Flash and PHP. Flash has been used for everything from basic banner ads to fully functional applications across the web and desktop.

Oftentimes you can find information required to write amazing Flash applications or the server-side counterpart but rarely both. This book builds both aspects and explains the process of working with PHP in your Flash projects.

The first part of the book is a step-by-step walkthrough of the installation and configuration process for PHP and all the necessary components. Once the components are installed, the next step is an overview of PHP and a guide to what features and techniques you will find in the book as you continue through the chapters.

Each chapter starts off with a basic overview and then moves quickly into the relevant information, leaving out any fluff to ensure you are getting all of the important information right away.

Part II focuses on the importance and best practices of making your applications more secure while maintaining functionality. The topic of security is repeated throughout the various examples in this book, but this part in particular is where you will find the majority of the security information.

Part III is extending Flash and PHP by working with various third-party applications and libraries. This chapter finishes with an overview of AMFPHP to build more-advanced and easier-to-maintain applications.

Part IV takes all the previous information and walks you through the process of building complete real-world applications in Flash and PHP. These real-world applications will help you build your own custom versions and ultimately allow you to create more-advanced and dynamic applications.

Examples and Source Files

You can find all the source code and starter files for the examples in this book on the following web site.

www.wiley.com/go/flashandphpbible

Introduction

What You'll Need

The ActionScript used in this book is not advanced, but a basic understanding of the fundamentals would allow you to better understand the examples. The Flash Bible is a perfect complement to this book and I highly recommend it.

A basic understanding of OOP practices would help you in the second portion of the book but is not required to understand the examples overall. You may want to pick up a book on advanced OOP practices to gain a more thorough understanding of the topic.

The PHP used in this book is assuming a very basic understanding of the subject. This means you will not only learn the advanced topics but how to get there by starting at the beginning. PHP also allows you to develop in a class-based format, so that will be utilized in the full-application chapters to ensure you are building a more complete and updatable application.

The last thing you will need is an Internet connection to download the code for the book and work with some of the third-party services. This is not used in the entire book, but to get the full experience the Internet connection will be needed.

That is everything you will need. Now is the time to jump in. Chapter 1 is only a few pages away.

Part I

Understanding the Basics

IN THIS PART

Chapter 1
Getting Started with Flash and PHP

Chapter 2
Exploring Flash and PHP

Chapter 3
Getting Connected

Chapter 4
Working with Data

Chapter 5
Interacting with the User

Chapter 6
Working with Cookies

Chapter 1

Getting Started with Flash and PHP

The process of getting started includes the installation and configuration of Apache, MySQL, and PHP. The examples in this book assume the installation will be done locally; however, you can modify the paths and URLs if you want to use a remote server.

The order in which you install these programs is important because they use paths and variables from each other, which results in the complete development environment.

This installation guide covers Windows and UNIX systems. If you have decided to work from the book on an existing server, you can skip to Chapter 2. However, there is some security and configuration information within this chapter you may find useful.

IN THIS CHAPTER

Apache installation

PHP installation

MySQL installation

Adding Apache to a Web Server

The first step to working with Flash and PHP is to install the necessary components. The installation process is defined by installing Apache, then MySQL, and finally PHP. This order is required because PHP needs paths to Apache and MySQL in order to provide that support.

You can recompile (build) any one of these components in the future. However, if you follow this installation order it will mean less work and rework in the future.

The components to be installed change from time to time, but the overall installation process remains fairly constant. This means you can download

Part I Understanding the Basics

the latest files from their respective project sites, or to ensure all the components work together, you can obtain these files from the book's site.

You should have a basic understanding of the system on which you will be installing. It is important to run a development system in a secured location. The best setup is a computer behind a physical firewall or on an internal network. If this is not possible, simply configure Apache to not allow remote connections and you can change the port number to hide it on your network.

 Development systems can require more advanced configuration depending on how they have been set up. You can find common issues explained on the book's Web site.

Installing Apache for Windows

Once you determine on which system you are installing the development system you can begin to download the necessary components. It is recommended that you use the files provided with the book. I also provide the necessary locations to download the latest files.

Access the latest version from Apache's Web site. It is easier to install from the binary installer version rather than compiling the source. However, compiling from source does offer a higher level of customization and allows you to understand what is running under the hood.

 Building from source is not for the beginner. It does require a certain level of experience and is only recommended to those who truly feel up to the challenge.

The latest Windows binary installer files for Apache can be found at `www.apache.org/dyn/closer.cgi/httpd/binaries/win32/`.

Installing

Start the installation process by opening the Windows installer file that was either downloaded from the book site or directly from Apache's Web site.

This installation will be mostly visual because the Windows installer is a graphical setup. The key to a successful installation is carefully following and reading the screens throughout the entire installation process. The first screen, as shown in Figure 1.1, requires no modification.

The next two screens are the license agreement, which you can take the time to read or you can simply click Next, because it is pretty standard information.

After that, you will find an introduction to Apache, which gives you a good overview of what Apache has to offer, as shown in Figure 1.2. The screen will also provide links to very valuable resources surrounding the Apache community.

Getting Started with Flash and PHP

FIGURE 1.1

The first screen requires no user modification. Simply click Next to continue the installation process.

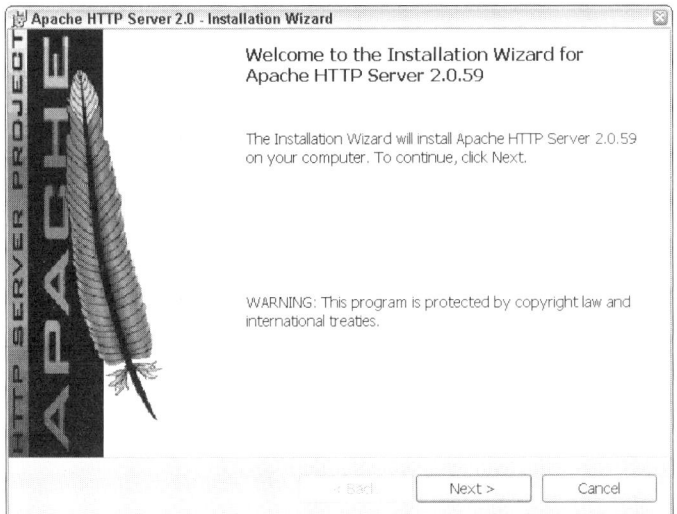

FIGURE 1.2

The Server Information for a development system does not need to be real, as this figure shows.

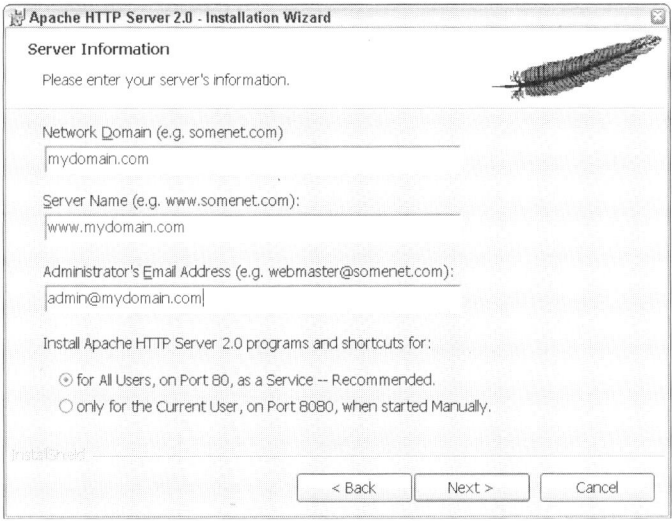

Part I Understanding the Basics

The server installation is where you define the specific configuration for your environment. If you were installing Apache on a real system, you would fill in this page with the correct information, otherwise Apache would not route requests correctly. You can accept the default options for a development setup, such as this.

Being that this installation is for a development server you don't have to fill in the screen with real data, unless you are using this guide to install on a live server.

The Install Apache HTTP Server 2.0 programs and shortcuts for: option is when you want to install Apache so only the current user can access it. If you want all users to be able to access Apache, then you will want to install it as a service.

The installation process of Apache can be done in two ways, as shown in Figure 1.3. The first option is to accept all of the default settings, which results in a quicker installation, but it's not always the best option.

The second more common option is the Custom alternative where you tell Apache which tools and libraries you want to install. Occasionally when installing an application you can experience a shortage of hard drive space.

Apache, on the other hand, is so small with all of the extra tools installed that you should not have a problem installing it.

FIGURE 1.3

The Custom option is selected to ensure all of the development tools are installed, such as library and module building capability.

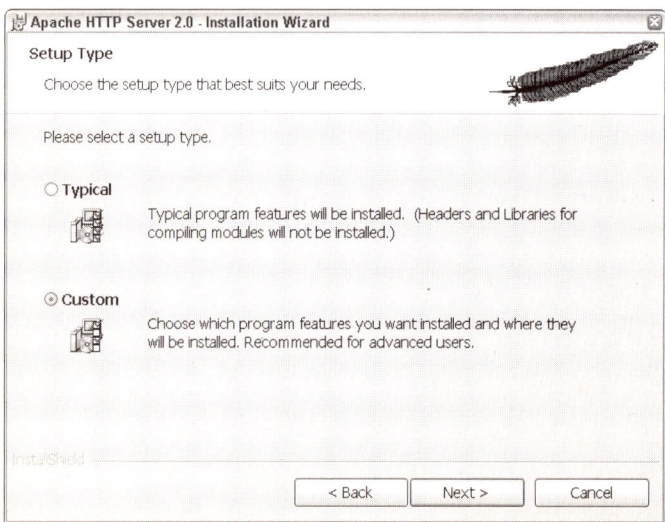

Getting Started with Flash and PHP

For the examples in this book, it is best to accept the Custom installation and make sure all of the libraries and extensions are installed. For example, some of the modules used to modify the user requests are only available when you install the full version.

Depending on the system, it may take a while to install Apache. Even if the status bar stops moving don't get concerned; some of the files take longer than others to install. The application notifies you if something happens during the installation process, which is very rare. Apache will update the progress bar, as shown in Figure 1.4, while the installation is occurring.

FIGURE 1.4

Apache installation status

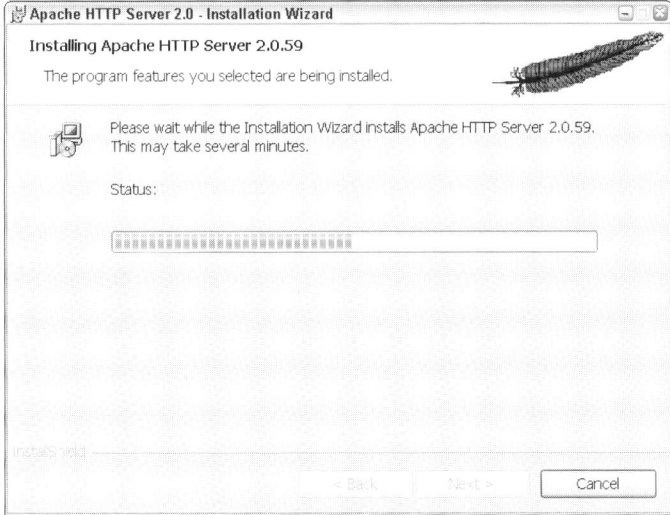

The last screen you should see is a note that the installation was successful. A DOS prompt may appear notifying you that the Apache service is starting. You may also get a Firewall warning, and you will need to grant Apache the access it requests.

Testing

Congratulations. If all went well you should now have Apache installed on your Windows machine. To test the installation, open a Web browser and point it to the local Apache Web server, which is also known as `localhost`.

```
http://localhost/
```

You should be presented with a screen similar to what is seen in Figure 1.5, which basically informs you that Apache is properly installed and is ready to start serving up your content.

Part I Understanding the Basics

Depending on the installation process, you can modify this location, which is sometimes required when installed on a remote server. You would not be able to access the Apache Web server on the `localhost` address. Instead, you would point to the IP address or the domain name of your Web site.

FIGURE 1.5

The default Welcome Screen for Apache

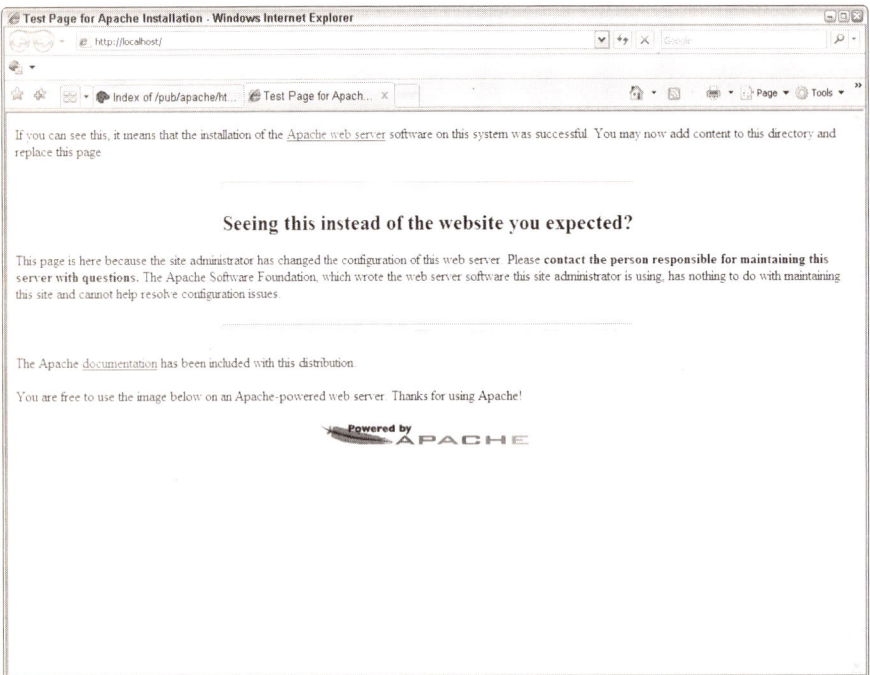

With Apache installed, you can modify the default page to truly see how Apache functions.

The Web files that Apache serves are located in the document root. This is similar to the `public_html` or www that you have most likely seen on a remote Web server. Unlike a remote Web server, permissions on these files are often unavailable to other users not viewing from your own personal computer.

The location of this Web directory in Windows using a default installation is:

    C:\Program Files\Apache Group\Apache2\htdocs

You will see many different files in this directory, such as the same index files in various languages.

You don't want to modify any of these files because it could mess up the core of Apache or introduce errors that would be very hard to track, so create a new file.

Using your favorite text editor, create a very simple HTML page, such as the following:

```
<!DOCTYPE html PUBLIC "-//W3C//DTD XHTML 1.0 Strict//EN"
   "http://www.w3.org/TR/xhtml1/DTD/xhtml1-strict.dtd">
<html xmlns="http://www.w3.org/1999/xhtml" lang="en">
<head>

<title>My Custom Page</title>

<body>

  <h1>Welcome to my custom page</h1>
  <p>This is a test of the customization of Apache!</p>
  <p>Pretty cool huh?</p>

</body>

</html>
```

Save this new file in the Apache Web directory and name it `myPage.html`. After saving the file, open it in your Web browser to witness the flexibility in Apache.

This is not the most advanced example, but it should give you the basic idea of how to modify and work with the Apache Web server. Now is the time to create more useful examples, because you have the basics down.

At this point, with Apache installed and tested, you can move on to the installation and configuration of PHP, or you can jump ahead to the configuration process of Apache.

Alternatively, you can read through the installation of Apache on UNIX, which is covered in the next section.

The installation of Apache in UNIX would be closer to working with a remote server, because you will find that most Web servers are built on Linux. This doesn't mean you will never find a Windows-based live Web server, but it certainly isn't as common.

Installing Apache for UNIX

The installation process in UNIX is more advanced than the Windows installation. However, the UNIX installation is often the more common scenario for a live server.

The first step to installing Apache is downloading the source. This source can either be downloaded from the book's site or directly from Apache's Web site. Using the source provided on the book site ensures you're running a nearly identical system to the one used for writing this book.

You will find the source, as shown in Figure 1.6, directly from Apache at the following URL: `http://httpd.apache.org/download.cgi`.

Part I Understanding the Basics

FIGURE 1.6

Here is a list of the possible versions of the source code to download from the Apache server.

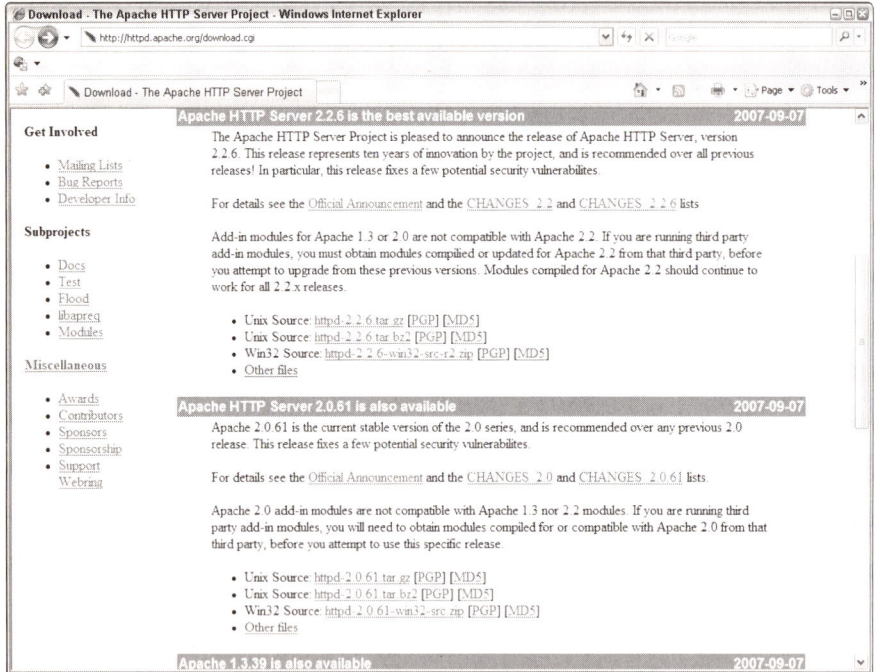

After downloading the source for Apache, you can begin the installation process.

Preinstallation

Before installation can begin, the source must be extracted from the downloaded file. This is done by simply uncompressing the `tarball` file and untarring the uncompressed file.

```
$ gzip -d httpd-2.2.6.tar.gz
$ tar xvf httpd-2.2.6.tar
```

Once the previous two processes are complete, you are left with a new directory containing the source code.

Before continuing, change to this directory, which means you will be in the directory the source code is located in.

```
$ cd httpd-2.2.6/
```

Installation

When the source code is extracted, you can begin the installation process. Apache will install using its own set of options, but you have the ability to modify these. If you want to configure Apache using the defaults, simply type `./configure`.

However, it is a better practice to tailor the installation process to your environment.

One of the most important options you can define is the `--prefix`, which is where Apache will be installed. This option is used throughout the application and also is used later during the PHP installation and configuration section.

For simplicity a partially modified configuration process is used, but feel free to look through the Apache documentation to gain a better understanding of what settings can be changed.

```
$ ./configure --prefix=/usr/local/apache
--enable-rewrite=shared \
--enable-spelling=shared
```

Once the configuration process begins, it can take a few minutes to complete. Most of the time you will see the process printing in your terminal window, but even if it is not, it is running.

After the configure command has completed you can run `make` to build the Apache package.

```
$ make
```

Again, this process may take time depending on your system, so please be patient. Once the `make` command is complete, the last command to run installs the package and wraps up the installation portion.

```
$ make install
```

Testing

With Apache installed, you can start it and test it in the browser.

Apache installs a very useful tool, `apachectl`, which can be found in the `bin/` directory of the installation location. Using the path chosen for this installation, the `apachectl` application would be found here.

```
$ usr/local/apache/bin/apachectl
```

Use the following command to start the Apache server:

```
$ usr/local/apache/bin/apachectl start
```

Use this command to stop the Apache server:

```
$ usr/local/apache/bin/apachectl stop
```

Part I   Understanding the Basics

To restart the Apache server, use this command:

```
$ usr/local/apache/bin/apachectl restart
```

Testing out the server is done by making a call to `localhost` from your web browser at http://localhost/.

As you can now see, the installation was a success. To further test and better understand how to modify the files Apache serves, create a new HMTL file and save it in the Apache Web root.

Using your favorite text editor, which in UNIX will most likely be vi, create this new HTML file. The following commands assume you are using vi.

Create a new file:

```
$ vi /usr/local/apache/htdocs/sampleFile.html
```

In order to begin entering the HTML code, you need to tell vi to enter Insert mode, which is done by pressing I. Press ESC to exit Insert mode.

Paste or type the following sample HTML code:

```
<!DOCTYPE html PUBLIC "-//W3C//DTD XHTML 1.0 Strict//EN"
   "http://www.w3.org/TR/xhtml1/DTD/xhtml1-strict.dtd">
<html xmlns="http://www.w3.org/1999/xhtml" lang="en">
<head>
<title>My Custom Page</title>
<body>
  <h1>Welcome to my custom page</h1>
  <p>This is a test of the customization of Apache!</p>
  <p>Pretty cool huh?</p>
</body>
</html>
```

Once the file is created, press ESC and type the following command to save and close the editor. Note, the `:` is part of the command.

```
:wq
```

Certain files you add or modify require you to restart Apache; however, basic Web files do not fall into that category. You can now display the new page by appending the filename to the `localhost` call at http://localhost/sampleFile.html.

As you can see, the Apache server has been properly installed and you were able to add a custom file that Apache properly served up. At this point, you should have a basic understanding of how Apache functions. The next section (platform independent) goes into more detail about how you can modify Apache.

Getting Started with Flash and PHP

Modifying Apache for Windows and UNIX

The following tips, tricks, and tweaks can be performed on Windows or UNIX installations. This is because they are specific to Apache and not the environment it runs on.

When working on development systems it isn't rare to require more than one installation of Apache. This could be to test bleeding-edge code, support more plug-ins, or just to ensure a project is running on a clone of the live system.

The installation process of Apache stays pretty much the same. You only need to change the prefix option by pointing it to a new/different location. You can run multiple versions of Apache; however, they require separate installation locations. Running multiple versions of Apache at the same time using only the default installation options isn't possible. This is due to Apache being set up to listen for requests on port 80 by default.

You can modify the port that Apache listens on by editing the configuration file. The configuration files are located in the `conf/` directory, which is located in the directory that you designate during the Apache install.

For example, you can change the port that Apache runs on. Start by opening the configuration file.

To open the configuration file in UNIX, use vi.

```
$ vi /usr/local/apache/conf/httpd.conf
```

To open the configuration file in Windows, navigate to the installation directory and open the `httpd.conf` file in your favorite text editor.

```
C:\Program Files\Apache Group\Apache2\conf\httpd.conf
```

When the file is open, scroll down or search for the `Listen` directive, which will look similar to the following:

```
#
# Listen: Allows you to bind Apache to specific IP addresses
   and/or
# ports, instead of the default. See also the <VirtualHost>
# directive.
#
Listen 80
```

NOTE Apache will only look at this file during startup. When you are finished editing, make sure you restart the Apache server.

Changing that one value allows you to run multiple copies of Apache. However, running multiple Apache instances can be processor intensive, so make sure you only run as many instances as required. In most cases, you will run only one instance on a live server.

Part I Understanding the Basics

Installing MySQL

Now that Apache is installed, the next component to install is MySQL. This would be the database that your application contents are stored in and managed using PHP.

Installing MySQL for Windows

Much like the Apache installation process, MySQL has a Windows installer that makes the entire process much easier. The installer guides you through the process of installing the core database and any additional components you need. For this setup, the default installation is used, but feel free to customize, which is a very good way to learn.

Downloading

The first step to installing MySQL is downloading the latest install files. You can use the files provided on the book's Web site to ensure compatibility or you can visit MySQL's Web site at `http://dev.mysql.com/downloads/mysql/5.0.html#win32` to get the latest stable version at this time.

Choose the Win32 installer with Setup to make the overall installation process easier. This allows you to use the GUI instead of the traditional command-line process of previous versions.

Installation

After you download and open the installer a Welcome page appears, followed by other pages that make up the install process, as shown in Figure 1.7. Similar to the Apache installation, MySQL also has various configuration options that need to be modified. Carefully look over the following steps to ensure your database will function properly.

Choose the Typical install option, which installs the core components necessary to run and maintain a MySQL database. Click Next to move to the next step.

At this point, MySQL has been installed. The final page gives you the option to launch the configuration section when you click Next.

Make sure you select this option. If you accidentally close this page you can rerun it or open the configuration application in the `mysql/` directory in `program files`.

The installation of MySQL does not offer all that much in modification. This is because the supporting application Configuration Wizard handles all the necessary configuration options.

Select the Detailed Configuration option, as shown in Figure 1.8. This allows you to fine-tune the MySQL configuration as opposed to using all of the defaults. Click Next to continue.

Getting Started with Flash and PHP

FIGURE 1.7

This page is the install process. The install can take several minutes, depending on the system.

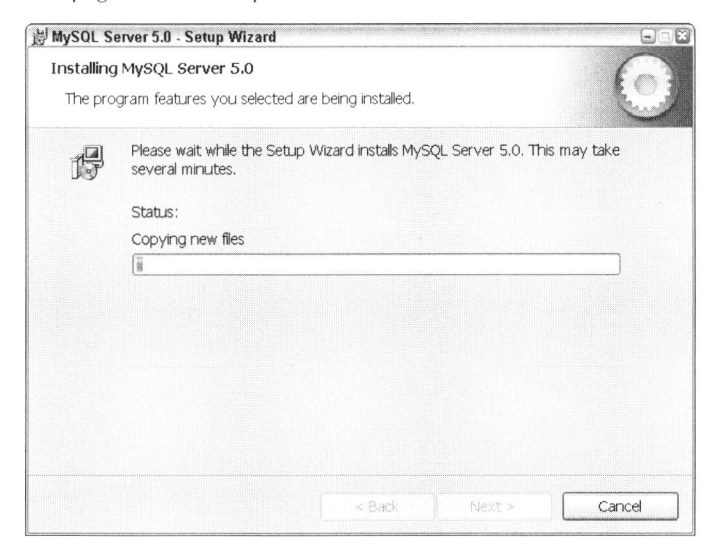

If you select the Standard Configuration option you are presented with a smaller list of configuration screens. This speeds up the configuration process, but doesn't allow you to customize the functionality of MySQL and could result in a less efficient system.

FIGURE 1.8

Select the configuration type.

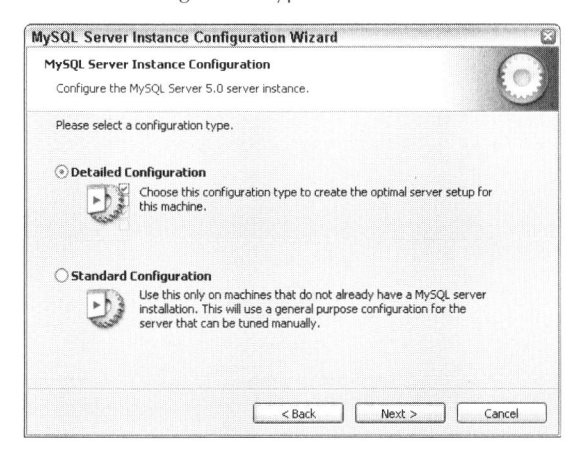

15

Part I Understanding the Basics

The server type determines the memory, hard drive, and CPU usage. This has been installed on your development machine so you want to ensure that MySQL doesn't become overly processor or resource intensive. Selecting the Developer Machine option ensures this doesn't happen.

The other two options are for dedicated servers. The Server Machine option would be used when you install MySQL on the same machine your Web server, such as Apache, is running. This is okay for a medium-trafficked site, but you may find a spike in resource usage as your site becomes more active.

When this happens, you will want to introduce a dedicated machine to run your MySQL database, which at this time you would select the Dedicated MySQL Server Machine option. This option tells MySQL it is installed on a dedicated machine and to use all the resources and memory that are present.

> **NOTE** Be sure you never accidentally select the Dedicated MySQL Server Machine option when installing on a Web server. Your system will not be able to manage resources properly and could eventually fail.

MySQL will constantly attempt to allocate all free memory whenever it is made available, which means when your Web server closes a stale connection, MySQL could potentially steal that free memory until there is no more room for connection available.

After you select an option (in this example Dedicated Machine), click Next (see Figure 1.9).

FIGURE 1.9
Select the Developer Machine option for your server type.

Select the Multifunctional Database option as the database usage type to allow the ultimate expandability of the system. This allows MySQL to optimize for both InnoDB and MyISAM storage engines. If this is your first time installing MySQL, which is very possible because many systems ship with it already installed, you may be asking how the other two options are used.

The Transactional Database Only option is used when you will be running a lot of transaction-based queries. This means you would be wrapping a bunch of queries (`UPDATE`, `SELECT`, `DELETE`, `INSERT`) in one run to ensure all the proper tables and data are modified. But if something goes wrong in one of those modifications it could ruin the remaining data.

This would mean a lot of unnecessary data editing and in some cases could result in bad data. A transaction looks for an error or trigger and if found all the modifications made during the start of the transaction are rolled back and reverted to their nonmodified state.

Here is a simple example of a MySQL-based transaction, which modifies two separate portions of data on the same table.

```
START TRANSACTION;

UPDATE users SET credits = credits - 100 WHERE id = 3002;
UPDATE users SET credits = credits + 100 WHERE id = 3002;

COMMIT;
```

During the process of a transaction those entries are made unavailable to other sessions to ensure the data cannot be read or modified while a transaction is being performed. You can think of this process as being similar to turning the power off in your house to ensure someone can't accidentally flip a light switch while you are working on something.

The Non-Transactional Database Only option is selected when you know you will never need transaction abilities. This only enables the MyISAM storage engine, which can provide better results, but also limits overall functionality.

Oftentimes you will find the Multifunctional Database option, as shown in Figure 1.10, to the best choice, but it is also good to know what the other options offer.

FIGURE 1.10

The Multifunctional Database option is selected as the database storage type.

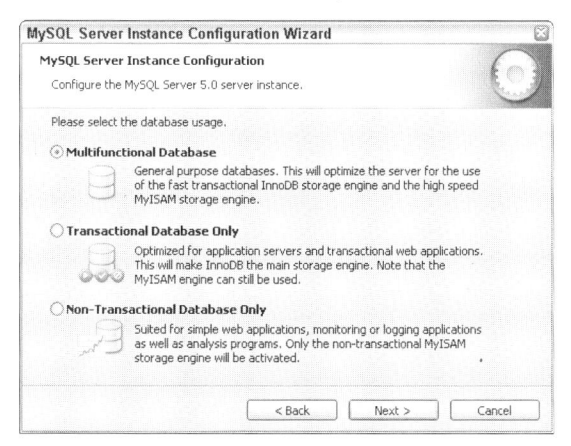

Part I Understanding the Basics

The next page allows you to customize the InnoDB storage system, but it is best to just leave it with the default settings.

In some instances, you may want to choose a separate location, which you can do by clicking the Browse button to the right of the installation box. Choosing a different location is only necessary when the Drive Info notice at the bottom of the window reports a small amount of Free disk space, which means your database could consume the remainder of your resources.

> **CAUTION** Make sure you never choose a removable drive as the storage location because you could harm the database if that drive is not attached at all times.

As stated earlier, most often it is best to leave this option at its default choice, as shown in Figure 1.11, to ensure your database functions properly.

FIGURE 1.11

InnoDB Tablespace settings

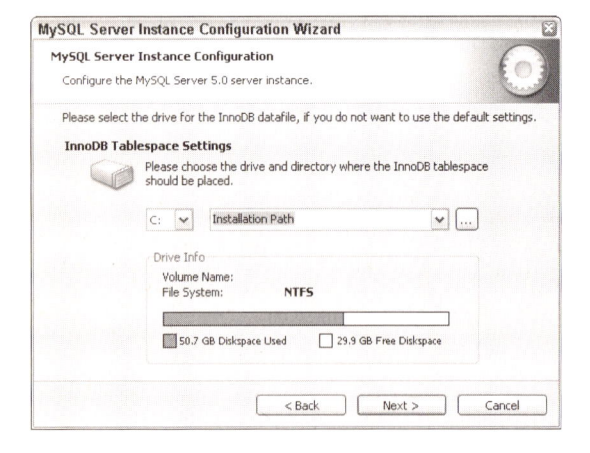

The next option is an approximation of how many concurrent connections your MySQL database will need to handle. Because this installation is being performed on a development server, an estimate of no more than 25 is a realistic assumption. Actually, it would be rare to have more than 5, but 25 is a good base number.

Select the Online Transaction Processing (OLTP) option under the "Decision Support" heading when you are developing a Web application to which the public has access. This is because you really have no idea how many people may attempt to access the system at any given time. As your application continues to grow you may even need to chain multiple databases together to handle the load, but for now one database is enough, especially considering this installation is being performed on your local system.

Getting Started with Flash and PHP

Select the Manual Setting option when you want to specify an exact number. This is only necessary when you want full control over your Web application. Oftentimes you see this manual number set to 300 on live Web applications. This appears to be a good average with the ability to handle many connections.

Be careful not to set the concurrent connections option, as shown in Figure 1.12, too high because your system will only have so many resources that can be split and shared by each connection. If you add more memory to your application you can increase this number, but that may not always be the best option.

FIGURE 1.12

Set the approximate number of concurrent connections.

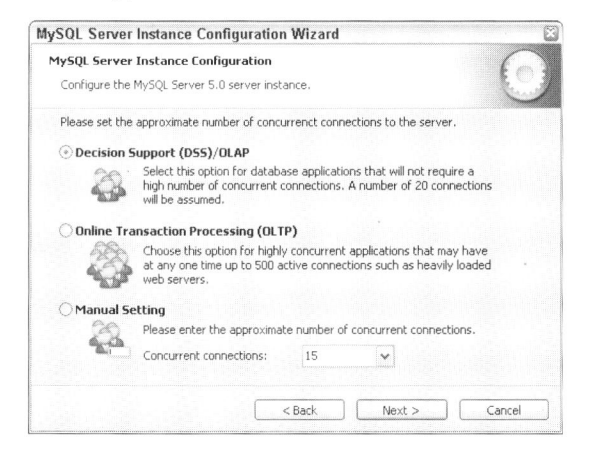

The networking options determine if your MySQL databases will be visible to other machines beyond the local setup. For the ultimate security, disable the Enable TCP/IP option. If you have multiple development machines, you can enable it and choose a nonstandard port.

For this installation, networking is enabled, as shown in Figure 1.13, and the default port is used because I do not intend to allow others to connect, but my Web server is located behind a hardware firewall for added security.

Choose a nonstandard port number if you install another version of MySQL on the same system. This is not very common, but sometimes you have to deploy backwards-compatible environments to test your code in various setups. This is a cost-effective alternative to building and maintaining another physical machine to handle the testing process.

Make sure you select the Enable Strict Mode option to ensure your database server functions properly.

FIGURE 1.13

Setting the networking options

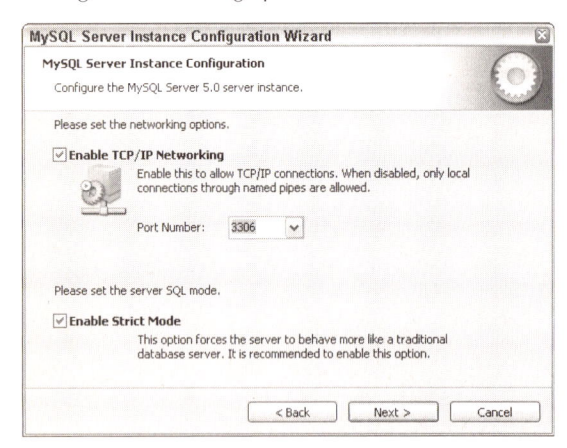

On the next page you can select the default character set used in your database. The Standard Character Set option is selected for this example (see Figure 1.14), but oftentimes this is not the best option because it does not allow the most compatibility with existing systems or allow for expansion over time. For this example it will work just fine because you will not have any advanced characters being used.

You can, of course, select any option that best fits your usage, but I prefer the Best Support for Multilingualism option. This option allows for greater expansion and is highly recommended when storing text in many different languages.

Select the Manual Selected Default Character Set/Collection option for the rare times when you want to specify a certain character set to use rather than choosing a selection of them. You will probably never use this option because it is too specific, but it is available if needed.

If you think you will be using multiple languages, I recommend the second option, Best Support for Multilingualism, to ensure your applications will be able to expand, and also allow you to experiment with different options later on.

The Windows Options page (see Figure 1.15) determines how MySQL is initialized. For example, if you choose to run MySQL as a service it will start or stop automatically, controlled by the operating system. If you have installed a previous version of MySQL you will want to choose a different service name. This is to ensure the existing service does not collide with this one.

Select the Launch the MySQL Server automatically option to ensure the database is available when the system starts. This is not required, but it makes it so you don't have to start the service manually each time you restart your machine. You can, of course, access the service application on your system and modify this option at any time, as well as turn off the service until the next time the machine starts up.

Getting Started with Flash and PHP 1

FIGURE 1.14

Selecting a default character set

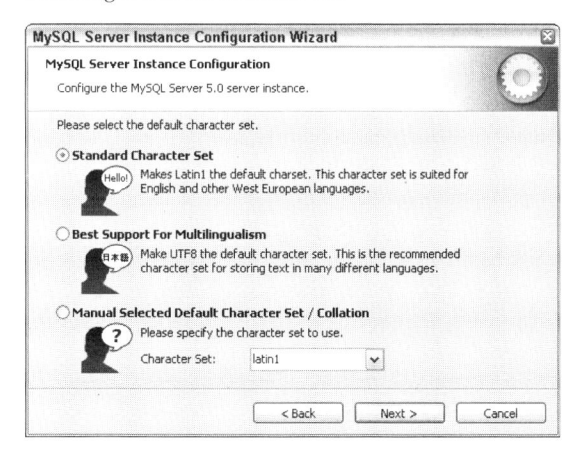

The Include Bin Directory in Windows PATH option, when selected, includes MySQL support from the command line by simply typing `mysql`. This means any command prompt will allow you quick access to your MySQL database. You can refer to your operating system instructions for modifying this PATH variable.

You can also add PHP and Apache to this same PATH variable, which would expose them to the command prompt as well. In fact, when you install PHP some instructional material for performing this modification is offered.

FIGURE 1.15

The Windows options determine how MySQL is started and accessed.

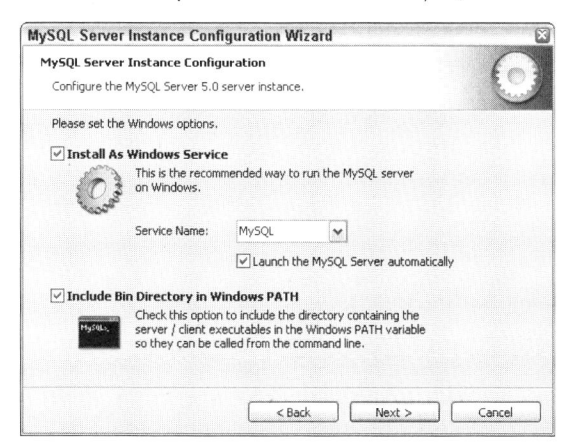

Part I Understanding the Basics

The final configuration is used to set a root password, as shown in Figure 1.16. The root user has global permissions over your databases, so you can imagine how important securing this user is. You do not have to choose a password, but by default, MySQL is installed with no root password, which means anyone has access to your databases.

It is best to choose a difficult-to-guess password, retype it once more and be sure that the Enable root access from remote machines option is not selected to disable the ability to administer the databases remotely. It may seem this option would allow for better usability, but there are some exceptions, one of which is overall security of a system.

Even though this setup is being performed on a development server, it is best to keep security in the forefront of the installation process. Doing so will ensure you follow the necessary precautions when you perform a similar installation on a remote setup.

If security is not a concern, you do have the option to create an Anonymous Account. However, creating such an account is nearly identical to a root login with no password and will suffer from the same overall security concerns.

FIGURE 1.16

Security options for MySQL

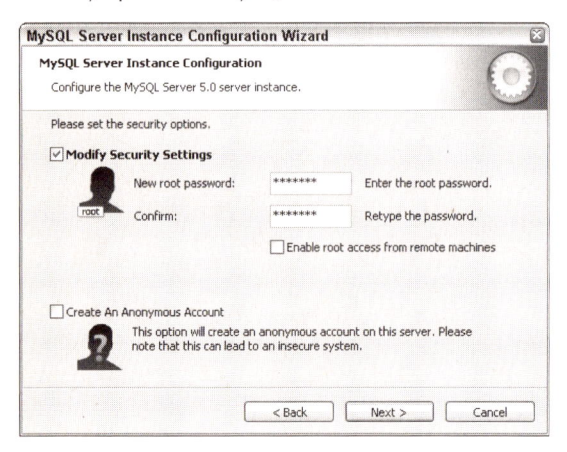

The last page, as shown in Figure 1.17, is for the processing of the configuration values set in the previous pages. If for some reason an error is encountered, MySQL will notify you.

Most of the time you will see each bullet point with a check mark applied as it is completed.

Getting Started with Flash and PHP

When processing is complete, you are presented with a notice informing you the configuration has been completed and MySQL is ready to use.

You have now successfully installed and configured MySQL to be used for the remainder of this book. Click Finish to close the configuration page and begin testing the installation.

FIGURE 1.17

Display of configuration processing with proper notices as each task is completed.

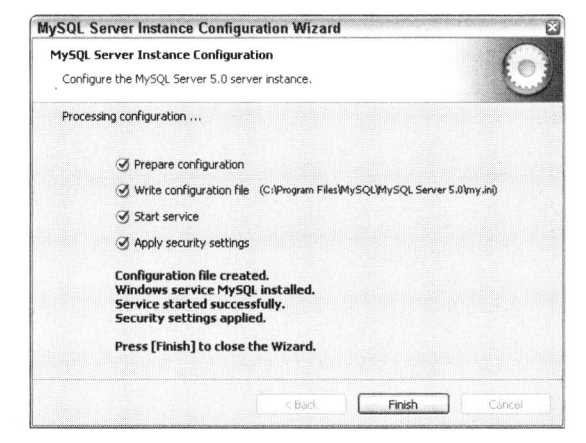

Testing

After you install MySQL you can test it. You can view the service status using the MySQL monitor, which determines if the database server is up and running. You can use the command line to log in and investigate the MySQL database just like you would on a remote server.

To open a new command prompt, as shown in Figure 1.18, press Windows key+R. When the prompt open, type the following command to log in:

```
$ mysql -uroot -p
```

NOTE If you get "command not found" you need to add MySQL to the path variable.

An Enter Password notice appears. Type the password you set in the configuration process.

NOTE When typing a password the prompt will not show any text updates.

23

Part I Understanding the Basics

FIGURE 1.18

Command prompt with the command entered to log in to the MySQL database server

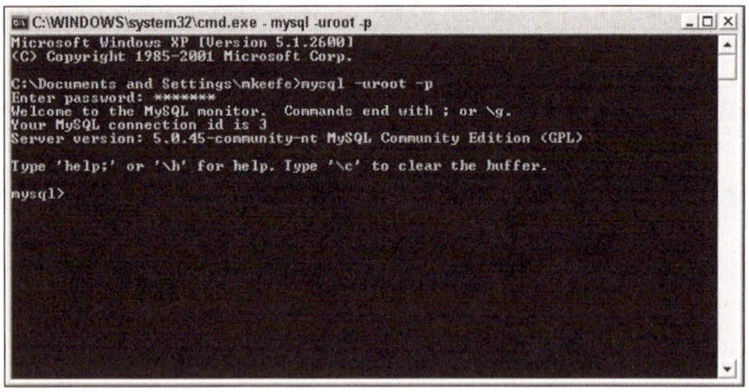

If the login is successful, a notice describing the MySQL server appears. The notice contains the version of MySQL that you are currently running. The following is an example of the notice:

```
Welcome to the MySQL monitor.  Commands end with ; or \g.
Your MySQL connection id is 5
Server version: 5.0T.45-community-nt MySQL Community Edition
    (GPL)
```

Once you log in to MySQL, your command prompt changes to `mysql>`. From this point on, until you log out, all commands are directed to the database server.

For example, to see what databases are available, type the following command:

```
mysql> show databases;
```

To test the database installation, create a new database:

```
mysql> create database flashphp;
```

When the database is created, you can select it with the following command:

```
mysql> use flashphp;
```

You can even pass in the database name during the login phase, such as:

```
$ mysql -uroot -p flashphp
```

At this point, MySQL should be successfully installed on your Windows development server. The next section covers how to install MySQL for UNIX and UNIX-like systems. The PHP installation process is directly following the UNIX instructions. Feel free to jump ahead if you only want to focus on a Windows system.

Installing MySQL for UNIX

You can install MySQL on your UNIX system using the provided source code on the book's site, or you can download the latest files from MySQL directly at `http://dev.mysql.com/downloads/mysql/5.0.html#linux`.

> **NOTE** The version to download depends on the environment on which you are installing. Consult the following guide for further information:
> `http://dev.mysql.com/doc/refman/5.0/en/which-version.html`.

After you download the necessary installation files, you can begin the preparation for the installation process. The first step is to add the user and group `mysql` for MySQL to run as. The following command creates the `mysql` group and adds a `mysql` user to that new group:

```
$ groupadd mysql
$ useradd -g mysql mysql
```

Choose the directory in which you want to install MySQL. You can choose the same location where you installed Apache to keep all of your development components in the same location.

```
$ cd /usr/local
```

> **NOTE** You may need to perform the MySQL installation as root if the directory is protected.

Unpack the distribution package and create a symbolic link to that directory.

```
$ gunzip < /usr/local/mysql-5.0.45-linux-i686-glibc23.tar.gz | tar xvf -
$ ln -s /usr/local/ mysql-5.0.45-linux-i686-glibc23 mysql
```

When the unpacking command is complete, change to the installation directory.

```
$ cd mysql
```

Change the ownership of the files to MySQL by running a recursive ownership command. The first command changes the ownership and the second changes the group attribute.

```
$ chown -R mysql
$ chgrp -R mysql
```

If you have not installed a previous version of MySQL on this machine, you must create the MySQL data directory and grant tables.

```
scripts/mysql_install_db --user=mysql
```

If you want MySQL to run automatically when the machine starts, you can copy the `mysql.server` file located in the `support/` directory to the location where your system has its other startup files. For more information regarding the location of that directory and other system specific concerns, go to `http://dev.mysql.com/doc/refman/5.0/en/UNIX-post-installation.html#automatic-start`.

Part I Understanding the Basics

When everything is properly unpacked and installed, you can begin testing.

To start the MySQL server, run the following command from the `mysql` installation directory:

```
$ bin/mysqld_safe -- user=mysql &
```

Use the following command to verify the server is actually running:

```
$ bin/mysqladmin version
$ bin/mysqladmin variables
```

The output from `mysqladmin version` will vary depending on the version installed. This is a sample returned from that command:

```
mysqladmin  Ver 14.12 Distrib 5.0.54, for pc-linux-gnu on i686
Copyright (C) 2000 MySQL AB & MySQL Finland AB & TCX DataKonsult
   AB
This software comes with ABSOLUTELY NO WARRANTY. This is free
   software,
and you are welcome to modify and redistribute it under the GPL
   license

Server version          5.0.54
Protocol version        10
Connection              Localhost via UNIX socket
UNIX socket             /var/lib/mysql/mysql.sock
Uptime:                 0 days 2 hours 2 min 07 sec

Threads: 1  Questions: 323  Slow queries: 0
Opens: 0  Flush tables: 1  Open tables: 7
Queries per second avg: 0.000
```

Protecting MySQL

It is important that you protect MySQL users from malicious activity. By default, MySQL installs the root and anonymous users with no passwords, which is the same as using a global default. It is a very good practice to immediately assign passwords and in some cases remove the anonymous users altogether.

Setting a password on Windows

The password for the root account was given a password when you ran the installer. However, if for some reason you want to change it, simply run the following command, substituting NEW_PASSWORD with the actual password you want to use:

```
$ mysql -uroot
mysql> SET PASSWORD FOR 'root'@'localhost' =
    PASSWORD(NEW_PASSWORD);
mysql> SET PASSWORD FOR 'root'@'%' = PASSWORD(NEW_PASSWORD);
```

Getting Started with Flash and PHP

Setting a password on UNIX

The installation of MySQL on UNIX leaves the root login with no password, unlike the Windows installation. It is very important to assign a password immediately:

```
$ mysql -uroot
mysql> SET PASSWORD FOR 'root'@'localhost' =
    PASSWORD(NEW_PASSWORD);
mysql> SET PASSWORD FOR 'root'@'host_name' =
    PASSWORD(NEW_PASSWORD);
```

Replace host_name with the name of the server host. If you do not know the server host, run this command while logged in to MySQL to determine that information:

```
SELECT Host, User FROM mysql.user;
```

To remove the anonymous account, log in to MySQL and issue the following command:

```
DROP USER '';
```

CAUTION Use caution when removing a user and double-check the spelling of the user's name before you issue that command.

Setting up PHP on the Web Server

PHP is the final component to install in order to complete the process of building the development system. The process of installing PHP is straightforward, but it requires some customization.

NOTE When installing the support for the XML and GD libraries, your system may require additional libraries and components.

Installing PHP for Windows

Installing PHP for Windows is actually fairly simple. A lot of the installation process consists of moving files around and editing existing files. You can find the PHP installation files on the book's Web site or you can download the latest files directly from the php.org site at www.php.net/downloads.php.

Installation

To begin the process of installing PHP, run the installer application that you downloaded. The Welcome page for the setup wizard appears, as shown in Figure 1.19.

The destination folder, as shown in Figure 1.20, is where you install PHP. By default, it chose a directory path with Program Files within it. This can cause issues on some servers. A common path is C:\php or C:\php5 if you intend to install multiple copies of PHP.

Part I Understanding the Basics

FIGURE 1.19

The PHP installation Welcome page

FIGURE 1.20

Choose the Destination folder.

Getting Started with Flash and PHP

The PHP installer is built to configure both PHP and Apache to work together. This includes the editing of the configuration files of Apache.

On the Web Server Setup page, as shown in Figure 1.21, select the version of Apache that you previously installed. If you are unsure which version is installed, you can run the following command in the prompt:

```
/usr/local/apache2/bin/httpd -v
```

The following is a sample output from the previous command:

```
Server version: Apache/2.0.59
Server built:   Aug 31 2007 01:58:43
```

FIGURE 1.21

The PHP Installer Web Server Setup page

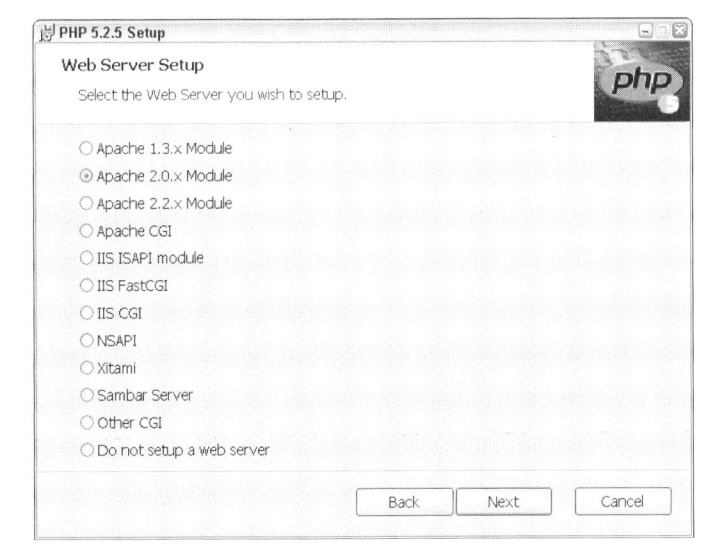

The next page, see Figure 1.22, is where you inform the installer of the location of the Apache configuration directory. For example, if you followed the Apache installation guide at the beginning of this chapter, the path would be the following:

```
C:\Program Files\Apache Group\Apache2\conf\
```

On the next page you choose the extra extensions needed for this book (see Figure 1.23). Those extensions are GD2, EXIF, MySQL, and PEAR. You can also choose to install any others that you think may be useful.

29

Part I Understanding the Basics

FIGURE 1.22

Apache Configuration Directory page

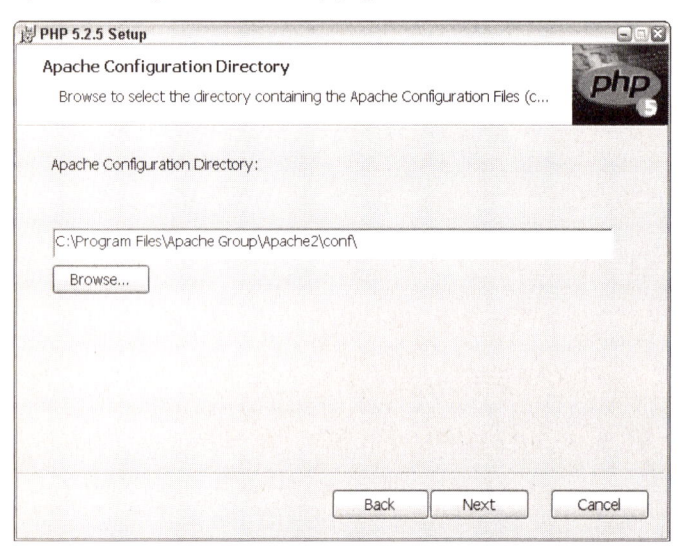

FIGURE 1.23

Choose which extensions you want to install in addition to PHP.

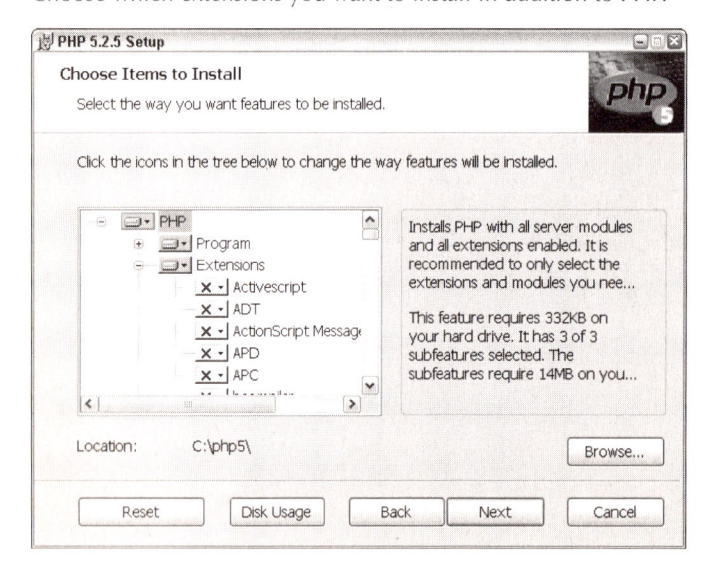

Getting Started with Flash and PHP 1

The entire configuration is set up at this point, and you can click Install to begin the process of installing PHP. When the installation is finished a Completed page appears.

You can open the directory in which PHP is installed and look at the various files. You can also edit the `php.ini` file to meet your specific needs.

```
C:\php5\php.ini
```

The default configuration of the `php.ini` should work for a development setup with the exception that you should enable `display_errors`. Enabling the display of errors tells PHP to print any errors to the screen. In a production setup this could be considered a security concern. A development server is generally only seen by authorized viewers, which means enabling this option is not a problem.

Open the `php.ini` file and search for the section referring to `error_reporting`.

```
display_errors = Off
```

Change the value to `On`.

```
display_errors = On
```

NOTE Changes to the `php.ini` file are not visible until you restart the server.

Make sure you restart the Apache web server before continuing because you made some modifications to the Apache configuration.

Testing

After you install PHP you can create a sample PHP file to test it out. A common sample file is the `phpinfo` file, which allows you to see the configuration variables for the PHP installation on the server.

You can use Notepad or any other text editor to create this sample file. If you install the full Web Suite from Adobe, you can use Dreamweaver to write PHP files (see Figure 1.24).

Here is the syntax for the `phpinfo` file.

```
<?php

phpinfo();

?>
```

Save this file as `info.php` in the Document Root of the Apache installation. For example, if you install Apache to the default location, the PHP file is saved to:

```
C:\Program Files\Apache Group\Apache2\htdocs\info.php
```

31

Part I Understanding the Basics

FIGURE 1.24

The sample PHP file as seen in Dreamweaver CS3

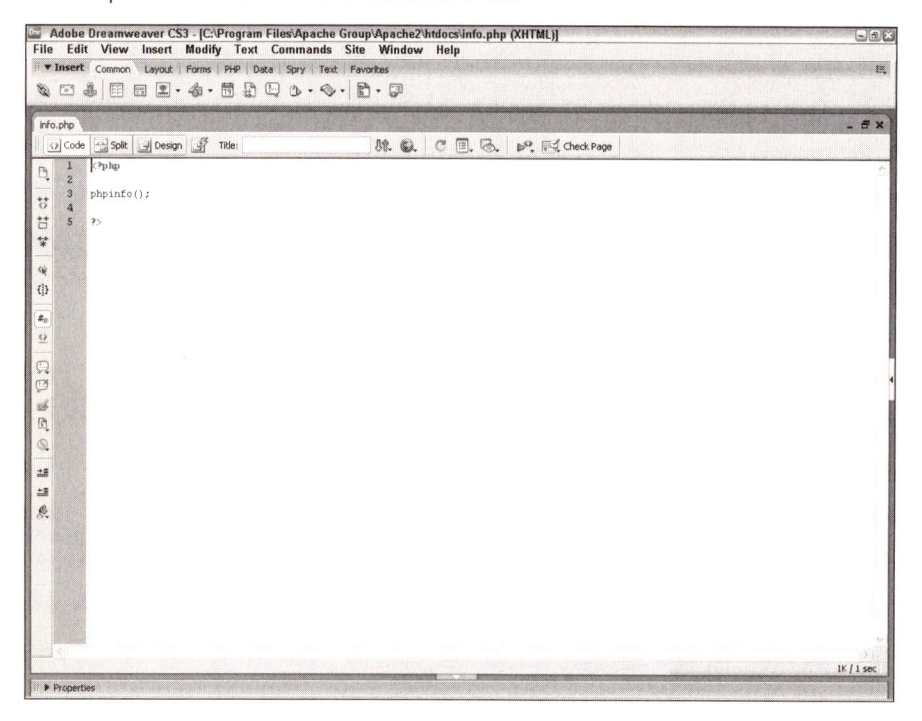

You can now open this file in your Web browser, as seen in Figure 1.25.

```
http://localhost/info.php
```

If you prefer, you can create a custom PHP file to test whether PHP is properly running, such as the following:

```
<?php

print "Hello, World! This is PHP.";

?>
```

When you run this file in the browser, you should see your message displayed.

Getting Started with Flash and PHP

FIGURE 1.25

PHP information displayed in a Web browser

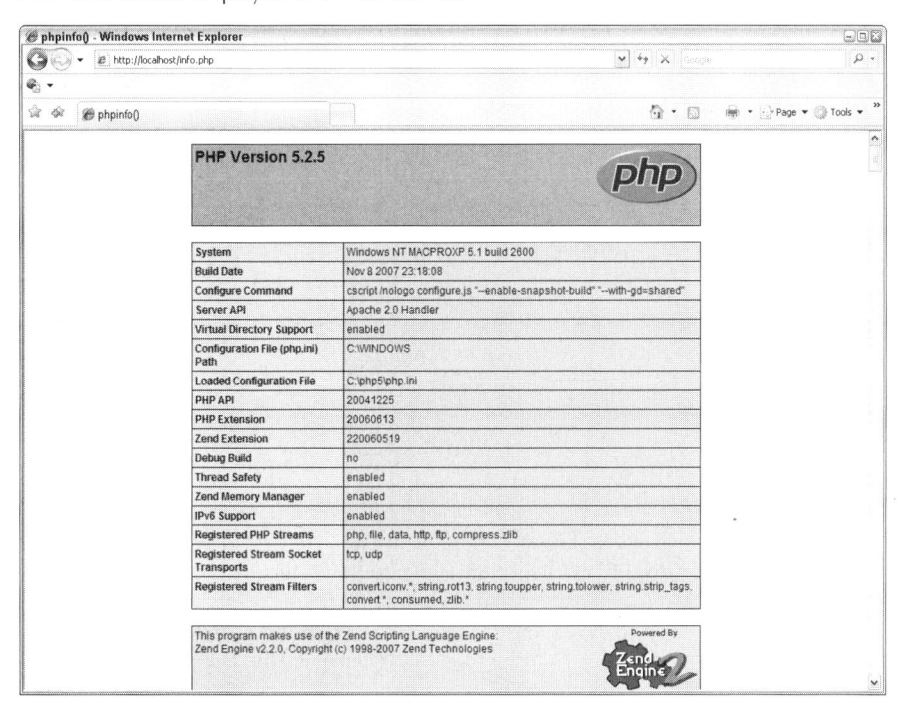

Installing PHP for UNIX

Installing PHP for UNIX is more detailed and requires more configuration. This is true for most command-line installation setups. You can download the installer files from the book's Web site or one the official PHP Web sites.

After you obtain the PHP installer files, you can begin the process of installation. Before you begin the installation, it is a good idea to stop Apache to ensure none of the files becomes corrupted.

```
/usr/local/apache/bin/apachectl stop
```

To start the installation, create the directory where PHP will be installed.

```
mkdir /usr/local/php5
```

You can substitute `php5` for simply `php`. However, adding the version number makes it easier to have multiple installations and will be easier to manage in the future.

```
cd /usr/local/php5
```

33

Part I Understanding the Basics

Unpack the files and type the installation directory:

```
gunzip php-5.2.5.tar.gz
tar -xvf php-5.2.5.tar
cd php-5.2.5
```

Building configuration parameters

The next step is to build the `config` line. This will contain all the necessary extensions and features you want to include in the installation. For example, you need to include database and image support to complete some of the chapters in this book, among others. Each option is contained within a set of single quotes (') and will include the path if necessary.

```
./configure' '--prefix=/usr/local/php5' '--with-
   apxs=/usr/local/apache/bin/apxs' '--with-gd' '--enable-exif'
   '--with-mysql=shared,/usr/local/php5' '--with-
   mysqli=shared,/usr/local/php5/bin/mysql_config' '--with-
   libxml-dir=shared,/usr/local/php5' '--with-
   xsl=shared,/usr/local/php5' '--with-jpeg-dir=/usr/local/php5'
   '--with-png-dir=/usr/local/php5' '--enable-gd-native-ttf' '--
   with-freetype-dir=/usr/local/php5' '--with-
   gettext=shared,/usr/local/php5'
```

When the configuration process is complete (which can take a while depending on the system), create and run the installer:

```
make
make install
```

After the `make install` command is completed, PHP should be installed.

Configuration

A few portions of PHP need to be configured to make sure it works seamlessly with Apache and your overall development system. This process is fairly easy to complete, but incorrect modification can result in a broken system. Also, when modifying configuration files, it is best to make a backup first.

The first step is to move the `php.ini` file to a central location that PHP will use when it starts up.

```
cp php.ini.recommended /usr/local/lib/php.ini
```

In order for Apache to load PHP files, add the necessary module references:

```
LoadModule php5_module modules/libphp5.so
AddType application/x-httpd-php .php .phtml
AddType application/x-httpd-php-source .phps
```

Getting Started with Flash and PHP

Restart Apache to have these changes take effect. Any time you edit the values in PHP or Apache, you must restart the server.

```
/usr/local/apache/bin/apachectl start
```

With everything properly installed, you can test the setup by running a sample PHP file:

```
<?php

phpinfo();

?>
```

Summary

In this chapter, you went through the steps necessary to install the complete development system. This process included the installation of Apache, PHP, and MySQL on a Windows or UNIX Web server. The next chapter walks you through the process of making this development setup more secure. This includes securing the files on the server as well as the overall server configuration through the `httpd.conf` configuration file.

Chapter 2

Exploring Flash and PHP

If you have installed all of the components on the server, you can configure the setup to be more secure. After security is explained, the next step is to set up the proper error handlers and look at ways to create a more usable setup for the end user.

After security and configuration of the Web server are complete, you will look at an overview of PHP to better understand how everything works. MySQL usage and basic integration with PHP are explained using various examples with descriptions and explanations.

The last section explores Flash, including class setup and overall IDE explanation.

IN THIS CHAPTER

Introducing the Web server

Exploring PHP

Exploring the basics of MySQL

Exploring Flash

Introduction to the Web Server

In the Chapter 1, you learned how to set up a development server, which included the installation of PHP, MySQL, and Apache. This section is an overview of how the Web server is set up, as well as how to make the system more secure.

Working with .htaccess files

The `.htaccess` file is used to modify how Apache functions for a specific directory. This file is similar to the `httpd.conf` file found in the global configuration of Apache, with the exception that it is not required and can be globally disabled, provided the admin modifies the settings of the Web server.

Part I: Understanding the Basics

The syntax of this file is not very advanced. It is basically a text file that informs the Web server of specific modifications.

For example, have you noticed a Web site that has specialized file extensions, such as the MediaTemple Web host, which has the following format?

```
http://www.mediatemple.net/contact.mt
```

Notice how the `url` has a `.mt` extension. This extension is not a standard file extension. This modification can be achieved using the `.htaccess` file:

```
# use custom file extensions
AddType application/x-httpd-php .me
```

This modification can also be done using the `httpd.conf` file if you prefer to have the entire Web server be able to use this custom file extension.

Apache handles many requests by default and can offer even more with additional modules installed. One module in particular allows you to have custom URLs, also commonly referred to as clean URLs.

The possibilities with `.htaccess` are varied and totally depend on your application. One more common usage of `.htaccess` is to redirect www and non-www requests to the same location. This not only limits redundant links but also provides better search engine optimization.

An example of this conversion, using the domain `example.org`, would look something similar to the following:

```
# Force www.domain.com to domain.com
RewriteCond %{HTTP_HOST} ^www.example.org [NC]
RewriteRule ^(.*)$ http://example.org/$1 [R=301,L]
```

Protecting your content

You can protect your content in a number of ways. You can build a custom authentication system or use the basic authentication that is packaged with Apache.

The basic authentication is set up in two steps. The first step is to create the password and user.

You use the `htpasswd` file to create the password file. This password-creation command is located in the `bin/` directory where you installed Apache. For example, you will most likely find the file at the following location, assuming you used the suggested installation path in Chapter 1.

```
$ /usr/local/apache/bin/htpasswd
```

The first time you create a user, you need to inform the password-creation application to create a new password file. From that point on you omit the -c flag.

Exploring Flash and PHP

CAUTION Failure to remove the -c flag after the first user setup will result in a new password file and remove any existing users.

While not required, it is a good practice to periodically back up this and any other important files in case your system encounters an unexpected crash or data corruption.

The command to create a password is simply a call to the password application with the username appended to the end.

```
$ cd /usr/local/apache/bin/
$ htpasswd -c /usr/local/apache/passwd/passwords USERNAME
```

Be sure to replace USERNAME with the actual username you want to add.

The `htpasswd` application will ask you for the password you want to assign, and then ask you to type the same password again to confirm it.

The generated password file is encrypted. However, you should still store it in a secure location. Under no circumstances should this file be stored in the public directory because it could compromise the integrity of your system.

This isn't as important in a development system, but it is a good practice to follow all proper security steps, even in a development setup, to become familiar with them. As you continue to work on servers, security will become second nature. You should never put it off to save time.

After you create the password file, add the security check in a `.htaccess` in whatever location you want to password protect. For example, let's add the authentication to the entire server because this a development server and you wouldn't want anyone viewing it.

Add the following to a new `.htaccess` file in the root of the Web directory.

```
AuthType Basic
AuthName "Authorization Required"
AuthUserFile /usr/local/apache/passwd/passwords
Require valid-user
```

This informs Apache that any request to this directory and below requires authorization. The last line allows any user in the password file to be able to log in.

Require valid-user

You can also add a specific username, but this is more difficult to maintain.

This is basic authentication so it does have various limitations. For example, you cannot modify the dialog box that displays in the user's browser. You can't modify the label values next to the input boxes and, most importantly, you cannot allow the user to log out.

If your application requires a more customized and integrated login system, it may be better to build a custom PHP/MySQL setup, depending on your requirements.

Part I: Understanding the Basics

Gathering information about Apache

As you continue to work with Apache, there are some commands and tools that can result in more time to develop an application instead of micromanaging the server.

Starting and stopping Apache

Sometimes Apache can act up just like any other piece of software or hardware on your system. Oftentimes when this occurs, a simple restart will fix the issue. For instance, as more users request files from Apache, it can start to fill up internal memory and temporary files.

To restart Apache you can simply call the following command in UNIX from the command line or restart the service on Windows:

```
$ /usr/local/apache/bin/apachectl restart
```

> **NOTE** The path to the `apachectl` application can vary depending on the installation of Apache.

If you want to stop Apache and not have it restart, use the following command. This would most likely be done when installing new modules or updating Apache itself.

```
$ /usr/local/apache/bin/apachectl stop
```

To start the server again after you complete the update, simply use the start option:

```
$ /usr/local/apache/bin/apachectl start
```

Determining the version of Apache

Occasionally, when installing new software, you need to know which version of Apache you are currently running. For example, when installing PHP you need to know which version of Apache you are using. This is found by running a simple command switch.

```
$ /usr/local/apache/bin/httpd -V
```

The result of that command would be something similar to Figure 2.1.

Determining which modules are installed in Apache

You can very easily determine which modules are currently installed in Apache by using the following command-line flags in UNIX.

```
$ /usr/local/apache/bin/apachectl -t -D DUMP_MODULES
```

To determine the modules in Windows, you would run the following command:

```
httpd -t -D DUMP_MODULES
```

Exploring Flash and PHP   2

FIGURE 2.1
Displaying the current version of Apache

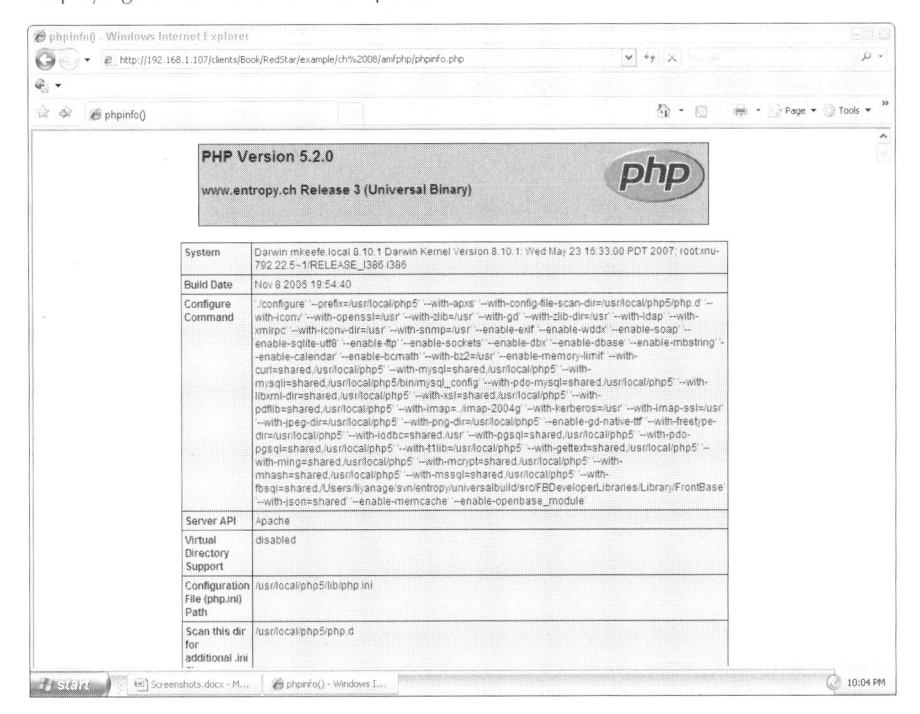

An example response from this command is something similar to the following:

```
Loaded Modules:
 core_module (static)
 mpm_worker_module (static)
 http_module (static)
 so_module (static)
 include_module (shared)
 deflate_module (shared)
 log_config_module (shared)
 env_module (shared)
 expires_module (shared)
 headers_module (shared)
 setenvif_module (shared)
 ssl_module (shared)
 mime_module (shared)
 status_module (shared)
 autoindex_module (shared)
 info_module (shared)
```

41

Part I Understanding the Basics

```
vhost_alias_module (shared)
negotiation_module (shared)
dir_module (shared)
imagemap_module (shared)
actions_module (shared)
userdir_module (shared)
alias_module (shared)
rewrite_module (shared)
...
Syntax OK
```

If you omit the `-D DUMP_MODULES` flag you will only see the `Syntax` response. This informs you if something is wrong or tells you everything is okay.

```
$ /usr/local/apache/bin/apachectl -t
```

For Windows the command would be

```
httpd -t
```

Using custom error documents

When you view a URL on a Web site, Apache serves a page to you based on your request. By default, if Apache is asked to serve a file it can't find, it returns an ugly 404 page that is not very informative and actually causes a potential security concern.

As you can see in Figure 2.2, Apache has printed the server information for the world to see. Now this isn't a huge security concern, but every piece of information can add up to a major problem.

FIGURE 2.2

Default error page from Apache

A more important issue with using the standard error pages is the fact the user is presented with a useless page. For example, the user now knows the file doesn't exist, but has nowhere to go and no idea what could be the problem. Oddly enough, if a user is shown a 404 page he or she will usually not stick around, and that means an abandoned user for your site.

Exploring Flash and PHP

Modifying Apache

Luckily, Apache allows you to modify this default error page. Some hosts allow you to modify the file using the included control panel that they installed when you purchased the server. In this case, however, the development server requires you to manually configure the majority of it.

Using custom error documents is as simple as adding the modification to a `.htaccess` file. This file is usually stored in the Document Root to ensure all files will see the file.

The following code is the syntax required to modify the error document.

```
# Customized Error Handler
ErrorDocument 204 /error.html
ErrorDocument 301 /error.html
ErrorDocument 302 /error.html
ErrorDocument 400 /error.html
ErrorDocument 401 /error.html
ErrorDocument 403 /error.html
ErrorDocument 404 /error.html
ErrorDocument 500 /error.html
ErrorDocument 501 /error.html
ErrorDocument 502 /error.html
ErrorDocument 503 /error.html
```

As you can see, the error documents will be replaced by one file. You can, of course, point to a separate file for each error encountered. If you do not assign a specific error page, Apache reverts to its default. The previous list is a robust record of possible error codes, but it is not a complete one.

Dynamic error documents

Using PHP, you can create a dynamic error handling system. The idea is to call one page like you did in the previous example, with the exception that a variable will be passed along to notify that page of which error was encountered.

You start by modifying the error handler in the `.htaccess` file, such as:

```
# Error Handler, request is sent to a php file
ErrorDocument 204 /errorHandler.php?e=204
ErrorDocument 301 /errorHandler.php?e=301
ErrorDocument 302 /errorHandler.php?e=302
ErrorDocument 400 /errorHandler.php?e=400
ErrorDocument 401 /errorHandler.php?e=401
ErrorDocument 403 /errorHandler.php?e=403
ErrorDocument 404 /errorHandler.php?e=404
ErrorDocument 500 /errorHandler.php?e=500
ErrorDocument 501 /errorHandler.php?e=501
ErrorDocument 502 /errorHandler.php?e=502
ErrorDocument 503 /errorHandler.php?e=503
```

Part I Understanding the Basics

That code tells Apache to redirect those errors to the `errorHandler.php` file, passing in the error code. The next step is to build the PHP file that will handle the error codes. This PHP will expect one argument and will be smart enough to return a valid response if no error is passed in.

The first part of the file captures the error code and initializes a variable to store the error string.

```
<?php

$errorCode = $_GET['e'];
$errorString = "";

...

?>
```

When an error code is found, a check to make sure it is a valid number is made to keep the application secure.

```
<?php

$errorCode = $_GET['e'];
$errorString = "";

if(!is_numeric($errorCode))
{
   $errorCode = -1;
}

...

?>
```

A basic switch is used to determine which error code was encountered. Switches are explained in the section "Exploring the Basics of PHP" later in this chapter.

```
<?php

$errorCode = $_GET['e'];
$errorString = "";

if(!is_numeric($errorCode))
{
   $errorCode = -1;
}
```

Exploring Flash and PHP

```php
switch($errorCode)
  {
  case 204: // No Content (Empty Document)
    $errorString = "No Content (Empty Document)";
    break;
  case 301: // Moved Permanently
    $errorString = "Moved Permanently";
    break;
  case 400: // Bad Request
    $errorString = "Bad Request";
    break;
  case 401: // Unauthorized User
    $errorString = "Unauthorized User";
    break;
  case 403: // Forbidden
    $errorString = "Forbidden";
    break;
  case 404: // Document Not Found
    $errorString = "Document Not Found";
    break;
  case 500: // Internal Server Error
    $errorString = "Internal Server Error";
    break;
  case 503: // Out of Resources
    $errorString = "Out of Resources";
    break;
  case -1: // No Error Code
    $errorString = "Unknown Error";
  }

?>
```

The last step is to display the error string to the user, which completes the custom error handling script. You will notice that some of the error codes were omitted from the switch to demonstrate the fact that the script silently moves on if an invalid error code is displayed.

```php
<?php

$errorCode = $_GET['e'];
$errorString = "";

if(!is_numeric($errorCode))
{
  $errorCode = -1;
}
```

Part I   Understanding the Basics

```
switch($errorCode)
  {
  case 204: // No Content (Empty Document)
    $errorString = "No Content (Empty Document)";
    break;
  case 301: // Moved Permanently
    $errorString = "Moved Permanently";
    break;
  case 400: // Bad Request
    $errorString = "Bad Request";
    break;
  case 401: // Unauthorized User
    $errorString = "Unauthorized User";
    break;
  case 403: // Forbidden
    $errorString = "Forbidden";
    break;
  case 404: // Document Not Found
    $errorString = "Document Not Found";
    break;
  case 500: // Internal Server Error
    $errorString = "Internal Server Error";
    break;
  case 503: // Out of Resources
    $errorString = "Out of Resources";
    break;
  case -1: // No Error Code
    $errorString = "Unknown Error";
  }

?>

<h2>An error occurred while processing your request</h2>
<h3><?=$errorString?></h3>
```

The $errorString variable is printed to the screen, informing the user that an error has occurred.

This custom error handler presents a much better error to the user. Some Web sites include relevant links of interest or use the query (if it was a search) to return relevant information. It is unfortunate that a user would see an error page, but is more common as technology changes and systems are updated.

It is a good idea to keep permanent links, because search engines will cache links. In the future, it will be beneficial for your traffic if that link still worked.

As a bonus to the previous script, which is located on the Web site for this book, there is a complete error-handling system that includes localized errors (can be tailored to a language setting) and utilizes PHP templates and a custom CSS file to modify the style.

Exploring the Basics of PHP

PHP (Hypertext Pre-Processor) is a server-side scripting language that runs on Apache or other similar Web server applications. PHP is one of the most popular server-side scripting languages because it is fairly simple to get started in and can handle robust applications.

The coding structure is based on C and can be written in a procedural (step-by-step) or Class-based structure (objects, properties, methods, and so on). Once you understand the basics of PHP, you can really start to see the true power it has.

This book is based around PHP 5, but a lot of the following tips, techniques, and styles explained in this section can be used for PHP 4 and PHP 5, as the versions are fairly similar.

Understanding variables

Variables, also commonly referred to as `vars` or properties (when working with classes), are probably the most-used item in programming. They are used to assign a value to a place that can be called in another part of the code. The usage of variables is not only a timesaver, but also makes the program more structured and easy to maintain.

Here is a very simple example of a variable definition in PHP:

```
$myVar = "hello world";
```

The previous example assigned the string `"hello world"` to the variable `$myVar`.

There are a few things to keep in mind when working with variables.

- They must be preceded by a dollar ($) sign (unless in a Class).
- They must end with semicolon (;).

Variables can accept many types of data, including, but not limited to String, Boolean, and Array, each of which is discussed in the following sections.

Strings

String variables contain text, such as:

```
"Hello, World!"
```

You can also build strings using concatenation techniques, such as:

```
$var = "Hello";
$var .= ", World!";
print $var; // Outputs: Hello, World!
```

Part I Understanding the Basics

Booleans

Booleans are special variables that can be one of two possible values: `true` or `false`. They are used mostly in `if` statements and other forms of conditional checks, such as:

```
$loggedIn = false;
if($loggedIn == false)
{
  print "Sorry, you are not logged in!";
}
```

Arrays

Arrays are complex data structures consisting of a group of elements that are accessed by indexing. In PHP, this index can either be a numeric value or a string.

Here is an example of an array and the two ways to access the data:

```
<?php

$fruit = array(
  "Orange",
  "Apple",
  "Strawberry",
  "Grape"
);

print $fruit[1]; // Apple

$fruit = array(
  "orange" => "Orange",
  "apple" => "Apple",
  "strawberry" => "Strawberry",
  "grape" => "Grape"
);

print $fruit['orange']; // Orange

?>
```

Objects

Classes in PHP describe an object or are the definition of an object. They consist of self-defined methods and properties, which allows you to create custom functionality.

Exploring Flash and PHP

Here is a very basic example of a class in PHP with a sample call at the bottom of the example:

```php
<?php

class Animals
{
    function Animal()
    {

    }
    public function speak($word)
    {
        print $word;
    }
}

class Dog extends Animals
{
    function Dog($word)
    {
        Animals::speak($word);
    }
}

// Create a new Dog
$dog = new Dog("Hello.. Woof!");

?>
```

Working with functions

When developing applications you tend to repeat various tasks. Constantly having to type those steps can be a long process. More importantly, repeating code makes an application less efficient.

Functions allow you to place repetitive tasks in a nice little container that you can call at any time as long as the function is accessible.

Here is an example function that adds two numbers and returns the sum:

```php
function addNumbers($num1, $num2)
{
  // return the sum of the two numbers
  return ($num1 + $num2);
}
```

You call a function by referencing the function name and passing any arguments the function requires. This example returns 10 as the sum.

49

Part I Understanding the Basics

An argument is a value that is passed into the function and later used within the function as a local variable.

```
addNumbers(4, 6); // outputs 10
```

Functions in PHP can have a default argument assigned, which means they won't require that argument to be passed in, such as:

```
function addNumbers($num1, $num2, $print=true)
{
  if($print)
  {
    print "Sum is: " . ($num1 + $num2);
  }
  else
  {
    return ($num1 + $num2);
  }
}
```

This function will print the result directly to the screen or return the value if the $print variable is false, which it is by default. You cannot exclude an argument in the middle of defining other arguments. For example, the following function call would be invalid:

```
function say($upperCase=false, $string)
{
  if($upperCase)
  {
    return strtoupper($string);
  }
  else
  {
    return $string;
  }
}

say("Hello, World!");
```

This would assign the passed-in string to the $upperCase value and ignore the $string variable. Because PHP does not worry about what type of value is passed in, this results in an error at the line where it returns the string.

Classes also have functions, called methods. Methods can retain special features that standard functions cannot.

Understanding control structures

Most programming languages have control structures that offer code fragments and overall provide a more dynamic path for an application. The following is some of the more common control structures, including the ones used in the majority of this book.

if

The `if` construct is found in any popular programming language, PHP included. It allows for conditional execution of code fragments. An example of an `if` statement would be:

```
$admin = getAdminStatus();
if($admin == true)
{
  print "Admin logged in, show admin controls";
}
```

You can nest `if` statements with other `if` statements an unlimited amount of times. A more realistic use of nesting `if` statements is a login application that has varied levels of authentication.

```
$loggedIn = true;
$admin = true;
$editable = true;

if($loggedIn)
{
  if($admin)
  {
    if($editable)
    {
      // allow the page to be
      // edited because a valid
      // administrator is logged in
    }
  }
}
```

else

Assume you want to display an error message to users not logged in and the proper control panel if the user is logged in. This is done using an `else` statement, which is executed if the condition in the `if` is not met.

```
$loggedIn = false;
if($loggedIn)
{
  // display control panel
}
else
{
  // display login form and error message
}
```

Part I Understanding the Basics

An `else` is not required and is placed after all other conditional checks, such as `elseif`, which is in the next section.

elseif

The `elseif` is the combination of an `if` and an `else`. This statement is placed after an `if` and allows the code to match another condition, which can be completely different than the `if` run before.

> **NOTE** An else or else..if will only be evaluated if the preceding conditional is not met.

```
$loggedIn = false;
$colorOfSky = "blue";

if($loggedIn)
{
  // user logged in
}
elseif($ColorOfSky == "blue")
{
  // color of sky is blue, log user in??
}
```

while

The `while` is a type of loop. The code within the curly braces {} runs "while" the condition is met. Once the condition is no longer valid, the loop stops.

> **CAUTION** Loops in PHP can run forever if not programmed correctly. Use caution when working with loops and always check for valid data first.

```
while($x < 50)
{
  print "x=" . $x . "<br />";
  $x++;
}
```

for

A `for` loop is the most complex loop in PHP. Here is an example:

```
for($x=0; $x < 10; $x++)
{
  print "x=" . $x . "<br />";
}
```

The first expression ($x=0) is executed unconditionally once at the start of the loop. The second expression ($x < 10;) is evaluated on each pass and the loop will continue until this condition is met or the loop is stopped using a `break`. On each pass, the third expression ($x++) is executed. In this example, it increments $x on each pass.

Exploring Flash and PHP

You can nest `for` loops and even define multiple variables in the first expression. This can make your code faster, but harder to read.

foreach

The `foreach` loop is used to iterate over an array. You assign the loop variable to the desired array, and on each pass the value is stored in that loop variable.

```
$fruits = array("Orange", "Apple", "Banana", "Grapefruit");
foreach($fruits as $fruit)
{
  print "Fruit: " . $fruit;
}
```

NOTE The variable `$fruit` will still exist once a `foreach` loop has been completed, so it is a good idea to destroy the variable using `unset()`, such as `unset($fruit)`.

break

The `break` control ends the execution of a loop, regardless if the condition is met or not. You can place an optional numeric value informing PHP of how many levels it should break out. This is useful when you have a nested loop that needs to tell the parent to exit if an error occurs.

```
for($i=0; $i < count($users); $i++)
{
  for($j=0; $j < 5; $j++)
  {
    if($users[$i][$j]['valid'] == false)
    {
      // found invalid user, group is compromised
      // exit both loops
      break 2;
    }
  }
}
```

continue

Unlike `break`, `continue` will exit the current iteration of a loop, but allow the remaining iterations to continue on.

This is useful when you are looping through a bunch of data and only want to act on valid data.

```
for($i=0; $i < count($users); $i++)
{
  if($users[$i]['valid'] == false)
  {
    // invalid user, continue with remaining list
    continue;
  }
  // more code logic here
}
```

Part I Understanding the Basics

Just like the `break`, `continue` will also accept a numeric argument telling it how many levels of enclosing loops to skip over.

switch

A `switch` is similar to a series of `if` statements using the same expression (variable). You would generally use a `switch` when you want to test a variable against a lot of conditions.

```
switch($userLevel)
{
  case 'ADMIN':
    print "User is an admin";
    break;
  case 'MODERATOR':
    print "User is a mod";
    break;
  case 'MEMBER':
    print "User is an member";
    break;

  case 'GUEST':
    print "User is an guest";
    break;


}
```

A `break` is used to ensure the remaining checks will not run; in fact, if you remove the breaks, every condition will be checked, which can cause problems if you intend to do a multilevel validation.

require

The `require()` statement attempts to load a file and will exit the script with a Fatal Error if that file is not found. This function checks for the file against the current `included_path` as well as the directory the file is running in.

```
require("importantFile.php");
```

The error that is displayed (see Figure 2.3) can sometimes cause a potential security concern in that it will display the path the file exited on. A better way to handle this is to create a check for the file first and display a cleaner, less crucial message to the user.

```
if(!file_exists("importantFile.php"))
{
  $error = "Sorry, one of the core components could not be
   loaded";
  exit($error); // display clean error and exit remaining script
}
require("importantFile.php"); // never runs, if file doesn't
   exist
```

54

FIGURE 2.3

PHP `require()` error as seen in the browser

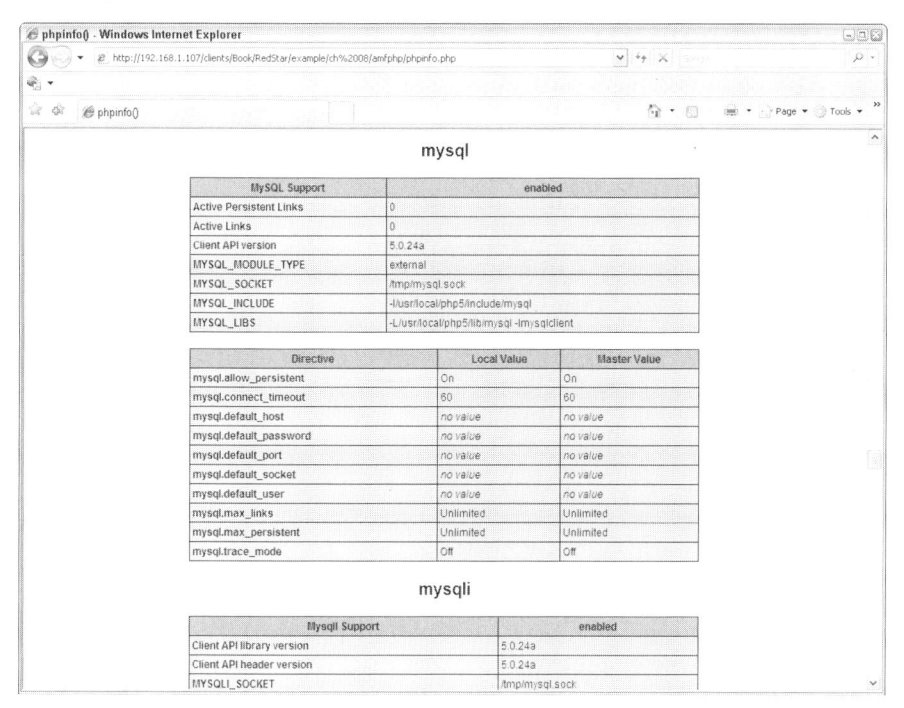

include

The `include()` statement is similar to the `require` with the exception it will display an error but not stop the execution of the script.

```
include("optionalFile.php");
```

require_once

The `require_once` statement behaves similarly to `require`, with the exception that if the current file is already loaded it will not attempt to load it again. This is more useful as you continue to build large applications that sometimes share many files. This ensures that no redundant code is loaded.

```
require_once("requiredFile.php");

// ... other code here

require_once("requiredFile.php");
```

The second `require_once` will not run because the file has already been loaded in the previous portion of the code.

include_once

The `include_once()` statement is similar to the `require_once` with the exception that if the file is not found, it only displays a simple error.

Using type checking in PHP

Unlike most programming languages, PHP doesn't require strict typing of variables. This means you don't have to define what type of data a variable will hold.

This may seem like a good thing because variables can be shared. However the potential downside to this approach is that a variable that you expect to be a string could potentially show up as an array. This would most likely break your code or cause an exploitable portion of code. Imagine code similar to the following:

```
$id = -1;

if(isset($id))
{
  // sql call here, set id to a string, for some reason
  $id = "user id";
}

// more logic here
if($id == -1)
{
  // user not logged in
}
else
{
  // user logged in
}
```

This is an overly dramatic example because it is full of worst-case scenarios, but you can see how untyped variables can cause headaches.

Type checking functions

PHP does offer some special functions that allow you to check the type of a variable, but this does not stop other code from overwriting the variables.

An example of one of these functions would be `is_string`, which checks to see if the passed-in variables contents are `string`.

```
$saying = "Hello, World!";

if(is_string($saying))
{
  print "$saying is a string";
}
```

PHP offers the ability to test for arrays, numbers, strings, and empty values.

Future version support
It has been mentioned that future versions of PHP could include strict type checking, but for now, these functions, when needed, will provide a higher level of integrity for your application.

Exploring the Basics of MySQL

MySQL is the storage application used with PHP to create a dynamic application. You can store pretty much any type of data in a MySQL database and have the ability to share that information with other applications and systems. Oftentimes a database is used when searching needs to be done or if data is changing frequently and many people will be requesting this updated data.

The alternative to a database is a flat file (text file) that has many limitations, the most devastating being the fact that only so many instances of the file can be used at once. Another limitation is the ability to quickly index and search a text file.

Using statements

The contents in a MySQL database are stored in tables. These tables are stored in databases that make up the MySQL system. The data stored in those tables is accessed using various statements and conditions, which are called queries.

There are many statements that can be used in SQL queries.

SELECT
The `SELECT` statement is the most common statement, which tells MySQL what contents (columns) you want returned from a table.

```
SELECT id,name,ip, bio FROM users WHERE id=3
```

You can select data from multiple tables using commas (,) to separate the column and table names.

```
SELECT users.id, users.name, members.posts, members.subs FROM
    users, members WHERE members.userID=users.id AND users.id=3
```

INSERT
The `INSERT` statement is used to add new rows to an existing table. There are multiple ways to define an `INSERT`.

If you only want to update some columns you need to define those columns.

```
INSERT INTO members (name, bio, ip) VALUES ($name, $bio, $ip);
```

Part I   Understanding the Basics

A shortcut is used to exclude the column definitions. However, this is only possible when all values are being updated or you have assigned default values when you create the table.

    INSERT INTO members ($name, $bio, $ip);

After an INSERT has completed, you can make a call to mysql_insert_id(), which will return the ID of the last successful insert.

    $result = mysql_query("INSERT INTO members (" .
        $name . ", " .
        $bio . ", " .
        $ip . ")");

    $rowID = mysql_insert_id($result);

DELETE

The DELETE statement is used to remove one or more rows from a table. Like the other statements, you can create a condition using WHERE, AND, OR, and so on.

    DELETE FROM users WHERE id=3

You can also remove all rows in a database by omitting the condition:

    DELETE FROM users

CAUTION   The DELETE statement is a very powerful one that should be used with extreme caution.

Conditions

Conditions in MySQL are used to limit the amount of data that is returned. For example, an SQL query such as the following would return all users in the database:

    SELECT * FROM users

WHERE

This would be okay if that's what you want to occur. You probably only would want to return certain users or even one specific user. This would be done using the WHERE condition.

    SELECT * FROM users WHERE id=3

AND

The AND condition is used when you need to match more than one condition. An example would be you want to return a database of members that have been registered and have a valid account.

    SELECT * FROM users WHERE active=1 AND registered="yes"

You can use any combination of the conditional statements, with the exception that there should only be one WHERE statement.

OR

The OR statement is used when you want only one condition to match. For example, you want users that have a level of `admin` or `mod`. Think of this as an if..else for SQL.

```
SELECT * FROM users WHERE level='admin' OR level='mod'
```

Conditions in MySQL can come in handy when trying to drill down data, especially when you start combining them. It is not rare to create very complex SQL statements in a matter of minutes.

Exploring Flash

Flash is not only a technology, it is also the name of a development tool from Adobe, which is used to create Flash-enabled content. This content can be anything from a simple banner advertisement all the way to a complete database-driven Web site with video and user interaction.

Flash IDE

The Flash IDE (Integrated Development Environment), as shown in Figure 2.4, is a robust development tool with many useful features.

FIGURE 2.4

Flash CS3 IDE with default layout

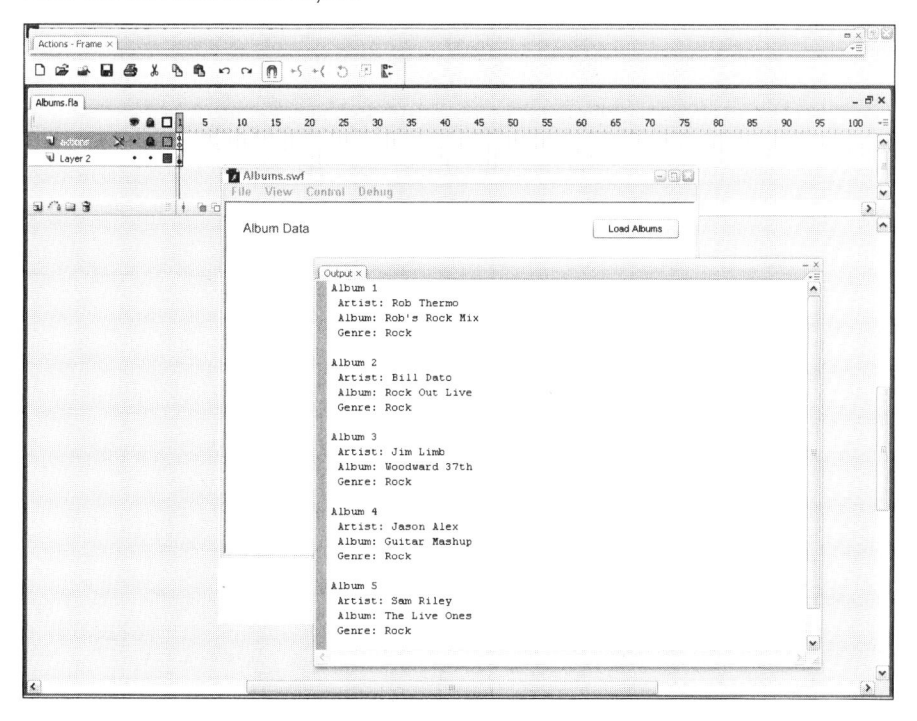

Part I Understanding the Basics

One of the updated tools is the code editor, also referred to as the ActionScript panel. This panel, as seen in Figure 2.5, is where you write your ActionScript code for your Flash applications. The latest version has robust code completion, advanced debugging, as well as syntax highlighting to name a few of the new features.

FIGURE 2.5

ActionScript panel found in Flash CS3

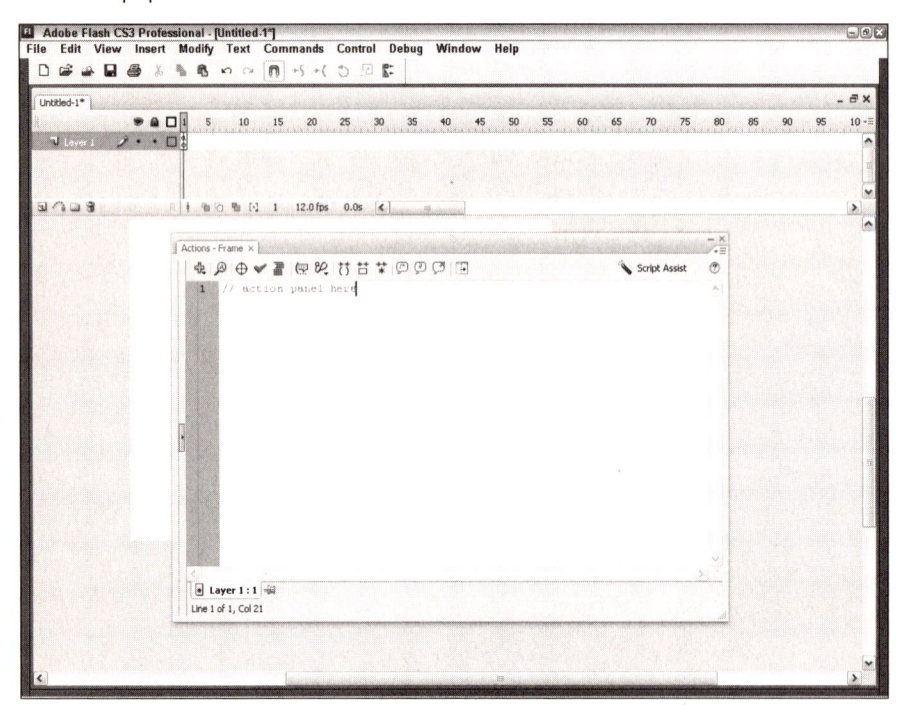

This is where the majority of your development life will be spent. The panel is not the only editor; you can create complete ActionScript files, as shown in Figure 2.6, and include them in your application.

To create a custom AS file, choose File ➪ New. Choose ActionScript 3 File from the middle column. Save the file as Sample.as to your desktop.

FIGURE 2.6

External ActionScript editor included with Flash CS3

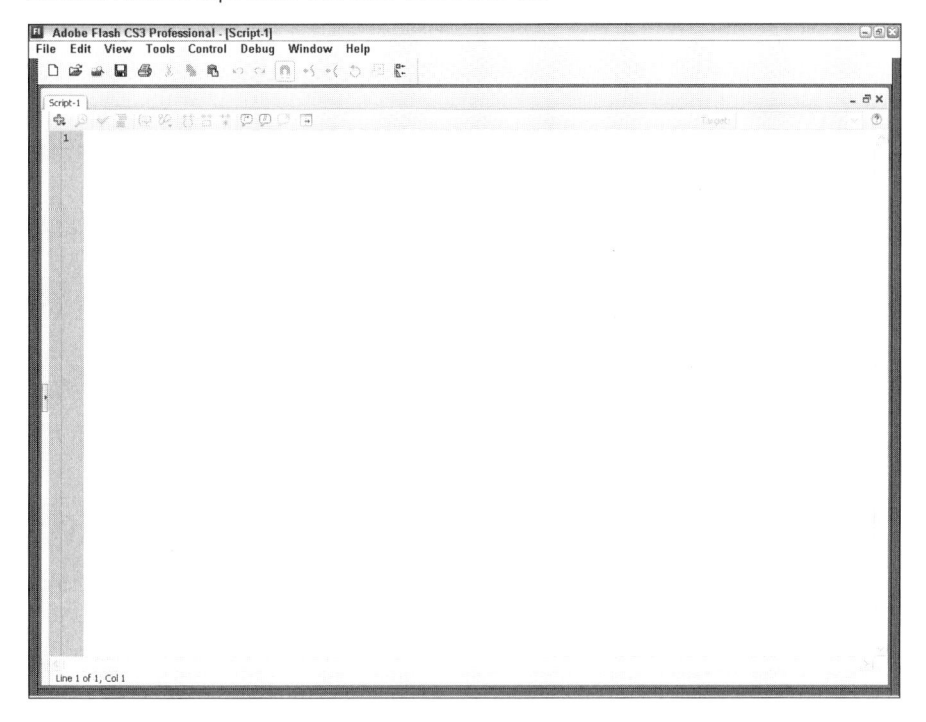

Alternative editors

You will find many ActionScript editors on the market. My personal favorite is FDT from powerflasher at `http://fdt.powerflasher.com/`. This editor offers the largest amount of customization and is built into the Eclipse editor, which many other companies depend on.

Create a new FLA and save that to your desktop as well. Now open the code editor and add the following code:

```
#include "Sample.as"
```

That line of code includes the contents of `Sample.as` in your application. This means you can write all of your ActionScript in the external file and Flash will know to include it when you test or build the application.

Flash-enabled devices

Flash is no longer a simple animation tool used to create flashy graphics for the Web. You can now find Flash installed on an array of products such as cell phones, media players, and even in some cameras. The cell phone technology is especially interesting because these devices tend to have active Internet connections, which means you can develop Rich Internet Applications (RIA) for mobile devices as well as the desktop.

Moving forward

You should now have a basic understanding of what Flash is and how it has advanced in the latest version. This book will explain the various aspects of Flash and ActionScript in regards to working with PHP and data management.

However, for a more detailed guide on Flash CS3, I highly recommend the *Adobe Flash CS3 Professional Bible*, published by John Wiley & Sons, Inc.

Summary

In this chapter, you learned about the Web server and how to modify the configuration files to set up your custom development or live environment. This information included custom error pages, application-specific modules, and best practices for protecting your content.

Once the basics of working with the Web server were understood, the next step was learning how to work with PHP. This covered the basics of PHP as well as specifics for the chapters in this book.

The second half of the chapter included information about MySQL and how to work with the data in your database.

The last part was an overview of Flash and how to work with the development environment. For a more detailed overview a few references were given.

Chapter 3

Getting Connected

etting connected is a phrase used to describe the process of connecting to various data sources. In this chapter, it is the process of connecting ActionScript (Flash), PHP, and MySQL in various ways. This data can be a simple Web site or a database-driven content management system for which Flash becomes the front-end display.

If these three components are not already installed, refer to Chapter 1 before continuing with this chapter.

The first part of each section focuses on what each connection type has to offer and moves on to examples to provide a complete picture of the end result.

IN THIS CHAPTER

Understanding communications in Flash

Connecting Flash to PHP

Connecting PHP to MySQL

Understanding Communications in Flash

Developing self-standing applications lacks certain functionality, primarily the ability to work with dynamic data. In smaller applications you can use flat files, such as XML files, but those would pose a problem as a project continues to grow.

Simple text file-based applications also suffer from file locking, which can occur if too many people are accessing the file. When this occurs, Apache and/or PHP can throw an error that results in users not being able to use the site.

Determining the status of PHP

The first step to setting up a connection to PHP in Flash is to determine if PHP is properly installed and running. This is done by creating a simple PHP file that outputs the current configuration settings for the version of PHP installed.

The PHP function `phpinfo()` outputs the configuration information by building a custom HTML page, as shown in Figure 3.1.

WARNING Leaving the `phpinfo` file on your server can be a security risk. It is best to only upload it when you need to look at it, and then delete it.

The following is a sample info file that makes a call to the `phpinfo()` function.

```php
<?php

// output php configuration settings
phpinfo();

?>
```

FIGURE 3.1

Here is the output of the `phpinfo` function, which shows the current PHP configuration settings.

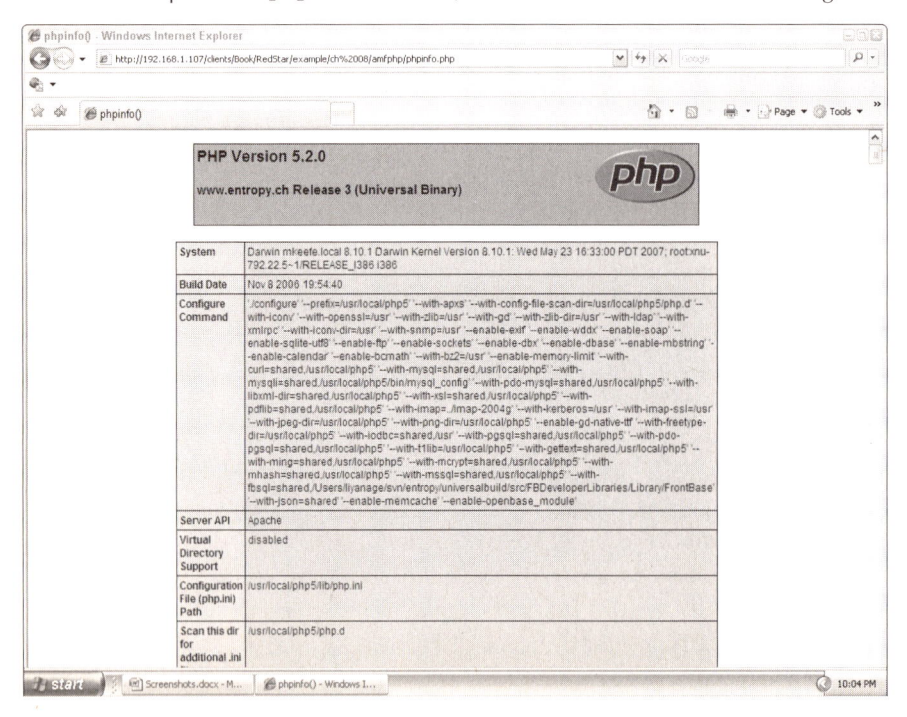

Getting Connected

If you are presented with the `phpinfo` file, which generally is in purple and starts with the version of PHP installed, then everything is installed properly.

However, if you see a dialog box to download your PHP file, it means Apache is improperly configured or has not been enabled for PHP support. This level of setup is covered in Chapter 1 and in the help files that ship with Apache. In rare cases you may be presented with a Server not found page, which could mean Apache is not installed or running.

Assuming that PHP and Apache are both properly running, you can move on with the process of connecting Flash to PHP.

Working with various connection types

Flash offers many different types of communication options. Determining which communication to use in your project is accomplished by the intended feature set of that specific application.

One-way communication

One-way communication in Flash is the process of sending data to a Web server and not looking or caring if a response comes back. This is mostly used to open a URL, but could also be used to update a file with no intention of handling the result. This type of communication is often used for simply firing off an event or running some sort of cleaning system.

For example, if your site needs periodic file cleaning (deleting, renaming, moving), it is a good idea to attach this to the front-end system because your server resources will only be in use when they are already providing content for that user. This would be started by a one-way communication behind the scenes.

> **NOTE** The update by viewing concept should not be used for backup solutions because a slow viewing could result in missing backups.

Here is an example of one-way communication in Flash:

```
var serverFile:String = "http://localhost/callLink.php";

var urlRequest:URLRequest = new URLRequest(serverFile);

navigateToURL(urlRequest);
```

The `navigateToURL` function accepts two parameters. The first parameter is the `URLRequest` instance, and the second parameter is the window or target. By default, the window is `_self`, which means the new page will load into the current browser if one exists.

However, in some cases, you may want to open a new browser window, which you can do by adding the second parameter.

```
var serverFile:String = "http://localhost/callLink.php";
```

Understanding the Basics

```
var urlRequest:URLRequest = new URLRequest(serverFile);

navigateToURL(urlRequest, "_blank");
```

The window parameter can accept one of the following strings, as shown in Table 3.1.

TABLE 3.1

Window Targets for Links

`"_self"`	Current frame in the current window
`"_blank"`	New window
`"_parent"`	Parent of the current frame
`"_top"`	Top-level frame in the current window

The window parameter can also accept a custom name, such as the name of a frame or specific window. For example, assuming you want to send a link to the window named `"childWindowBox"`, the code would look like the following block:

```
var serverFile:String = "http://localhost/callLink.php";

var urlRequest:URLRequest = new URLRequest(serverFile);

navigateToURL(urlRequest, "childWindowBox");
```

You substitute the prebuilt window names and add your custom name. Although this is a small change, it offers some great added functionality.

Opening a new or existing window is just one of the possibilities for connecting with other data.

Another type of one-way communication in Flash can be performed by using `sendToURL()`.

The `sendToURL()` is used to silently communicate with a script. Silent communication is a form of one-way communication which does not load a separate Web page. This form of communication offers the ability to send data to a server without interfering with the user's browsing experience.

Here is the previous example, with the new function added, along with some basic error handling to manage invalid and unavailable requests.

```
var serverFile:String = "http://localhost/callLink.php";

var urlRequest:URLRequest = new URLRequest(serverFile);

try
{
   sendToURL(urlRequest);
}
```

Getting Connected

```
catch (e:Error)
{
  // handle error here
}
```

Sending data to the server

There may be times when you want to not only silently request a URL, but also send data along with it. This is done using the `URLVariables` class, which allows you to create an object of name/value pairs. These would be the same as those found in a standard HTML request.

```
var serverFile:String = "http://localhost/callLink.php";

var variables:URLVariables = new URLVariables();
variables.id = 1004;
variables.user = "James";

var urlRequest:URLRequest = new URLRequest(serverFile);
urlRequest.data = variables;

try
{
  sendToURL(urlRequest);
}
catch (e:Error)
{
  // handle error here
}
```

Another example of one-way communication is blindly sending POST data to a server. This adds a little bit more security to your application by removing the parameters from the `url`, and is done by including the parameters within the request.

The code for the POST data request is simply assigning a value to the method property of the `URLRequest` instance. ActionScript has a static variable on the `URLRequestMethod` Class that will be assigned to the method variable.

```
var serverFile:String = "http://localhost/callLink.php";

var variables:URLVariables = new URLVariables();
variables.id = 1004;
variables.user = "James";

var urlRequest:URLRequest = new URLRequest(serverFile);
urlRequest.method = URLRequestMethod.POST;
urlRequest.data = variables;

try
{
  sendToURL(urlRequest);
}
```

Part I Understanding the Basics

```
catch (e:Error)
{
  // handle error here
}
```

Here is a sample request that would be sent to the server. As you can see, the Content and POST elements have the information that was sent. The remaining parts of the request are standard data attributes and are not specific to this example.

```
POST /callLink.php HTTP/1.1
Accept-Language: en
Accept-Encoding: gzip, deflate
Cookie: login=usernames;session-id=1206701
Referer: http://www.example.org/
User-Agent: Mozilla/5.0 (Macintosh; U; Intel Mac OS X; en)
  AppleWebKit/522.11.1 (KHTML, like Gecko) Version/3.0.3
  Safari/522.12.1
Content: id=1004%2Fuser=James
Content-Type: application/x-www-form-urlencoded
Accept: text/xml, text/html;q=0.9,text/plain;q=0.8,image/png
Pragma: no-cache
Content-Length: 327
Connection: keep-alive
Host: www.example.org
```

Two-way communication

In some cases, you will want to receive a response when you send data. One would be when attempting to load a specific user's data from a database. You would pass a user `id` and expect to receive some data type containing that user's information.

The response of a two-way communication is handled by assigning an event listener and attaching a `handler` function.

```
var serverFile:String = "http://localhost/callLink.php";

var variables:URLVariables = new URLVariables();
variables.id = 1004;
variables.user = "James";

var urlRequest:URLRequest = new URLRequest(serverFile);
urlRequest.method = URLRequestMethod.POST;
urlRequest.data = variables;

var urlLoader:URLLoader = new URLLoader();
urlLoader.addEventListener(Event.COMPLETE, userResponseHandler);

try {
  urlLoader.load(urlRequest);
} catch (e:Error) {
  //handle error here
```

Getting Connected 3

```
   }

// handler function
function userResponseHandler(e:Event):void
{
  var urlLoader:URLLoader = URLLoader(e.target);
  var args:URLVariables  = new URLVariables(urlLoader.data);

  trace("User Data: " + args.response);
}
```

The `response` function is passed a reference to the Event. The `URLLoader` and `URLVariables` instances handle the process of pulling apart the response and returning just the data that was sent back. The response comes back with other values and parameters, but most of the time you will only be interested in the data property of the `URLLoader` instance.

More complete applications often return XML format, which is covered in Chapter 3 with other various data-loading examples.

Now that you understand how to work with one-way and two-way communication, the next section expands on these practices by connecting to PHP.

Connecting Flash to PHP

The process of connecting Flash to PHP is done using the prebuilt classes that were introduced in the previous section. If you haven't installed PHP at this time, refer to Chapter 1 to fully understand and install PHP.

To start this example, open the starting file that is included in the book source files. The source files can be found on the book's Web site. The starting file for this example has the design and components already added, as shown in Figure 3.2, allowing you to focus on the code that makes it all work.

The first part of this example is to define the variable of where the PHP file is located on your local or remote server.

```
var phpFile:String =
   "http://localhost/connecting/exampleConn.php";
```

Once the location of the PHP script is defined, the next step is to create the function that is called when the button is clicked.

```
function callServer(e:MouseEvent):void
{
  var urlRequest:URLRequest = new URLRequest(phpFile);

  var loader:URLLoader = new URLLoader();
  loader.addEventListener(Event.COMPLETE, serverResponse);
  loader.load(urlRequest);
}
```

Part I Understanding the Basics

FIGURE 3.2

Here is the completed design of the sample application you will be working with.

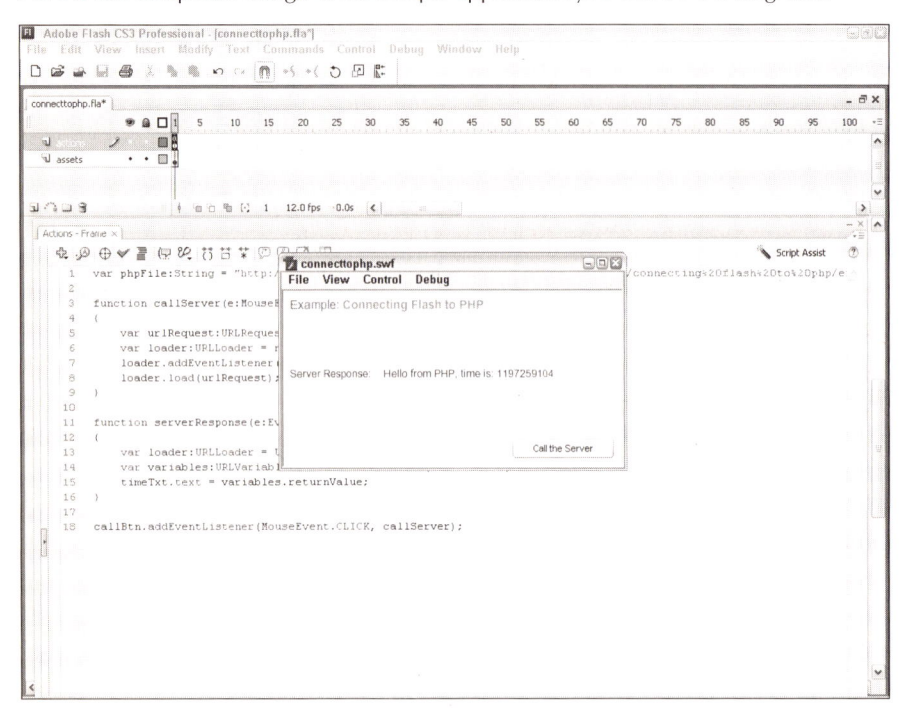

This function creates `URLLoader` and `URLRequest` instances. The `phpFile` is passed in to the `URLRequest` to create the object. Finally, the event listener is attached to the `loader` variable making reference to the `serverResponse`, which is the function that is called when the data is loaded.

```
function serverResponse(e:Event):void
{
  var loader:URLLoader = URLLoader(e.target);
  var variables:URLVariables = new URLVariables(loader.data);
  timeTxt.text = variables.returnValue;
}
```

The server handler function `serverResponse()` is responsible for capturing the data passed back from the PHP file. After that data is properly loaded, it is passed into the `URLVariables` class to generate a dynamic object.

This dynamic object holds the response data passed from the server, so a simple object call is all that is required to load the sample data. In this example, that sample data will be the UNIX timestamp captured and returned by PHP.

The last part is a simple button handler that calls the `callServer` function when a user clicks the button.

```
callBtn.addEventListener(MouseEvent.CLICK, callServer);
```

The PHP code for this example is a very a simple print statement. The `time()` function is used to grab the current UNIX timestamp. The `returnValue` variable located in the string is a custom variable definition so Flash knows what to call once the data is loaded.

This variable can be named any number of things and can even be a series of these:

```
<?php

print "returnValue=Hello from PHP, time is: " . time();

?>
```

Concatenating data

The `.=` is used to concatenate or join multiple variables used into one long string. In this case, it is building on the previous line to create the user data string that will be returned to Flash.

```
<?php

$userData = "username=James";
$userData .= "&id=1004";
$userData .= "&level=Reader";

print $userData;

?>
```

The result that will be passed back to Flash will look something similar to the following:

```
username=James&id=1004&level=Reader
```

You may notice that the name/value relationship is very similar to the format in which POST data is sent. However all you need to know to work with this data in Flash are the variable names.

Multiple pieces of data

Take the existing `serverResponse()` function and modify it to include these new variables being sent from the modified PHP code. The following example is returning hard-coded values; however, in a real-world application, that data would most likely be coming from a dynamic data source.

As you learned in the previous section, the data format of Flash becomes a very simple and easy-to-use set of objects.

```
function serverResponse(e:Event):void
{
  var loader:URLLoader = URLLoader(e.target);
  var variables:URLVariables = new URLVariables(loader.data);
```

```
      userTxt.text = "Welcome back, " + variables.username;
      levelTxt.text = "Your current level is: " + variables.level;
}
```

One limitation of the previous function is the `variables` var is only accessible within that function. To ensure the data returned is accessible by the entire application, it is a good idea to store that data in an external variable.

For example, this example will build on the previous code by adding the new variable assignment and definition. The first change is to create an `Object` variable that will store the data.

```
var phpFile:String =
   "http://localhost/connecting/exampleConn.php";
var storedResult:Object;

function callServer(e:MouseEvent):void
{
  ...
}

function serverResponse(e:Event):void
{
  ...
}

callBtn.addEventListener(MouseEvent.CLICK, callServer);
```

After the new `Object` variable is defined, the next step is to modify the `serverResponse` function to store the loaded data into the newly created variable.

```
function serverResponse(e:Event):void
{
  var loader:URLLoader = URLLoader(e.target);
  var variables:URLVariables = new URLVariables(loader.data);

  // check for valid data
  if(uint(variables.itemLength) > 0)
  {
    storedResult = variables;
  }

  userTxt.text = "Welcome back, " + variables.username;
  levelTxt.text = "Your current level is: " + variables.level;
}
```

The loaded object data is stored within the `storedResult` Object, but only if a valid `itemLength` is found. The `itemLength` variable is also returned by the PHP and validated using a simple `if` statement.

With this new addition to the code you can share the loaded data to other variables and sections within this same application.

Getting Connected 3

> **NOTE** The stored data is not accessible until the loading process is complete.

The last step is to modify the PHP to return the newly created `itemLength` variable, which is done with another addition to the `$userData` string.

```php
<?php

$userData = "username=James";
$userData .= "&id=1004";
$userData .= "&level=Reader";
$userData .= "&itemLength=3";

print $userData;

?>
```

Now that you have an understanding of how to load static data from PHP into Flash, the next section expands on this static data format and introduces a MySQL database.

Connecting PHP to MySQL

Loading data in Flash from a static PHP file is a great way to learn the process. However, a real-world application is probably not going to use that format. Data is always changing and no one wants to update PHP files by hand.

Determining the status of MySQL

Before the connection to MySQL is established, ensure that MySQL is installed and properly running.

> **NOTE** The default installation of MySQL leaves the password blank. This is okay for a testing site, but the password should never be left blank on a live server.

The most common installation of MySQL for use in PHP is by including the MySQL library during the PHP installation process. This means the MySQL information will be displayed on the `phphinfo`, which was explained in the previous section.

Checking for MySQL is done simply by creating a `phpinfo` test file and running it in your browser, as shown in Figure 3.3.

```php
<?php

phpinfo();

?>
```

This result is a massive HTML page that displays all of the information regarding the current installation of PHP. To determine the status of MySQL, search for `"MySQL"`. Keep in mind there could be more than one.

73

Part I Understanding the Basics

FIGURE 3.3

Here is the portion of the `phpinfo` file that explains the MySQL installation available.

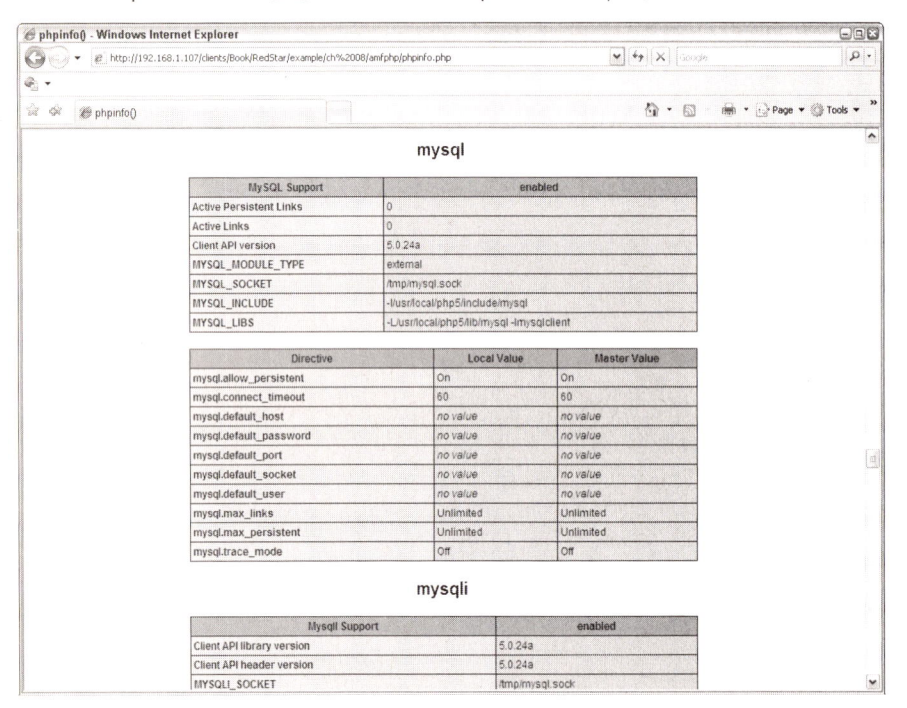

MySQL Support	enabled
Active Persistent Links	0
Active Links	0
Client API version	5.0.24a
MYSQL_MODULE_TYPE	external
MYSQL_SOCKET	/tmp/mysql.sock
MYSQL_INCLUDE	-I/usr/local/php5/include/mysql
MYSQL_LIBS	-L/usr/local/php5/lib/mysql -lmysqlclient

Directive	Local Value	Master Value
mysql.allow_persistent	On	On
mysql.connect_timeout	60	60
mysql.default_host	no value	no value
mysql.default_password	no value	no value
mysql.default_port	no value	no value
mysql.default_socket	no value	no value
mysql.default_user	no value	no value
mysql.max_links	Unlimited	Unlimited
mysql.max_persistent	Unlimited	Unlimited
mysql.trace_mode	Off	Off

mysqli

Mysqli Support	enabled
Client API library version	5.0.24a
Client API header version	5.0.24a
MYSQLI_SOCKET	/tmp/mysql.sock

NOTE The MySQL section in the `phpinfo` file will not be visible at all if not installed.

Assuming that MySQL is properly installed and running, you can move on to the next section, which explains how to connect PHP to a MySQL database.

Connecting to MySQL

The process of connecting to MySQL from PHP is fairly simple. The first step is to obtain the connection information from your server admin or, if you just installed, the login details would be the defaults.

Here is the very basic, no frills code to connect to a MySQL database.

```
<?php

$host = "localhost";
$user = "";
$pass = "";
```

```
$link = mysql_connect($host, $user, $pass);

?>
```

The `mysql_connect` function accepts three arguments. The `hostname` is the first argument, which is almost always set to `"localhost"`. The second is the username that was chosen when you installed MySQL, and finally, the password of your MySQL database, which is blank for a default setup.

The `mysql_connect` function returns a resource `id`, which is a reference to the current MySQL connection. This `id` can be used in future SQL calls, such as `mysql_query`, and many other functions. If you happen to print this `$link` variable you will see a resource code. The following code sample returns that resource ID:

```
<?php

$link = mysql_connect("localhost", "root", "");
print "Response: " . $link;

?>
```

The previous block of code produces a response, such as:

Response: **Resource id #32**

Persistent connection

The standard `mysql_connect` function will close the connection once the script finishes executing. However, there are some cases where you will want to maintain a connection that doesn't close once the script is finished.

The function `mysql_pconnect` is exactly what accomplishes this. This function maintains a connection after the script executes. The advantage to `mysql_pconnect` is it removes the necessity for a new connection. However, the disadvantage is that the persistent connections are stored in a pool and you aren't guaranteed the same connection each time, which can produce unexpected results.

Here is an example of a persistent connection, where the only change is a p in front of the word `"connect"` on the connection function.

```
<?php

$link = mysql_pconnect("localhost", "root", "");
print "Persistent Resource ID: " . $link;

?>
```

Closing the connection

After the SQL finishes executing, a best practice is to remove the connection to free up resources and memory. This is done by simply making a call to `mysql_close()`, which closes the connection.

Part I Understanding the Basics

Closing the connection isn't always required because it will automatically close when the script stops executing. That being said, in a larger application it is best to free up resources as soon as possible to maintain a responsible usage.

Here is the previous `mysql_connect()` example with the `close` addition.

```php
<?php

$link = mysql_connect("localhost", "root", "");
print "Response: " . $link;

// close connection
mysql_close($link);

?>
```

The `mysql_close` function can accept a resource `id` reference, which comes in handy when you have multiple connections. This argument is not required; by default the last connection will be closed.

> **NOTE** A persistent connection created by `mysql_pconnect()` cannot be closed using `mysql_close()`.

Selecting the database

After you establish the MySQL connection you can select a database. You will not be able to query the database until a proper connection and database are chosen. The `mysql_select_db` function allows you to select the database to query. You can also use this function to switch databases.

> **NOTE** An active connection can only have one database connected at a time.

The `mysql_select_db` function accepts two parameters. The first parameter is the database name. The second (optional) parameter is a link to the active connection resource. This is important to use when you have a few different connections or you want to properly track the active connection.

Here is an example using the previous code for connecting and selecting a database:

```php
<?php

$link = mysql_connect("localhost", "root", "");

mysql_select_db("db_name", $link);

// close connection
mysql_close($link);

?>
```

Bringing it all together

You can use your understanding of how to connect to MySQL from PHP to expand on this concept and build a complete application.

The first part of the development process is to create the database and tables, and fill it with data. This example will be the start of a CD listing site where the user requests a genre category and the specified albums are returned.

Start by creating the two MySQL tables for this example. The first table is for the genres and the second table is the list of albums.

```
CREATE TABLE genre (
  id int(11) NOT NULL auto_increment,
  name varchar(100) default '',
  dateAdded int(11) default '0',
  PRIMARY KEY  (id)
) ENGINE=MyISAM;

CREATE TABLE albums (
  id int(11) NOT NULL auto_increment,
  genreID int(11) NOT NULL default '0',
  artist varchar(200) NOT NULL default '',
  albumName varchar(200) NOT NULL default '',
  PRIMARY KEY  (id)
) ENGINE=MyISAM;
```

Using whichever browser or editor you want, create a music database and add those two tables to get started. After creating the tables, you can fill them with predefined data for this example, which is done by executing a series of MySQL INSERT statements.

```
INSERT INTO genre (name, dateAdded) VALUES ('Blues', 1197090235);
INSERT INTO genre (name, dateAdded) VALUES ('Country',
   1197090146);
INSERT INTO genre (name, dateAdded) VALUES ('Jazz', 1197090525);
INSERT INTO genre (name, dateAdded) VALUES ('Rock', 1197090230);

INSERT INTO albums (genreID, artist, albumName) VALUES (4, 'Rob
   Thermo', 'Rob\'s Rock Mix');
INSERT INTO albums (genreID, artist, albumName) VALUES (4, 'Bill
   Dato', 'Rock Out Live');
INSERT INTO albums (genreID, artist, albumName) VALUES (4, 'Jim
   Limb', 'Woodward 37th');
INSERT INTO albums (genreID, artist, albumName) VALUES (4, 'Jason
   Alex', 'Guitar Mashup');
INSERT INTO albums (genreID, artist, albumName) VALUES (4, 'Sam
   Riley', 'The Live Ones');
```

With the database created and the tables assigned and filled with sample data, you can continue with the PHP portion of the application.

Connecting the PHP

The PHP code starts by connecting to the newly created database using the techniques learned in the previous section.

```php
<?php

$link = mysql_connect("localhost", "username", "password");
mysql_select_db("music", $link);
```

When a connection is established, you can create the query that handles the loading of the album data. First, create the genre to look for by setting a static variable. In a more complete application, this variable would most likely be passed via URL or some other form of a call.

```php
$genreID = 4;

$query = "SELECT g.name, a.artist, a.albumName";
$query .= " FROM albums a, genre g";
$query .= " WHERE a.genreID=g.id";
$query .= " AND g.id=" . $genreID;
```

A call to `mysql_query()` is made, which is responsible for executing the previous SQL query. This function will return a resource `id` to be used in the remainder of the SQL calls.

```php
$result = mysql_query($query);
```

This loaded album data will be stored in a name/value string for simplicity but a more real-world example would most likely use XML or another form of structured data.

```php
$response = "resp=loaded\n";
```

CROSS-REF XML data usage is explained in Chapter 3. This includes the loading and saving of XML while working with PHP/MySQL data objects.

At this point, the connection to MySQL and the call should be created, but you still can't test the code because nothing is outputted. The next section explains the outputting of the data using a common `while` loop to traverse the data returned from the tables in the `music` database.

The data will be returned in a basic list format, but there needs to be a way to differentiate the data. This is done by creating a unique `id` on each instance of the result and assigning it to the value name.

```php
$index = 0;
```

The next part is the meat of the application, which is the `while` loop.

```php
while($row = mysql_fetch_array($result))
{

   ...

}
```

Getting Connected 3

The contents of the `while` loop build the string response.

```
while($row = mysql_fetch_array($result))
{
   $response .= "&artist" . $index . "=" . $row['artist'];
   $response .= "&album" . $index . "=" . $row['albumName'];
   $response .= "&genre" . $index . "=" . $row['name']. "\n";

   $index++;
}
```

You will notice the `$response` variable is assigned a name and value for each individual piece of data returned from the database. The data returned from the `mysql_fetch_array` function comes in as a multidimensional array. The `$row` variable stores each row of data, and you use the column name to access the specific piece of data, such as:

```
$response .= "&artist" . $index . "=" . $row['artist'];
```

This process is repeated for each piece of data you want to capture. The data that is available to this `while` loop is determined in the SQL query that was defined in the previous section.

You might have noticed that the SQL query was forced to only include the columns needed. This is done to limit the amount of data and use less memory, which adds up as a system continues to grow.

If you need all columns from the tables you can use an asterisk (`*`), which modifies the previous SQL call to look something like:

```
$query = "SELECT g.*, a.*";
$query .= " FROM albums a, genre g";
$query .= " WHERE a.genreID=g.id";
$query .= " AND g.id=" . $genreID;
```

Two letters are assigned stars because those are references to the two tables needed for this example. Using multiple tables in one SQL call is very common to keep the data relationship known, and doing so allows the data to be stored in smaller, more manageable chunks.

The last portion of PHP creates a `"total"` value that tells Flash how much data is being returned. This is needed because the data is in string format. When using a data type of XML or Arrays, you won't need this extra variable.

The index created for each row of data becomes the count because it was only incremented when a new row of data was found, meaning it is in sync with the amount of data in the string.

```
$response .= "&total=" . $index;
```

The last part is the `print` statement, which exposes this data for Flash or a Web application to load.

```
print $response;
```

79

Part I Understanding the Basics

Here is a sample response:

```
resp=loaded
&artist0=Rob Thermo&album0=Rob's Rock Mix&genre0=Rock
&artist1=Bill Dato&album1=Rock Out Live&genre1=Rock
&artist2=Jim Limb&album2=Woodward 37th&genre2=Rock
&artist3=Jason Alex&album3=Guitar Mashup&genre3=Rock
&artist4=Sam Riley&album4=The Live Ones&genre4=Rock
&total=5
```

That is the complete application, which loads in a block of album data using the genre as the key.

Here is all of the PHP code in one listing for copying/pasting or to closely examine and better understand how it is all working together.

```php
<?php

$link = mysql_connect("localhost", "username", "password");
mysql_select_db("music", $link);

$genreID = 4;

$query = "SELECT g.name, a.artist, a.albumName";
$query .= " FROM albums a, genre g";
$query .= " WHERE a.genreID=g.id";
$query .= " AND g.id=" . $genreID;

$result = mysql_query($query);

$response = "resp=loaded\n";

$index = 0;

while($row = mysql_fetch_array($result))
{
  $response .= "&artist" . $index . "=" . $row['artist'];
  $response .= "&album" . $index . "=" . $row['albumName'];
  $response .= "&genre" . $index . "=" . $row['name'] . "\n";

  $index++;
}

$response .= "&total=" . $index;

print $response;

?>
```

Building the Flash

The Flash portion of this application is responsible for loading the data and looping through it to print each album. For simplicity, this application is all ActionScript, which means the display of the data is done in the Output panel.

A more complete application would take this loaded data and display it in a list or another custom data component.

The first step is to define the PHP file that will be called, which would look similar to this, depending on how your system is set up:

```
var phpFile:String = "http://localhost/getAlbums.php";
```

When the PHP variable is defined, the next step is to build the function that calls the server.

```
function loadHandler():void
{
   ...
}
```

This function first sets up the URLRequest instance, passing the PHP variable as an argument.

```
var urlRequest:URLRequest = new URLRequest(phpFile);
```

The URLLoader is used to create an event listener and to start the loading process at the completion of this function. The urlRequest variable is passed in to the load function of the URLLoader class instance, which is required for any type of data loading.

```
var urlLoader:URLLoader = new URLLoader();
urlLoader.addEventListener(Event.COMPLETE, callServerHandler);
urlLoader.load(urlRequest);
```

The next function to define is the callServerHandler, which is called once the data is sent back from the PHP file written in the previous section. This function is passed an Event reference that contains the loaded data.

```
function callServerHandler(e:Event):void
{
   ...
}
```

The first step in this function is to create the URLLoader instance, which is used to capture the loaded data. The event instance contains a target property, which is used here by passing it into a new URLLoader.

The result is stored in the local loader variable, which will be used in the remainder of this function.

```
var loader:URLLoader = URLLoader(e.target);
```

Part I Understanding the Basics

You may remember from the PHP section of this example that the data is returned in name/value object pairs. That data is stored in the `data` property of the newly created loader instance.

This data is passed into an instance of the `URLVariables` class, which creates an ActionScript Object so other portions of the script can handle the data.

```
var dataObj:URLVariables = new URLVariables(loader.data);
```

Now that the data is loaded, you can test it using a simple `trace` statement that should display the total entries returned.

```
trace("Total Albums: " + dataObj.total);
```

That `trace` call should display the following in the Output panel:

```
//Output: Total Albums: 5
```

This means the PHP file is being called and the data is being loaded properly from the database using PHP as the data handler in the middle.

You could end the script here, because it all works, but continue using a `for..` loop to display the information from each album using a series of `trace` calls for simplicity.

The `for..` loop is set up using the `total` property of the `dataObj` to determine how many times the loop should run.

```
for(var i:uint = 0; i < dataObj.total; i++)
{
   ...
}
```

The first trace within the `for..` loop displays the current album being displayed. The current album number is created using the `i` variable of the loop with 1 added to it. The reason for this is because the `i` variable starts at zero, and for display purposes the first album should be 1.

```
trace("Album " + (i + 1));
```

The next `trace` statement is set up to display the current artist. The value is captured from the `dataObj` Object instance using a dynamic object reference. The `"artist"` name is appended to the `i` variable, which creates an instance name.

```
trace(" Artist: " + dataObj['artist' + i]);
```

The remaining trace statements are duplicates of the previous one, with the instance name and description slightly modified.

```
trace(" Album: " + dataObj['album' + i]);
trace(" Genre: " + dataObj['genre' + i]);
```

At this point, the loop is completed and so is the entire sample application. You can now test the example and should see the trace statements displayed in the Output panel, as shown in Figure 3.4.

Getting Connected 3

FIGURE 3.4

Here is an example of the album data displayed in the Output panel.

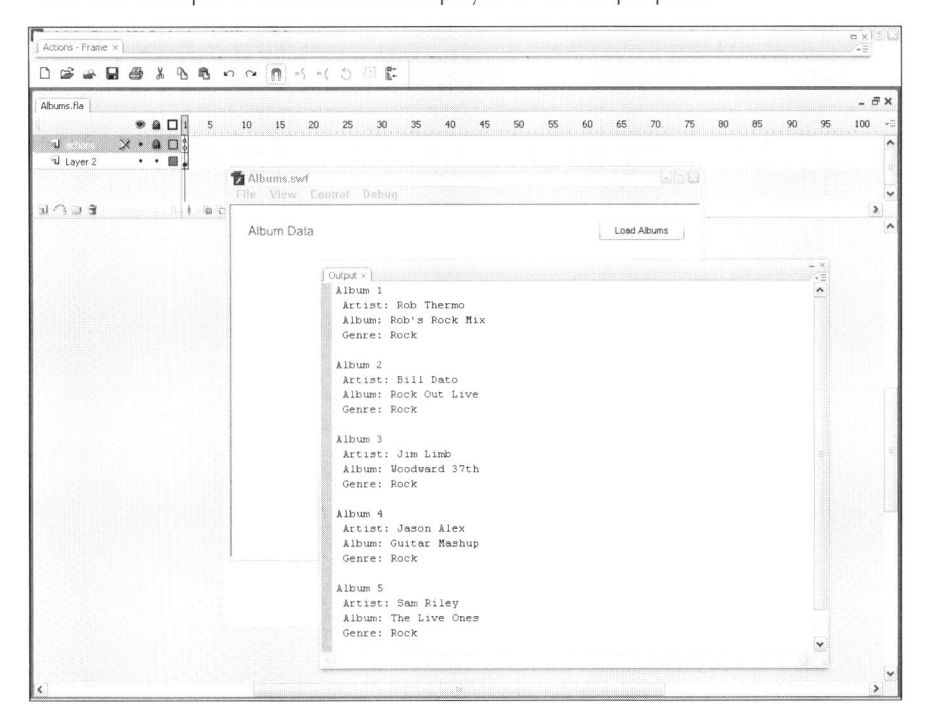

The complete ActionScript portion of this application follows:

```
var phpFile:String = "http://localhost/getAlbums.php";

function loadHandler():void
{
  var urlRequest:URLRequest = new URLRequest(phpFile);

  var urlLoader:URLLoader = new URLLoader();
  urlLoader.addEventListener(Event.COMPLETE, callServerHandler);
  urlLoader.load(urlRequest);
}

function callServerHandler(e:Event):void
{
  var loader:URLLoader = URLLoader(e.target);

  var dataObj:URLVariables = new URLVariables(loader.data);

  // Simple trace for example
```

83

Part I Understanding the Basics

```
      for(var i:uint = 0; i < dataObj.total; i++)
      {
        trace("Album " + (i + 1));

        trace(" Artist: " + dataObj['artist' + i]);
        trace(" Album: " + dataObj['album' + i]);
        trace(" Genre: " + dataObj['genre' + i]);
      }

    }
    loadHandler();

    loadHandler();
```

Summary

The previous example should have given you a pretty good understanding of working with a MySQL database in Flash using PHP as the script in the middle. You can expand on this example to create a more robust application since this sample application was used to illustrate the concept and did not focus on display or the application itself.

MySQL data is only one example of data that can be displayed in Flash.

The next chapter expands on this example and introduces more advanced data objects, such as XML, along with other forms of data such as image and text files.

Chapter 4

Working with Data

W orking with data is the process of sending and loading information for ActionScript to interpret. There are two types of data that can be used in ActionScript. These would be static and dynamic. In most common cases, the dynamic process is preferred over static. Mainly because dynamic data oftentimes includes a database component.

This chapter is about working with dynamic data in both Flash and PHP. You start by loading simple text files, then move on to XML and more advanced loading. The chapter concludes with a complete demo application that loads image data to display a thumbnail and normal size image.

IN THIS CHAPTER

How to load data

Sending data

Loading XML

Loading images using PHP

Loading Data in Flash

Loading data in Flash is a very common practice. In almost every project, you want to have some dynamic (updatable) portion. The purpose of dynamic data is to limit the amount of updating necessary. For instance, if you look at a news site, you will see that most of the outer content doesn't change (logos, navigation, etc.). This is also true for a Flash application where you will most likely only have a certain portion that actually needs to be updated. This section walks you through the process of loading data from XML all the way to images and sound.

The process of loading data in Flash becomes familiar fairly quickly as most types of data you will be loading have similar requirements.

Start by looking at a simple example that would load a text file. This example will look for the text file in a couple of different locations depending on where the application is being run. If you execute this code within the Flash

Part I Understanding the Basics

IDE it will look in the same place the `FLA` is saved or in the user's temp directory if the file has not been saved. If the code is in a compiled `SWF`, the text file will be loaded from the same directory the `SWF` is stored in.

```
var txtFile:String = "sample.txt";
var urlRequest:URLRequst = new URLRequest(txtFile);
var loader:URLLoader = new URLLoader();
loader.addEventListener(Event.COMPLETE, loadHandler);
loader.load(urlRequest);

function loadHandler(e:Event):void
{
  var loader:URLLoader = URLLoader(e.target);
  trace("Loaded Data: " + loader.data);
}
```

The previous example loads a `"sample.txt"` file and traces all of its contents to the Flash Output panel, which opens automatically. Another way to open or close the Output panel is by choosing Window ⇨ Output.

Understanding the classes used to load data

ActionScript in Flash has a series of prebuilt classes that are used to load data. The following section will explain the function of each of those classes.

URLRequest

This class is used to set up the file that is loaded. You can either assign this directly to a variable, or to keep your overall code more compact, assign it directly within the `load()` of the `URLLoader`. In fact, you can apply this process to many of the classes. This has no impact on the functionality of the class and is not a required step.

```
...
    loader.load(new URLRequest(txtFile));
```

URLLoader

As stated in the Adobe Live Docs, "The URLLoader class downloads data from a URL as text, binary data, or URL-encoded variables. It is useful for downloading text files, XML, or other information to be used in a dynamic, data-driven application."

The `URLLoader` serves two purposes when sending and loading data in ActionScript. The first purpose of the `URLLoader` is to set up the complete handler. The other purpose is to capture the loaded data within the complete handler. One noticeable difference of the second purpose is the fact the `URLLoader` does not have a new keyword before it.

Set up the callback

The final step in setting up a data loader is the callback. The callback is another name for the "handler" function that is called when the data is completely loaded. This function is assigned to the `Event.COMPLETE` event on the `URLLoader` class.

```
var loader:URLLoader = new URLLoader();
loader.addEventListener(Event.COMPLETE, loadHandler);
```

This callback function requires one argument of the type `Event`, which is automatically passed in when the ActionScript is called. This argument is where the contents of the loaded data will be stored.

> **NOTE** If you forget to include the argument in the event Handler you will get an argument count mismatch error.

```
ArgumentError: Error #1063: Argument count mismatch on
   sendtophp_fla::MainTimeline/serverResponse(). Expected 0,
   got 1.
   at flash.events::EventDispatcher/dispatchEventFunction()
   at flash.events::EventDispatcher/dispatchEvent()
   at flash.net::URLLoader/onComplete()
```

Putting it all together

Now that you have an understanding of how the code to load data using ActionScript works you can move on to more specific examples of sending and loading. In this example, you can experiment and build from the `URLLoader` class because it has a lot more `Events` than just the simple `COMPLETE` you used. For example, there is an `IOError` event that is called when the `load` or `send` fails. The code for various `Events` is pretty much the same; for your `IOError` example it would look like this:

```
var loader:URLLoader = new URLLoader();
loader.addEventListener(Event.COMPLETE, ioHandler);
function ioHandler(e:Event):void
{
   trace("File loading was terminated");
}
```

You will quickly notice the only thing that changed is the `Event` string and the `handler` function. Multiple events can also be assigned, and it is often a good idea to maintain a high level of compatibility. You also are able to quickly debug code if you set up the proper events.

Assigning multiple events

Assume that you want to handle the `IOError` and `Complete` event for the loader instance. You could enter each event handler; however, this may become a long process when working with multiple loaders. One way to achieve the intended result is to use a function to assign the handlers. You basically pass in the target as an argument and dynamically assign your event handlers.

```
var txtFile:String = "sample.txt";
var urlRequest:URLRequest = new URLRequest(txtFile);
```

Part I   Understanding the Basics

```
var loader:URLLoader = new URLLoader();
assignHandlers(loader);
loader.load(urlRequest);

function assignHandlers(target:*):void
{
  target["addEventListener"](Event.COMPLETE, completeHandler);
  target["addEventListener"](IOErrorEvent.IO_ERROR,
    ioErrorHandler);
}

function completeHandler(e:Event):void
{
  ...
}
function ioErrorHandler(e:Event):void
{
  ...
}
```

A new concept introduced in this function is the dynamic way of assigning event listeners. The `[]` are used to define a string within them as a variable. In this case, the string `"addEventListener"` is actually the method to invoke and the values with the () are the arguments to pass to the method. Using this example for just one event listener is kind of overkill, but if you are working with multiple events it quickly becomes beneficial.

Handling Loaded Data

After using the previous steps to load the data, you will want to use this data in some way. However, before you dive into working with loaded data you need an understanding of what is passed back and how to work with it. In the next sections you will learn how to handle the data that has been loaded. Once you have completed this section you will fully understand how to load data and how to work with that loaded data.

One-way loading

Loading a text file or image is considered one-way loading, mostly because you don't pass along any rules or steps to the loaded file. A call to load an image would expect an image to be returned and nothing more. This type of loading process is most commonly understood if you look at a Web site. The logo on that site is requested and is loaded; no extra data is managed to accomplish this.

Two-way loading

Two-way loading is the process of loading data by passing along arguments that the requested process will handle. For instance, a call to an ad server would pass along the account id and most likely some other information to determine which ad should be displayed.

Working with Data

When working with PHP applications or other dynamic scripting you will most likely pass along parameters to work with. Even more important is the fact you may get different data types back. For example, you may expect an Object but get an error code instead. The purpose of this section is to develop a way in which to handle this case.

```
var phpFile:String = "sample.php";
var urlRequest:URLRequest = new URLRequest(phpFile);
var loader:URLLoader = new URLLoader();
loader.addEventListener(Event.COMPLETE, serverHandler);
loader.load(urlRequest);

function serverHandler(e:Event):void
{
  var loader:URLLoader = URLLoader(e.target);
  var vars:URLVariables = new URLVariables(loader.data);


  if(vars.response == 'ERROR')
  {
    trace("An Error occurred, response not loaded");
  }
  else
  {
    trace("Server Response: " + vars.response);
  }
}
```

This handler is very similar to previous examples, with the exception that the response variable has been given an untyped definition. This allows various data types to be stored in it, such as a string for an error and an object for the expected response.

> **NOTE** Be careful when setting a variable as untyped. This removes error checking and makes it hard to know what a variable contains.

Loading XML in Flash

More than likely you will find yourself working with lots of data. Ideally this data will be passed back in XML format. XML is an industry standard; after you start working with it you quickly understand why. It is based on tags to define the data objects, similar to a multidimensional array. The developer is allowed to define custom tags, so easily building a usable XML style is very painless.

Using E4X with XML

A major update to ActionScript 3 is the ability to parse XML using E4X. This allows us to quickly get data hidden deep within an XML file and with a lot less code than needed in previous versions.

89

Part I Understanding the Basics

For example, you can start with an XML file such as this:

```
<store>
  <item>
    <name>Book</name>
    <section>Learning</section>
    <price>19.95</price>
    <inStock>yes</inStock>
  </item>
  <item>
    <name>Football</name>
    <section>Sports</section>
    <price>4.99</price>
    <inStock>no</inStock>
  </item>
  <item>
    <name>Bike</name>
    <section>Sports</section>
    <price>89.95</price>
    <inStock>yes</inStock>
  </item>
  <item>
    <name>Basketball</name>
    <section>Sports</section>
    <price>8.95</price>
    <inStock>no</inStock>
  </item>
  <item>
    <name>Magazine</name>
    <section>Periodicals</section>
    <price>5.95</price>
    <inStock>yes</inStock>
  </item>
</store>
```

Now you want to load this file and display only the items that are in stock. Using E4X this will be a very simple task.

You can start off with the standard loading sequence that has been seen in previous examples. The path to the XML file we want to load in this example is "storeItems.xml".

```
var xmlFile:String = "storeItems.xml";
loadXML();

function loadXML():void
{
  var urlRequest:URLRequest = new URLRequest(xmlFile);
  var urlLoader:URLLoader = new URLLoader();
  urlLoader.addEventListener(Event.COMPLETE, xmlHandler);
  urlLoader.load(urlRequest);
}
```

Working with Data

After the XML file is completely loaded the xmlHandler function is called. This function is where the XML file is read and the point where E4X is used.

This function is a little more advanced than we have seen in previous code examples, so the function will be broken down into more manageable pieces.

```
function xmlHandler(e:Event):void
{
  var urlLoader:URLLoader = URLLoader(e.target);
  var xml:XML = new XML(urlLoader.data);

  // Loop through all items, ONLY show items in stock
  for each(var item in xml..item)
  {
    if(String(item..inStock) == 'yes')
    {
      trace("Product: " + item.name);
      trace("\tSection: " + item.section);
      trace("\tPrice: " + item.price);
    }
  }
}
```

The first step in this function is to grab the loaded data and pass it to the XML class, which ensures that you will be working with valid XML objects in the next sections.

```
var urlLoader:URLLoader = URLLoader(e.target);
var xml:XML = new XML(urlLoader.data);
```

A for..each loop is used to walk through the XML file and look for items that are in stock. This loop also has a special operator .. "descendant accessor" which is looking for each item in the XML object. The "descendant accessor" was introduced in ActionScript 3 for accessing descendants or children and children within children. This is done using two dot operators in succession (..) followed by the name of the descendant element.

```
for each(var item in xml..item) { ... }
```

This is a huge advancement from ActionScript 2 where you would set up nested loops and traverse the entire XML document. However one thing to note is that the descendant accessor is case sensitive so it is best to use a consistent naming convention.

```
<items>
  <item>
    <objectName>Example</objectName>
  </item>
</items>
```

The most common naming convention for the node names when working with XML is camel-case. *Camel-case* is starting the first word with a lowercase character and then the first letter of every word after that is uppercase.

91

Part I Understanding the Basics

```
firstSecondThird
```

Now that the overall for..each loop is defined the next step is to add in the actual check for in-stock items. This is achieved by creating a conditional statement to go inside the loop.

```
var urlLoader:URLLoader = URLLoader(e.target);
   var xml:XML = new XML(urlLoader.data);
for each(var item in xml..item)
{
  if(String(item..inStock) == 'yes')
  {
    trace("Product: " + item.name);
    trace("\tSection: " + item.section);
    trace("\tPrice: " + item.price);
  }
}
```

This portion looks at each item in the loop, and using the descendant accessor, it looks for the inStock variable. The inStock variable will either be set to yes or no; if the variable is set to yes then we simply print out the item data. In a more advanced example this data would most likely be passed to a display function or possibly a DataGrid component.

That is all there is to quickly looking through an XML file and checking for specific node values. You can expand this example to look for multiple types and use the results to build a mini-store which should only show items that are in stock.

> **NOTE** When working with XML it is a good idea to maintain a consistent format. This allows you to work with various files without having to rebuild the overall program logic. It also is a good idea so you can work with other developers on the same project.

Working with XML in PHP

In the next section you will learn how to load and manage XML data using PHP. This will allow you to develop more dynamic applications.

Loading XML

The process of loading XML in PHP can be achieved in a couple of different ways. You can quickly take a look at using PHP to load XML because this process is fairly straightforward. You then look at how to dynamically build and send XML data. This process can be achieved in a couple of different ways.

Old-fashioned Dom XML

Dom XML is the old way of working with XML. In a way it is very similar to working with XML in older versions of ActionScript. You need to use a series of loops to find nodes, and this simply requires a lot more code than needed.

Working with Data

```php
<?php

$doc = domxml_open_file('sample.xml');
$node = $doc->document_element()->first_child();
while($node)
{
   if(($node->node_name() == 'sampleNode') &&
   ($node->node_type() == XML_ELEMENT_NODE))
   {
     $content = $node->first_child();
     print $content->node_value();
     break;
   }
   $node = $node->next_sibling();
}

?>
```

> **NOTE** The domxml code requires PHP 4.3, or you must have PECL installed separately. You can find more information on the PHP Web site (http://us.php.net/manual/en/ref.domxml.php).

The previous example loads in the XML file and using Dom XML parses through it to find the `sampleNode`. Working within the loop, you are looking for the chosen node and when that node is found you print the contents to the screen. Not a very elaborate example, but it shows the overall process that would be found in a more advanced example.

Simple XML

Working with *Simple XML* quickly shows how easy loading XML can be. This block of code is achieving the same result as before, but with a lot fewer lines of code. Two lines of code instead of 13 is a considerable improvement.

```php
<?php
$xml = simplexml_load_file('sample.xml');
print $xml->sampleNode;?>
```

Sending XML

The process of sending XML from PHP into Flash is explained in the following section. Overall, the code for this is very similar to loading XML.

Printing dynamic XML

Oftentimes you will want to work with dynamic XML. Usually when a database is involved this becomes a lot more common practice. The process of building dynamic XML is very simple: You set the correct file header type and print the raw XML. The following block of code is an example of how to achieve this.

93

Part I Understanding the Basics

```php
<?php

header("content-type: text/xml");

$xmlData = "";
$xmlData .= "<store>\n";

$xmlData .= "   <item>\n";
$xmlData .= "      <name>Book</name>\n";
$xmlData .= "      <section>Learning</section>\n";
$xmlData .= "      <price>19.95</price>\n";
$xmlData .= "      <inStock>yes</inStock>\n";
$xmlData .= "   </item>\n";

$xmlData .= "   <item>\n";
$xmlData .= "      <name>Football</name>\n";
$xmlData .= "      <section>Sports</section>\n";
$xmlData .= "      <price>4.99</price>\n";
$xmlData .= "      <inStock>no</inStock>\n";
$xmlData .= "   </item>\n";

$xmlData .= "   <item>\n";
$xmlData .= "      <name>Bike</name>\n";
$xmlData .= "      <section>Sports</section>\n";
$xmlData .= "      <price>89.95</price>\n";
$xmlData .= "      <inStock>yes</inStock>\n";
$xmlData .= "   </item>\n";

// add more 'item's here

$xmlData .= "</store>\n";

print "response=" . $xmlData;

?>
```

The magic line in that example would be the `print` function that sends the XML to the output buffer and ultimately passes it along to Flash. As you can see, this is a fairly simple example.

Dynamic XML from the database

Say you want to build the XML from a MySQL database call. A database is a more common approach when developing an application because the data is often dynamic. Static prints in the case would not be very easy to maintain. Here is the code, which will be broken down and gone through.

```php
<?php

header("content-type: text/xml");
```

Working with Data 4

```php
$query = "SELECT * FROM store WHERE inStock=yes";

$link = mysql_connect("localhost", "user", "pass");
$result = mysql_query($query, $link);


$xmlData = "";
$xmlData .= "<store>\n";

while($row = mysql_fetch_array($result))
{
  $xmlData .= "   <item>\n";
  $xmlData .= "      <name>" . $row['name'] . "</name>\n";
  $xmlData .= "      <section>" . $row['section'] . "</section>\n";
  $xmlData .= "      <price>" . $row['price'] . "</price>\n";
  $xmlData .= "      <inStock>" . $row['inStock'] . "</inStock>\n";
  $xmlData .= "   </item>\n";
}

$xmlData .= "</store>\n";

print "response=" . $xmlData;

?>
```

You looked at loading the contents of a database in Chapter 2, and for the most part it's the same process. Actually, the only difference is found inside the `while` loop. This is the point at which you build the XML tree structure and finally print that response back to Flash.

There you have it, multiple ways to send and load XML data in both PHP and Flash. You can take these simple examples and build full applications. In fact, you will be building on this example in Chapter 11 for the Mini Shopping cart exercise.

Loading Images Using PHP

ActionScript can load much more than simple text and XML files. One more advanced concept is to load images, but you will take that a step further and load images determined by a PHP file.

Load the starter file which can be found on the books Web site. This file has a `UILoader` and vertical `TileList` to hold the images, as shown in Figure 4.1. The contents of this file are not particularly important for this example, but you can experiment with other components to build more advanced applications.

95

Part I Understanding the Basics

FIGURE 4.1

Showing the completed application with loaded images

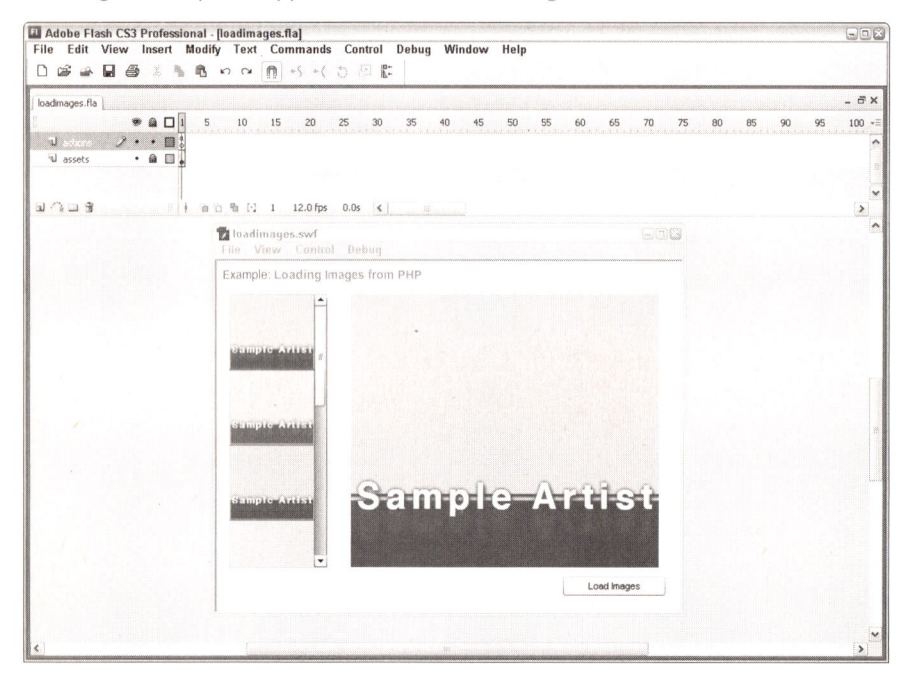

Setting up the image loader

The first step to building the image loader is to construct the ActionScript portion of the application, which is shown here. The following code assumes the `thumbSP` ScrollPane is already located on the stage.

```
var xmlFile:String = "http://localhost/ch03/loadImages.php";
var imageDir:String = "images/";

function callServer(e:MouseEvent):void
{
  var urlRequest:URLRequest = new URLRequest(xmlFile);
  var loader:URLLoader = new URLLoader();
  loader.addEventListener(Event.COMPLETE, xmlLoaded);
  loader.load(urlRequest);
}

function xmlLoaded(e:Event):void
{
  var loader:URLLoader = URLLoader(e.target);
  var xml:XML = new XML(loader.data);

  var thumbContainer:TileList = thumbSP;
```

Working with Data 4

```
thumbContainer.removeAll();
thumbContainer.sourceFunction = sourceHandler;
thumbContainer.addEventListener(Event.CHANGE, loadMainImage);

for each(var item:XML in xml..product)
{
  var smImage:String = item.smImage.toString();
  var lgImage:String = item.lgImage.toString();
  thumbContainer.addItem({source:{sm:smImage, lg:lgImage}});
}
}

function sourceHandler(item:Object):String
{
  return imageDir + item.source.sm;
}

function loadMainImage(e:Event):void
{
  imageUI.source = imageDir + e.target.selectedItem.source.lg;
}

callBtn.addEventListener(MouseEvent.CLICK, callServer);
```

This example has some code purely for working with the components, which you don't need to understand at this point. However, the loader `xmlLoaded` function is the focus. The first one, `xmlLoaded`, is used to walk through the loaded XML file and place the thumbnail images in the `TileList` component.

You will notice the XML is using E4X to find the image nodes. This example assumes the nodes to be called product, which is where the small and large image sources can be found.

You use the `addItem` method to pass in an object containing the small and large image sources. This saves time when you write the logic for clicking on a thumbnail. The `TileList` fires off a CHANGE event when an item is clicked. This is used to attach the handler, which loads the big image.

```
thumbContainer.addEventListener(Event.CHANGE, loadMainImage);
function loadMainImage(e:Event):void
{
  imageUI.source = imageDir + e.target.selectedItem.source.lg;
}
```

The `sourceFunction` handler is used to add in the path to the images. This function is called each time an item is added to the `TileList`.

```
thumbContainer.sourceFunction = sourceHandler;
function sourceHandler(item:Object):String
{
  return imageDir + item.source.sm;
}
```

97

Part I Understanding the Basics

Summary

In this chapter you learned how to send and load data using PHP and Flash You then expanded upon this by sending and loading XML data, which allowed you to develop a more dynamic application.

You should now have a pretty good understanding of how to work with data in Flash and PHP. You also learned a few different reasons why you should use a specific form of data in your application.

Chapter 5

Interacting with the User

An application will often times have some level of interaction with the end user to enrich the overall application experience. This is most commonly a contact or some other type of form, which allows the site owner to allow communication without providing an e-mail address or requiring the user to have an e-mail client. Another form that you would find in an application is a login form, which allows you to limit access to certain aspects or sections of your application.

This chapter will explain the process of building forms in Flash and how to make them interactive using PHP. You will also obtain an overview of sending data using Flash; however, I recommend you look at Chapter 4 to completely understand the process of sending and loading data.

> **IN THIS CHAPTER**
>
> Form development
>
> Developing a contact form
>
> Creating a login module

Form Development Using Flash

Forms generally consist of input boxes, buttons, list boxes, and radio buttons, as shown in Figure 5.1. Each of these elements is available as a component within Flash. You can access the Components pane by choosing Window ➪ Components. Using one of these prebuilt components is as simple as clicking and dragging it to a layer in your Flash document.

Part I Understanding the Basics

FIGURE 5.1

Sample form built using the default components that ship with Flash

NOTE If the component doesn't appear on the Stage, ensure the layer is not displaying a locked icon in the Layer list.

If you ran this Flash movie, you would see some cool components on the Stage but they would be nonfunctional. The process of using them is very straightforward. You assign an instance name to the component and reference the name in your ActionScript.

For example, if you had a `TextInput` and wanted to prefill it, you would add the following code:

```
textInstance.text = "please enter your name";
```

As useful as that code is, you should also capture user input. This is achieved by adding a Submit button component to the stage.

```
userName.text = "please enter your name";
submitBtn.addEventListener(MouseEvent.CLICK, submitHandler);
   function submitHandler(e:MouseEvent):void
   {
     trace("User input: " + userName.text);
   }
```

You can expand this example to add error checking and enforcing required fields:

```
function submitHandler(e:MouseEvent):void
   {
     if(userName.text.length == 0)
     {
       trace("Please enter a name!");
     }
   }
```

Very often you will want to get feedback from a viewer of your site. This is accomplished by adding a contact form, which generally consists of a Flash form that talks to a PHP file.

Creating a Contact Form

For this section, you will be using the starting file that is included on the book's Web site. This file has all of the components located in the `contactMC` `MovieClip` already on the Stage and has been assigned instance names that you will use in the ActionScript.

Here is the complete contact form ActionScript:

```
var phpFile:String = "http://localhost/ch04/contact.php";
var form:MovieClip = contactMC;

function sendMessage(e:MouseEvent):void
{
  // first check the fields

  var nameStr:String    = form.nameTxt.text;
  var subjectStr:String = form.subjectTxt.text;
  var messageStr:String = form.msgTxt.text;

  var allFields:Boolean = true;

  // check name
  if(nameStr.length < 2)
  {
    allFields = false;
  }

  // check subject
  if(subjectStr.length < 2)
  {
    allFields = false;
  }

  // check message
  if(messageStr.length < 2)
  {
    allFields = false;
  }

  if(!allFields)
  {
    trace("All required fields not filled in!");

    form.statusTxt.htmlText = "<font color=\"#FF0000\">"+
      "All required fields not filled in!</font>";
    return;
  }
  var variables:URLVariables = new URLVariables();
  variables.name = nameStr;
```

Part I   Understanding the Basics

```
    variables.subject = subjectStr;
    variables.msg = messageStr;

    var urlRequest:URLRequest = new URLRequest(phpFile);
    urlRequest.method = URLRequestMethod.POST;
    urlRequest.data = variables;

    var loader:URLLoader = new URLLoader();
    loader.addEventListener(Event.COMPLETE, sendHandler);
    loader.load(urlRequest);
}

function sendHandler(e:Event):void
{
    var loader:URLLoader = URLLoader(e.target);
    var variables:URLVariables = new URLVariables(loader.data);

    if(variables.resultCode == "SENT")
    {
      // message sent
      form.statusTxt.htmlText = "<font color=\"#009933\">Email"+
     " sent, thank you.</font>";
    }
    else if(variables.resultCode == "ERROR")
    {
      // message not sent
      form.statusTxt.htmlText = "<font color=\"#FF0000\">Email"+
     " not sent, please try again.</font>";
    }
    else
    {
      // unknown response
      form.statusTxt.htmlText = "<font color=\"#FF0000\">Unknown"
      + " ERROR</font>";
    }
}
form.sendBtn.addEventListener(MouseEvent.CLICK, sendMessage);
```

The focus of this section will be on the `sendMessage` and `sendHandler` functions. The `sendMessage` function assigns the variables that are passed to the PHP, instantiates the necessary Classes, and sets up the event listeners.

```
function sendMessage(e:MouseEvent):void
{
  ...

  var variables:URLVariables = new URLVariables();
  variables.name = nameStr;
  variables.subject = subjectStr;
  variables.msg = messageStr;
```

Interacting with the User

```
    var urlRequest:URLRequest = new URLRequest(phpFile);
    urlRequest.method = URLRequestMethod.POST;
    urlRequest.data = variables;

    var loader:URLLoader = new URLLoader();
    loader.addEventListener(Event.COMPLETE, sendHandler);
    loader.load(urlRequest);
}
```

CROSS-REF Some of the code in the previous section is explained in greater detail in Chapter 4.

Calling the PHP

The call to the PHP is broken up into three classes: the `URLVariables`, `URLRequest`, and `URLLoader` classes, the jobs of which are to set up a container for the contact form data, make a request object, and finally call the PHP file.

The `URLVariables` class stores the contact form data in an object format `name.value`, which is then attached to the `data` property of the `URLRequest`.

The `URLRequest` sets up a request method using the static `POST` property of the `URLRequestMethod` class, which tells Flash whether to send the data in `GET` or `POST` format. `GET` sends the data out attached to the end of the URL:

```
file.php?var1=value1&var2=value2
```

`POST` sends the data in the request, which in most cases is more secure.

The last class used in this contact form is `URLLoader`. This class adds the event listener that is called when the PHP is fully loaded and any expected response has been returned. This class also makes a call to the `load()` method, passing along a reference to the `URLRequest`. This ultimately makes the call to the PHP and passes along the contact form variables you have assigned. That is all that's required to set up and make the call to the PHP.

Contact form event handlers

The next step in the process is to set up the event handler that is called when the PHP sends a response.

```
function sendHandler(e:Event):void
{
   var loader:URLLoader = URLLoader(e.target);
   var variables:URLVariables = new URLVariables(loader.data);

   if(variables.resultCode == "SENT")
   {
     form.statusTxt.htmlText = "<font color=\"#009933\">Email"+
    " sent, thank you.</font>";
   }
```

103

Part I Understanding the Basics

```
    else if(variables.resultCode == "ERROR")
    {
      form.statusTxt.htmlText = "<font color=\"#FF0000\">Email"+
    " not sent, please try again.</font>";
    }
    else
    {
      form.statusTxt.htmlText = "<font color=\"#FF0000\">Unknown"
      +" ERROR</font>";
    }
}
```

You will quickly notice that the `URLLoader` class is used again, but this time to retrieve the PHP response. This is then placed into the `URLVariables` class to pull out the result from the overall response. The PHP is set up to simply respond with a `SENT` or `ERROR` response; however, you also use an `else` statement to catch any unknown responses, some of which could include network errors or simple parse errors in the PHP code.

A Label component is located in the contact form `MovieClip`, which is where the response is sent for the user to see. In a more advanced script you would most likely return a result number and leave the text response in the Flash, which would allow the ability to tailor the responses to specific languages, also called localization.

With the ActionScript set up, you can move on to the PHP code:

```
<?php

error_reporting(0); // disable all error reporting
set_time_limit(120); // let script run for no more than 2 minutes

$emailTo = "you@yourdomain.com";

$name     = $_POST['name'];
$from     = $_POST['fromEmail'];
$subject  = $_POST['subject'];
$msg      = $_POST['msg'];

if(!empty($_POST))
{
  $headers = "";
  $headers .= "";

  $date = date("F j, Y", time()); // Grab todays date
  $email_info .= "Below is the visitors contact info and
   message.\n\n";
  $email_info .= "Visitor's Info:\n";
  $email_info .= "----------------------------------------\n";
  $email_info .= "Name:  " . $from . "\n";
  $email_info .= "Date Sent:  " . $date . "\n\n";
```

104

Interacting with the User

```
    $email_info .= "Message\n";
    $email_info .= "----------------------------------------\n";
    $email_info .= "" . $msg . "\n";

    // Mail headers, do not alter
    $mailheaders = "From: " . $from . " <" . $name . "> \n";
    $mailheaders .= "Reply-To: " . $from . "\n\n";

    if(mail($emailTo, $subject, $email_info, $mailheaders))
    {
      print "resultCode=SENT";
    }
    else
    {
      print "resultCode=ERROR";
    }
  }

?>
```

Mailing in PHP

Most of this PHP is similar to what you have been working with in previous sections, with some exceptions, of course. The most notable exception is the introduction of the `mail()` function, which takes a series of arguments:

```
mail($to, $subject, $emailBodyInfo, $emailHeaders);
```

The first two are e-mail to send to and subject of the e-mail, which is pretty standard. The last two are the most important: `$emailBodyInfo` contains the contents of your e-mail, and `$emailHeaders` defines the file as an e-mail. This variable holds the routing info, reply-to, and all the other e-mail-specific variables that a mail server looks for.

Globals

You assign variables to hold the data passed in from Flash, which is done by using the global `$_POST` data array. Globals in PHP handle overall site information and values that any script has access to. You go over reasons why globals can be the wrong approach in the security chapter.

Getting back to your e-mail script, use the global `$_POST` data variable to access the variables passed in from Flash.

```
    $emailTo   = "you@yourdomain.com";
    $name      = $_POST['name'];
    $from      = $_POST['fromEmail'];
    $subject   = $_POST['subject'];
    $msg       = $_POST['msg'];
```

105

Part I Understanding the Basics

That is all the code that is needed to develop a fully functional contact form using Flash and PHP. You can expand on this example and give the contact form a lot more functionality. A few things to think about adding would be a more robust validation process, more form fields, and possibly more informative responses to the user.

Keep security in mind

One very important element to note about this contact form example is the code does not honor security procedures and actually lets the user pass any data to PHP. A more robust and live example would require a much stronger level of security; however, for demonstration purposes overall security has been left out.

Login Module in Flash

More often than not you will want to have a secure portion to a Web site. A very popular example of this would be a review section for a photographer where a client can log in and look at the photos.

The form portion of this application is almost identical to the contact form. You need a Username and Password box and a Submit button to fire off the login handler routine.

Here is a sample layout that can be found in the starting file, or you can create it from scratch.

The instance names for this example are displayed in Table 5.1.

TABLE 5.1

Form Components for Login Module

usernameTxt	Username to be logged in
passwordTxt	Password to be attempted
resetBtn	Reset button, clears the fields
loginBtn	Login button, fire the `loginHandler`

Now that you have the form visually complete you can move on to the ActionScript, which makes the form functional.

Code skeleton

In previous examples, you looked at all of the code in one long section, but sometimes that can be overwhelming. Looking at the skeleton of code offers a quick way to evaluate the program variables, functions, and other elements.

Interacting with the User

Here is the code skeleton for the login module:

```
stop(); // stop the playhead

var phpFile:String = "http://localhost/ch04/login.php";
var form:MovieClip = loginMC;
var loggedIn:Boolean = false;

function loginHandler(e:MouseEvent):void {...}
function resetHandler(e:MouseEvent):void {...}
function clearIndicators():void {...}
function sendHandler(e:Event):void {...}

form.usernameTxt.tabIndex = 1;
form.passwordTxt.tabIndex = 2;
form.resetBtn.tabIndex = 3;
form.loginBtn.tabIndex = 4;

form.passwordTxt.displayAsPassword = true;
form.resetBtn.addEventListener(MouseEvent.CLICK, resetHandler);
form.loginBtn.addEventListener(MouseEvent.CLICK, loginHandler);
```

Login event handlers

Similar to the contact form example, you need to assign event handlers that handle the login, clearing, and UI changes for the login module.

The first event handler is the `loginHandler`, which is responsible for calling the server and ensuring valid data is passed to the server. Its last task is to assign the handler for the result event.

```
function loginHandler(e:MouseEvent):void
{
  clearIndicators();

  var user:String = form.usernameTxt.text;
  var pass:String = form.passwordTxt.text;
  var allFields:Boolean = true;

  if(user.length < 2)
  {
    allFields = false;
    form.userRequiredIndicator.alpha = 1.0;
  }

  if(pass.length < 2)
  {
    allFields = false;
    form.passRequiredIndicator.alpha = 1.0;
  }
```

Part I Understanding the Basics

```
if(!allFields)
{
  form.statusTxt.htmlText= "<font color=\"#FF0000\">Username"
 + " and Password required!</font>";
  return;
}

var variables:URLVariables = new URLVariables();
variables.user = user;
variables.pass = pass;

var urlRequest:URLRequest = new URLRequest(phpFile);
urlRequest.method = URLRequestMethod.POST;
urlRequest.data = variables;

var loader:URLLoader = new URLLoader();
loader.addEventListener(Event.COMPLETE, sendHandler);
loader.load(urlRequest);
}
```

This handler starts off by assigning the username and password fields to internal variables. Those new variables are then checked for valid length, which if correct sets the `allFields` variable. This `allFields` variable is used to determine if the error message should be displayed and the function should be exited. If `allFields` is not set you can continue setting up the call to the server. This portion is identical to the contact form example. In fact, you will quickly notice that ActionScript has a very similar format for all types of loading and sending of data.

The next handler you will focus on is the `clearHandler`, which is assigned to the `resetBtn`. Its job is to clear all of the form fields and make a call to the `clearIndicators` function, which you look at in a moment.

```
function resetHandler(e:MouseEvent):void
{
  form.usernameTxt.text = "";
  form.passwordTxt.text = "";
  form.statusTxt.htmlText = "";

  clearIndicators();
}
```

The `clearIndicators` function changes the alpha opacity of the icons that can be found to the right of the username and password `TextInput` components in the starter file. If you are creating this module from scratch you would most likely omit this function and the call to it in the `resetHandler`.

Interacting with the User   5

```
function clearIndicators():void
{
  form.userRequiredIndicator.alpha = 0;
  form.passRequiredIndicator.alpha = 0;
}
```

The last handler needed for this module is the `sendHandler`, which is called when the PHP code sends back a response.

```
function sendHandler(e:Event):void
{
  var loader:URLLoader = URLLoader(e.target);
  var variables:URLVariables = new URLVariables(loader.data);

  if(variables.resultCode == "LOGGED_IN")
  {
    loggedIn = true;
    gotoAndStop(2);
  }
  else if(variables.resultCode == "NOT_LOGGED_IN")
  {
    form.statusTxt.htmlText = "<font color=\"#FF0000\">"+
      "Username/Password not correct.</font>";
  }
}
```

The response passed from PHP is evaluated to determine if the user is valid and whether or not the secure page should be displayed.

```
if(variables.resultCode == "LOGGED_IN")
{
  loggedIn = true; // user logged in,
  gotoAndStop(2); // sample has secure page on frame 2
}
else if(variables.resultCode == "NOT_LOGGED_IN")
{
  form.statusTxt.htmlText = "<font color=\"#FF0000\">"+
    "Username/Password not correct.</font>";
}
```

Assuming the user is logged in, you set a `loggedIn` variable and move to the second frame, which in the example is a top-secret section, as shown in Figure 5.2. Your example will most likely have a more important reason to be logged in, but maybe not.

109

Part I Understanding the Basics

FIGURE 5.2

Example secure page that is only visible if the user is logged in

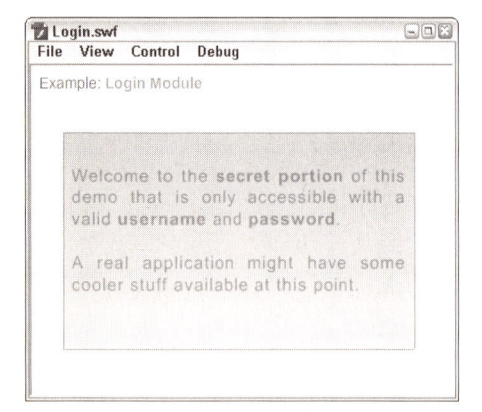

[Login.swf window showing:
Example: Login Module

Welcome to the **secret portion** of this demo that is only accessible with a valid **username** and **password**.

A real application might have some cooler stuff available at this point.]

Server integration for login module

The PHP code for the login module is the next part in the process.

```
<?php

error_reporting(0); // disable all error reporting

$user = $_POST['user'];
$pass = $_POST['pass'];

// sample password response, normally
// would be sent from database
$storedPassword = "83e4a96aed96436c621b9809e258b309";

if(!empty($_POST))
{
  if($user == "guest" && md5($pass) == $storedPassword)
  {
    print "resultCode=LOGGED_IN";
  }
  else
  {
    print "resultCode=NOT_LOGGED_IN";
  }
}

?>
```

Your focus in this section is on the $_POST data and conditional check to determine if the password is correct or not. This result is then sent back to Flash where it is used to set logged-in status and whatever else a valid user would see.

A more robust example would have the PHP be evaluated against a database instead of a static string. The $storedPassword variable has an md5() hashed string. MD5 is a hashing algorithm that is available in many programming languages, one of which is PHP and is most frequently used when storing passwords in a database. You will look at MD5 a little more in depth in the security chapter, but for now the most important thing to note is that hashed string is your password.

You now have a complete login module using Flash and PHP. You could easily expand this example to include database integration and more importantly, an added level of security.

Summary

In this chapter you learned how to build forms in Flash and how to make them interactive using PHP. As a more advanced project you then created a login component utilizing the previous information you learned about form development overall.

Chapter 6

Working with Cookies

ookies are very common in Web browsing. In fact, you would find it very hard to navigate the Internet in the way we are accustomed to if cookies stopped working. This chapter is how to work with cookies in both Flash and PHP. It covers loading and sending of cookies and investigates how a cookie is deleted.

The second half of the chapter is about shared objects, which are cookies in Flash. They act almost the same as standard browser cookies with some differences, which you will investigate.

Once you have completed this chapter you will fully understand how to work with cookies and why they are important for a successful application and user experience.

IN THIS CHAPTER

Using cookies in PHP

Using cookies in Flash

Understanding shared objects

Loading Cookies

A *cookie* is a small file placed on the user's computer by a Web server. This file is then sent back to the server unchanged each time the user accesses the server. Most often a cookie will contain the username for a Web site. A cookie can also be used to save user settings and any other small pieces of information.

The process of loading cookies is explained in multiple pieces to better understand how they work. You will notice that the process of loading cookies is very similar to loading other forms of data.

Using cookies with PHP

Using cookies with PHP is necessary in order to develop a usable Web application. You will find many opportunities to implement cookie support from user login to styles and many other uses.

As you begin to work with dynamic data more often you will want to save portions to the user's machine. Doing this allows the program to log a user in automatically or modify a style based on the user's settings.

Cookies are saved per domain and directory. This means that any page within the same domain or path can read that cookie. This is very useful when building multiple examples and also means another Web site cannot read cookies from a different site.

> **NOTE** The common workaround for sharing cookies across a domain is to create a subdomain. A cookie is only specific to the overall domain and simply ignores paths, parameters, and subdomains.

Loading a cookie

Now that you have an understanding of what a cookie is, take a look at how to load and work with one in PHP: The following code attempts to load a cookie and display the response as shown in Figure 6.1.

```php
<?php

$username = "Jimmy";

if (!isset($_COOKIE['user'])) {

  setcookie("user", $username);

  print "Welcome " . $username;

}
else
{
  Print "Welcome back, " . $_COOKIE['user'];
}

?>
```

The previous code checks for the existence of the cookie `"user"` in the global array of cookies. If the cookie is found, the user is welcomed back. If the cookie is not found, the cookie is set and the user is welcomed for the first time.

The `$_COOKIE` variable is a multidimensional array that can contain many different cookies. This variable is automatically filled by PHP and doesn't require you to add to it.

Working with Cookies 6

FIGURE 6.1

The print statement as displayed in the browser window

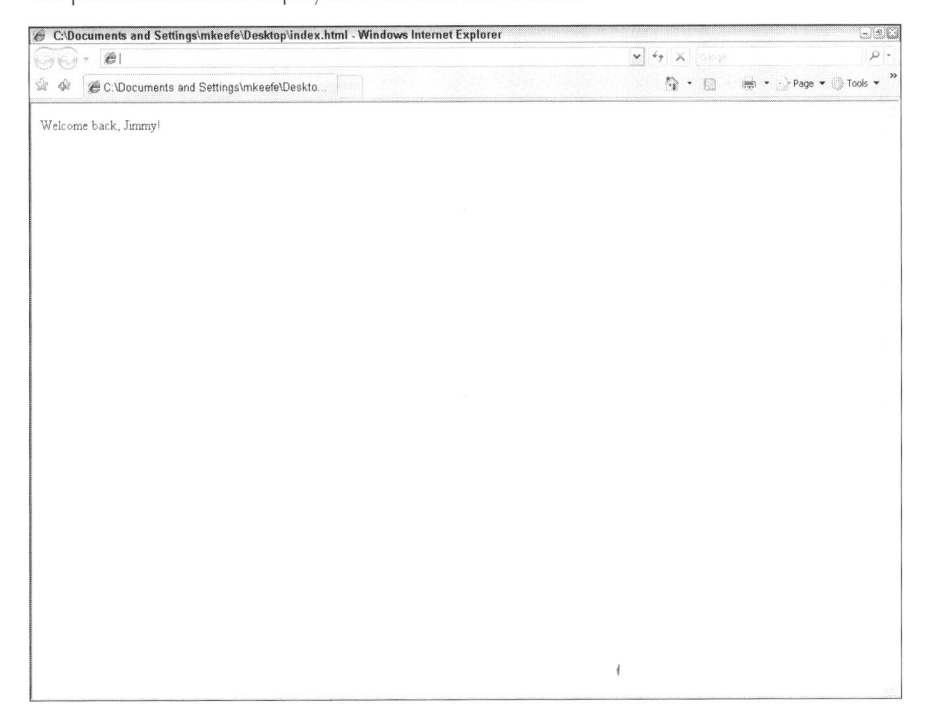

[Browser window screenshot showing "Welcome back, Jimmy!"]

Saving a cookie

Setting or saving a cookie in PHP is very simple: you make a call to the `setcookie` function. The first argument is the cookie name; the second argument is the cookie value. For example, say you want to set a `time_logged_in` cookie.

```
setcookie("time_logged_in", time());
```

Anytime you want to save a cookie you can call the `setcookie` function. If the cookie exists, it is updated, and if it doesn't exist it is created.

> **NOTE** A cookie's ability to be saved depends on whether or not a user allows cookies.

The `setcookie` function accepts more than two arguments, but actually only requires the first argument, which is the name.

115

Cookie expiration

By default, a cookie expires when the session ends or the user closes the browser. The way a session ends is by a predefined amount of time on the server. By default, this amount is 0 seconds because the session ends when the browser closes. Normally, you as the developer do not need to know how long a session lasts. You would, of course, be more interested in whether or not the cookie exists.

Occasionally, you will want to ensure a cookie is deleted after a certain amount of time. This is the case when working with secure data or a content management system. Assume you want the cookie to expire soon after the cookie is created.

```
setcookie("username", "adminDave", (time() + 7200));
```

This tells the user's browser to delete the cookie 2 hours after the cookie is created. The expiration time of a cookie is in seconds, so for this example 7200 is 2 hours. Another way to look at it is (60 * 60 * 2).

Have you ever opened your browser, visited a site, and were introduced to custom content that you had applied in a previous session? This data was determined by a cookie saved on your machine that was not deleted when the session ended.

Look at an example of a cookie that doesn't expire for three months.

```
<?php

$secondsInDay = 86400;
$daysBeforeExpiration = 90;
setcookie("userStylePref", "blueTheme", (time() + ($secondsInDay
    * $daysBeforeExpiration)));

?>
```

You start by setting the number of seconds in a day — 86400. Then you set our `$daysBeforeExpiration` variable that is holding how many days you want the cookie to live. The last step is to set the cookie. Multiply the seconds by the days, add to the `time()` function, and this becomes your expiration date.

Three months is only an example; you can set a cookie to expire years later. However, users have a tendency to clean up their browser storage. So, you should never allow an application to rely on the existence of a cookie.

Deleting a cookie

At some point in your application you will probably want to delete a cookie. However, the local Web browser that your user is on does not allow a Web server to directly delete a cookie. Instead, set the expiration date behind the current date and basically make the cookie expire. This tells the Web browser to delete the cookie because it is no longer in use.

```
setcookie("time_logged_in", "", (time() - 300));
```

Assigning multiple cookies

The process of assigning multiple cookies is fairly straightforward. You basically make multiple calls to the `setcookie` function ensuring that each cookie has a unique name.

```php
<?php

$username = "jimmy";
$userID = 5;
$loggedInTime = time();

setcookie("username", $username);
setcookie("userid", $userID);
setcookie("logged_in_since", $loggedInTime);

?>
```

The previous code sets three cookies by making three unique calls to the `setcookie` function. You could also place the `setcookie` call into a custom function if the passed-in code requires more security. For example, you can create a `saveCookie` function that ensures the data is clean.

```php
<?php

function saveCookie($name, $value, $expires=0)
{
  if($name == "")
  {
    print "Name not provided, cookie not saved";
  }
  if($value == "")
  {
    print "Value not provided, cookie not saved";
  }

  setcookie($name , $value, $expires);
}

$username = "jimmy";
$userID = 5;
$loggedInTime = time();

saveCookie("username", $username);
saveCookie("userid", $userID);
saveCookie("logged_in_since", $loggedInTime);

?>
```

Your `saveCookie` function is used as a proxy to the prebuilt `setcookie` function. This allows you to check the passed in data and ensure that it is filled in properly. In the previous example, you print an error if either the name or value is empty. You could take this simple security check a step further by ensuring the data is, in fact, a string and doesn't contain any potentially malicious

Part I Understanding the Basics

code. As you begin to develop Web applications you will learn to follow rigid guidelines as far as security is concerned.

Now that you have looked at how to use cookies in PHP, you can look at using cookies in Flash. The process of using cookies in Flash is very similar, but offers some advantages that you will look at.

Using cookies in Flash

Cookies in Flash are actually called shared objects and share similar attributes to cookies in PHP. Some of these attributes include the ability to store small amounts of data locally and retrieve them by any file in the same basic domain. Just like cookies in PHP, the user is able to disable them per site or globally. However, they have some distinct differences. One major advantage to shared objects is the ability to bind to them. This means multiple movies have the ability to watch the file and be alerted when it is updated. For example, say you have a multiplayer game and want each client to track the score in sync. With shared objects you can allow each of the clients to have read/write access and the others will update the score as it changes.

Loading shared objects

The following code attempts to load a shared object and creates one if it doesn't exist. As you can see, loading a shared object is fairly simple and only requires one line of code. Cookies in PHP don't offer the ability to natively create one if it doesn't exist; you have to check for the cookie and manually create it.

```
var so:SharedObject = SharedObject.getLocal("sample");
trace("Object is " + so.size + " bytes in size");
```

Saving shared objects

The process of saving a shared object is also straightforward. Start by creating a new instance of the `SharedObject` class.

```
var so:SharedObject = SharedObject.getLocal("sample");
```

After the object is created, you can attach data to the shared object by adding elements to the `data` object, such as:

```
var so:SharedObject = SharedObject.getLocal("sample");
so.data.user = "guest";
```

You can call and recall that above block of code and the value won't be saved just yet. The reason is because you need to alert the object to write it to the local filesystem by calling the flush method.

```
var so:SharedObject = SharedObject.getLocal("sample");
so.data.user = "guest";
so.flush();
```

Working with Cookies

> **NOTE:** When using `flush()`, check whether the user has disabled local storage using the Settings Manager (www.macromedia.com/support/documentation/en/flashplayer/help/settings_manager07.html).

If the object doesn't exist, one is created. In some cases, you will want to know if the shared object exists. The way to achieve that is by checking the `size` property.

```
var so:SharedObject = SharedObject.getLocal("sample");
if(so.size == 0)
{
  // Shared object doesn't exist.
  trace("Shared Object doesn't exist.");
}
```

Assuming the size test came back equal to zero, you would know the shared object doesn't exist. You can then take this result and replace the simple trace with the code to create the object.

```
var so:SharedObject = SharedObject.getLocal("sample");
if(so.size == 0)
{
  // Shared object doesn't exist.
  so.data.user = "guest";
}
```

Deleting a shared object

Unlike PHP, shared objects can explicitly be deleted from the local storage system. Making a call to the `clear()` method removes the shared object and its data, but the reference to the object will remain.

```
var so:SharedObject = SharedObject.getLocal("sample");
so.data.user = "guest";

trace("Username is: " + so.data.user); // guest

so.clear();

trace("Username is: " + so.data.user); // undefined
```

The second trace returns undefined because the previous call to `clear()` has removed the value. You can now reassign the value. However, you do not need to delete an object to reassign it. You can simply rewrite to it.

Bringing it all together

Now that you have looked at each individual concept, bring it all into one final example. This example will create, save, edit, and delete a shared object.

Start by opening the starting file which can be found on the book's Web site, which has been pre-built for this example.

Part I Understanding the Basics

After opening the file in Flash, open the Action pane (press F9 or Alt+F9) and add the ActionScript.

```
var soDomain:String = "sample";
var so:SharedObject = null;
function loadObject():void
{
  so = SharedObject.getLocal(soDomain);
  trace("Shared Object Loaded");
}

function addDataToObject(name:String, value:String):void
{
  if(so == null)
  {
    trace("You must first load the Shared Object");
  }

  so.data[name] = value;
  so.flush();

  trace("Value added: " + so.data[name]);
}

function deleteObject():void
{
  if(so == null)
  {
    trace("You must first load the Shared Object");
  }

  so.clear();

  trace("Shared Object deleted");
}

function readObject(name:String):void
{
  if(so == null)
  {
    trace("You must first load the Shared Object");
  }
  else
  {
    trace("Shared Object Value : " + so.data[name]);
  }
}

function loadHandler(e:MouseEvent):void
```

Working with Cookies

```
{
  loadObject();
}
function saveHandler(e:MouseEvent):void
{
  addDataToObject('test', valueTxt.text);
}
function deleteHandler(e:MouseEvent):void
{
  deleteObject();
}
function readHandler(e:MouseEvent):void
{
  readObject('test');
}

loadBtn.addEventListener(MouseEvent.CLICK, loadHandler);
saveBtn.addEventListener(MouseEvent.CLICK, saveHandler);
deleteBtn.addEventListener(MouseEvent.CLICK, deleteHandler);
readBtn.addEventListener(MouseEvent.CLICK, readHandler);
```

The most important parts of this code are the `addDataToObject` function and two variables that are references to the shared object: property name and the value to store.

```
var soDomain:String = "sample";
var so:SharedObject = null;

function addDataToObject(name:String, value:String):void
{
  ...
}
```

The `addDataToObject` function checks to make sure the shared object is properly loaded and attempts to assign the value using a dynamic object.

```
function addDataToObject(name:String, value:String):void
{
  if(so == undefined)
  {
    trace("You must first load the Shared Object");
  }

  so.data[name] = value;
  so.flush();
}
```

After the `addDataToObject` function is called, you can read in the shared object by simply making a call to the data object.

```
trace("Shared Object Data: " + so.data.test);
```

121

Understanding the Basics

That is all there is to working with shared objects in Flash. You now know how to load, save, and delete shared objects and cookies in Flash.

NOTE Shared objects can also be used in a remote setting, but require a more advanced system.

Discovering the benefits of using PHP cookies

Now that you have looked at using cookies in both PHP and Flash, look at some reasons why using cookies in PHP is a better option. When working in Flash it would seem that shared objects are the best option, but they aren't always.

Cookies in PHP offer the ability to share them between both HTML and Flash sites. Shared objects only are accessible from within Flash, which can be both good and bad. The good side is that no other application can change the cookies. On the bad side, it also means you can't share them and add a level of consistency between your applications.

There is a pretty common workaround to this problem, however, and that is to use regular cookies in Flash by passing them through a PHP middleman.

First, look at the PHP code that will pass the cookie data back to Flash.

```
<?php

if(isset($_POST['act']) && $_POST['act'] == 'getcookie')
{
  if(isset($_COOKIE[$_POST['cookieName']]))
  {
    print "resp=" . $_COOKIE[$_POST['cookieName']];
  }
  else
  {
    print "resp=" . "cookie_not_found";
  }
}

?>
```

This code ensures the proper POST data is sent before it continues. Assuming valid data is passed, the next step is to determine if the cookie does, in fact, exist. Use a conditional test to determine if cookie data or an error message will be sent to Flash.

```
if(isset($_COOKIE[$_POST['cookieName']]))
{
  print "resp=" . $_COOKIE[$_POST['cookieName']];
}
else
{
  print "resp=" . "cookie_not_found";
}
```

Working with Cookies   6

Either way, the variable passed in to Flash is `"resp"`. This way you can easily program the ActionScript to handle the response accordingly.

The reason that you use `isset()` in the first `if` statement is so PHP can't accidentally send a notice to Flash alerting the variable is not sent. This sort of application is a very good candidate for XML, which is explained in depth in Chapter 3. XML would make it so only the value you are interested in would be returned. For this simple example, you will continue with a standard print-based return.

Now that you have the PHP in place you can move on to the ActionScript. The ActionScript makes a call to the PHP and expects a cookie or error to be returned.

```
var phpFile:String =
    "http://localhost/ch05/cookies/loadCookie.php";

var variables:URLVariables = new URLVariables();
variables.act = 'getcookie';
variables.cookieName = 'sample';

var urlRequest:URLRequest = new URLRequest(phpFile);
urlRequest.method = URLRequestMethod.POST;
urlRequest.data = variables;

var loader:URLLoader = new URLLoader();
loader.addEventListener(Event.COMPLETE, serverHandler);
loader.load(urlRequest);

function serverHandler(e:Event):void
{
  var loader:URLLoader = URLLoader(e.target);
  var variables:URLVariables = new URLVariables(loader.data);

  if(variables.resp == 'cookie not found')
  {
    trace("Requested Cookie Not Found");
  }
  else
  {
    trace("Cookie Data: " + variables.resp);
  }
}
```

The overall call to the server is similar to other calls in this book. The focus on this call is the variables passed to the PHP and the response. You use the `URLVariables` class to assign the act and `cookieName` variables. The `act` variable tells PHP that your request is valid, and the `cookieName` variable contains the name of the cookie you are looking for.

```
var variables:URLVariables = new URLVariables();
variables.act = 'getcookie';
variables.cookieName = 'sample';
```

123

Just like the other loader examples, you need to assign a function to handle the server response. This is the function that is called after the PHP passes back either your cookie or an error message. Start by using the `URLLoader` class to get the data contained in the response. You then make a call to the `URLVariables` class, which returns an object of the response variables. In this case, you are looking for the `"resp"` property. First, check to see if the response is `"cookie_not_found"`, which is self-explanatory. More than likely, the cookie will be set and the second trace statement would get called, but it is never good programming to assume this. That is why that conditional statement is added.

```
function serverHandler(e:Event):void
{
  var loader:URLLoader = URLLoader(e.target);
  var variables:URLVariables = new URLVariables(loader.data);

  if(variables.resp == 'cookie_not_found')
  {
    trace("Requested Cookie Not Found");
  }
  else
  {
    trace("Cookie Data: " + variables.resp);
  }
}
```

You can take this example to the next step by setting the cookie if one is not found, or even pass along an array or object of cookie names to quickly load all the cookies for a site. AMFPHP, which you will look at in Chapter 8, would be a great way to load in multiple cookies.

As you can now see, there are multiple ways to work with cookies in both PHP and Flash. You even developed a common way in which both PHP and Flash can share the same cookie data.

NOTE Sharing cookie data still has the limitation that the PHP needs to be on the domain you are loading the cookies from. One thing to be aware of with this script is the fact that this simple example is not checking the input passed to the PHP. You would certainly want to add that to a real-world application.

Summary

In this chapter you learned how to load and work with cookies in Flash and PHP. To start you learned how to load an existing cookie from the user's machine and then learned how to modify and update that cookie.

You should now understand how to work with cookies in Flash and PHP and understand why they are important when you develop an application.

Part II

Developing Interactive Content

IN THIS PART

Chapter 7
Maintaining Security while Working with User Input

Chapter 8
Using Sockets

Chapter 7

Maintaining Security while Working with User Input

Working with user input focuses on the best practices of storing and returning data while maintaining a high level of security.

This chapter is broken into sections that focus on a specific aspect of handling user data. This is not a step-based guide on working with user data, which can be found in Chapter 4. Instead, this chapter focuses on the specifics of security when handling that data.

The subtopic covered in this chapter is working with and understanding the sandbox in Flash. Basically, the sandbox is a container that each application runs in, but the section goes into greater detail and provides visual examples to better explain the sandbox and how it affects your applications.

The practices provided in this chapter can be adapted to future applications you develop. Maintaining a secure application is about as important as locking your home before you leave. An application will technically still work if it is not secure. However, the lifespan of that application is not certain. There are many aspects to security in an application: sanitized data, secure logins, file storage, and exploitability, to name a few. In this chapter, the focus is the security of user input. User input is any piece of data the user can modify. This list of data includes cookies, logins, sessions, and file uploads.

IN THIS CHAPTER

Using caution with user input

Cleaning user data

Storing data

Returning data

Understanding the Flash security sandbox

Using Caution with User Input

User data expands far beyond a simple text box on a contact form. Now that you know what data is considered user input, you're probably wondering how something as harmless as a file upload system poses a security risk.

As with most security, it isn't the technology or feature that is flawed, but how it is implemented.

Part II Developing Interactive Content

Safely handling file uploads

For example, assume there is a basic PHP file that accepts file uploads and stores the uploaded file information in a database.

The first question to ask is what parts of this simple application are potential security concerns?

- The form itself?
- The database component?
- The file being uploaded?

Checking for valid file extensions

The uploaded file would be the least obvious point of a security breach, but look at some sample code that explains how it can very easily become an issue. A very common, but misleading attempt to secure the file uploading process is to check for a valid extension, such as:

```php
<?php

$file = $_FILES[0];

if(strpos($file['name'], '.jpg') !== false)
{
  if(!move_uploaded_file($file['tmp_name'], 'storage/'))
  {
    print "File uploaded";
  }
}

?>
```

As you can see, the code is set up to look for the `.jpg` file extension. The `strpos` function is used to return the index or placement of the checked value, which in this example is `.jpg`. At first glance this seems pretty secure and should stop malicious uploading, but it doesn't. This code doesn't care where the file extension is, so you could have `imagename.jpg.php` as the filename and it will pass. Even worse, if this is for a publicly accessible photo gallery, that file can execute PHP freely because it is already on the server. The ability to execute arbitrary code becomes a great concern when the malicious user is able to place code directly on an unsuspecting server.

Imagine an image being uploaded that is actually a PHP file with code such as the following:

```php
<?php
error_reporting(E_ALL);

phpinfo();

mysql_connect('localhost', 'anyuser', 'anypass');

?>
```

Maintaining Security while Working with User Input

> **NOTE**: Error reporting can be forced off by disabling the `display_errors` directive in the `php.ini` file. This ensures error reporting can't accidentally be turned back on.

When accessed through the browser, this code would allow all errors to be visible, display vital server information, force a failed attempt to the database exposing the true path of file, as you can see in Figure 7.1, and determine if a database exists.

Using a better way to check for file extensions

Going back to the simple upload example, let's add more robust security measures. The major change to the code is the `if` statement that checks for a valid file extension. Instead of looking for the existence of a file type, it looks at the end of the filename and retrieves the actual correct extension.

```
if(strrpos( $file['name'], '.jpg') !== false)
{
    ...
}
```

FIGURE 7.1

Error message returned when database is intentionally set to fail on connection

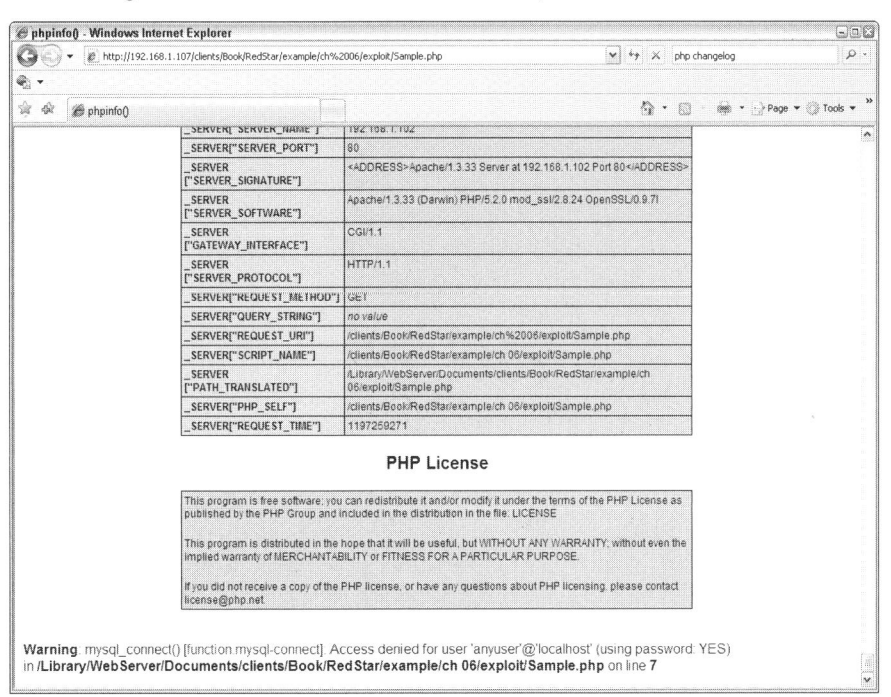

129

Part II   Developing Interactive Content

At first glance it seems nothing has changed, but in fact it has. The `strpos` function has been replaced with the less common `strrpos`, which looks for the file type starting at the end of the string and moving toward the front. This ensures the final file extension is found and not one buried within the name.

As with code in general, security can be expanded, and this example allows a great deal of expansion. Here is a more dynamic method of looking for valid file types that can easily be placed in an existing project or a brand-new project.

```php
<?php

function checkForFileType($file, $type)
{

  $fileTypePos = strrpos($file,'.');

  if($fileTypePos === false)
  {
    return "File not valid.";
  }

  if(substr($file, ($fileTypePos+1), strlen($file)) == $type)
  {
    return "Valid file type";
  }
  else
  {
    return "Invalid or malicious file type detected.";
  }

}

checkForFileType("sample.jpg", "jpg");

?>
```

The above code is a custom function that accepts two arguments. The first argument addresses the file to validate, and the second is the extension to recognize. This expandable solution returns a string determining whether the file type is found or not. Less common is the third possibility, an invalid match. An invalid match means the passed-in file does not have a valid filename at all.

Now that the upload portion of the code is secure, the next point of security is the actual form itself. This part would most likely consist of the file upload box and input boxes for extra data. Generally, an automated attack (computer set up to exploit Web sites) is the security issue developers are most concerned with, but an input form in Flash can also pose a security risk.

Maintaining Security while Working with User Input 7

Checking for valid input

Checking the validity of the input boxes is a good start. An example of an input check in ActionScript is something such as the following:

```
if(length(fileNameTxt.text) > 0)
{
  // file name is valid
}
```

This is simply checking the `fileNameTxt` variable for a length that is greater than 0, meaning the input box has some amount of text in it. Now that the input box is known to be valid, a call to the server is made and this results in the PHP being called. The PHP for a simple unsecure example could look something like this.

```
<?php

$name = $_POST['fileName'];

// database info goes here...

mysql_query("INSERT INTO uploads (name) VALUES (" . $name .
    ")");

?>
```

This is basically taking the filename and directly inserting it into the database. You might be wondering at this point how if the filename is validated in Flash this could be a security concern. The problem isn't in the data passed in from Flash, but more importantly, the fact that the PHP could potentially be called by another method. This is one of the most important reasons to properly secure all points of an application.

A more secure alternative to the previous code would be

```
<?php

$name = $_POST['fileName'];

// database info goes here ...

if(!empty($name) && strlen($name) > 0)
{
  mysql_query("INSERT INTO uploads (name) VALUES (" . $name .
    ")");
}

?>
```

131

This code is not only checking for a valid value but also ensuring that value is of a valid length.

```
if(!empty($name) && strlen($name) > 0)
```

In a real-world application you would probably check for a value of at least two to three characters, but that all depends on the intended use. This small update to the code ensures that a call from Flash or any other method will be secured.

Validating ZIP codes

Of course, securing data is not limited to basic form fields. Assume there is a portion to the application that accepts a five-digit ZIP code when the user submits an image. The way to ensure a valid ZIP code is by testing for a numeric value and a valid length.

```
<?php

$zipCode = $_POST['zip'];

if(is_numeric($zipCode) && strlen($zipCode) == 5)
{
  // valid zip code found
}

?>
```

The `is_numeric()` function accepts a variable as an argument that is tested to determine whether or not that value is a number. This function will return a true/false response so it can easily be used within an `if` statement or you could assign the result to a variable.

Looking for valid types

If you want to perform this same basic validation within Flash, you would use the `typeof` and `length` functions. The `typeof` function returns a string value defining what the type is for the passed-in item. This function can be used for more than just number validation, but it works perfectly for this example:

```
if(typeof(zipCode) == "number" && zipCode.toString().length == 5)
{
  // valid zip code found
}
```

Cleaning User Data

Now that you have a better understanding of security in your application, the next step is to sanitize or clean more advanced data before it is stored.

Maintaining Security while Working with User Input   7

The process of storing data covers both database usage and a more simple approach of using standard text files. The advantage to standard text files is the fact you don't need database access. The disadvantage to this approach is it is a less robust solution that results in much slower searching possibilities. Most often you would use a database, unless it was a fairly small application that didn't need the potential to scale in to a larger application.

Sanitizing the data

The first step to sanitizing data is covered in the previous section, which is to ensure that at least the data is valid. This process is necessary as various functions that interact with a database or file system will create pretty substantial errors if empty data sets are used.

The process of sanitizing data should be done in the PHP because it is always a good practice to assume any passed-in data is dirty. This means that even though the data was sent from your Flash app it could have been tampered with in the submission process.

CROSS-REF Sent data from Flash is easily viewed using Charles, which is discussed in Chapter 13. Charles can be used to be 100 percent sure what data is being sent from Flash.

There are a couple of very useful functions in PHP that can assist in the process of sanitizing data before it is stored. The first function is `addslashes()`, which will escape characters such as quotes and slashes in the data passed to it. The following snippet of code shows how `addslashes` properly sanitizes the data.

```
<?php

$quote = "I hope to finish the "coolest" Flash application ever.
   Which will use Flash and PHP";

?>
```

Creating safe SQL queries

If you ran the preceding code, it would generate an error because the PHP processor does not allow quotes within quotes. With multiple quotes, it would not be able to determine where one string starts and another ends. Assume the `$quote` variable is filled dynamically by a call from Flash. The variable will properly be filled at runtime because the compiler does not validate content on the fly; however, entering that data in SQL will cause an error. Even worse, in some cases the string could be partially entered. Here is a real-world SQL query where you can easily see the issue with unescaped quotes.

```
$sql = 'UPDATE users SET business=Tom's Diner WHERE id=' . $ID;
```

Once again, running the code with it previously entered into the PHP causes an error, but assume this string is built from a `$_GET` request. At first, the request seems safe, but notice the SQL query begins with a single quote (') and there is an apostrophe in `Tom's Diner`. The actual SQL call will become:

```
$sql = 'UPDATE users SET business=Tom
```

133

Part II Developing Interactive Content

This basically sets every business name in the application to Tom, which is probably not the intended result. It would also be very hard to revert unless the application took proper backups. That example is fairly extreme, because a double quote is more common for an SQL call, but you can definitely see how unsanitized data could cause a very bad day for the system administrator.

Now that you know how bad unsanitized data can be, go back to that `addslashes()` function and see what the SQL call turns into:

```
$business = addslashes($_GET['name']);
$sql = 'UPDATE users SET business=' . $business . ' WHERE id=' . $ID;
```

The properly sanitized SQL call looks something like this:

```
$sql = 'UPDATE users SET business=Tom\'s Diner WHERE id=' . $ID;
```

Look at another malformed SQL call that has drastic results. This one deals with logging into a secure portion of a Web page. An SQL call for authorization would look something like this:

```
<?php
$user = "admin";
$pass = "password here";
$query = "SELECT * FROM staff WHERE user='" . $user . "' AND
   pass='" . $pass . "'";
?>
```

Notice how once again the SQL blindly accepts the values. This really becomes a problem when a user enters a password such as

```
$pass = "' OR ''='";
```

The resulting SQL call is an empty password because the quotes force the SQL to end and the OR allows it to equal itself. It creates an empty password, which means only the username is stopping someone from logging in, but nine times out of ten, `admin` is a valid username.

```
SELECT * FROM staff WHERE user='admin' AND pass='' OR ''=''
```

That simple \ means the difference between an effective SQL call and a very dangerous one. This function is only one possible way to sanitize data.

The next function, when working with a database, is `mysql_real_escape_string`, which sanitizes data before entering it into the database. When using this function you must first make a proper connection to the database; otherwise you will receive an error.

The syntax for `mysql_real_escape_string` is pretty much the same as `addslashes()`. You pass in the value you want cleaned and an optional `mysql` link. If a link is not passed, the last SQL link is used.

Maintaining Security while Working with User Input

```php
<?php

// connect to database, generate $link

$business = mysql_real_escape_string($_GET['name'], $link);
$sql = 'UPDATE users SET business=' . $business . ' WHERE id=' .
    $ID;

?>
```

The advantage to using this function is that it takes care of all the various escaping, which goes beyond single and double quotes. The obvious problem is it requires a MySQL link, so it cannot be used unless the data will be stored in a database. Or, at the very least, you need to have access to a database. An incorrect usage of this function will result in an error, as seen in Figure 7.2.

FIGURE 7.2

Error message displayed when a MySQL database link is not available

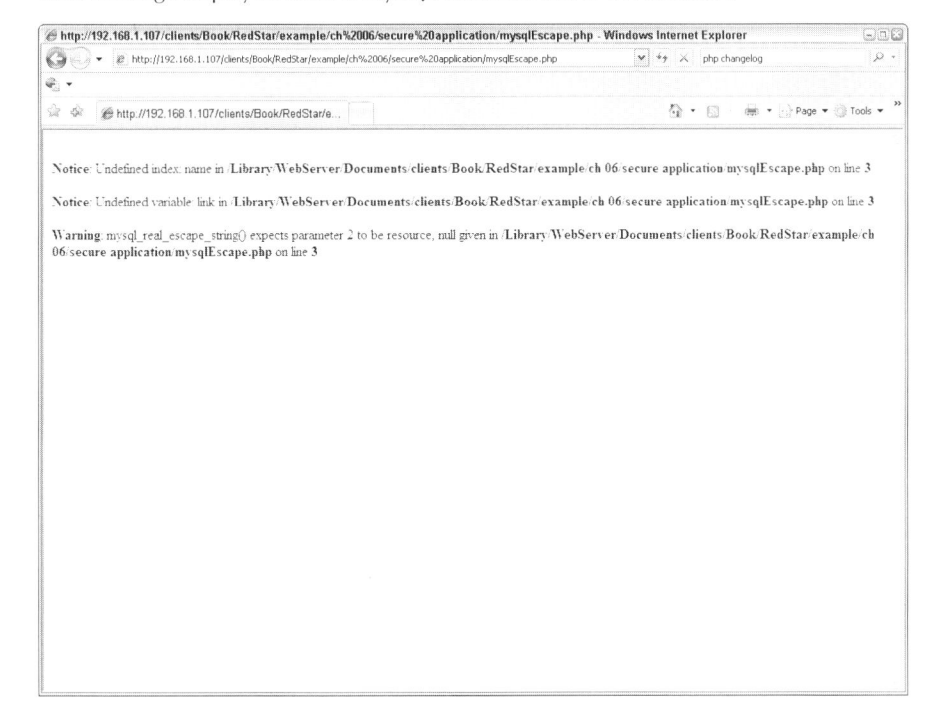

Properly cleaning HTML data

The final function to look at is `htmlentities()`. Basically, this function takes HTML characters and converts them to numeric values. These are better because things like `""` become `&quot;` and this pretty much eliminates the need for advanced sanitizing of data.

```php
<?php

$str = "The 'red' fox <b>jumped</b>";

// The &#039;red&#039; fox &lt;b&gt;jumped&lt;/b&gt;
echo htmlentities($str, ENT_QUOTES);

?>
```

The second argument in the `htmlentities()` function determines if both single and double quotes should be converted, The possible values for this second argument are shown in Table 7.1.

TABLE 7.1

Available Quote Styles

Constant Name	Description
ENT_COMPAT	Converts double quotes; leaves single quotes alone
ENT_QUOTES	Converts both double and single quotes
ENT_NOQUOTES	Leaves both double and single quotes unconverted

It is a good idea to run all three of these functions to ensure your data is as clean as possible. It only takes a little bit more processing power, but can make the difference between a secure and an insecure application.

More importantly, as you continue to practice these good security concepts you will spend less time patching and debugging in the future.

Storing Data

The database is not the only storage method, as explained in the beginning of this section. You can also use simple text files to store information, and the majority of the sanitizing steps would work here as well. The one exception is `mysql_real_escape_string`, which, as stated earlier, requires an SQL link.

Securely writing to a file

A simple example of securely writing to a file would go something like this. First, validate the data before opening the file. Doing this ensures the file can't accidentally be written to.

```php
<?php

if($fileContents != "")
{
  $handle = fopen("sample.txt" , "w+");
  fwrite($handle, $fileContents);
}
else
{
  print "File content not written, invalid data";
}

?>
```

Working with data in a logical order

It is important to keep a logical order when working with data. For example, if the `addslashes()` was run before the `if` statement, the length of the content could be thrown off and produce a false result. At the same time, if the file is opened prior to the data being validated, a malicious exploit could potentially inject content into the opened file. Think of it as the same precautions you take when logging on to a secure Web site in a public location.

Creating a class to handle sanitization

At this point you should fully understand how to sanitize data that can be saved in a database or a simple text file. You can expand on these best practices to create a more reusable set of tools. For example, you could create a sanitization class that automatically takes care of the process. A basic class would be something similar to the following:

```php
<?php

class Sanitization
{

  function cleanSQL($str)
  {
    return mysql_real_escape_string($str);
  }

  function cleanHTML($str)
  {
    return htmlentities($str, ENT_QUOTES);
  }
```

Part II Developing Interactive Content

```
function cleanText($str)
{
  $s = $str;

  if(!ini_get('magic_quotes_gpc'))
  {
    $s = addslashes($s);
  }

  return $s;
}

function checkLength($str, $acceptableLength)
{
  if(strlen($str) >= $acceptableLength)
  {
    return true;
  }
  else
  {
    return false;
  }
}

}

?>
```

The class defines three methods, each one being a replacement for a technique learned in the previous section. This approach offers the ability to be reusable as you continue to work on more applications. The class also contains more logic than previously used because `addslashes` adds slashes to existing slashes. The result will be three slashes escaping each quote.

> **NOTE** A double slash will render a slash in front of the quote because it tells the compiler to escape the slash and not think of it as code.

```
The \\\'red\\\' fox jumped.
```

Working with magic_quotes options

There is a setting in PHP called `magic_quotes_gpc`, which is responsible for escaping data automatically, as shown in Figure 7.3.

138

Maintaining Security while Working with User Input 7

FIGURE 7.3
A sample value from the `magic_quotes_gpc` property as seen in the `phpinfo()` listing

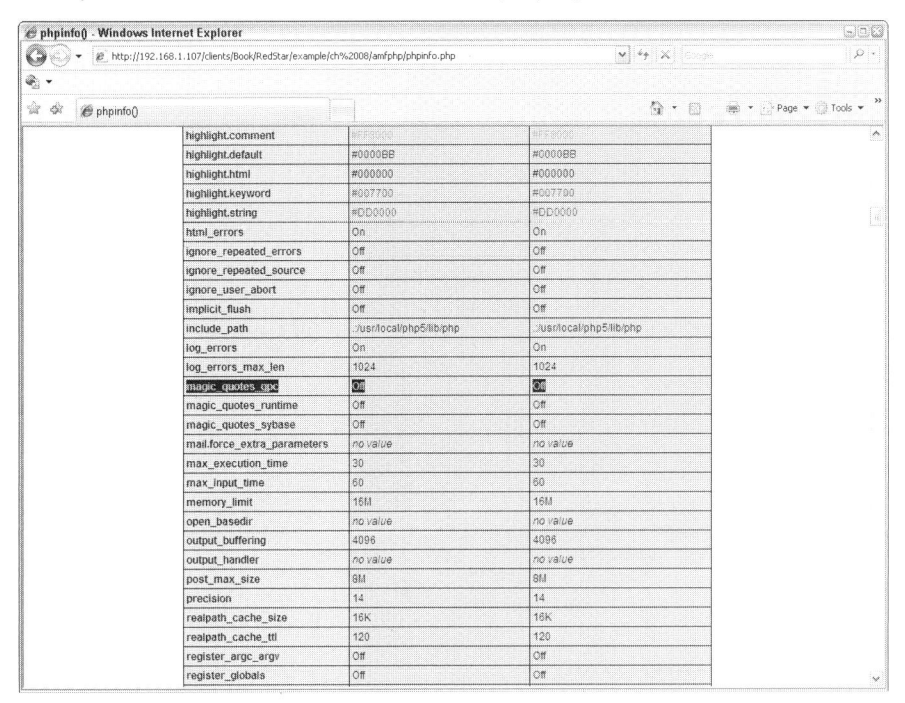

Disabling magic_quotes

In less common server configurations this feature cannot be turned off. A quick test to determine if that setting is enabled ensures extra slashes will not be added.

```
if(!ini_get('magic_quotes_gpc'))
{
    $s = addslashes($s);
}
```

The other two functions in the sanitization class simply clean the passed-in data and return it.

Using shared objects

As you begin to build more complete applications you will come to a point where storing some small amounts of data on the user's machine becomes necessary. These small pieces of information generally hold a user `id` or session that maps to a database entry on the live server. A Shared Object Flash cookie is used in this case because it is a small piece of data stored on the user's machine but isn't required for the application to run.

139

Part II Developing Interactive Content

When the application that makes use of the Shared Object reopens, it would be configured to look for this small piece of data and make a call to a server based on the result. However, just like normal cookies that your browser uses, a Shared Object can be edited by the end user, which can have harmful results.

As stated in the previous section, it is best to not trust data that a user submitted. This common guideline ensures a more secure application and overall makes it easier to work with.

> **NOTE** The majority of holes in an application are exploited by user-submitted data.

Imagine an example application, which would be used to work with a shared object. This application could be set up to open a shared object and pass that data to a remote server.

Once the shared object has been loaded, a call to the remote server could be made passing along the small piece of information from the shared object. In this example, the small piece of information could be a user ID that would have been saved in a previous usage.

Using PHP to handle data from shared objects

The PHP code is responsible for loading this piece of information and querying the database. However, before a call to the database is made, the `user id` is validated ensuring it is a valid number and within range.

```php
<?php

$userID = $_GET['user_id'];
$idRange = 500;
if(is_numeric($userID) && $userID > 0 && $userID < $idRange)
{
  // connect to database at this point
  mysql_connect("localhost", "user", "pass");
  mysql_select_db("db_name");
  $r = mysql_query("SELECT * FROM user WHERE userID=" . $userID);

  while($row = mysql_fetch_array($r))
  {
    print "resp=success&username=" . $row['username']
      . "&userlevel=" . $row['user_level']
      . "&userstyle=" . $row['user_style'];
  }

}
else
{
  print "resp=" . "User ID not found or is invalid";
}
?>
```

Assuming the user id is valid, a block of information is passed back in simple text format. This data is then loaded into an array and used in the rest of the application. If the user id is not valid, a string is returned informing the user that something happened and the existing session cannot be loaded. In most cases, if the existing session cannot be loaded, the Flash application knows to start over rather than attempting to use incomplete or erroneous data.

> **NOTE** ActionScript 3 `corelib` from Adobe (external library) has an MD5 class that can be used in place of PHP.

Creating and storing a safe password using PHP

The process of modifying a password that can be stored is fairly simple. You first create a connection to the PHP file passing along the clear text password. However, this process is not the most secure and it would be better to return an md5 response of the password when a login attempt is made.

To explain the process, here is an example of the simple (less secure) option:

```
var phpFile:String = "http://localhost/md5creator.php";

var query:String = "?pass=" . "password";
var urlRequest:URLRequest = new URLRequest(phpFile + query);
var urlLoader:URLLoader = new URLLoader();

urlLoader.addEventListener(Event.COMPLETE, response);
urlLoader.load(urlRequest);

function response(e:Event):void
{
  var loader:URLLoader = URLLoader(e.target);
  var param:URLVariables = new URLVariables(loader.data);

  trace("User Information Loaded");
  trace("\tUser: " + param.username);
  trace("\tLevel: " + param. userlevel);
  trace("\tStyle: " + param.userstyle);
}
```

A call to the PHP on the server is made using a basic URLRequest, which should be familiar to you from previous examples and chapters. Once the URLRequest is established, a callback function is assigned to handle the server response. This example will either contain an md5 string or an error.

The PHP simply checks for a valid string and returns an md5 hash (encrypted string). If an incomplete or empty string is sent from the Flash, the PHP returns an error message.

```
<?php

$string = $_GET['string'];

if(strlen($string) == 0)
```

Part II Developing Interactive Content

```
{
  print "response=" . "String not provided.";
}
else
{
  $md5 = md5($string);
  print "response=" . $md5;
}

?>
```

This would be a fairly simple example for creating an md5 hash. In real-world usage you would want to seed the md5 encryption to make the response more unique and harder to break open.

A seed is a known value that is used in the md5 process. If you want to create a truly random seed, using the time() is a good idea because nearly every call produces a different result.

The hash for this example needs to be verifiable when the user attempts to log in. For this example, the name of the application used will be "securepass".

```
cfcd208495d565ef66e7dff9f98764da
```

The seed is appended to the existing string that will be encrypted, either at the beginning or the end.

```
$md5 = md5($string + "securepass");
```

The position of the seed needs to be consistent because it will be re-created when the user attempts to log in the next time.

The PHP code with the unique seed applied would look something like this:

```
<?php

$string = $_GET['string'];

if(strlen($string) == 0)
{
  print "response=" . "String not provided.";
}
else
{
  $md5 = md5($string + "securepass");
  print "response=" . $md5;
}

?>
```

At this point in the application the seed is created, and you can continue on with the process of storing that value into a shared object.

Returning Data

It is safe to assume that you will want to be returning data back to Flash at some point in your application. The overall security concern in this process is similar to sending data, with the exception that more exploits would be attempted on the returning of data.

Securely returning data

The idea of securely passing data back to Flash is a much less talked about topic. This is mostly due to the fact that Flash doesn't need to be secure; however, it is still a good practice to ensure it is.

If you fail to validate data coming back into Flash you can open a security hole that could, for example, allow a user to access a private section of an application. Even worse, it can have negative effects on the user experience, and your users can lose faith in your application.

The data coming back into Flash can be altered in the same way the data going out can. For the previous example, a string of data is returned, but is never checked to make sure the data is valid. Let's expand upon the previous example to add this extra security. The response function is the only section of code that needs to be modified because the request will be the same.

```
function response(e:Event):void
{
  var loader:URLLoader = URLLoader(e.target);
  var param:URLVariables = URLVariables(loader.data);

  var username:String;
  var userLevel:uint;
  var userStyle:String;
  var validData:Boolean = true;

  if(param.username != "")
  {
    username = param.username;
  }
  else
  {
    validData = false;
  }

  if(param.userlevel!= "")
  {
    userLevel = param.userlevel;
  }
  else
  {
    validData = false;
  }

  if(param.userstyle != "")
```

Part II Developing Interactive Content

```
  {
    userStyle = param.userstyle;
  }
  else
  {
    validData = false;
  }

  if(!validData)
  {
    trace("User data was not properly loaded");
  }
  else
  {
    trace("User Information Loaded");
    trace("\tUser: " + param.username);
    trace("\tLevel: " + param. userlevel);
    trace("\tStyle: " + param.userstyle);
  }

}
```

Basically, this code first initializes variables to store the user data and then checks each passed-in value for a valid entry. The validation variable is assigned to true from the start because if any of the `if` statements fail it will be changed to false. This process is considered reverse logic, but works quite well for validation routines.

Using a more secure approach for returning data

In the previous example you learned how to securely work with returned data. The problem with this simplified approach is that other ways exist to intercept information passed between Flash and the server.

Using unique responses

There are a few options to creating an even more secure application, which all depend on development time and cost. It is a common thought to ignore cost for the ultimate security, but this is simply not possible all of the time. Oftentimes you will work on a project that gets to a "good enough" point and the app will ship with issues; this is a downside to application development, but very common.

The best way to keep cost realistic is to look at all your options. One option is to use md5 to create unique response codes and ensure the data is valid, which will work, but nothing stops the "hacker" from decompiling your SWF and looking directly at the code.

Securing your files

In previous versions of ActionScript you were able to create obfuscated SWFs, which meant that most applications couldn't decompile them. However, at the time of this writing no tool exists for AS3 applications.

Understanding the Flash Security Sandbox

The sandbox in Flash determines which files can be accessed depending on where the SWF file is located. An SWF file functions differently when it runs locally on the user's machine than it does on a server.

For example, an SWF in the local sandbox cannot access both local and remote objects. This enforces a level of security on the application to ensure sources can't cross each other.

Local files can be placed in one of three sandboxes:

- `local-with-filesystem`: This ensures the user that local content cannot accidentally be sent to a network or shared.
- `local-with-networking-sandbox`: Allows local SWFs to access remote objects, if a valid policy file is found.
- `local-trusted`: An SWF in this sandbox can access data from anywhere, both local and remote. Only users and administrators can move an SWF to this sandbox.

The `local-trusted` sandbox cannot accidentally be set by a stand-alone SWF. This is done to ensure the level of security a user would expect.

In order to allow access to a remote domain you must first add it to the `Security` class by making a call to `allowDomain()`.

```
Security.allowDomain("www.example.org");
```

You can also use a cross-domain policy file that allows access from specific domains or all domains using a wildcard (`"*"`).

```
<allow-access-from-domain="*" />
```

Setting the sandbox type

When publishing an SWF, you can choose the specified sandbox type depending on the resources required in that use. To set the sandbox type, follow these steps:

1. Choose File ⇨ Publish Settings.
2. Click the Flash tab.
3. In the drop-down list, click Playback Security.
4. Click OK.

Using the sandboxType property

An SWF file can use the read-only static `Security.sandboxType` property to determine which sandbox the Flash player has assigned the current SWF.

Part II Developing Interactive Content

In some cases, you will want to use the current value of the `sandboxType` property in programming to determine how an application should interact. Using a simple switch statement, you can construct a custom function that will trace out the current sandbox type, as shown in Figure 7.4.

FIGURE 7.4

Output window displaying an example result from the `whichSandbox` function

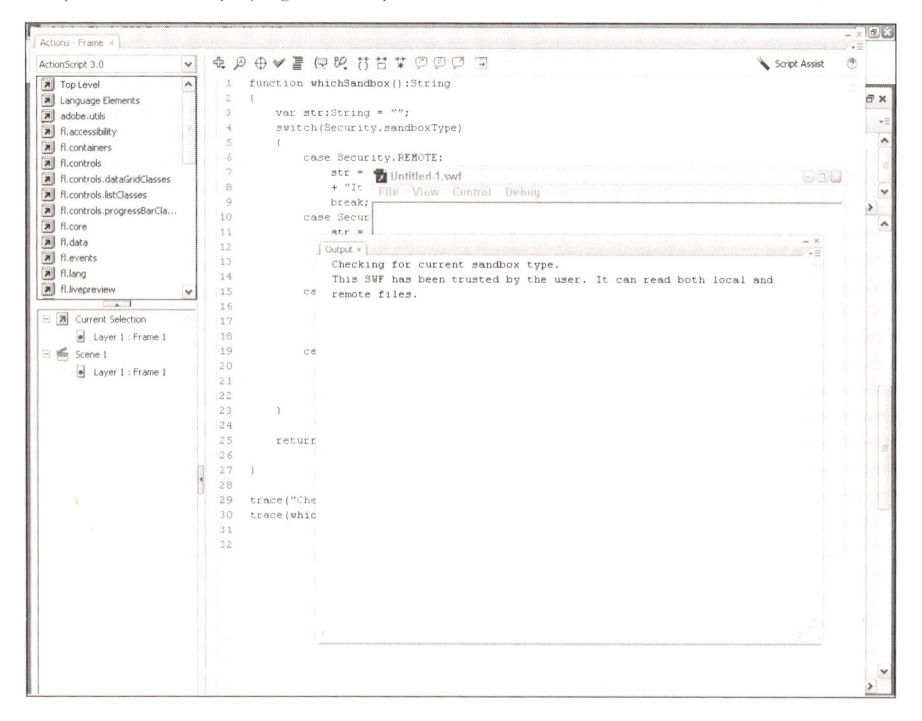

```
function whichSandbox():String
{
  var str:String = "";
  switch(Security.sandboxType)
  {
    case Security.REMOTE:
      str = "This SWF is from an Internet URL. "
      + "It cannot access local files";
      break;
    case Security.LOCAL_WITH_FILE:
      str = "This SWF is local, but not trusted by "
      + "the user. It does not have access to "
      + "remote files.";
      break;
    case Security.LOCAL_WITH_NETWORK:
      str = "This SWF can communicate with remote "
```

146

Maintaining Security while Working with User Input

```
      + "files, but can with local files.";
      break;
    case Security.LOCAL_TRUSTED:
      str = "This SWF has been trusted by the user. "
      + "It can read both local and remote files.";
      break;
  }

  return str;

}

trace("Checking for current sandbox type.");
trace(whichSandbox());
```

Determining the active sandbox

Determining the current sandbox type is not limited to a simple trace response. You can present the user with a warning screen notifying him or her that the current SWF cannot access remote resources because it is running locally. You can also forcefully stop a movie from running if a local sandbox is found, which means the movie is no longer running from your Web site. For example, a movie running locally could have been stolen from your site, so it is a good idea to check for this and act accordingly.

Running applications in the local sandbox

This example shown in Figure 7.5 checks the sandbox type and displays a countdown if the movie is running locally.

FIGURE 7.5

Example of the completed application showing an active countdown

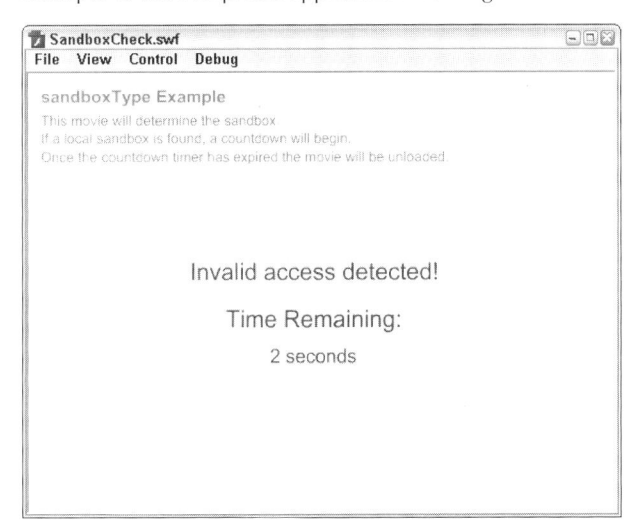

```
SandboxCheck.swf
File  View  Control  Debug

sandboxType Example
This movie will determine the sandbox
If a local sandbox is found, a countdown will begin.
Once the countdown timer has expired the movie will be unloaded.




              Invalid access detected!

                Time Remaining:

                    2 seconds
```

147

Part II Developing Interactive Content

To get started, open the starting file that can be found on this book's Web site.

The assets for this example have already been completed so you can focus on the programming. The first step is to create the necessary variables.

```
var timer:Timer;
var sandbox:String;
var startingTime:uint = 5;
```

After the variables are assigned, you can build the initial function `init`, which is called as soon as the movie begins.

```
function init():void
{
   timerMC.alpha = 0;
   sandbox = Security.sandboxType;


   if(sandbox.indexOf('local') == -1)
   {
      startTimer();
   }

}
```

The main portion of this function is the `if` statement, which checks for the presence of the string `"local"` in the sandbox type. This covers any of the local versions and determines the movie is not running on the remote sandbox. If a local sandbox is detected, a call to `startTimer` is made, which initializes and starts the countdown timer.

```
if(sandbox.indexOf('local') != -1)
{
   startTimer();
}
```

The `startTimer` function first initializes a new `timer` instance and then adds an event listener, which is called every millisecond. The last action in this function is to display the timer text, by setting the alpha property to `1.0` which makes it fully visible.

> **CAUTION** Using a timer update of 1 millisecond for a long period of time can create an unresponsive movie. For an immediate check, such as in this example, it is not a great concern.

```
function startTimer():void
{
   startingTime *= 1000;
```

Maintaining Security while Working with User Input

```
    timer = new Timer(1, 0);
    timer.addEventListener(TimerEvent.TIMER, tickHandler);
    timer.start();
    timerMC.alpha = 1.0;
}
```

The event handler in the previous section assigns a function for each call to the timer. This function is that handler. The argument passed in is a reference to the timer object. You can also reference the global `Event`; however, this is more understandable if you return to this code in the future.

```
function tickHandler(e:TimerEvent):void
{
  var time:Timer = e.target as Timer;

  var milli:uint = (startingTime - getTimer());
  var sec:uint = Math.round(milli / 1000);

  timerMC.timerTxt.text = String(sec)
  + ((sec == 1) ? " second" : " seconds");

  if(sec == 0)
  {
    timer.stop();
    stage.removeChildAt(0);
  }
}
```

The target of the event object is cast as `Timer`. Once again, this step is not required, but makes it easier to work with the code.

The idea is to display the seconds remaining, which is determined using the remaining milliseconds. The remaining milliseconds are obtained using the `getTimer()` function, which returns the milliseconds the current movie has been running. The `startingTime` is subtracted by this value and the result is total milliseconds.

```
    var milli:uint = (startingTime - getTimer());
```

> **NOTE** The `getTimer()` function always returns the total time the current movie has been running. This means if this test is done later in the playback process the value would not be correctly displayed.

The remaining milliseconds are then converted to seconds using some basic math. The current value of the `milli` variable divided by 1000 equals the seconds remaining.

```
    var sec:uint = Math.round(milli / 1000);
```

Once the seconds are determined, that value is sent to the `timerTxt` textfield on the Stage. For correct grammatical display, the `sec` variable is used to determine if second or seconds should be

Part II Developing Interactive Content

displayed. That `sec` variable is tested on each running of this function to determine when the timer should be stopped and to unload the entire application.

```
if(sec == 0)
{
  timer.stop();
  stage.removeChildAt(0);
}
```

Unloading an application

The action of unloading the entire application is done by making a call to `removeChildAt` on the Stage instance. In this case, the whole movie should be removed, so 0 is passed meaning from index 0 and down.

```
if(sec == 0)
{
  timer.stop();
  stage.removeChildAt(0);
}
```

The last step of the code is to make a call to `init`, which starts the entire process.

```
init();
```

That is the complete application, which will run if the current sandbox is local. You can adapt the overall logic in this application and add it into your own to ensure your movie is not improperly run.

Here is the completed code:

```
var timer:Timer;
var sandbox:String;
var startingTime:uint = 5;

function init():void
{
  timerMC.alpha = 0;
  sandbox = Security.sandboxType;
  
  if(sandbox.indexOf('local') == -1)
  {
    startTimer();
  }
  
}

function startTimer():void
```

Maintaining Security while Working with User Input 7

```
{
  startingTime *= 1000;
  timer = new Timer(1, 0);
  timer.addEventListener(TimerEvent.TIMER, tickHandler);
  timer.start();
  timerMC.alpha = 1.0;
}

function tickHandler(e:TimerEvent):void
{
  var time:Timer = e.target as Timer;

  var milli:uint = (startingTime - getTimer());
  var sec:uint = Math.round(milli / 1000);

  timerMC.timerTxt.text = String(sec)
  + ((sec == 1) ? " second" : " seconds");

  if(sec == 0)
  {
    timer.stop();
    stage.removeChildAt(0);
  }
}

init();
```

At this point you should have a good understanding of how the Flash security sandbox works and what it is. As you can see, the sandbox can prove to be a problem in some cases, but overall its purpose is to protect the user. In the last example, the code was expanded and now the sandbox is able to protect the owner of the content as well as the user.

You can take the practices and techniques learned in this section and begin to adapt them into your own applications.

Ensuring an application cannot be shared

As a bonus to this section, the last example will be to create a similar sandbox style check, but this time using the objective that a movie should not be viewable on any other Web site except the one it was built for.

This is achieved by using the `url` property on the `loaderInfo` object. This property is accessible on any loaded object. For this example, the loaded object would be the stage, because it is the root Display Object. The code to determine the current location a movie is running is:

```
stage.loaderInfo.url
```

151

Part II Developing Interactive Content

This code returns a string displaying where a movie is running. An example response from a movie running locally would be:

```
file:///MacPro%20HD/Library/Server/Documents/DomainCheck.swf
```

Using this property you could display a warning message as was done in the sandbox test. For demonstration purposes, an invalid domain is provided to cause the movie to be immediately removed.

```
if(String(stage.loaderInfo.url).indexOf('example.org') != -1)
{
   stage.removeChildAt(0);
}
```

Assuming the previous code is run in a movie that is not located on the `example.org` domain, the movie removes itself and the application is no longer accessible. For a more complete application you would check for the www and non-www version of the Web site. You could also expand on this code and check for a list of valid sites, which could be achieved using a simple `for` loop and an array of allowed domains.

> **NOTE** This check is not 100 percent secure due to limitations in how a `url` can be accessed.

Now you should have an understanding of how to secure your application, and add a level of protection to stop other sites and locations from benefiting from your content without permission.

Summary

In this chapter you learned how to properly sanitize user data while being aware of how it can affect your application functionality. You then learned how to properly load and clean user data to ensure the storage process will not be harmed. Storing the secure data was introduced next with examples of how simple SQL calls can cause headaches in your applications.

The next step that was introduced was the process of returning data to Flash and analyzing this data to ensure it was properly handled.

The last section was an introduction and overview of the Flash sandbox and how it can affect your applications. As a bonus you learned how to create an application that will remove itself if it is not running on the correct domain.

Chapter 8

Using Sockets

When working with multiuser applications, there are different ways to send and receive data. You can use an XML-based delivery method. Another alternative to the standard delivery is to build a "pull" application that checks for updates using a timer.

Sockets allow a "push" method that leaves out the timers and only updates when new data is sent across. The use of sockets is not limited to simple data; you could actually build a multiuser drawing application that would pass the coordinates across the various logged-in clients.

This chapter is broken into two parts. The first part explains sockets. The second part is a simple Flash-based chat application using sockets as the delivery of the messages.

IN THIS CHAPTER

Understanding sockets

Working with sockets in PHP

Working with sockets in Flash

Building a chat client with sockets using Flash and PHP

Understanding Sockets

A *socket* is a communication endpoint or computer part of a network connected to another computer on the same protocol. The difference between a traditional connection (Internet) and a socket is the ability to make a distinction between which machines you are talking to.

When you request a Web site from the Internet, you get the page you requested, but the Internet cannot push new data directly to you (the client) without requesting it once again.

A socket provides this direct communication by allowing the master connection to send new data to you (the client). This is most commonly used in direct connection applications, such as instant messengers, video applications, and team collaboration environments.

Security in sockets

The use of sockets does require a more direct connection, which means security is a larger concern. Generally, whatever tool you are using to implement the socket client or server allows a level of security directly within its own library. For example, Flash requires a trust to be set up in a different domain that allows both parties to authorize the connection. In contrast, a simple connection made by the command line does not have any implied security beyond standard protocol limits.

> **NOTE** Sockets can be a poor choice when implemented into certain systems or setups due to their direct connection nature.

Implementing a socket server

The socket server master can be implemented using many common programming languages.

For a persistent or production-level socket, you would most likely run it from a live server to ensure other users can connect to it and limit the risk of an open connection on your local system.

Understanding the socket connection

The socket connection in the following example will be responsible for communicating with the user. The following sections explain that process.

Parts of a socket

A socket connection is made of two pieces. The first part is the master connection or server, and the second part is the clients that connect to the master. The clients can talk directly to the master but cannot generally talk to other clients. If you want the clients to talk with each other you would implement a talkback system within the master.

Binding

The master socket is bound to a specific IP address and port. This means the master connection is made to this specific point to ensure the connection is unique. Clients that want to communicate with that socket server must connect to the same IP address and port as the master.

Listening

This is similar to the standard Web server. Once the socket server starts, it listens for active clients and new ones that want to connect. These clients are then added to the queue and begin to receive communications from the group.

Working with Sockets in PHP

Building a socket server in PHP requires some prior configuration. A socket server within PHP cannot be run from the standard graphic version due to its persistent connection. A standard Web browser-based connection would timeout or possibly crash the host machine.

Using Sockets

A socket connection would be run using the nongraphic command-line version of PHP (CLI). The first step to working with sockets in PHP is to determine if you have this CLI version of PHP installed, as it is not normally included in a Web server package.

Looking for command-line version of PHP

The command-line version (CLI), if installed, is usually accessible directly from the Terminal on a Mac or the command prompt on a PC (see Figure 8.1).

To determine if you have this version, simply open the command line. In Windows, click Start and then Run. Type **cmd** in the Run dialog box and click OK. If you're using a Mac, open the Finder, navigate to Applications/Utilities, and open the Terminal.

FIGURE 8.1

Example of a command prompt in Windows XP

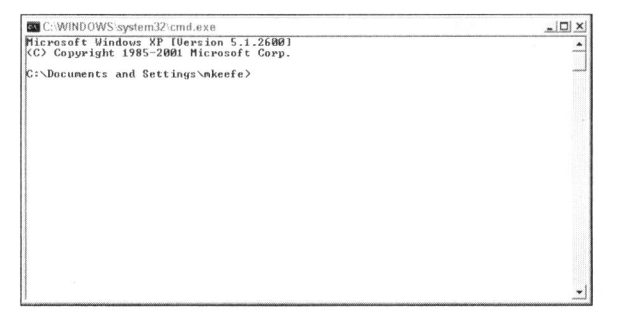

With the command line open, type the following:

```
$ php -v
```

That command tells PHP to report the version information and exit. The results should look something similar to the following:

```
PHP 5.2.5 (cli) (built: Dec 20 2007 02:55:52)
Copyright (c) 1997-2007 The PHP Group
Zend Engine v2.2.0, Copyright (c) 1998-2007 Zend Technologies
```

If you get a response similar to the following, it means the PHP version may be installed but not globally accessible from any command line and will require configuration.

```
-bash: php: command not found
```

You will need to locate the command-line version or install it to continue with this chapter.

155

CROSS-REF See Chapter 1 for information on how to install the command-line version of PHP.

Building a socket server

To build a simple socket server using PHP, start by creating a file and saving it to a commonly accessible location. This file does not need to be in your Web directory and will probably only be harder to work with if it is.

NOTE You want to ensure the socket file is not visible to the Web because it could cause your PHP to not work properly if a malicious user attempted to run the file.

To better understand how sockets work, start with a very simple socket server example.

Simple PHP-based socket server

The first part of the socket server is to determine the server IP address and port number. If you are running the server locally you don't need to determine your physical IP address. Instead, you can use the local address.

```
<?php

$host = "127.0.0.1";
$port = "8888";
```

The port number is not specific, but it needs to be unique on the same machine to ensure it won't collide with any other application on your system or network (if used remotely).

This script will need to inform PHP to continue running because it needs to check for and manage connections indefinitely. This is achieved by passing the `set_time_limit` function a value of 0, meaning this script should never stop until properly exited.

```
set_time_limit(0);
```

With the configuration out of the way, you can create the master socket connection.

```
$sock = socket_create(AF_INET, SOCK_STREAM, SOL_TCP);
```

The three arguments passed into the `socket_create` function define which type of connection it is and are PHP constants. For this example they are not important, but they will be explained later in the chapter.

The `$sock` variable now contains an active socket resource id. The next step is to bind the socket to the port defined in the first part of the code.

```
socket_bind($sock, $host, $port);
```

After the socket is bound to the port, you can start listening for connections. The first argument is the `$socket` variable, which holds the socket resource id. The second argument is a backlog variable that tells PHP how many messages to queue up before an error is passed to the client. This

Using Sockets

variable is a suggestion because some systems will define or override this value. For example, Windows sets this based on the underlying service provider and basically ignores any user-submitted value.

```
socket_listen($sock, 4);
```

At this point, you have built a socket server that doesn't do anything. This basically means the server starts and waits for incoming connections but does not handle them in any way. The next step is to set up the portion of the socket server that handles the incoming connections.

You need to create another socket that handles the incoming connections by making a call to `socket_accept` passing in the `$socket` resource id.

```
$childSocket = socket_accept($sock);
```

From this point the `$childSocket` variable is used to handle all client communications. The data sent from a connection is read using the `socket_read` function.

```
$incomingData = socket_read($childSocket, 2048);
```

This function takes two arguments. The first argument is the client socket handler, and the second argument is the number of bytes to read from the client. This can be useful when trying to run a more efficient socket server. It is also a good idea to limit the output on the client side (if possible).

The `socket_read` function continues to load information into the `$incomingData` variable until the data limit is hit or one of the following characters is found: carriage return (\n), tab (\t), or \0. PHP treats those as end-of-input characters and moves to the next line in the script when one is found.

Responding to the client connection

After the data is loaded, the next step is to act on that data and in most cases respond to the client. For example, the following is a simple question/answer demo that has PHP responding to one question:

```
if(substr($incomingData, 0, -2) == "are you hungry?")
{
  $response = "Server Response > I could eat!\n";
  socket_write($childSocket, $response, strlen($response));
}
```

The `socket_write` function takes three arguments. The first is the child socket resource id; the second argument is the response being sent to the client. The third argument, which is optional, is the length of the `$response`. This example only sends a response back to the client when you ask PHP if it is hungry. As you can see, this is not a very practical application, but does clearly explain how sockets are set up and how to interact with them.

The last step to the sample application, before testing it, is closing the two socket connections to free up the resources and allow new connections to be made.

157

Part II Developing Interactive Content

> **NOTE** If you want to still receive connections you would only want to remove the $childSocket variable.

```
socket_close($childSocket);
socket_close($sock);
```

The sockets can be closed in any order, but it is a good practice to close the master last in case you have to loop through multiple client connections first.

Testing the socket server

Testing of the socket server can be done using a simple prompt or terminal, as shown in Figure 8.2. With the command line open, start the command-line version of PHP, passing in the sample file using the -f option.

```
$ /path/to/php -f /path/to/socket/sample/simpleSocket.php
```

FIGURE 8.2

Simple socket server running in the command prompt

You will notice that the prompt indicator disappears and the PHP file reports no updates. This may not be a very desirable result because nothing is letting you know the server is currently running. You can add a very simple print statement to the top of the file, such as:

```
<?php

$host = "127.0.0.1";
$port = "8888";

set_time_limit(0);

print "Starting Socket Server...\n";

...
```

Using Sockets   8

If you stop and start the socket server you should see the message printed, similar to the following:

```
$ /usr/bin/php -f /path/to/simpleSocket.php
Starting Socket Server...
```

> **NOTE** If you restart the socket server often you may see a warning stating the port is in use. You can either try again or choose another port to continue testing.

When the socket server is properly running you can open a new prompt and attempt to connect the client with the socket server.

```
$ telnet 127.0.0.1 8888
```

Upon a successful connection a message similar to the following should appear:

```
$ telnet 127.0.0.1 8888
Trying 127.0.0.1...
Connected to localhost.
Escape character is '^]'.
```

This application only accepts one message to be sent before being terminated. If you type anything other than "are you hungry?" you will not see a response, unless you modified the question that is asked in the socket application.

Here is the complete code for this example:

```
<?php

$host = "127.0.0.1";
$port = "8888";

set_time_limit(0);

print "Starting Socket Server...\n";

$sock = socket_create(AF_INET, SOCK_STREAM, SOL_TCP);

socket_bind($sock, $host, $port);
socket_listen($sock, 4);

$childSocket = socket_accept($sock);
$incomingData = socket_read($childSocket, 2048);

if(substr($incomingData, 0, -2) == "are you hungry?")
{
   $response = "Server Response > I could eat!\n";
   socket_write($childSocket, $response, strlen($response));
```

159

```
       }

       socket_close($childSocket);
       socket_close($sock);

       ?>
```

The connection is automatically terminated when the message is returned because there is no system in place to look for additional messages. A more realistic application would assume some sort of loop is in place to look for more than one message.

Creating a persistent socket server

The persistent socket server would be very similar to the previous example, with the exception of a looping check for new messages.

Recursive loops

PHP does not offer an asynchronous system (event based) like you would find in ActionScript, but you can create a loop to achieve the same result.

For example, here is a very simple `while` loop similar to the one that will be used in the persistent connection example:

```
x = 0;
while(x < 50)
{
  x++;
}
```

Managing multiple communications

The key to allowing a user to send more than one message per connection is to wrap the `socket_read` calls that are responsible for checking for new messages in a loop.

```
       do
       {
         // look for new messages

         $incomingData = socket_read($childSocket, 2048);

         if(trim($incomingData) == "are you hungry?")
         {
           $response = "Server Response > I could eat!\n";
           socket_write($childSocket, $response, strlen($response));
         }
         else if(trim($incomingData) == "exit")
         {
           $response = "Goodbye!\n";
           socket_write($childSocket, $response, strlen($response));
```

```
        socket_close($childSocket);
        break;
    }
    else
    {
        $response = strtoupper(trim($incomingData)) . "\n";
        socket_write($childSocket, $response, strlen($response));
    }

}
while(true);
```

If you test the example, the connection stays active until you either close the prompt or you type "exit" when connected to the application, which informs the socket server to close your connection. You can also type anything besides "exit" or the previous question and the response will be your input in uppercase.

This simple example does not have support for multiple clients, so once the client is closed, the server ends as well. In the second part of this chapter you build a complete socket-based multiuser chat application that by definition will allow more than one connection at a time.

You should now understand how sockets work in PHP as well as how to implement them in different ways, depending on the application. The next part explains how sockets work in Flash. Then in the final chapter, you combine Flash and PHP to send/receive information using sockets.

Working with Sockets in Flash

Flash is considered the client side of a socket connection. This means you can't deploy a socket server directly from Flash, because Flash is a client-side application. Being able to use Flash as a socket server, if it was possible, wouldn't be very beneficial due to the fact that Flash is a graphical application. It would essentially be a waste of resources to use Flash in a command-line environment.

That being said, Flash makes an excellent socket server client. Telnet was used in the previous section, which is one way to initialize a client connection to a socket server. Flash allows the TCP connections, which require more code and more setup in the beginning.

The majority of the connection code in the next section could be built into a common class or library to minimize the amount of code required to create a socket connection.

Initializing a socket connection

The first part to initializing a socket connection is to define the host and port to connect on.

```
var host:String = "127.0.0.1";
var port:uint = 8888;
```

These two variables will need to be the same as the PHP code you wrote in the previous section. Or, if you are using the supplied code, you can keep the sample values just shown.

Once the variables are defined, create an instance of the Socket class. The constructor of this class accepts two parameters. The first is the host, and the second is the port to connect on.

```
var socket:Socket = new Socket(host, port);
```

As you continue to work with dynamic data sources, you quickly find that proper event handlers make it easier to understand how something is working. This means that adding event listeners to the socket process is a good idea. Start by building the calls, and then create the event handlers later on.

```
socket.addEventListener(Event.CLOSE, closeHandler);
socket.addEventListener(Event.CONNECT, connectHandler);
socket.addEventListener(IOErrorEvent.IO_ERROR, ioErrorHandler);
socket.addEventListener(SecurityErrorEvent.SECURITY_ERROR,
   securityErrorHandler);
socket.addEventListener(ProgressEvent.SOCKET_DATA,
   socketDataHandler);
```

Event handlers

The event handler functions used in this sample application trace the errors to the Output window. A more realistic application would require some logic to handle these errors and respond to the user accordingly.

```
function closeHandler(event:Event):void
{
   trace("Connection to [" + host + "] closed");
}

function ioErrorHandler(event:IOErrorEvent):void
{
   trace(event.text);
}

function securityErrorHandler(event:SecurityErrorEvent):void
{
   trace(event.toString());
}
```

Special handlers

This example has two special event handlers. The first special event handler is called when a connection is successful, informing you that messages can be sent to the socket server. Messages sent before a proper connection is made could result in errors or missed messages.

```
function connectHandler(event:Event):void
{
  trace("Connected to [" + host + "]");
}
```

The `connectHandler` function is the place any calls to the server should be made. It would be a good place to add the sample message call, such as:

```
function connectHandler(event:Event):void
{
  trace("Connected to [" + host + "]");

  try
  {
    socket.writeUTFBytes(("are you hungry?\n");
  }
  catch(e:IOError)
  {
    trace(e);
  }
}
```

The second special event handler is called when a response is fully gathered from the socket server. This is used to ensure partial messages are not evaluated, as they could potentially cause programming errors that would be hard to track.

```
function socketDataHandler(event:ProgressEvent):void
{
  trace("Socket Server Response Loaded");
}
```

This is the function in which all response code should be placed, similar to the following:

```
function socketDataHandler(event:ProgressEvent):void
{
  var str:String = socket.readUTFBytes(socket.bytesAvailable);
  trace("Socket Server Response: " + str);
}
```

As you can see, working with sockets in Flash is not that different from any other data object. The consistency of the code across different packages is one very great aspect of ActionScript.

Remote socket connections

The previous example was connecting to a local socket (on the same machine), but it is more realistic that your application would be connecting to a remote socket. This means you must set up a trust between the client and server running the socket server application.

Part II Developing Interactive Content

Security trust

A trust uses the `crossdomain.xml` file with the ports that are allowed, such as:

```
<?xml version="1.0"?>
<!DOCTYPE cross-domain-policy SYSTEM
    "http://www.macromedia.com/xml/dtds/cross-domain-policy.dtd">
<cross-domain-policy>
  <allow-access-from domain="*" to-ports="8888" />
</cross-domain-policy>
```

This access file is allowing any client to connect on port 8888 and no other. You can also define a domain if this socket application will be accessible only from another Web site, such as.

```
<?xml version="1.0"?>
<!DOCTYPE cross-domain-policy SYSTEM
    "http://www.macromedia.com/xml/dtds/cross-domain-policy.dtd">
<cross-domain-policy>
  <allow-access-from domain="anothersite.com" to-ports="8888" />
</cross-domain-policy>
```

The second part of the security trust is a call to `allowDomain` in the Flash file. This method of the Security class is responsible for defining a domain that is allowed to connect to this client. This connection will only occur if the remote site has a proper `crossdomain` file.

```
Security.allowDomain("example.com");
```

Loading the policy file

In rare cases, the cross-domain policy file is not in the default location, so a call to `loadPolicyFile` can be made to inform Flash where to find the `crossdomain.xml` file.

```
Security.loadPolicyFile("http://example.com/newloc/crossdomain
    .xml");
```

You should now know how to set up a client-based socket connection in Flash. As you can see, the majority of the code used in a socket connection is handled by Flash.

As stated in the beginning of this section, the code used to build a socket connection can be reused throughout your projects.

Using a class for socket connections

To better understand socket connections in Flash, let's start off by building a basic socket example. Then once the basics are in place, the next section will cover building a complete socket-based chat application using Flash and PHP.

Basic socket class

Here is a basic socket class that easily defines the customizable elements. Simply save this code in an ActionScript file with the name `SimpleSocket` in the same directory as your sample Flash document.

```
package
{

import flash.errors.*;
import flash.events.*;
import flash.net.Socket;

public class SimpleSocket extends Socket
{

  public var host:String;
  public var port:uint;
  private var socket:Socket;

  public static var SOCK_CONNECTED:String = "onSockConnect";
  public static var SOCK_IOERROR:String = "onSockIOError";

  function SimpleSocket(h:String, p:uint)
  {
    host = h;
    port = p;
    socket = this;
    super(host, port);
    initListeners();
  }
  public function sendMessage(str:String):void
  {
    if(connected)
    {
      socket.writeUTFBytes(str + "\n");
    }
    else
    {
      trace("Not connected, message not sent!");
    }
  }

  public function readMessage():void
  {
    if(connected)
    {
      var str:String =
      socket.readUTFBytes(socket.bytesAvailable);
      trace("Socket Server Response: " + str);
    }
```

Part II Developing Interactive Content

```
    else
    {
      trace("No message read, not connected!");
    }
}

private function initListeners():void
{
  socket.addEventListener(Event.CLOSE, closeHandler);
  socket.addEventListener(Event.CONNECT, connectHandler);
  socket.addEventListener(IOErrorEvent.IO_ERROR,
 ioErrorHandler);
}

private function closeHandler(event:Event):void
{
  trace("Connection to [" + host + "] closed");
}

private function ioErrorHandler(event:IOErrorEvent):void
{
  dispatchEvent(new Event(SOCK_IOERROR));
}

private function connectHandler(event:Event):void
{
  trace("Connected to [" + host + "]");
  dispatchEvent(new Event(SOCK_CONNECTED));
}

private function socketDataHandler(event:ProgressEvent):void
{
  readMessage();
}
}
} // last two braces are lined up for printing purposes
```

Using the SimpleSocket class

The process of using the `SimpleSocket` class is fairly simple. Start by setting up a new Flash movie. This movie makes an import call, which is responsible for loading the custom class.

```
import SimpleSocket;

var sock:SimpleSocket;
```

To create a socket connection, start by making a new instance of the `SimpleSocket` class, passing in the host and port information for the socket server you want to connect to.

```
sock = new SimpleSocket('127.0.0.1', 8888);
```

Using Sockets 8

When the socket connection call is finished, you will want to assign listeners to the custom events. This simple class only has events for a successful connection and another for any connection error. You can expand the class and add more event handlers as needed.

```
sock.addEventListener(SimpleSocket.SOCK_CONNECTED, connected);
sock.addEventListener(SimpleSocket.SOCK_IOERROR, ioError);
```

The final step is to define the event handler functions, such as:

```
function ioError(e:Event):void
{
   trace("Can't connect to " + sock.host + " on port " +
   sock.port);
}
function connected(e:Event):void
{
   sock.sendMessage("are you hungry?");
}
```

You can now run the movie and should see the following output if you built or loaded the socket server code and the server is currently running.

```
"Connected to [127.0.0.1] Socket Server Response: ARE YOU THERE?"
```

This class can be expanded upon to allow for more specific requirements, but you should have a basic understanding of how the socket system works in Flash. At this point you should also know how to construct a custom class to handle the majority of the socket connecting and communicating process.

The final section focuses on building a custom multiuser chat client using the information learned in the previous sections.

Building a Chat Client with Sockets Using Flash and PHP

In the previous sections, you learned how to construct a simple PHP socket server. You then built a basic Flash client to communicate with the PHP socket server. In this section, you combine the steps into one real-world application. The application you will be building is a multiuser chat client running in Flash with a PHP socket server to handle the connections.

This multiuser chat application will allow multiple client connections to talk to each other with the admin being able to send specific messages about status and connection details.

PHP socket server for the chat client

The PHP portion of the application will be two files: the actual socket server class and the calling page to start the socket server.

Part II Developing Interactive Content

The socket server class skeleton looks like the following block of code. As you can see, the socket class has many methods. Breaking them up into easy-to-maintain portions will create a better product in the end.

```
class ChatServer
{
  ...

  function ChatServer($ip='192.168.1.110', $port=8888) {}

  public function startServer() {}

  public function stopServer() {}

  private function initLoop() {}

  private function createMasterClient() {}

  private function notifyClient($sockID, $buffer) {}

  private function notifyClients($clients, $sock, $buffer,
    $admin) {}

  private function handleError($str, $err) {}

  private function endSocket($sockID=null) {}

  private function serverMessage($str) {}

}
```

Chat properties

The first part to focus on in the class is the properties, which are responsible for storing the various error messages, as well as connection details.

```
private $ipAddress = null;
private $port = null;

private $masterClient = null;
private $clients;

// Server Messages
private static $SOCKET_CREATE_FAIL  = "socket_create() failed";
private static $SOCKET_BIND_FAIL    = "socket_bind() failed";
private static $SOCKET_LISTEN_FAIL  = "socket_listen() failed";
private static $SOCKET_ACCEPT_FAIL  = "";

private $LINE_ENDING     = "\n";
private static $SHOW_ERRORS  = 1; // display errors (0=off, 1=on)
```

Using Sockets

These methods are all set as private to ensure they are not accidentally accessible to other scripts. You can set up getters and setters if you decide that you want to share these or any properties in a class.

> **CAUTION** Use caution when allowing methods and properties to be globally accessible. Failure to properly lock down these elements can result in major security flaws.

The constructor method is responsible for storing the host and port information. This method also creates a new array that will store the connected client's information. You will notice the most common values in the constructor are predefined. This means that if no host or port is defined by the calling script these default values are used:

```
function ChatServer($ip='127.0.0.1', $port=8888)
{
  $this->ipAddress = $ip;
  $this->port = $port;

  $this->clients = array();
}
```

The next function is called by the second PHP file and is where the master server function as well as the listening system function are called from. The `stopServer` function is left empty because the socket server is turned off when the connection ends. You could add more logic that could allow remote turnoff or possibly even shutdown at a certain time.

```
public function startServer()
{
  $this->createMasterClient();
  $this->initLoop();
}

public function stopServer() { /* empty */ }
```

The `initLoop` function, which is called when the server starts, is the core of the socket server. This function is responsible for initializing new connections and listening for messages sent from the existing connections. This function covers the majority of this application. You will look at it in parts.

The first step of this function is to reset the `$socketsChanged` variable that holds the modified list of active socket connections.

```
private function initLoop()
{
  $socketsChanged = null;

  while(true)
  {
    // connection and message loop
  }
}
```

169

Part II Developing Interactive Content

The contents of the `while` loop is where the majority of client and message checking occurs. The `socket_select` function is responsible for changing the read status of a socket if new data is found, which marks it and adds the socket to the array of changed sockets to be looped through. This is used to limit the data checking in the `foreach` loops.

> **NOTE** The `socket_select` function modifies the array. It is a good idea to make a copy first.

```
...
while
{
   $socketsChanged = $this->clients;

   $write  = NULL;
   $except = NULL;

   socket_select($socketsChanged, $write, $except, NULL);

   foreach($socketsChanged as $socket)
   {
      ...
   }
}
```

You could expand this functionality to multiple methods in the class, but it is a good idea to keep all relevant code together.

The `foreach` loop runs through each active socket connection. It is verified against the master server and then checked to make sure an active client exists. If no active client exists the script exits because something has gone wrong and the code will not be able to continue.

```
foreach($socketsChanged as $socket)
{
  if($socket == $this->masterClient)
    {
      if (($client = socket_accept($this->masterClient)) < 0)
      {
        $this->handleError(ChatServer::SOCKET_ACCEPT_FAIL,
           '');
        continue;
      }
      else
      {
        array_push($this->clients, $client);
      }
    }
    else
    {
      ...
    }
}
```

Using Sockets

If the client has been added and the master server instance exists, the `else` portion of the code is run. This part checks the message buffer for a valid message. If no valid buffer is found, the client's connection ends. This cleanup routine ensures that the resources are not being wasted.

Excluding the master server from communication

Assuming a valid message is found, the value is stored in a new string variable and the master server is removed from the array. This is done to ensure any messages or maintenance will not occur on the master connection. For example, a broadcast message informing clients of the service is not something the master server needs to receive.

The `array_shift` function removes the first element and rekeys the array, basically shifting all of the elements down by one.

```
if($socket == $this->masterClient)
{
   ...
}
else
{
  $buffer = ''; // filled by socket_recv (undocumented)
  $bytes = socket_recv($socket, $buffer, 2048, 0);
  if($bytes == 0)
  {
    $this->endSocket($socket);
  }
  else
  {
    $allclients = $this->clients;
    array_shift($allclients); // remove master
    $specialString = $buffer;
  }
  ...
}
```

Special chat parameters

When a valid message is found, it is checked for special parameters. This could be a simple `"exit"` request or a more advanced admin flag that is used to notify clients with service messages. The special message types are just a use case example. You can easily change, add, or remove the special messages, depending on how you set up your chat client.

```
// look for admin beacon
if(substr($specialString, 0, 7) == "[admin]")
{
  $this->notifyClients($allclients,
    $socket, substr($buffer, 7), true);
}
```

The `"exit"` message is called by a client that wants to exit chat. If the user simply closes the Flash movie, the socket server removes the user from the list on the next loop pass. This gives the user a way to cleanly leave the system and see a `"Goodbye"` message as he or she is exiting.

```
else if(substr($specialString, 0, 4) == "exit")
  {
  $this->serverMessage("Closing Connection: " . $socket);
  $this->notifyClient($socket, "Goodbye");
  $this->endSocket($socket);

}
```

A more advanced chat application would probably have documentation on the Web site. This `"help"` command shows you another way to deliver the more commonly used commands directly to your connected clients. You will notice this command is very similar to the `"man"` command that is found in UNIX terminals.

```
else if(substr($specialString, 0, 4) == "help")
{
   $this->notifyClient($socket, "Chat Help:\n"
     . "Type exit to leave chat");
}
```

If no special message is found, then simply broadcast the unedited message to all of the other clients. This system will even display your comment back to you. A more complete application would need to be set up to exclude the author of the comment from being updated.

```
else
{
  $this->notifyClients($allclients, $socket, $buffer);
}
```

As you can see, the `initLoop` method has a lot of responsibilities and handles a good portion of the entire socket server.

Master client connection

The `createMasterClient` method is called when the socket server starts. This method initializes the socket server and creates the master connection to which all other clients connect.

```
private function createMasterClient()
  {
  if(($this->masterClient = socket_create(AF_INET, SOCK_STREAM,
    SOL_TCP)) < 0)
    {
      $this->handleError(ChatServer::SOCKET_CREATE_FAIL,
        $this->masterClient);
    }
```

The socket options are set to allow the reuse of the local address, which informs PHP that overwriting the existing connection is allowed. You would set this to `false` if you want to retain a unique connection.

```
socket_set_option($this->masterClient, SOL_SOCKET,SO_REUSEADDR,
  1);
```

Before the initial connection can be made, you must ensure that the address is available and not in use by an existing application.

```
if(($bindRes = socket_bind($this->masterClient,
  $this->ipAddress, $this->port)) < 0)
{
   $this->handleError(ChatServer::SOCKET_BIND_FAIL, $bindRes);
}
```

Assuming the address is available, a call to `socket_listen` is made, which makes the socket ready to receive connection requests. Once the connection is made, the master client is added to the `client` array and the initialization process is complete.

```
if(($ret = socket_listen($this->masterClient, 5)) < 0)
{
   $this->handleError(ChatServer::SOCKET_LISTEN_FAIL, $ret);
}

$this->clients = array($this->masterClient);
```

The last step in the `createMasterClient` method is to send a server message that informs the server operator that a new chat server has been initialized. In this example, the operator is you, so you will notice a print statement in the prompt when you start the server.

```
    $this->serverMessage("Chat Server Started");
}
```

Notifying a specific client

There are two types of client notifications in this chat application. The first type is a global notification and the second type is for a single user. The single-user notification is most commonly used to send status messages to a client.

The single-user method accepts two parameters defining the specific socket ID and the message to send to that client. A `foreach` loop is used to find the specific client, and, if found, a call to `socket_write` is made, sending the message.

```
    private function notifyClient($sockID, $buffer)
    {
      foreach($this->clients as $client)
      {
        if($client == $sockID)
```

```
        {
            socket_write($client, $buffer . $this->LINE_ENDING);
        }
    }
}
```

Notifying all clients

The global notification is similar to the single-user method, with the exception that it checks to see if the message being sent is to be marked as an admin message. The admin flag can be set when a call to `notifyClients` is made. The default value is `false`, ensuring that client messages can't be marked as coming from the admin.

```
private function notifyClients($clients, $sock, $buffer, $admin)
{
  foreach($clients as $client)
  {
    if($admin == true)
    {
      socket_write($client, "ADMIN NOTICE: " . $buffer);
    }
    else
    {
      socket_write($client, $sock . " wrote: " . $buffer);
    }
  }
}
```

Handling errors

As the application continues to run, it is bound to have an error or two. Rather than throw these errors away, it is a good idea to capture them and at least display them to the server. An example of a basic error handler can be seen here:

```
private function handleError($str, $err)
{
  if(ChatServer::SHOW_ERRORS)
  {
    $this->serverMessage(($str . ": reason: "
      . $err) . $this->LINE_ENDING);
  }
}
```

The `handleError` method first checks that errors should be displayed by checking the static `SHOW_ERRORS` property, defined at the top of the class file. The passed-in error message is relayed to the `serverMessage` method, which prints it.

Using Sockets

You could call the `serverMessage` method directly, but using this relay system allows you to trap errors and keep your code clean. It wouldn't make sense to have the `SHOW_ERRORS` condition in the `serverMessage` because a message isn't always an error.

Ending a connection

The connection ends if the client closes the browser or application. However, the user can also close the connection by sending the special `"exit"` parameter. A socket termination method is used to ensure the array of active connections is properly handled. This method will also remove the master if no active clients exist, ultimately ending the socket server connection itself.

The `array_search` function is used to find the socket id to close. This function returns the id from the array. This is used to remove the connection from the list and terminate the specific socket connection.

```php
private function endSocket($sockID=null)
{
  // close master if no socket is defined
  if($sockID == null)
  {
    $sockID = $this->masterClient;
  }

  $index = array_search($sockID, $this->clients);
  unset($this->clients[$index]);
  socket_close($sockID);
}
```

Server monitoring

The last method of the chat class is used to print messages about the socket server directly to the active prompt, generally running on the Web server to which the clients are connecting.

```php
private function serverMessage($str)
{
  print $str . $this->LINE_ENDING;
}
```

Connecting to the socket server

The connection to the chat class built in the previous section is handled by the second PHP file. This file will be the one you would call when you want to start the chat server. Building the system in this manner allows you to leave the chat class on its own and duplicate the connection without modifying the code.

175

Part II Developing Interactive Content

Building the connection file

Here is an example connection on the `localhost` domain, also commonly referred to as the loopback address of your machine or server.

```
#!/usr/bin/php -q
<?php

include 'ChatServer.php';
```

The first line is used to define the command to the terminal. It is not required, but does mean you can exclude the switches, in this case the `-q` which is used to suppress HTTP header output, when you call the `php` file. The next line includes the `ChatServer` class, allowing it to be called from that point.

Once the file is properly included you can make a new chat instance, passing in the host and port that you would like to begin listening on. In this example, the local host is used and is bound to port 8888. The port number does not need to be the same; it only needs to be open. It is a good idea to choose a port number that won't be used by other applications on your system.

```
$chatServer = new ChatServer("127.0.0.1", 8888);
```

The last step is to start the server and allow others to connect to it. To stop the server you can close the terminal or press Ctrl+C, which in most terminals will end the active process.

```
$chatServer->startServer();
```

Here is the complete code for this simple test:

```
#!/usr/bin/php -q
<?php

include 'ChatServer.php';

$chatServer = new ChatServer("127.0.0.1", 8888);
$chatServer->startServer();

?>
```

Testing the connection

For simple testing, you can attach to the chat server using the telnet method, as shown in Figure 8.3, which was explained at the beginning of the chapter. This method poses a graphical and usability limitation, so the next section is the process of developing the Flash application that will connect to this PHP socket server.

Using Sockets 8

FIGURE 8.3
Example of the chat server running in the command prompt

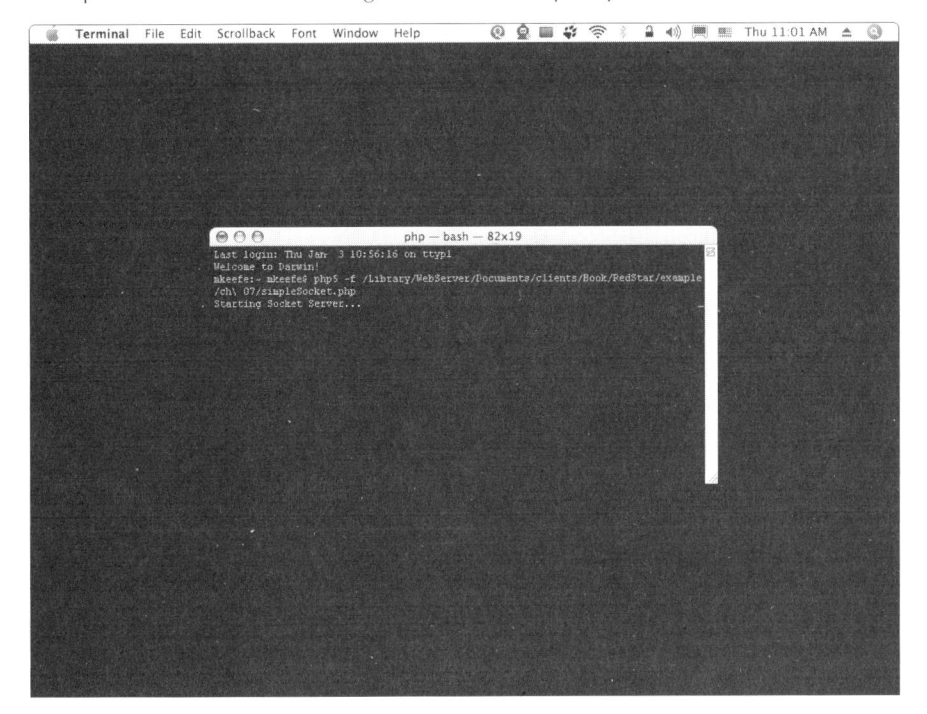

Building the Flash client

The Flash chat client is used to interact with the socket server. This client application can be used locally or on a Web site, depending on how the socket server is configured. For this example, the code assumes the socket server is running locally.

The design portion of the Flash client has been completed for you, as shown in Figure 8.4. This starting file can be found on the Web site for this book, along with the code for all the other sections.

The first part of the Flash code initializes the host and port information, which is passed into a new instance of the Socket class.

```
var host:String = "127.0.0.1";
var port:uint = 8888;

var socket:Socket = new Socket(host, port);
```

177

Part II Developing Interactive Content

FIGURE 8.4

The completed application, which can be found on the book's Web site

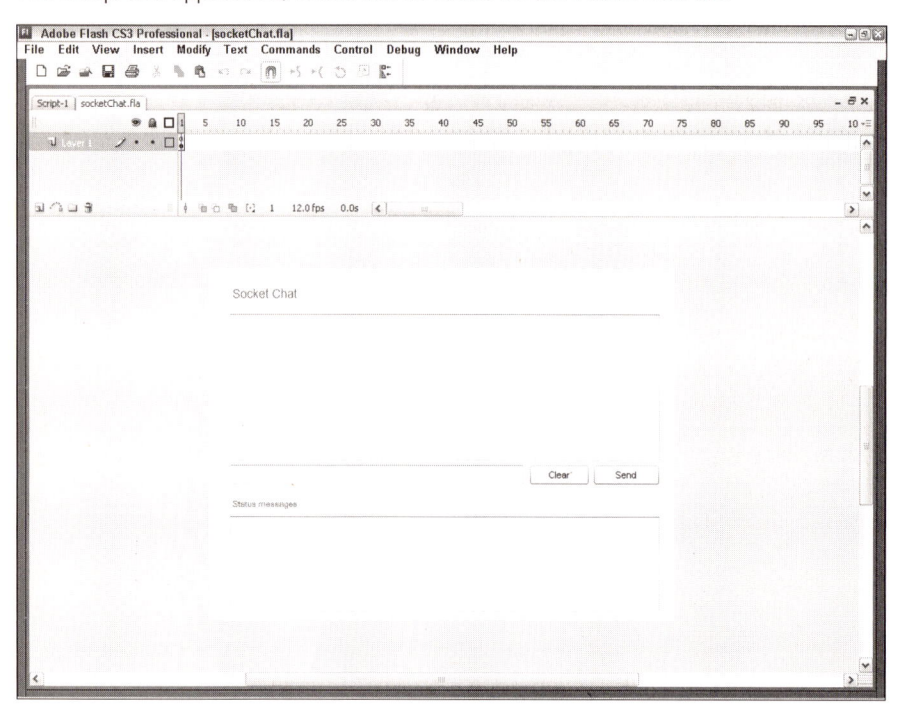

After the connection is made, assign the event listeners, which will be called when new data is sent or loaded.

```
socket.addEventListener(Event.CLOSE, closeHandler);
socket.addEventListener(Event.CONNECT, connectHandler);
socket.addEventListener(IOErrorEvent.IO_ERROR, ioErrorHandler);
socket.addEventListener(SecurityErrorEvent.SECURITY_ERROR,
    securityErrorHandler);
socket.addEventListener(ProgressEvent.SOCKET_DATA, sockHandler);
```

The chat client also needs event handlers that will be assigned to the message box and text input submission buttons, such as:

```
msgTxt.addEventListener(Event.CHANGE, inputHandler);

clearBtn.addEventListener(MouseEvent.CLICK, clearButtonHandler);
sendBtn.addEventListener(MouseEvent.CLICK, sendButtonHandler);
```

Using Sockets

The last event handler will be assigned to the keyboard to allow the use of the Enter key for sending messages. This is not a required step, but adds functionality to the application.

```
addEventListener(KeyboardEvent.KEY_DOWN, keyDownHandler);
```

Event handler functions

The functions that are assigned to the event handlers can be seen in the following code. As you can see, these event handlers have basic functionality for this example, but could be expanded in a more real-world application.

```
function closeHandler(event:Event):void
{
  statusMessage("Connection to [" + host + "] closed",
    "#FF0000");
  disableInterface();
}

function connectHandler(event:Event):void
{
  statusMessage("Connected to [" + host + "]", "#006600");
  sendRequest();
}

function ioErrorHandler(event:IOErrorEvent):void
{
  statusMessage(event.text, "#FF0000");
}

function securityErrorHandler(event:SecurityErrorEvent):void
{
  statusMessage(event.toString(), "#FF0000");
}

function sockHandler(event:ProgressEvent):void
{
  readResponse();
}
```

Trapping key presses

The key event handler has special code. This event traps the currently pressed key and checks to see if it is the Enter key. For this example, the only key to look for is Enter. If you required more than one, you could define them in an array or use a `switch..case` statement.

179

Part II Developing Interactive Content

If the Enter key is pressed, a call to the `dispatchEvent` is made, forcing the click of the Submit button.

```
function keyDownHandler(e:KeyboardEvent):void
{
  if(e.keyCode == Keyboard.ENTER)
  {
    sendBtn.dispatchEvent(new MouseEvent(MouseEvent.CLICK));
  }
}
```

Submit message handler

The key handler makes a call to the Submit button click event, which is assigned to the following function. This function checks the length of the `msgTxt TextInput` and, if length is greater than zero, the message is prepared and sent.

The last step of this function is to clear the message box to ensure the same message is not resent. You could add this clearing code in the status handler. This would clear the field once you know the message has been sent. This allows you to preserve the message and avoid lost messages due to glitches in the network.

```
function sendButtonHandler(e:MouseEvent):void
{
  if(msgTxt.text.length > 0)
  {
    writeLine(msgTxt.text);
    clearBtn.dispatchEvent(new MouseEvent(MouseEvent.CLICK));
  }
}
```

Clearing the message input

The `clearButtonHandler` function is called whenever you want to clear the text input field and disable the Submit button until a new message is entered. The buttons will be disabled when you dispatch the CHANGE event in the next section.

```
function clearButtonHandler(e:MouseEvent):void
{
  msgTxt.text = "";
  msgTxt.dispatchEvent(new Event(Event.CHANGE));
}
```

Checking the text input length

When a new message is entered or the input box is cleared, a call to the CHANGE event on the `msgTxt` box is made. This event is responsible for checking the length of text in the input box and enabling or disabling the Submit and Clear buttons, as shown in Figure 8.5, depending on the result of the length check.

Using Sockets

```
function inputHandler(e:Event):void
{
  if(e.target.text.length > 0)
  {
    clearBtn.enabled = true;
    sendBtn.enabled = true;
  }
  else
  {
    clearBtn.enabled = false;
    sendBtn.enabled = false;
  }
}
```

FIGURE 8.5

Showing the application in the disabled state

Maintaining a stable interface

To create a stable application, the interface and buttons are disabled when a connection is not present.

```
function enableInterface():void
{
  msgTxt.enabled = true;
  bodyTxt.enabled = true;
}
function disableInterface():void
{
```

181

```
    bodyTxt.editable = false;
    msgTxt.enabled = false;
    clearBtn.enabled = false;
    sendBtn.enabled = false;
}
```

These `enable` and `disable` functions are called from other portions of the code, depending on the result of the active connection. For example, the `disableInterface` function is called from the `closeHandler`, which is dispatched when an active connection is terminated.

```
function closeHandler(event:Event):void
{
    ...
    disableInterface();
}
```

Sending the initial request

The `sendRequest` function is called when a connection is made. This function sends data to the status function and clears any existing queued information in the socket connection.

```
function sendRequest():void
{
    statusMessage("Send initial request to [" + host + "]",
      "#006600");
    socket.flush();
    enableInterface();
}
```

Sending messages to the socket server

The process of actually sending the messages to the socket server is handled in the `writeLine` function. This `writeLine` function is called from the input and submit handlers, which are defined in the previous portion of code.

```
function writeLine(str:String):void
{
    ...
}
```

The first part of the function is appending a new line to the message, which you may remember is the end of message indicator in PHP.

```
    str += "\n";
```

This function also makes use of the `try..catch` programming style to ensure errors in the sending process are properly captured and hidden from the user. For simplicity, the error is displayed in

Using Sockets

the Output window. In a more realistic application, you would want to inform the user if the message was not sent as well as store the message to attempt to send it again later.

```
try
{
   socket.writeUTFBytes(str);
}
catch(e:IOError)
{
   trace(e);
}
```

Handling status updates

This application has a status box, which is used to notify the user of the possible connection or message issues. All of these status updates are sent to the `statusMessage` function, which inputs them into the status box and colors them accordingly.

```
function statusMessage(str:String, color:String="#000000"):void
{
   statusTxt.htmlText += "<font color=\""
      + color + "\">"
      + str + "</font>";
}
```

A default color is applied in case the caller forgets to define one. Failure to include a default color could result in the text not being added.

The last function in this socket-based chat application is called when a new message is received from the socket server.

```
function readResponse():void
{
}
```

The first part of this function retrieves the new message from the socket class and assigns it to the `str` variable, which is used in the remaining portion of this function.

```
var str:String = socket.readUTFBytes(socket.bytesAvailable);
```

Before the message can be displayed, you must remove any extra new lines that could affect how the text is displayed. This is performed using a very basic `substring` function that returns the message excluding the last two characters, which in this case would be `"\r\n"`.

```
// strip off line feeds
if(str.substring((str.length-2), str.length) == "\r\n")
{
   trace("found \\n\\r");
```

183

Part II   Developing Interactive Content

```
    str = str.substring(0, (str.length-2));
}
```

Once the new lines have been removed, the next step is to determine if this message was sent from an admin. This example allows any *user* to be an admin. In a more complete application, you would want to require login before an admin account could be used. If the message is from an admin, the contents of the message are colored in red, to make the admin messages stand out.

```
if(str.substring(0, 12) == "ADMIN NOTICE")
{
   bodyTxt.htmlText += "<font color=\"#FF0000\">" + str +
   "</font>";
}
```

If the message is standard, then it is simply added to the `TextArea` and the function ends, waiting for the next message to be retrieved.

```
else
{
   bodyTxt.htmlText += "<font color=\"#000000\">" + str +
   "</font>";
}
```

That is all there is to the Flash-based chat client with a socket server in PHP. At this point, you can start the socket server (unless it's already running) and test the chat client, as shown in Figure 8.6. Being that this system is intended for multiple connections, you can call over some of your friends and have them test it.

Or, you can modify the code to allow remote connections and let many users connect by sending a link to the Flash application.

Here is the complete code for the chat client example:

```
var host:String = "127.0.0.1";
var port:uint = 8888;

var socket:Socket = new Socket(host, port);

socket.addEventListener(Event.CLOSE, closeHandler);
socket.addEventListener(Event.CONNECT, connectHandler);
socket.addEventListener(IOErrorEvent.IO_ERROR, ioErrorHandler);
socket.addEventListener(SecurityErrorEvent.SECURITY_ERROR,
    securityErrorHandler);
socket.addEventListener(ProgressEvent.SOCKET_DATA, sockHandler);
msgTxt.addEventListener(Event.CHANGE, inputHandler);
addEventListener(KeyboardEvent.KEY_DOWN, keyDownHandler);
```

Using Sockets

```
clearBtn.addEventListener(MouseEvent.CLICK, clearButtonHandler);
sendBtn.addEventListener(MouseEvent.CLICK, sendButtonHandler);

this.align = StageAlign.TOP_LEFT;
this.scaleMode = StageScaleMode.NO_SCALE;

function writeLine(str:String):void
{
  str += "\n";
  try
  {
    socket.writeUTFBytes(str);
  }
  catch(e:IOError)
  {
    trace(e);
  }
}

function sendRequest():void
{
  statusMessage("Send initial request to [" + host + "]",
   "#006600");
  socket.flush();
  enableInterface();
}

function readResponse():void
{
  var str:String = socket.readUTFBytes(socket.bytesAvailable);

  // strip off line feeds
  if(str.substring((str.length-2), str.length) == "\r\n")
  {
    trace("found \\n\\r");
    str = str.substring(0, (str.length-2));
  }

  if(str.substring(0, 12) == "ADMIN NOTICE")
  {
    bodyTxt.htmlText += "<font color=\"#FF0000\">" + str +
   "</font>";
  }
  else
  {
```

Part II Developing Interactive Content

```
    bodyTxt.htmlText += "<font color=\"#000000\">" + str +
    "</font>";
  }
}

function enableInterface():void
{
  msgTxt.enabled = true;
  bodyTxt.enabled = true;
}
function disableInterface():void
{
  bodyTxt.editable = false;
  msgTxt.enabled = false;
  clearBtn.enabled = false;
  sendBtn.enabled = false;
}

function statusMessage(str:String, color:String="#000000"):void
{
  statusTxt.htmlText += "<font color=\"" + color + "\">" + str +
    "</font>";
}

function clearButtonHandler(e:MouseEvent):void
{
  msgTxt.text = "";
  msgTxt.dispatchEvent(new Event(Event.CHANGE));
}

function sendButtonHandler(e:MouseEvent):void
{
  if(msgTxt.text.length > 0)
  {
    writeLine(msgTxt.text);
    clearBtn.dispatchEvent(new MouseEvent(MouseEvent.CLICK));
  }
}

function inputHandler(e:Event):void
{
  if(e.target.text.length > 0)
  {
    clearBtn.enabled = true;
    sendBtn.enabled = true;
  }
```

186

Using Sockets 8

```
    else
    {
      clearBtn.enabled = false;
      sendBtn.enabled = false;
    }
}

function closeHandler(event:Event):void
{
  statusMessage("Connection to [" + host + "] closed",
    "#FF0000");
  disableInterface();
}

function connectHandler(event:Event):void
{
  statusMessage("Connected to [" + host + "]", "#006600");
  sendRequest();
}

function ioErrorHandler(event:IOErrorEvent):void
{
  statusMessage(event.text, "#FF0000");
}

function securityErrorHandler(event:SecurityErrorEvent):void
{
  statusMessage(event.toString(), "#FF0000");
}

function sockHandler(event:ProgressEvent):void
{
  readResponse();
}

function keyDownHandler(e:KeyboardEvent):void
{
  if(e.keyCode == Keyboard.ENTER)
  {
    sendBtn.dispatchEvent(new MouseEvent(MouseEvent.CLICK));
  }
}

// disable interface until connected
disableInterface();
```

187

Part II Developing Interactive Content

FIGURE 8.6

Chat application running in the browser

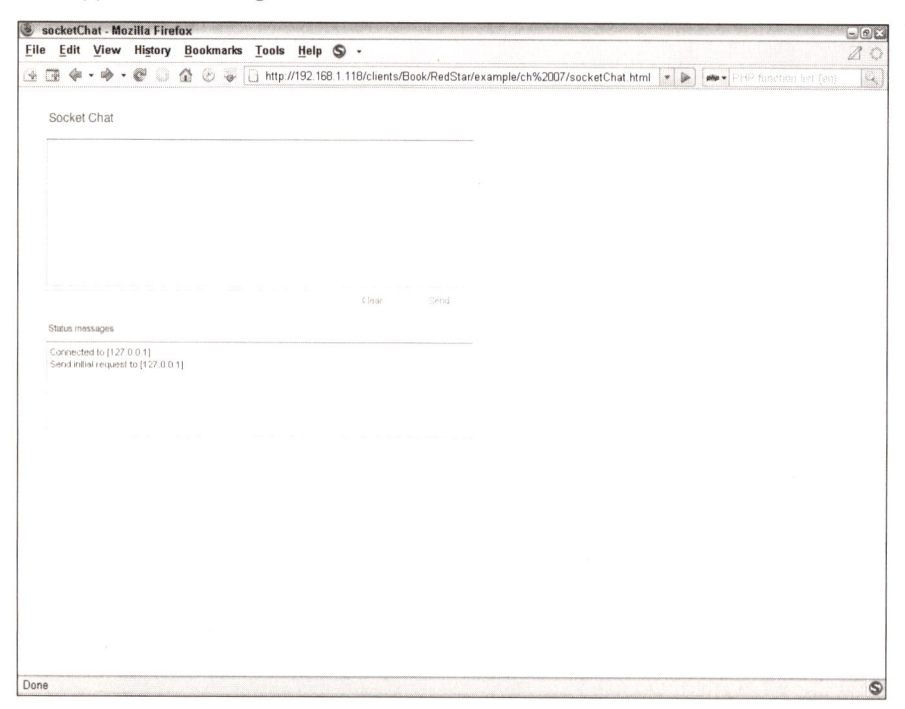

Summary

In this chapter, you have learned what a socket server is and how they are built. You then learned how to build a simple socket server and connect to it using Flash. Once you had an understanding of the Flash and PHP portions of the process, the final step was to build a complete multiuser chat application with a socket server in PHP running behind the scenes.

You can take the information learned in this chapter and expand it to create a fully functional chat application. You can add features such as moderation, members, timers, chat rooms, and so on. It is important to realize that socket server systems are not limited to chat applications. You can use this same technology to build a multiuser drawing application or even build a multipoint server monitoring architecture.

As you can see, sockets can be used in a variety of ways. Once you learn the basics, your imagination is the only limit to your development.

Part III

Extending Flash and PHP

IN THIS PART

Chapter 9
Working with Third-Party Libraries

Chapter 10
Using Object-Oriented Programming

Chapter 9

Working with Third-Party Libraries

The use of third-party libraries continues to grow as more demanding applications are being developed. Third-party libraries often solve a problem or make a common task easier to handle, which lets the developer focus on the more important aspects of the application.

The first part of this chapter is devoted to explaining what third-party libraries are, how to use them, and what is needed to install a library.

The second part of this chapter focuses on the use of AMFPHP in Flash. AMFPHP is basically a PHP library that offers a common link between Flash and a database, as well as other data types.

IN THIS CHAPTER

Going over third-party libraries

Installing third-party libraries

Using third-party libraries

Glancing at AMFPHP

Going over Third-Party Libraries

A third-party library is a custom package or piece of code that is developed by a company or organization to work with another company's product. For example, if you look at the Firefox Web browser, there is a series of plug-ins and enhancements that are released by developers not working for Mozilla.

Developers have different views on third-party libraries; one of the most important concerns about these libraries is security. You have to be careful working with other portions of code, especially if you don't have the time or expertise to thoroughly investigate how that code functions.

Security concerns are even more important when you don't know the party that developed the library or if the library itself is connected to some secure aspect of your application.

For example, it's not a good idea to use a cookie or session library from an unknown developer. Doing so can introduce security holes in your application.

Part III Extending Flash and PHP

There are some notable exceptions to working with third-party libraries and secure applications. For example, if you are building a store application, it is a reasonable guess that you will be interacting with some form of a merchant system, such as Authorize.net, Miva, or PayPal.

These systems offer third-party libraries that you can easily connect to your application and are known to be secure because they have been thoroughly tested in various environments.

Other types of third-party libraries

These external libraries are not limited to security or data handling. This is due to the fact that Flash is a design program as well. There are many excellent third-party libraries available to speed up the development and design process.

In some cases, these external libraries provide functionality that isn't possible directly in Flash/ActionScript.

Commercial Flash libraries

There are some libraries being built that have commercial licenses, which means you get more extensively developed code. You won't have a problem getting support for these libraries.

For example, gskinner.com has a robust spell-check library and component set that is available for purchase. This library allows you to build a real-time spell-check engine into your application with only a few lines of code. You can find more information about the gskinner Spell Check library at the company's Web site At `www.gskinner.com/products/spl/`.

Open source Flash libraries

You will also find a large selection of free open source libraries for all aspects of application development and deployment. One example of an open source library is AMFPHP, which is examined in detail in the section "Glancing at AMFPHP."

There are many other open source libraries available, such as MCtweener, which is similar to the included Tween library with more functionality. Also, the project documentation contains a lot of example code.

A few other open source libraries available to assist in your development process are shown in Table 9.1.

TABLE 9.1

Open Source Libraries

Red5	Open Source Flash Server	`http://osflash.org/red5`
Papervision3D	Open Source 3D engine	`http://code.google.com/p/papervision3d/`
as3corelib	AS3 library for several basic utilities	`http://code.google.com/p/as3corelib/`

Working with Third-Party Libraries

This is only a small portion of the full line of open source libraries available for ActionScript 3. It should give you a good idea of not only how expandable ActionScript 3 is, but also how many developers have spent long hours developing these awesome tools. Even more amazing is the fact these libraries are free, which means more developers, including you, can create more interesting and engaging content at no additional costs.

Libraries in PHP

There are also many libraries available for PHP, which include session management, image handling, database connectivity, and overall server management to name a few. Basically, PHP is built using third-party libraries because PHP in itself is an open source project. This means many different developers contribute code to the project.

Some of the more common PHP libraries include the GD library, which is discussed Chapter 12. Table 9.2 lists other common PHP libraries that you will use in your development process.

TABLE 9.2

Common PHP Libraries

Library	Description	Source
Pear	A structured library of opensource code	http://pear.php.net/
ImageMagick	Software suite to create, edit, and compose bitmap images	www.imagemagick.org/
PDF Library	PDF creation library for PHP	www.php.net/pdf

Installing Third-Party Libraries

You should now have an understanding of what third-party libraries are available for you to use in your ActionScript 3 development.

The process of installing these third-party libraries is very similar no matter which library it is.

NOTE Check the version requirements on libraries to make sure they will work with ActionScript 3 or the version of PHP you happen to be using.

Installing libraries in Flash CS3

After you select the third-party libraries that you want to use, the next step is to install them. The process of installing a code library in CS3 depends on the specific class.

Part III Extending Flash and PHP

Installing as an MXP file

One way a library or component set can be distributed for portability is in the MXP format. These files are loaded into the Extension Manager that ships with Flash CS3 and many other Adobe applications (see Figure 9.1).

The advantage to using this included application to manage your libraries is that you can enable, disable, or update the individual libraries in a nice, manageable GUI. This application also contains direct links to the developer's Web site for support or online documentation.

FIGURE 9.1

Extension Manager ships with Flash CS3 and other Adobe applications.

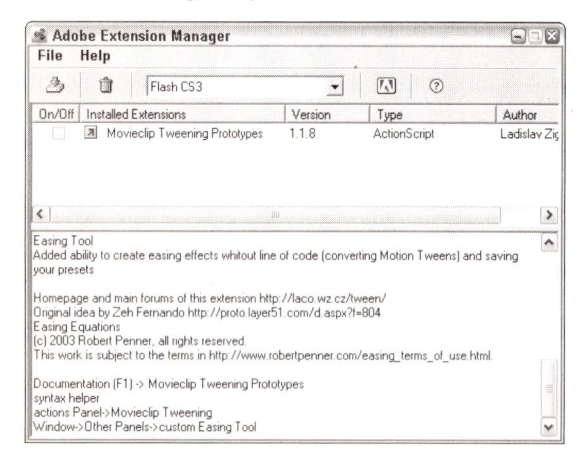

Installing as a standard class package

The other more common installation method is to manually add the classes to the classpath of Flash CS3. You also need to copy the class files to the sharing directories that Flash knows to look in for third-party libraries.

It is a good idea to create a new folder on a separate part of your computer so you don't accidentally modify the default classes that ship with Flash CS3.

Creating a custom classpath

In order to add a custom classpath, you must first create a directory on your computer to store your classes. After you determine which directory you will use, add this new path to the existing classpath listing.

To add a new classpath to the existing list, follow these steps:

1. Choose Edit ⇨ Preferences (Windows). On a Mac, choose Flash ⇨ Preferences to open the Preferences dialog box.

Working with Third-Party Libraries

2. Click ActionScript in the Category list, and then click ActionScript 3.0 Settings.
3. Click Browse To Path, and browse to the directory you want to add. Click OK.

You can also add a classpath to the specific Flash project by modifying the ActionScript settings in the Publish Settings dialog box. Adding the classpath to a project has the benefit that it will move with the FLA, which means this file can be shared and the global classpaths won't need to be modified.

Default classpaths

The default classpath of all Flash documents can be modified so you don't have to update each individual Flash file. The following are the locations where Flash expects to find the class files, based on a default installation.

Windows: Hard Disk\Documents and Settings\user\Local Settings\Application Data\Adobe\Adobe Flash CS3\language\Configuration\Classes.

Macintosh: Hard Disk/Users/user/Library/Application Support/Adobe/Adobe Flash CS3/language/Configuration/Classes.

NOTE Do not delete the absolute global classpath. Flash uses this classpath to access built-in classes. If you accidentally delete this classpath you can re-add it by using the following piece of code as a new class path: `$(LocalData)/Classes`.

Installing libraries in PHP

PHP libraries are often compiled directly into the PHP installation process. However, with the use of PEAR and other common structured library systems, you can install new libraries after the initial installation has been completed.

An example of an external library that is commonly used and can be added after you install PHP is the MySQL library. This library is used to communicate with a database directly in PHP.

The first step is to open the `php.ini` file, uncomment the `mysql` library file, and modify the location of the MySQL socket path and the port if you choose a different one when installing MySQL.

NOTE You must restart the Apache server after you modify the `php.ini` file.

If once you restart Apache, and MySQL still isn't functioning properly, then you may have an outdated version installed. This means you may have to recompile PHP.

CROSS-REF To learn about recompiling PHP, see Chapter 1.

Part III   Extending Flash and PHP

Using Third-Party Libraries

The first step to working with third-party libraries is to download the library files from the developer's Web site. Once you have successfully downloaded the class library files, the next step is to install and configure the third-party libraries.

Normally the library will come with a testing kit to ensure everything is working properly. This step is not required, but does minimize debugging needed in your final application.

If the library does not come with a test kit, you can quickly create one, which is explained in the following section.

Working with libraries in Flash CS3

To determine if the classes are properly loaded, you can build an application to test a specific portion of a class contained in the library.

For this example, the as3CoreLib library from Adobe is used. This class contains a series of utility classes for everything including image manipulation all the way to security such as MD5 hash creation tools.

Here is an example application using the MD5 functionality:

```
import com.adobe.crypto.MD5;

function createHash(e:MouseEvent):void
{
   responseTxt.text = MD5.hash(origStrTxt.text);
}

createBtn.addEventListener(MouseEvent.CLICK, createHash);
```

The first part of this application imports the necessary classes. In this example, that would be the `MD5` class found in the `crypto` package.

The function is called when the button is clicked. Once the function is called, the next step is to create a new hash by calling the static `hash` method of the `MD5` class. Finally, the newly created string is returned to the `responseTxt TextInput` component located on the Stage.

That is the complete application. It is a very simple usage but informs you when the proper classes are installed and are functioning properly.

Working in this unit style is very common in development because if an application gets too big it is much harder to debug and manage.

Working with Libraries in PHP

Libraries in PHP are very similar to compiled portions of PHP, but you still should test them after you install a new library. You normally will also have to restart Apache in order for new changes to PHP to take effect. Oftentimes the installation instructions for a library will mention this, but either way it needs to be done.

Testing the MySQL library

For testing the MySQL support you don't have to create an elaborate example; in fact, you can create a script that is guaranteed to not run properly, but will inform you whether MySQL is properly installed or not.

This is not a very common practice, but in the interest of rapid testing it works very well.

> **NOTE** After you run code that you know is going to fail it is a good idea to clear the error logs so they don't confuse you later on down the road.

Here is the code for the simple test.

```
<?php

// no password is sure to fail,
// unless it is a default installation

mysql_connect("localhost", "root", "");

?>
```

The simple application attempts to connect to the database, and if you are shown invalid user or no database selected then you know MySQL is properly installed.

However, if you see a Fatal Error: function not found... it means MySQL has not been properly configured or installed to work with PHP.

You can create a quick `phpinfo` file to determine whether or not MySQL has been installed and to track down the specific error.

Installing the MySQL library

The MySQL library is normally included with PHP, but doesn't come enabled, by default. The first step is to open the `php.ini` file for the version of PHP that you have installed.

You will find a section in the php.ini file with the heading "[mysql]". This is where you would configure the installation of MySQL.

Once the configuration is finalized, the next step is to uncomment the line in the library list that has the name "mysql" within it.

197

At this point the configuration is complete; the last step is to restart Apache and test the previous script once again, which should display a connection error and not the PHP Fatal Error.

Glancing at AMFPHP

AMFPHP is an open source implementation of the Action Message Format (AMF). AMF allows for binary serialization of ActionScript objects to be sent to server-side scripts.

AMFPHP for AS3 and PHP Developers

PHP developers can leverage their PHP experience by connecting to data such as Web services and databases. AMF allows for native data types and complex object mapping between the client and the server. AMFPHP is one of the most popular and fastest client server communication protocols available to Flash Player developers. Communication is arranged into binary format, which is generally more compact than other representations.

AMFPHP and ActionScript 3

ActionScript 3 allows for the compression of communications, which means faster output of calls and overall better performance. In addition, AMF3, which is available in ActionScript 3, also compresses the binary communication for increased performance.

Installing AMFPHP

Installing AMFPHP is simple. The scripts require a PHP server and do not need any additional services or libraries installed. This offers the advantage of near instant setup, which allows the developer to focus on the actual application instead of worrying about what is going on behind the scenes.

To install AMFPHP, first download the latest version, which is available free from the SourceForge Web site at `http://sourceforge.net/project/showfiles.php?group_id=72483#files`. SourceForge is the largest open source Web development Web site that hosts a number of different projects like AMFPHP.

The contents of the downloaded archive are placed in the root of your Web server in a new directory such as `flashservices` or any name you choose.

AMFPHP is almost ready to go right out of the box. The only file you need to modify is `gateway.php`, which is located in the root of the installation directory. In this case, the path would be `flashservices/gateway.php`. In some cases, you can leave all of the settings on the default, which is what is used for this example.

Working with Third-Party Libraries 9

Testing the installation

When everything is properly installed you can test the installation of AMFPHP by opening the `gateway.php` in your Web browser. For example, assuming the installation is done locally, the URL would be `http://localhost/flashservices/gateway.php`.

A screen, as shown in Figure 9.2, should appear that informs you that the installation was successful. If an error occurs, a PHP error or a series of errors appears that will help you determine what possibly went wrong.

AMFPHP debugging tools

Before beginning any development, look at some of the debugging and viewing tools that ship with AMFPHP. These various tools can be used to debug your services.

CAUTION Be sure to remove these debugging tools on a live server to minimize security concerns.

FIGURE 9.2

Example of the AMFPHP welcome message seen from calling `gateway.php` from your Web browser

Part III Extending Flash and PHP

AMFPHP service browser

The AMFPHP service browser, as shown in Figure 9.3, is a Flash-based application that lets you view individual services and closely examine their methods and properties. You can also use the service browser to test new code before you write the ActionScript in Flash.

Using these added debugging tools allows you to more rapidly develop applications and test new concepts with less overhead. They also assist in the debugging of your code.

AMFPHP debug gateway

The Debug Gateway is script that sits in between Flash and the `gateway.php` file to wrap up errors. It is a best practice to use this script when debugging or developing locally. The only change in your code is to point to the `debuggateway.php` file instead of the standard `gateway.php` file.

FIGURE 9.3

Here is an example service as seen from the AMFPHP service browser.

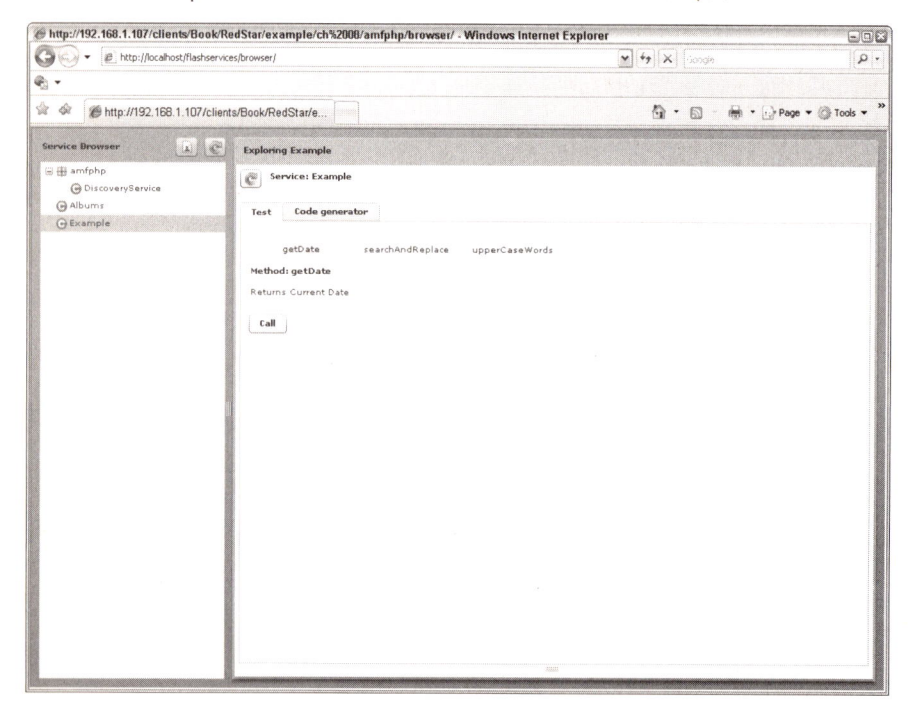

Working with Third-Party Libraries

The following are a few important points to keep in mind with using this specialized gateway:

- Sessions won't work properly.
- cURL must be enabled in PHP.
- The server will experience a drop in performance.
- It should only be used on a development system.

Testing AMFPHP with a custom service

With AMFPHP properly installed, you can test a very simple service using the service browser. Later, you build a small search application in Flash and PHP.

An AMFPHP service is a standard PHP file that is built in a known order. For example, the first part of a service file is the method table, which is used to expose the available methods and define the access restrictions of that service.

A method table is a multidimensional array containing each of the methods. This sample method table defines the method `getDate`, which returns the current UNIX timestamp from PHP. The method table is located within the constructor of the class seen in the next portion of code.

```
$this->methodTable = array
(
  "getDate" => array
  (
    "access" => "remote",
    "description" => "Example, returns Unix timestamp"
  )
);
```

Continuing with this example, you would create the sample PHP class, which will become the AMFPHP service. Here is the sample class, which contains one method and the constructor.

```
<?php

class Example
{

  function Example()
  {

    $this->methodTable = array
    (
      "getDate" => array
      (
        "access" => "remote",
        "description" => "Returns the current date."
      )
```

201

Part III Extending Flash and PHP

```
    );
  }
  /**
   * Returns Current Date
   */
  function getDate()
  {
    // return current date
    return "Current Date: "  . date("F j, Y", time());
  }

}

?>
```

> **NOTE** The comment above the `getDate` function will be seen by the service browser and display it below the method. This is not required, but it helps you understand what a service does at a glance.

Save this file as `Example.php` in the `/services` directory found in the root of the AMFPHP directory.

Here is the location of this file if you install AMFPHP on the root of your Web server: `http://localhost/flashservices/services/Example.php`.

Now that this simple service is created you can test it by going to the service browser. You will see your new service located in the left-side list along with any other services already installed. If you don't see the service, click Refresh or reload the page by refreshing your browser.

To test the service, click the name in the left-side list, which loads the service in the Exploring pane to the right. The name of the method is located on the Test tab, which in this example is named `getDate`.

Click the Call button to run the service. You will see the services output in the Results tab located on the bottom of the Exploring pane.

The output of the sample service should be the current date in string format, such as.

```
"Current Date: October 5, 2007"
```

The other tabs are for viewing the service data, which would be used for debugging and overall tracking of your services.

This example is fairly simple. It has no parameters and doesn't create any real code. You can expand on the previous service by adding another method, which capitalizes the first letter of each word found in the string. The capitalization portion of the code is done using a built-in function of PHP called `ucwords`. This function accepts one parameter and returns the capitalized string.

Working with Third-Party Libraries

```php
<?php

class Example
{

  function Example()
  {

    $this->methodTable = array
    (
      "getDate" => array
      (
        "access" => "remote",
        "description" => "Returns the current date."
      ),

      "upperCaseWords" => array
      (
        "access" => "remote",
        "description" => "Converts arg to uppercase"
      )

    );
  }
  /**
   * Returns Current Date
   */
  function getDate()
  {
    // return current date
    return "Current Date: "  . date("F j, Y", time());
  }

  function upperCaseWords($str)
  {
    return ucwords($str);
  }

}

?>
```

After the new method is added it is visible in the service browser (after a refresh). After looking at the service browser, you will notice an advantage of the method table is that AMFPHP automatically adds textboxes with the name of the variable for each argument found.

The new method accepts one argument as defined in the service code. If you type some text in the TextBox and execute the method, your string is capitalized.

Part III   Extending Flash and PHP

For example, if you use the string `"hello world"`, you see the following output:

```
"Hello World"
```

AMFPHP services can, of course, have more than one argument in a method. Create another new method that has three arguments. The first argument is a string, the second a word to search for, and the third is the replacement word. Basically, you are creating a PHP-based search-and-replace method.

Start off by updating the method table.

```
$this->methodTable = array
  (
    "getDate" => array
    (
      "access" => "remote",
      "description" => "Returns the current date."
    ),
    "upperCaseWords" => array
    (
      "access" => "remote",
      "description" => "Converts arg to uppercase"
    ),
    "searchAndReplace" => array
    (
      "access" => "remote",
      "description" => "Searches and replaces text"
    )

  );
```

When the method table is updated, the new method is added. You are not limited to the code within the method. AMFPHP allows you to call other methods and properties within the same class or even include other PHP files for added functionality.

```
/**
 * Searches and replaces text
 */
function searchAndReplace($haystack, $needle, $replacement)
{
  $string = str_replace($needle, $replacement, $haystack);
  return $this->upperCaseWords($string);
}
```

NOTE If you create a new method and do not add it the method table, it will not be exported for remoting. This is useful when you want to have private methods, such as database connectivity, or overall security layers.

After the new method is added, you can test it by refreshing the service browser. Notice the methods are listed in alphabetical order. The new method should be found in the middle of the horizontal list.

Working with Third-Party Libraries

The service browser adds a text field for each argument; in this case there are three. Type a string in the first text field, choose one of the words from that string as the needle, and then enter that into the second `TextField`. Finally, type the replacement into the third text field. After all three text fields are filled in, you can click the Call button and see the output in the Results tab.

Assuming you use the string `"hello world"` with the needle of `"world"` and a replacement of `"earth"`, you should see the following result. The word is replaced and the first letter of each word is capitalized using the `upperCaseWords` method.

```
"Hello Earth"
```

Now that you have thoroughly tested the AMFPHP services, you can move on to installing the necessary classes required for Flash to actually be able to make use of this setup. That process is explained in the next section.

Using AMFPHP in Flash

Unlike previous versions, ActionScript 3 has all of the necessary classes for remoting and interacting with AMFPHP already installed. You simply load those Classes and write in the ActionScript, which is all fairly simple. This section walks you through the process of building a simple Flash application to better understand the process of working with AMFPHP in Flash.

Loading the remoting classes

The first step to working with AMFPHP in Flash is to load the classes. This is required for any AMFPHP project you build as it contains the core of the remoting system.

```
import flash.net.*;
```

When the classes are loaded, you can define a variable that points to the AMFPHP gateway file.

```
var gatewayURL:String =
    "http://localhost/flashservices/gateway.php";
```

The next step is to create the `NetConnection` instance, which is assigned to the gateway variable. At this point, you can also set up the method events that are called when a button is clicked.

```
var gateway:NetConnection;

getDateBtn.addEventListener(MouseEvent.CLICK, getDate);
searcBtn.addEventListener(MouseEvent.CLICK, searchAndReplace);
upperCaseWordsBtn.addEventListener(MouseEvent.CLICK,
    upperCaseWords);
debugTxt.wordWrap = false;
```

Here is the skeleton for the button handlers that will be created in the next portion. Each of these functions makes a call to the AMFPHP service.

```
function getDate(e:MouseEvent):void
{
```

```
    ...
}

function searchAndReplace(e:MouseEvent):void
{
    ...
}

function upperCaseWords(e:MouseEvent):void
{
    ...
}
```

The first method on which to focus is `getDate`, which will make a call to the server with no arguments and receives a string of the current date. The `Responder` class is used to handle the object response for both the success and failure calls.

```
var responder:Responder = new Responder(onResult, onFault);
```

The next portion of the function assigns a new instance of the `NetConnection` class. A call to the `connect` method is called passing in the `gateway url` variable. Once the connection is established, a call is made where the first argument is the service name and method. The second variable is a reference to the `Responder` class instance.

```
gateway = new NetConnection();
   gateway.connect(gatewayURL);
   gateway.call("Example.getDate", responder);
```

Here is the complete `getDate` function responsible for establishing the AMFPHP connection and calling the requested service.

```
function getDate(e:MouseEvent):void
{
   var responder:Responder = new Responder(onResult, onFault);
   
   gateway = new NetConnection();
   gateway.connect(gatewayURL);
   gateway.call("Example.getDate", responder);
}
```

The other two functions are very similar with the exception of the method name and arguments passed to the service.

The `searchAndReplace` function accepts three arguments.

- **arg1**: The string to search in
- **arg2**: The word to search for
- **arg3**: The replacement word

Working with Third-Party Libraries

The service located in the AMFPHP setup is responsible for running the `searchAndReplace` method, but also makes a call to the `uppercase` method before returning the string.

```
function searchAndReplace(e:MouseEvent):void
{
  var responder:Responder = new Responder(onResult, onFault);

  gateway = new NetConnection();
  gateway.connect(gatewayURL);
  gateway.call("Example.searchAndReplace", responder,
    "hello world",
    "world",
    "earth"
  );
}
```

The final function is `upperCaseWords`, which takes one argument and returns a new string with the first letter of each word converted to uppercase. The rest of the function is the same as the previous two. This is a good example of AMFPHP being able to accomplish something that is not native to ActionScript, which, of course, is the uppercase portion.

```
function upperCaseWords(e:MouseEvent):void
{
  var responder:Responder = new Responder(onResult, onFault);

  gateway = new NetConnection();
  gateway.connect(gatewayURL);
  gateway.call("Example.upperCaseWords", responder, "hello
    world");
}
```

Once the three functions responsible for calling the services are defined, the next part is the debugging and result functions that are called when the service returns a valid response.

The `onResult` function is called when a successful message is received. In this simple example, the raw contents of the output are sent to the `TextArea` component located on the Stage. You can also replace the `TextArea` portion of the code with simple `trace()` statements for quicker testing.

```
function onResult(responds:Object):void
{

  debugTxt.text = "Response: " + responds;

}
```

If an error occurs, the `onFault` function is called, which contains the specific error. To better view the error, the contents of the object are run through a `for..in` loop, which displays each item. This function also clears the `TextArea` to ensure the old data is not mixed in, which could cause confusion while trying to debug an application.

Part III Extending Flash and PHP

The `appendText` method is the AS3 replacement to the `"+="` way of concatenating strings in older versions of ActionScript. This method is much faster, which means quicker execution of code.

```
function onFault(responds:Object):void
{
  debugTxt.text = "";
  debugTxt.appendText("Debug::Error\n");
  for(var i in responds)
  {
    debugTxt.appendText("   " + responds[i] + "\n");
  }

}
```

Figures 9.4, 9.5, and 9.6 show example responses from sample applications within AMFPHP. You can expand on these examples to build a more complete application, which is done in the next section.

The first example is displaying the response from the `getDate` method of the sample AMFPHP classes. This example will return the current date in string format.

FIGURE 9.4

Here is a sample response from the first AMFPHP service method.

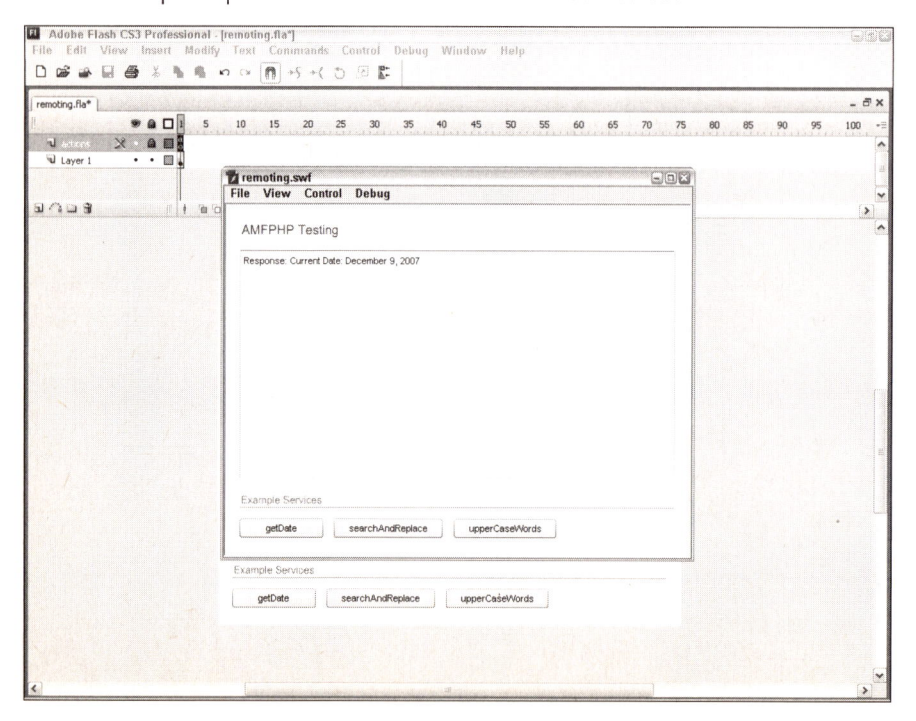

Working with Third-Party Libraries

The second example accepts one argument and replaces the text. All of this is a simple example, showing the process of working with arguments in AMFPHP.

FIGURE 9.5

Here is a sample response from the second AMFPHP service method.

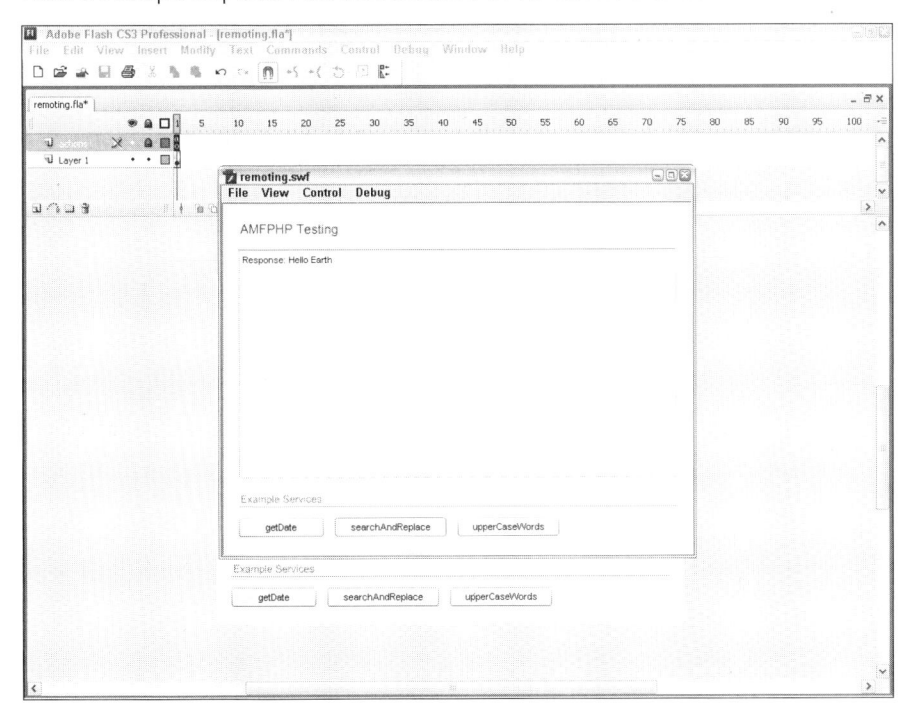

The third and final example is a carbon response. It basically takes the passed-in string and returns it exactly as it was sent.

209

Part III   Extending Flash and PHP

FIGURE 9.6

Here is a sample response from the third AMFPHP service method.

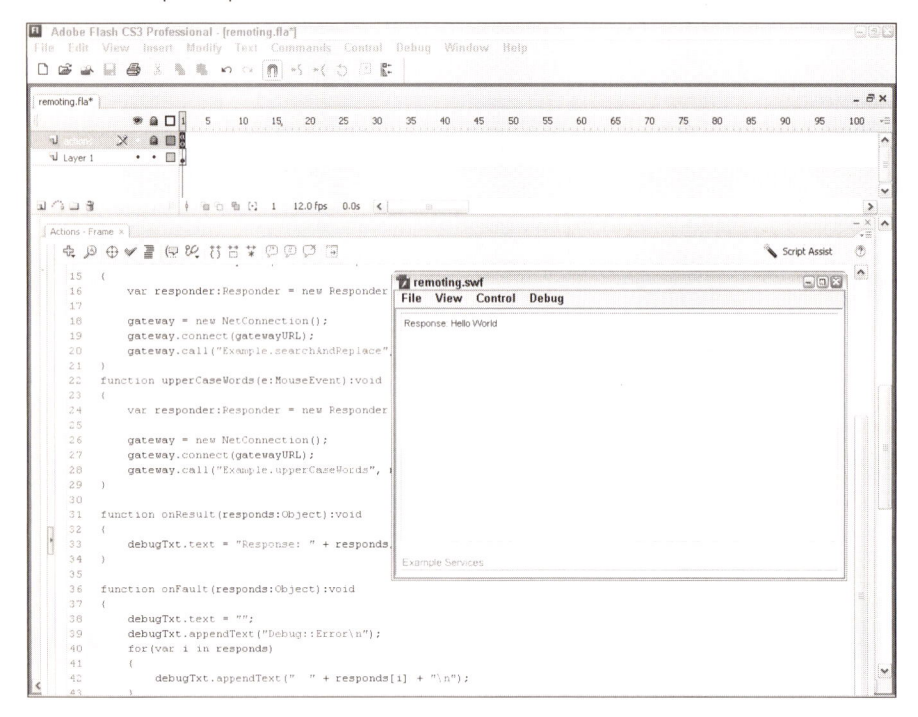

Building a Real-World Application Using AMFPHP

Now that you have seen AMFPHP service usage and how to implement it in Flash, you can continue by building a real-world application. A good example of a real-world application is a Flash-based album listing applications, which is explained in the next sections.

The database used for this example is the same one that is created in Chapter 2. If you haven't completed that chapter at this point, I recommend starting there.

AMFPHP services

The AMFPHP services needed for this example are responsible for querying the database based on passed-in arguments. This also requires a database connection system that will need to be secure. This means methods will not be exportable or viewable by AMFPHP.

Working with Third-Party Libraries 9

For simplicity, all of this functionality is contained in one service. However, in a more complete application, you would want to separate the classes into different services for a more portable solution. Figure 9.7 shows the completed application.

FIGURE 9.7

Here is the completed application from the real-world example.

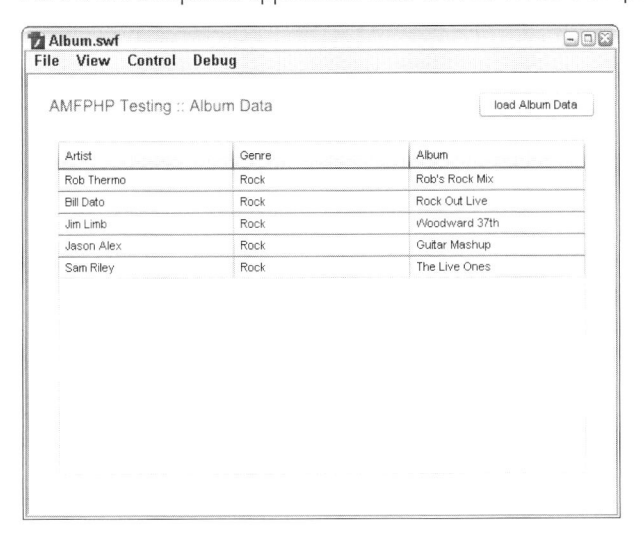

The first part to the application is the AMFPHP services. Here is the class skeleton for the Album service, which gives you a better understanding of the functionality.

```
<?php

class Albums
{
   function Albums()
   {
      ...
   }
   function connect()
   {
      ...
   }

   function getAlbumByGenreID($genreID)
   {
      ...
   }
```

211

```
}

?>
```

The start to any AMFPHP project should be the method table either included in the same service file or in a separate file that is included. The advantage to using the same file is you can quickly make changes and not have to maintain a different file.

The method table in this example is included in the service constructor function. The `connection` method is set to private to ensure a higher level of security.

```
function Albums()
{

  $this->methodTable = array
  (
    "connect" => array
    (
      "access" => "private"
    ),
    "getAlbumByGenreID" => array
    (
      "access" => "remote"
    )
  );

}
```

The `connection` method first checks for an existing connection to limit resources. If an existing connection is not found, a new one is created and stored in the private variable `_connection`.

```
/**
 * @access private
 * @desc Connect to database - **PRIVATE**
 */
function connect()
{

  if($this->_connection == null)
  {
    $this->_connection = mysql_connect(
      $this->dbHost,
      $this->dbUser,
      $this->dbPass
    );
    mysql_select_db($this->dbName, $this->_connection);
  }

}
```

Working with Third-Party Libraries

The connection parameters are stored in private variables within the class. For an added level of security, the variables are made private to prohibit external access of the sensitive database credentials.

```
// Database info
private $dbHost = "localhost";
private $dbUser = "username";
private $dbPass = "password";
private $dbName = "database name";

private $_connection = null;
```

The last method of the service class is the getAlbumByGenreID, which returns an array of album data based on the genre ID passed in as a single argument. The part of the function establishes a connection to the database using the private connect() method defined in the previous step.

```
function getAlbumCatID($genreID)
{
   $this->connect();

   ...
}
```

Once the database connection is established, the next step is to build the $sql string.

```
$sql = "SELECT g.name, a.artist, a.albumName
   FROM albums a, genre g
   WHERE a.genreID=g.id
   AND g.id=" . $genreID;
```

The $sql string is passed in to the mysql_query() with the database connection as the second argument.

```
$result = mysql_query($sql, $this->_connection);
```

The last step of the function is to create the associative array of album data.

```
$rows = array();

while($row = mysql_fetch_array($result, MYSQL_ASSOC))
{
   array_push($rows, $row);
}
return $rows;
```

An alternative to creating the array in PHP using a while loop is to pass the resource ID back to Flash and use a custom record set class to parse the data row by row. Doing this in Flash takes some of the strain off of the server and makes better use of the client's machine.

Part III Extending Flash and PHP

Previous versions of Flash had a native `RecordSet` class. In AS3, you would have to create your own class. This class has been added to the extra content available on the book's Web site and properly mimics the AS2 `RecordSet` class.

The first step in working with the `RecordSet` class is to modify the `album` method.

```
/**
 * List of albums for RecordSet
 */
function getAlbumByGenreID($genreID)
{

  $this->connect();

  $sql = "SELECT g.name, a.artist, a.albumName
    FROM albums a, genre g
    WHERE a.genreID=g.id
    AND g.id=" . $genreID;

  return mysql_query($sql, $this->_connection);

}
```

Here is the completed `Album` class:

```
<?php

class Albums
{

  // Database info
  private $dbHost = "localhost";
  private $dbUser = "username";
  private $dbPass = "password";
  private $dbName = "db name";

  private $_connection = null;

  function Albums()
  {

    $this->methodTable = array
    (
      "connect" => array
      (
        "access" => "private"
      ),
      "getAlbumByGenreID" => array
      (
        "access" => "remote",
```

Working with Third-Party Libraries 9

```
        "description" => "List of albums from           category
ID."
    )
  );

}
/**
 * @access private
 * @desc Connect to database - **PRIVATE**
 */
function connect()
{

  if($this->_connection == null)
  {
    $this->_connection = mysql_connect(
      $this->dbHost,
      $this->dbUser,
      $this->dbPass
    );
    mysql_select_db($this->dbName, $this->_connection);
  }

}

/**
 * List of albums from genre ID.
 */
function getAlbumByGenreID($genreID)
{

  $this->connect();

  $sql = "SELECT g.name, a.artist, a.albumName
    FROM albums a, genre g
    WHERE a.genreID=g.id
    AND g.id=" . $genreID;

  $result = mysql_query($sql, $this->_connection);

  $rows = array();

  while($row = mysql_fetch_array($result, MYSQL_ASSOC))
  {
    array_push($rows, $row);
  }
```

Part III Extending Flash and PHP

```
    return $rows;

}

/**
 * List of albums for RecordSet
 */
function getAlbumByGenreID_recordset($genreID)
{

  $this->connect();

  $sql = "SELECT g.name, a.artist, a.albumName
     FROM albums a, genre g
     WHERE a.genreID=g.id
     AND g.id=" . $genreID;

  return mysql_query($sql, $this->_connection);

}

}
?>
```

ActionScript for AMFPHP integration

The next step is to build the Flash portion of the application, which is responsible for displaying the album data in a prebuilt `DataGrid` component.

The only function changes are within the onResult function for this more complete example.

```
function onResult(responds:Object):void
{
  albumsDG.removeAll();
  for(var i:uint=0; i < responds.length; i++)
  {
    albumsDG.addItem(responds[i]);
  }

}
```

Clearing old results

The `onResult` function clears any existing data in the `DataGrid` by making a call to the `removeAll` method of the `DataGrid` component.

```
albumsDG.removeAll();
```

Working with Third-Party Libraries 9

After the `DataGrid` has been cleared a `for..` loop is used to insert the row data from the database. The `addItem` accepts an Object as an argument. The `DataGrid` is also smart enough to match up the Object names to be used as the column titles.

```
for(var i:uint=0; i < responds.length; i++)
{
  albumsDG.addItem(responds[i]);
}
```

The remainder of the example is the same as the proof-of-concept application. While not an addition to the application, the method name of the service needs to be modified if you decide to use the `RecordSet` way of displaying the row data.

Here is the complete source from the Album application example.

```
import flash.net.*;

var gatewayURL:String =
    "http://localhost/flashservices/gateway.php";
var gateway:NetConnection;

function loadAlbumData(e:MouseEvent):void
{

  var responder:Responder = new Responder(onResult, onFault);

  gateway = new NetConnection();
  gateway.connect(gatewayURL);
  gateway.call("Albums.getAlbumByGenreID", responder, 4);

}

function onResult(responds:Object):void
{

  albumsDG.removeAll();
  for(var i:uint=0; i < responds.length; i++)
  {
    albumsDG.addItem(responds[i]);
  }

}

function onFault(responds:Object):void
{

  for(var i in responds)
  {
```

217

Part III Extending Flash and PHP

```
      trace("[" + i + "]\t" + responds[i]);
   }

}

      loadAlbumBtn.addEventListener(MouseEvent.CLICK, loadAlbumData);
```

As you can see, working with dynamic data using AMFPHP does have many advantage over normal methods of working with data.

This section should have given you a good understanding of how to work with AMFPHP in ActionScript 3. You can take the concepts learned in this section and build upon the other information in this book to create a very robust application.

Summary

You learned the process of working with third-party libraries in the first part of the chapter. Then in the second part you were introduced to how you properly install the third-party libraries. Once the initial setup and installation process was completed, the next step was to build some custom code to work with the installed libraries.

The final portion of the chapter focused on working with AMFPHP to create more robust applications and strengthen the concepts of working with libraries.

Chapter 10

Using Object-Oriented Programming

This chapter focuses on classes and object-oriented programming. Understanding how classes work and where they should be used will help you write more efficient code. The key to successfully writing in an object-oriented programming format (OOP) is to properly evaluate the application you will be writing.

This chapter starts by explaining the individual aspects of OOP in both Flash and PHP. The last section of this chapter is the construction of an example class to strengthen your understanding of the practices learned in the previous sections.

It is important to note that this is not an in-depth guide to OOP, which actually would require its own book, but is more an overview to support the usages in this book.

IN THIS CHAPTER

Understanding classes in PHP

Understanding classes in Flash

Using methods

Using properties

Writing a custom class

Understanding OOP

The key to understanding object-oriented programming (OOP) is to think of each element as a separate piece. In traditional programming, the code flows from line 1 until it reaches the end of the document, with the occasional function to accomplish repetitive tasks. The problem with this approach is scalability, or the ability to let a program grow is it evolves in the future.

I am sure you're wondering why you should care if an application is scalable or not. It actually is a very important concern that is often overlooked in applications. Making a program scalable from the beginning means less code reworking and editing in the future. In a way, OOP and scalable code actually go together quite nicely when used properly.

Part III   Extending Flash and PHP

Overview of OOP practices

Now that you have an understanding of what OOP is and how it can benefit your code, you can look at what is involved in writing it. The first O in OOP is for "object" or a collection of information contained in one easy-to-manage piece.

As you begin to work with OOP practices you will quickly understand how easy it is implement and will be using OOP all of the time.

Classes

A *class* is a definition of all objects of a specified type. The class defines the objects structure and behavior. This approach not only allows the code to be distributed, but also allows you to maintain a certain level of security.

To better understand classes, here is a very basic example:

```
public class Hello
{
  function Hello()
  {

  }
  public function getSaying():String
  {
    return "Hello World!";
  }
}
```

The previous code is a simple example of a class and is merely meant to visually demonstrate how a class is constructed. The `public` before the class defines the entire class as globally accessible. In certain instances, this is not the desired result. You can also assign each method and property as public, private, or other types depending on the requirements.

Here is a common example of applying protections to a class to ensure security:

```
public class UserLogin
{
  function UserLogin()
  {
  }
  public function login():void
  {
    callDatabase();
  }
  private function callDatabase():void
  {
  }
}
```

It is safe to assume that you would not want the `callDatabase` method to be called directly because a malicious call could actually harm your database and weaken the overall integrity of the application. Forcing the method as private ensures the method cannot be called. The user must call the `login` method where you can validate the request before the database is called. This is, of course, a very simple usage of public and private types, but it should help you understand why they are important.

Constructor

The first method in a class is generally the constructor. The constructor is automatically called by the system and cannot return data. It is usually where initialization tasks would take place, such as drawing an object on the stage or calling a database.

Packages

Packages are containers for multiple classes that offer the ability to share the information within the global container. This is similar to the employees in an office who share information within their own department, but at the same time can pass information along to upper management without it ever leaving the organization. In a way, a package is an organization of classes.

There are two ways to define a package. The first is the current directory, which just becomes:

```
package {
  class Example
  {
    function Example()
    {
    }
  }
}
```

The other option is to define a package structure, usually defined by the developer or company's domain name in reverse order, such as:

```
com.companywebsite.projectname
```

The structure is placed after the `package` keyword.

```
package com.companywebsite.projectname {
  class Example
  {
    function Example()
    {
    }
  }
}
```

A reverse domain package path is used to make sure the package is unique. It is also used to properly define the application or library. Another advantage to using this approach is it stops class collisions, which is when two different classes have the same name. This happens more often when third-party libraries are used in an application because you have no control over the names used in those classes. If the library is properly built, it will have a unique package structure to avoid collisions.

Importing

Importing when working with classes is referring to loading in, or connecting classes together. For example, in Flash the stage is an instance of the `DisplayObject` class. However, when you create a `movieclip`, which is an instance of the `MovieClip` class, it is also loading in an instance of the `DisplayObject`, along with a lot of other classes and packages.

You can place imports within the class so they are only visible to that class, or you can load them into the package allowing them to be shared across the entire package. For example, if you had a `Member` class it is safe to assume that you would always want that member's credentials visible to validate them in various portions of the application. You would start off by defining the `Member` class and then import the `UserCredentials` class for validation, such as:

```
import UserCredentials;

public class Member
{
   function Member()
   {
   }
}
```

This would allow the `UserCredentials` to be viewed by any method or property in the `Member` class. However, there are some cases where you would want all classes to share another class.

```
package
{
   import UserCredentials;
   public class Member
   {
      function Member()
      {
      }
   }
}
```

In ActionScript 3 you don't have to worry about importing a class more than once because the AS compiler is intelligent enough to only import it one time. PHP, on the other hand, throws an error if you attempt to load a class more than once. This actually isn't a bad thing and can easily be avoided by loading all classes in one file. Just think of this master class as the parent of all others. The next section will focus on the differences and similarities of class in PHP and Flash.

Using Object-Oriented Programming

Static methods and properties

A static method is one that doesn't require a class instance to be called. It also allows the code to have a certain level of consistency. For example, there is a `Date` class, and in that a method that returns the days of the week. It is safe to assume the days of the week aren't going to change, so you can access that method by simply calling it directly.

```
Date.getDaysOfWeek();
```

A static method is called in the following way: `Class.method`. There is no need for an instance name or constructor; in fact, a constructor isn't even needed in this type of class. However, it is good practice to have a constructor for complete compatibility.

A static property is similar to a static method in that it can be accessed without an instance. However, it does have one special attribute; its type and data can't be changed, with the obvious exception of an Array or Object, which can have no elements added to it.

```
trace("Days in Week: " + Date.daysInWeek);
```

The preceding code would access the static property `daysInWeek`, which would return a numeric value representing the total days in a week. A static property is useful when you have a value that never changes, such as a URL or company information to be used in an application.

Singletons

A singleton is a design pattern. The subject of design patterns requires its own book, but basically they are rules and practices formed between various developers. You are not required to follow any design pattern, but doing so offers cleaner and more scalable code. The singleton is likely the most common design pattern. It is commonly used to pass around a piece of information that never changes and will be needed quite a bit during an application.

> **NOTE** In most programming languages it is common to declare the constructor of a singleton private. This keeps developers from accidentally creating more than one instance of a singleton. However, ActionScript does not support private constructors.

As you learned previously, an instance of a class is made by using the new keyword. That is one way you can access a class; another is to reuse the existing instance, such as:

```
public class User
{
  private static instance:User;
  function User(){}
  public static function getInstance():User
  {
    if(instance == null)
    {
      instance = new User();
    }
```

223

Part III Extending Flash and PHP

```
    return instance;
  }
  public function exampleName():String
  {
    return "Joey";
  }
}
```

The majority of this class is the same as previous examples, with the exception of the addition of the `getInstance` method. This method is used to ensure that a unique instance of the class is always used. Any call to this class is done through the `getInstance` method, such as:

```
import User;
trace("Example Call: " + User.getInstance().exampleName);
```

The first time the class is referenced the unique instance is generated. Any call from that point simply returns the existing instance. This ensures any changes to this class will be seen by all callers. The magic behind this class is the static method and properties, which are used to essentially put a gate between the methods and the caller. All calls going through `getInstance` also allow you to place an authorization check on all calls.

> **NOTE** A singleton should only be used when needed. Turning every class you create into a singleton is not a good practice; in fact, most programs have one singleton that stores all of the necessary information.

Getters and setters

You may have noticed that a lot of class usage is focused on passing data back and forth. In fact, that is pretty much what all programming is, in a way. The idea behind a getter and setter is to gain access to private properties. In fact, it is a pretty safe bet that most of your properties will be private, because that is sort of the idea of a class. Here is an example of a getter and setter, using a class skeleton as an example:

```
class People
{
  private var _person:String;
  public function get person():String
  {
    return _person;
  }
  public function set person(u:String):void
  {
    if(u.length > 0 && u.length < 25)
    {
      _person = u;
    }
  }
}
```

Using Object-Oriented Programming

The preceding code simply returns the current value of the private `_person` property. Or, a call to `person` will modify that private property if the new value is at least 1 and no more than 25 characters in length. You can add any level of security or data modification to these setters. The advantage to using a setter is the ability to lock access to the private properties, also called encapsulation. This ensures the code can't be broken by passing in the incorrect data, or worse, compromising a system due to an open class.

Now that you understand what a getter and setter are, it is probably a safe bet to say you probably also want to know how to call them. That is done by accessing the public variable, such as:

```
var people:People = new People();
people.person = "Timmy";
trace("The new person is: " + people.person);
```

Like most aspects of programming, it is the developer's responsibility to determine where and when the use of a getter/setter is a good idea. The easiest way to determine this is by first creating a proper application outline.

Using Classes in PHP

Now that you have an understanding of what OOP is and how it works, the next step is looking at the class differences in Flash and PHP.

To start, here is a quick example of a class in PHP:

```
<?php

class Example
{
  public $sample = "Hello, World!";
  function Example()
  {
    return $sample;
  }
}

?>
```

That is the basic way to set up a class in PHP. The main aspects are property definitions that start with public, private, or protected. A property will still require the $, just like in standard PHP code. The only other real difference is the fact PHP does not declare the return type. In fact, PHP really doesn't strictly care what type a variable holds, which is actually not a good thing. The developer can lose the ability to know what type of data a variable holds.

225

Importing classes in PHP

Importing a class in PHP is done by loading the file using `include` or `require`. Using `include` will attempt to load the file, but will continue if the file isn't found. Require, on the other hand, also looks for the file, but exits the script with a fatal error if the file is not found, as shown in Figure 10.1. Using `require` offers the ability to halt a script if the proper files aren't found. Here is an example of loading a class by requiring it:

```php
<?php

if(!file_exists('Interface.php'))
{
  print "Class 'Interface' not loaded, exiting script!";
}
@require('Interface.php');

class Example
{
  function Example()
  {
    $i = new iExample();

    print "My i: " . $i->samplr();
  }
}

$example = new Example();

?>
```

An `if` statement is used to first check for the existence of the file, because `require` will create a fatal error, which means the script will be unable to report any proper error messages. If for some reason the file is not found, the message is sent to the browser and the script ends silently when it reaches the `require` line. The `@` is used to silence the internal errors that more often then not cause a security concern because they display crucial file paths. An alternative way to hide errors is to disable error reporting, which is explained in Chapter 13.

Instantiation

Class instantiation is the act of making a class instance. The action is the same in any OOP language, but each language has a different way of setting it up. In PHP, you first create a variable and then assign the class to that variable. Once the new instance is created, you can access the public methods and properties of that class.

```php
$myNewInstance = new Example();
```

Using Object-Oriented Programming 10

FIGURE 10.1

Here is the error message displayed in the browser, which is a result of the class not being found.

Methods in PHP are accessed using:

    $instance->methodName();

However, when you want to access a method inside the same class, you can substitute the instance variable and use $this. So, assuming you want to access the helloWorld method in the Speak class, it would look like this:

    $this->helloWorld();

You can also use the Scope Resolution Operator (also called Paamayim Nekudotayim, which is Hebrew for double-colon) to access methods and properties. The difference is instead of using $this, you would use the actual Class name. This approach makes the code easier to read.

    Speak::helloWorld();

227

Part III   Extending Flash and PHP

Multiple classes

PHP allows a class script to hold multiple classes. This is both a good and bad idea, because too many classes in one file result in bloated code that is hard to manage. On the other hand, having the classes all in one file makes it easier to distribute. I am sure you are asking yourself how exactly are multiple classes defined in one file; here is an example of a pseudo-class package.

```
<?php

class Animals
{
  function Animal()
  {

  }
  public function speak($word)
  {
    print $word;
  }
}

class Dog extends Animals
{
  function Dog($word)
  {
    $this->speak($word);
  }
}

// Create a new Dog
$dog = new Dog("Hello.. Woof!");

?>
```

In fact, PHP really doesn't follow all of the standard OOP practices, which I think will change as newer versions are developed. For now, you can create your own version of a package and get the same basic functionality. It is important to note that a pseudo-package does not offer the same level of separation and security that a real package does, but with some creative programming and proper creation of your classes, you can keep the code secure.

CROSS-REF   See Chapter 6 for more in-depth information on code security.

That is all there is to using and understanding classes in PHP, up to the point needed for this book. You can, of course, extend this newfound knowledge and start exploring the more advanced aspects of classes in PHP.

NOTE   PHP offers a lot of "magic" methods and properties that make classes more fun and less painful to work with.

Using Classes in Flash

As stated previously, classes in Flash and PHP are similar in most aspects. Let's look at how you use and modify classes in ActionScript Flash.

Importing

Importing a class in ActionScript is a little less forgiving if the class is not found. In fact, the compiler that runs when you export a movie stops if a class is not found. This basically means you don't need error messages if a class is not loaded, because the movie is never able to be seen by the general public.

The exception to this compiler check is if the class is dynamic, which means its overall structure can change, but that is beyond the scope of this book. Now back to importing classes, which would be set up like this:

```
import com.organization.project.Example;
var example:Example = new Example();
trace("Call a method: " + example.methodName());
```

You may have noticed the use of `import` instead of `require` or `include`. The other obvious difference in the preceding example is the `:Example` type definition. This actually isn't required, but it allows better error checking when the movie is being compiled or is running.

Document class

The Document class is used as the main class for an application. Think of it as the Timeline class, similar to the days of adding basic code on frame 1 of a movie. Those days are over and it is a good thing, too. However, there are some things to know about when using a Document class, as shown in Figure 10.2. First, look at what a Document class looks like:

```
package
{
  import flash.display.MovieClip;
  public class DocRoot extends MovieClip
  {
    function DocRoot
    {
      trace("I am the Document Class");
    }
  }
}
```

Part III Extending Flash and PHP

FIGURE 10.2

The Document class, which can be found in the Properties inspector

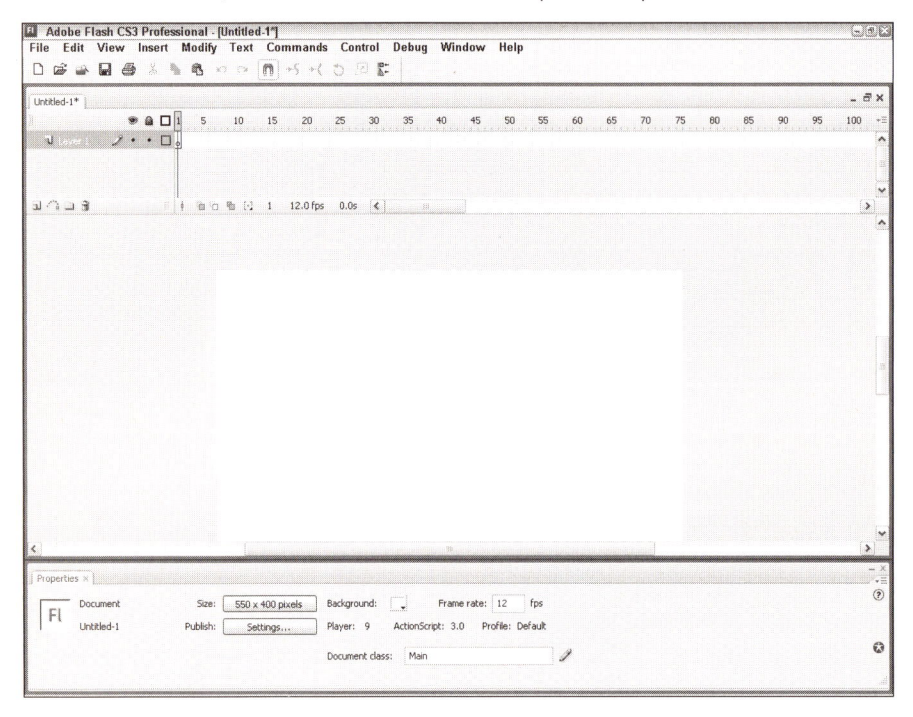

The assignment of the Document class is fairly unique. You can add or edit the class file using the following steps:

1. Click on the Stage, to ensure nothing is selected.
2. Open the Properties inspector if it isn't already open.
3. Click in the Document Class `TextBox` and add the name of the class.

You may have noticed the Document class extends the `MovieClip` Class, but it can also extend the `Sprite` class. In fact, this extension is required because the Document class is in fact a `MovieClip`.

Library classes

A library class is the new way to attach ActionScript to a `MovieClip` in the Timeline. In previous versions of Flash you would assign a Linkage Identifier to your `MovieClip`. In ActionScript 3, you take the same basic steps of opening the Properties inspector, select the Export for ActionScript option, and add the class name, as shown in Figure 10.3.

Using Object-Oriented Programming

FIGURE 10.3

The Properties inspector with the Export for ActionScript option selected

Just like the Document class, you need to make sure the `MovieClip`'s custom class extends the `MovieClip` class. In fact, the Document and Library classes are very similar when setting them up.

Using Flash and PHP to Build Custom Classes

You may have noticed that there is less to explain with class usage in Flash than there is in PHP. This section focuses on a complete class-based example in Flash and PHP. It is used to strengthen the concepts learned in the previous pages.

Let's start with PHP that will be used in this example. The idea is to build a basic application that allows PHP and Flash to communicate, while taking advantage of custom classes.

```php
<?php

class Communication
{
    public $MESSAGE_NOTIFY = "Hi, from PHP! You said: ";

    function Communication()
```

231

Part III Extending Flash and PHP

```
    {

    }

    public function respond($str)
    {
      return $this->MESSAGE_NOTIFY . $str;
    }
}

$communication = new Communication();

if($_GET['a'] == "newMessage")
{
  // send message back to Flash
  print "resp=" . $communication->respond();
}
?>
```

The PHP portion of this example allows Flash to communicate by passing along a request for the `respond()` method to be called. Inside the class, PHP then builds a string and returns it to the Flash, where at that point it is read in and displayed on the Stage.

The next step is to build the Document class and caller in Flash. Here is the Document class:

```
package
{

  import flash.display.MovieClip;
  import flash.text.TextField;

  import Communicator;

  public class Document extends MovieClip
  {
    function Document()
    {
      makeCall();
    }

    public function makeCall():void
    {
      var mc:MovieClip = new MovieClip();
      var txt:TextField = new TextField();

      mc.addChild(txt);
      addChild(mc);

      var communicator:Communicator = new Communicator();
```

Using Object-Oriented Programming 10

```
      communicator.action = "newMessage";
      communicator.container = mc;
      communicator.callServer();
    }
  }
}
```

The constructor is responsible for calling the `makeCall()` method. This method creates a new `TextField`, attaches it to the Stage using `addChild`, and finally sets up the call to the custom `communicator` class.

As the call to the `communicator` class is being set up, it is also responsible for assigning the `TextField` instance and the action. The action in this example is used to tell PHP which code to run. Of course, in this example there is only one action assigned. However, it is easy to quickly have ten or more actions in a real-world application.

The `TextField` class is similar to the `createNewTextField` method that would have been used in ActionScript 2. The change in code for ActionScript 3 was done to be consistent with custom library items, such as the ones in the previous section.

The next step is to build the `custom` class, which will be used to communicate with PHP on the Web server.

```
package{
    import flash.net.URLRequest;
    import flash.net.URLLoader;
    import flash.net.URLVariables;
    import flash.display.MovieClip;
    import flash.events.*;

    public class Communicator
    {
      private var _action:String;
      private var _txtBoxContainer:MovieClip;

      function Communicator() {}

      public function callServer():void
      {
        var variables:URLVariables = new URLVariables();
        variables.a = _action;

        var request:URLRequest = new
       URLRequest("http://localhost/flashphp/Communicate.php");
        request.data = variables;

        var loader:URLLoader = new URLLoader();
```

233

Part III Extending Flash and PHP

```
      loader.addEventListener(Event.COMPLETE, serverHandler);
      loader.load(request);
    }

    public function serverHandler(e:Event):void
    {
      var loader:URLLoader = URLLoader(e.target);
      var variables:URLVariables = new URLVariables(loader.data);

      _txtBoxContainer.text = variables.resp;
    }

    public function set action(a:String):void
    {
      _action = a;
    }

    public function set container(mc:MovieClip):void
    {
      _txtBoxContainer = mc;
    }
  }
}
```

The class is pretty straightforward and has the concepts that have been used in prior examples. The main focus points of this class are the `callServer` and `serverHandler` methods, which are responsible for calling and dealing with the response from the server.

The first method, `callServer`, sets up the variable `_action` that is passed to PHP using the value that was set in the Document class in the previous section. You may have noticed the _ before the variable name, which is used to clearly define a private variable. It is not required, but it makes your code easier to read.

The last two methods in this class are responsible for setting the container of the `TextField` and the action. These two setters are called from the document class.

As you can see, building this application as a custom class offers the ability to quickly update it or extend it to another application and best of all keeps it all secure. This basic application is just a sampling of what classes can offer, but should give you a better understanding of how the Document class is set up.

The following, Table 10.1, is a table quickly and graphically explaining the differences of classes in PHP and Flash. You can always refer back to this page if you have a question of whether a feature exists in the language you are working in.

TABLE 10.1

Differences Between Classes in PHP and Flash

Class	PHP	Flash
Instantiation	X	X
Multiple classes in one file	X	
Importing	X include or require	X
Constructor	X	X
Packages		X
Static methods and properties	X	X

Summary

A lot of information was covered in this chapter and at this point you should have a pretty good understanding of how object-oriented programming works and when to use it. As you may now notice, classes and OOP in general offer a lot of advantages. However, you might also notice OOP development does take more time. This isn't necessarily a bad thing, because in the long run you will notice less development time on future updates. It also offers the less obvious advantage of more secure code that the developer can control. At this point you know how to set up and use classes in PHP and Flash, and will probably want to experiment with some of the more advanced topics that were not covered in this chapter.

Part IV

Developing Applications

IN THIS PART

Chapter 11
Developing Basic Applications

Chapter 12
Developing Real-World Applications

Chapter 13
Using Advanced Real-World Applications

Chapter 14
Debugging Applications

Chapter 11

Developing Basic Applications

In this chapter, you develop a series of full applications. The objective of this chapter is to end up with complete applications while explaining common pitfalls and how to overcome them. You will investigate some new concepts as well, such as multiple event handlers, custom classes, and remote services.

This chapter also focuses on the best way to work with MySQL in an efficient and safe way. The chapter concludes by evaluating best practices for maintaining the applications and allowing the ability to add new functionality.

IN THIS CHAPTER

Understanding elements of an application

Developing a chat client

Building a Gallery using PHP

Using MySQL to create a series of other dynamic applications

Understanding Elements of an Application

Building applications isn't only about jumping into Flash or your favorite editor and writing line after line of code. The best place to start in application development is the evaluation stage. This is the point where you look at the list of what your application should do, who the audience is, and how you plan to develop the application. Table 11.1 illustrates the three points of the evaluation stage.

TABLE 11.1

The Three Points of the Evaluation Stage

What	Defines what the application will do
Who	The target audience of your application
How	Techniques you use to develop your application

The following examples skip over the "how" step because this is a Flash and PHP book. Once the "how" is defined you can think about the "who." This is, of course, your target audience. An application will not always have a rigidly defined who, especially if it is a service Web site, but it is best to define one. The best way to determine your target audience is to think about the type of application. For example, will it be an e-commerce application or maybe video player. Knowing who will be using the application is crucial to its success.

Now that the "how" and "who" are defined, you can think about what exactly your application will do. You would never go to the hardware store, buy all the materials, and then decide what to build. The same is true for developing applications. As you begin to follow these practices they become second nature.

Understanding application design

With the evaluation stage completed you would naturally move into the design stage. But, just like the evaluation stage, it is always a good idea to plan first. This would be a sketch with paper and pencil or using Flash with primitive shapes. For example, Figure 11.1 shows an example sketch.

Working with pseudo-code

After you have the overall layout of the application developed, you can move on to functionality. This would be the point where you start to write pseudo-code, such as functions, variables, events, and any other concepts you will use in your application. The following is an example of pseudo-code for a user management program.

```
// Pseudo-code

function loadUser(id:uint):void
{
  // make call to server passing
  // along the id as the user id
}
function handleServerResponse(e:Event):void
{
  // capture server response
  // make necessary calls to application
}

function drawInterface():void
```

Developing Basic Applications

```
{
  // paint "draw" the interface that
  // the user will interact with
}

function redraw():void
{
  // redraw interface as info is loaded,
  // to keep things up to date
}

// Assign event handlers
```

You will notice that pseudo-code is not a complete application, but a skeleton of the overall application. This allows you to quickly develop how the application will work and what it will do. Writing pseudo-code becomes a lot more important when developing large-scale applications, but it is good practice to evaluate, sketch, and plan no matter how large the project is.

FIGURE 11.1

An example application sketch using primitive shapes in Flash

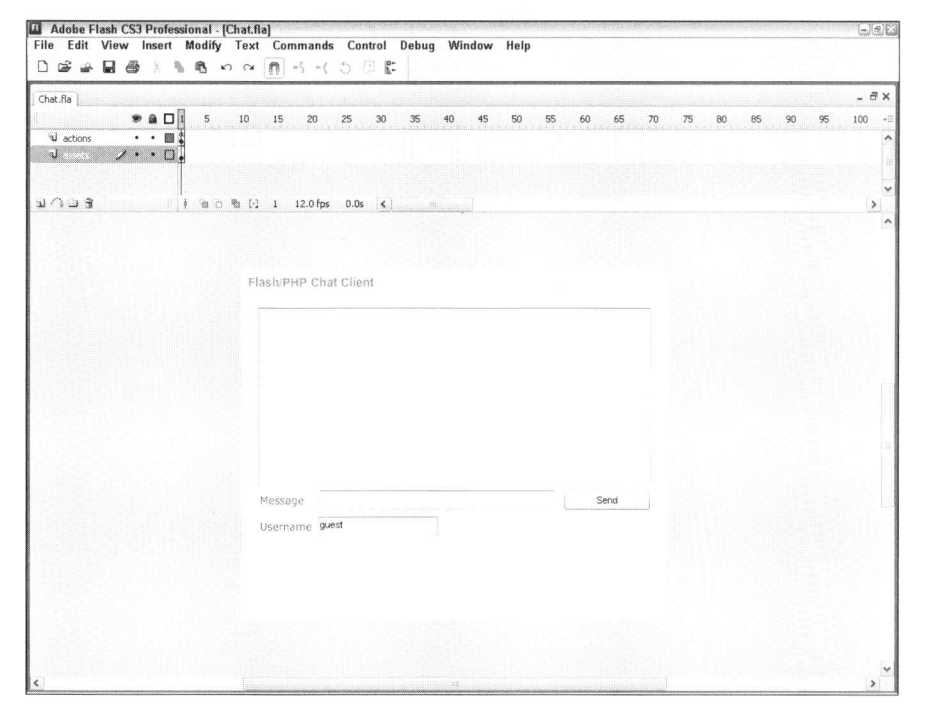

241

Finalizing the planning stage

The last step to planning an application is not definitive because you can either wrap up the planning stages or begin the development process. This choice can sometimes be determined by your client or creative director if one has been assigned.

At this point in the planning process, you have determined what the application will do, who will be using it, and how it will be built. You have also designed a layout and begun the programming process. The next step is up to you as the developer. You can either continue and finalize the design process or begin developing the code the application will use.

Normally, you would design the application enough to get started in the programming because things are more than likely going to change as you continue to develop. However, with the proper amount of planning you can minimize these revision phases.

Developing a Chat Client

Now that you have looked at the best practices for application development you can begin developing your first complete application. This application will be a Flash chat client using PHP to interface with a MySQL database. After developing the basic application you will continue to add features and look at the best way to build a scalable application.

A scalable application is developed keeping in mind that two users may use the application at first, but it could easily be used by millions over time. The idea is to account for this and develop the application in a manner that allows for expansion.

The Flash portion

You begin this project by designing the application. For this application, the design is provided, but feel free to modify it. In fact, you are encouraged to expand upon all the examples, which is how you become familiar with new concepts and also how you grow as a developer. Figure 11.2 shows the interface for the chat application.

Basically the interface consists of a `TextArea` component, which is used for displaying the chat messages, two `TextInput` components for the message and username items, and a `Button` instance for the submit button.

Developing Basic Applications 11

FIGURE 11.2

The design from your chat application built using prebuilt components in Flash

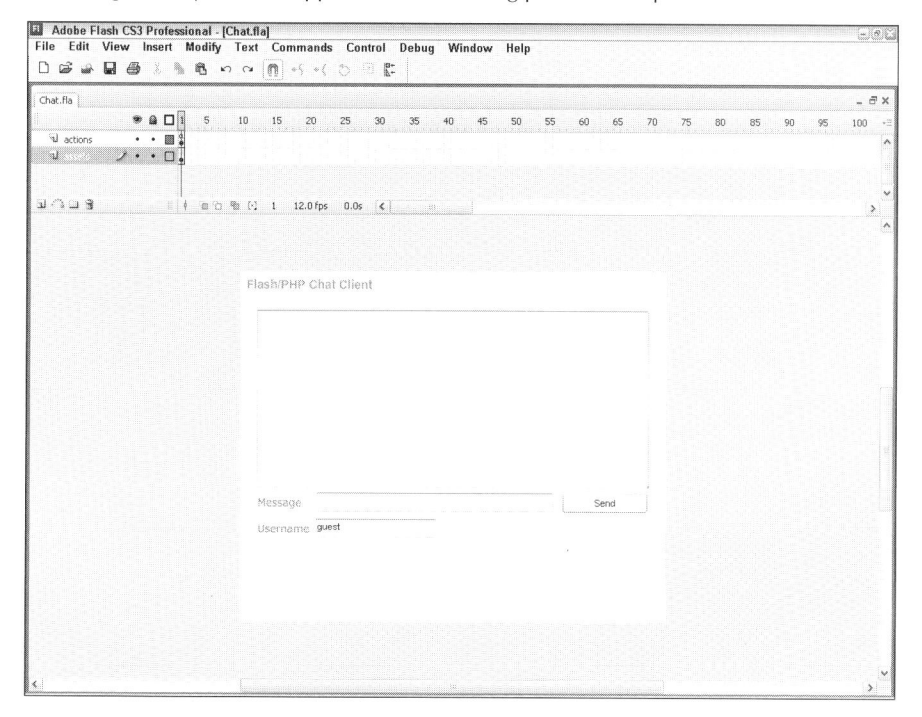

Table 11.2 shows the instance names for each component.

TABLE 11.2

Instance Names for the Components

Component	Instance Name	Result
TextArea	messagesTxt	Display the chat messages
TextInput	newMsgTxt	New message
TextInput	usernameTxt	Name of the chat person
Button	sendBtn	Send new message to the server

Part IV Developing Applications

You will be referencing the instance names during the development of the ActionScript for your chat application.

With the user interface "design" portion completed or in this case loaded, you can begin development of the code.

The first part of the chat application code is a block of variables that are used throughout. The first variable is the absolute path to the PHP files. Then next two variables are the PHP files responsible for sending and loading the chat messages from the database. After that are two Boolean variables to ensure multiple message calls can't be made. The last set of variables is a reference to the `Timer` object and the cache buster.

```
var phpPath:String = "http://localhost/ch10/chatClient/";
var phpSendMessage:String = phpPath + "message.php";
var phpLoadMessages:String = phpPath + "getMessages.php";

var loadingMessages:Boolean = false;
var sendingMessage:Boolean = false;

var timer:Timer;
var cacheBuster:String = "?cb=1";
```

The first function you will build is the `init()` or initialization function. This is called only once, when the application starts. It is responsible for setting up a `timer` handler for loading the messages from the server and making the first call to a cache buster, which is explained in the next section. The last action of the `init()` function is to call the `loadMessages` function and populate the message list.

```
function init():void
{
  // start timer for loading of messages
  timer = new Timer(5000, 0);
  timer.addEventListener(TimerEvent.TIMER, timerHandler);
  timer.start();

  cacheBuster =  getCacheBuster();
  loadMessages(); // first time
}
```

The `Timer` class ships with Flash and has a lot of great uses. This example takes advantage of the `TIMER` event, which is called every time the countdown is reached. The countdown time and number of repeats are passed into the constructor. Set countdown to 5000 or 5 seconds and the repeats to 0, which actually tells ActionScript to repeat continuously. After a new `Timer` instance is created you assign the event handler and start the timer immediately. The timer handler simply makes a call to the `loadMessages` function.

Developing Basic Applications 11

This portion of the code could be condensed by placing the `loadMessages` function in place of the `timerHandler`, but doing it this way allows us to add more functionality down the road. It is all good development practice to create proper handlers for events so the code can be updated, and it makes it overall a lot easier to read.

```
function timerHandler(e:TimerEvent):void
{
  loadMessages();
}
```

The `loadMessages` function is responsible for calling and handling the response from the server. The call to the server is very similar to other examples with a few new elements. One new element is the `cacheBuster` variable, which is used to ensure we don't receive a cached result.

Stop caching with dynamic data

You just created a variable to stop caching, but what exactly is that? Caching on the server is when dynamic data is stored for quicker loading on all future calls. At first glance this would seem like a good idea, and in most cases it is. However, in the example of loading chat data that is constantly changing it is probably safe to say you want this data to be fresh. This is accomplished by adding a variable referred to as a "cache buster," which fools the browser into thinking each call to the same file is different.

Here is a very simple example of a cache buster and the actual string that is sent to the server:

```
function getRandom(length:uint):void
{
  return Math.round(Math.random() * (length - 1)) + 1;
}

var rand:String =  "?cb=" + getRandom(8);
var php:String = "http://localhost/ch04/getMessages.php" + rand;

trace("URL: " + phpFile); // getMessages.php?cb=65378426
```

CAUTION Cache busters add to download time and force any file with a cache buster to be downloaded every time it is requested.

Everything after the ? in the URL is telling the browser and server that the call is dynamic and results in the file not being cached.

The next part to the process of sending the message is ensuring the message is at least three characters long. If the message is not at least three characters, an error message is displayed. There are two ways you can write this conditional check.

245

Part IV Developing Applications

The first option is:

```
if(newMsgTxt.text.length > 2)
{
}
```

The second option, which is easier to quickly understand:

```
if(newMsgTxt.text.length >= 3)
{
}
```

Both options achieve the same result, but the second option is much easier to read from a logical point of view.

Now, assuming you have a message of the correct length you can continue with the process of sending the message to the server. The next part is constructing the call to the server.

```
var variables:URLVariables = new URLVariables();
variables.user = usernameTxt.text;
variables.msg = newMsgTxt.text;
var urlRequest:URLRequest = new URLRequest(phpSendMessage +
    getCacheBuster());
urlRequest.method = URLRequestMethod.POST;
urlRequest.data = variables;

var urlLoader:URLLoader = new URLLoader();
urlLoader.addEventListener(Event.COMPLETE, sendMessageHandler);
urlLoader.load(urlRequest);
```

When calling the server, you must set up a `URLVariables` object in order to pass along the username and message that was entered. A call is also made to the custom cache buster function to ensure the data is always fresh.

The last step in the sending function is to immediately add the user's message instead of waiting for the message list to update from the server. This gives the application a more responsive feel and makes it so the message doesn't appear to have been ignored.

```
addMessage(usernameTxt.text, newMsgTxt.text);
```

This function accepts two arguments: the username and the message gathered from their respective components. This information is then built into an HMTL string that is assigned to the `messagesTxt TextArea`. The username is placed within bold tags to emphasize the name. In fact, you can use a lot of common HTML tags within HTML-enabled textboxes.

```
function addMessage(user:String, msg:String):void
{
  messagesTxt.htmlText += "<b>" + user + "</b>" + ": " + msg +
    "\n";
}
```

Table 11.3 shows the supported HTML tags that can be used.

TABLE 11.3

Supported HTML Tags

Label	HTML Tag
Anchor Tag	`<a>`
Bold Tag	`<b>`
Break Tag	` `
Font Tag	`<font>`
Image Tag	`<img>`
Italic Tag	`<i>`
List Item Tag	`<li>`
Paragraph Tag	`<p>`
Span Tag	`<span>`
Underline Tag	`<u>`

The `sendMessageHandler` function is called once the message is successfully sent to the server. The only important part of this function is the last line, which clears the message box and allows the user to type a new message. You could clear the message in the `send` function, but doing it this way ensures the message stays intact until you are sure it has been added.

NOTE The PHP does not alert you to an error if the SQL fails, only if the page is not loaded. You can certainly add more advanced error handling to this example.

```
function sendMessageHandler(e:Event):void
{
   ...
   newMsgTxt.text = "";
}
```

Now that you have completed the code for sending and handling calls to the server, you can begin the function that manages the messages and displays them in `TextArea`.

The `loadMessages()` function is called from two different points. The first point is the `init()` function, which you looked at earlier; the second is the timer handler.

The function first checks to see if another call has already been made to load the messages. Adding this check ensures you can't flood the server and potentially force it to become unresponsive. If another load has already begun, you simply back out of the function and stop processing.

Part IV Developing Applications

Assuming that another load is not already under way, you set the `loadingMessages` variable, which is similar to locking your door after you enter a room. Most of the `loadMessages` functionality is similar to the sending process.

You basically set the correct PHP file to load and set up an event handler for when the server sends back the message data.

```
function loadMessages():void
{
  if(loadingMessages) return;
  loadingMessages  = true;

  var urlRequest:URLRequest = new URLRequest(phpLoadMessages +
    getCacheBuster());
  var urlLoader:URLLoader = new URLLoader();

  urlLoader.addEventListener(Event.COMPLETE,
    loadMessagesHandler);
  urlLoader.load(urlRequest);
}
```

Handling XML response

The loading response function is responsible for working with the XML data and passing the messages to be displayed.

```
function loadMessagesHandler(e:Event):void
{
  var loader:URLLoader = URLLoader(e.target);
  var xml:XML = new XML(loader.data);

  messagesTxt.htmlText = "";

  for each(var item in xml..message)
  {
    addMessage(item.name, item.msg);
  }

  cacheBuster = getCacheBuster();
  loadingMessages = false;
}
```

> **NOTE** The item names within the XML response are case sensitive. The standard is lowercase, or camel case, for multiple words.

After the XML is properly loaded and ready to use, you set up a `for..each` loop just like you used in the loading XML example in Chapter 3. The loop is based on all `"message"` nodes found in the example response. A sample of the response passed back would look something like this:

248

Developing Basic Applications

```
<messages>
  <message id='29'>
    <name>guest1</name>
    <msg>Flash is a lot of fun</msg>
  </message>
  <message id='30'>
    <name>guest2</name>
    <msg>PHP and Flash is better</msg>
  </message>
  <message id='32'>
    <name>guest1</name>
    <msg>You can do so many things with it</msg>
  </message>
  <message id='33'>
    <name>guest2</name>
    <msg>For sure, just look at this cool chat client</msg>
  </message>
</messages>
```

The final step of the `loadMessagesHandler` function is to create a new cache buster and set the `loadingMessages` variable to `false`, which allows future calls to get the latest messages.

Cache busters were explained earlier in the section. However, there are multiple ways to create a unique string. The date is always changing and ActionScript has a `getTime` method that returns the milliseconds since January 1, 1970. This date method is used because it is constantly changing and never repeats, which leaves a unique string each time it is called.

At this point, you have completed the ActionScript for your chat application. Here is the complete code for reference:

```
var phpPath:String = "http://localhost/ch10/chatClient/";
var phpSendMessage:String = phpPath + "message.php";
var phpLoadMessages:String = phpPath + "getMessages.php";

var loadingMessages:Boolean = false;
var sendingMessage:Boolean = false;
var chatMessages:Array = new Array();

var timer:Timer;
var cacheBuster:String = "?cb=1";

function init():void
{
  // start timer for loading of messages
  timer = new Timer(5000, 0);
  timer.addEventListener(TimerEvent.TIMER, timerHandler);
```

249

Part IV Developing Applications

```
  timer.start();

  cacheBuster = getCacheBuster();

  loadMessages(); // first time
}

function sendMessage(e:MouseEvent):void
{
  if(usernameTxt.text == "")
  {
    trace("Username required");
    return;
  }

  if(newMsgTxt.text.length >= 3)
  {
    var variables:URLVariables = new URLVariables();
    variables.user = usernameTxt.text;
    variables.msg = newMsgTxt.text;

    var urlRequest:URLRequest = new URLRequest(phpSendMessage +
    getCacheBuster());
    urlRequest.method = URLRequestMethod.POST;
    urlRequest.data = variables;

    var urlLoader:URLLoader = new URLLoader();
    urlLoader.addEventListener(Event.COMPLETE,
    sendMessageHandler);
    urlLoader.load(urlRequest);

    // force message into display
    addMessage(usernameTxt.text, newMsgTxt.text);
  }
}

function sendMessageHandler(e:Event):void
{
  var loader:URLLoader = URLLoader(e.target);
  var variables:URLVariables = new URLVariables(loader.data);
  trace("Response: " + variables.resp);

  // clear message box
  newMsgTxt.text = "";
}

function loadMessages():void
{
  if(loadingMessages) return;
```

Developing Basic Applications

```
  loadingMessages  = true;

  var urlRequest:URLRequest = new URLRequest(phpLoadMessages +
    getCacheBuster());
  var urlLoader:URLLoader = new URLLoader();

  urlLoader.addEventListener(Event.COMPLETE,
    loadMessagesHandler);
  urlLoader.load(urlRequest);
}

function loadMessagesHandler(e:Event):void
{
  var loader:URLLoader = URLLoader(e.target);
  var xml:XML = new XML(loader.data);

  loadingMessages = false;
  messagesTxt.htmlText = "";

  for each(var item in xml..message)
  {
    addMessage(item.name, item.msg);
  }

  cacheBuster = getCacheBuster();
}

function getCacheBuster():String
{
  var date:Date = new Date();
  cacheBuster = "?cb=" + date.getTime();
  return cacheBuster;
}

function addMessage(user:String, msg:String):void
{
  messagesTxt.htmlText += "<b>" + user + "</b>" + ": " + msg +
    "\n";
}

function timerHandler(e:TimerEvent):void
{
  trace("Timer hit");
  loadMessages();
}

sendBtn.addEventListener(MouseEvent.CLICK, sendMessage);

init();
```

251

PHP for chat application

At this point, you have completed the ActionScript portion of the chat application. The second step is to develop the PHP code, which is called from the ActionScript.

The PHP code is broken up into three files, which are illustrated in Table 11.4.

TABLE 11.4

Breakdown of PHP Files

PHP Code File	Action
getMessages.php	Grabs all of the messages in the past 15 minutes
messages.php	Handles the writing of a new message to the database
dbConn.php	The database connection shared with the other files

The first file you work with is `getMessages.php`. The first part of the code loads or includes the database connection file, which you will look at in just a moment. The next part is the SQL call, which queries the MySQL database and grabs all the latest messages posted in the last 15 minutes.

```
$sql = "SELECT * FROM flashChat WHERE dateAdded > " .
(time() - (60 * 15));
$result = mysql_query($sql);
```

The condition of the last 15 minutes is determined by the following code. The `time()` returns a UNIX timestamp that is subtracted by 60 and multiplied by 15. The 60 is for seconds in a minute and the 15 is how many minutes you are referring to. You could also write this basic math equation by removing the multiplication step. Doing so makes it harder to read the code, but it also increases the speed of the application.

```
time() - 900
```

This SQL string is passed into the actual function that makes the call to the server `mysql_query()`, which is assigned to the `$result` variable. Now that you have successfully made the call to the MySQL database, the next step is to generate a loop that builds the messages. Figure 11.3 shows the query display in MySQL Query Browser, which is available for free from www.mysql.com.

This loop is done using a `while`, which is set to run until a valid row is not returned from the database. You could also place this in a `for` loop and use `mysql_num_rows()` to determine how many rows are being returned.

FIGURE 11.3

The SQL query returned within the MySQL Query Browser

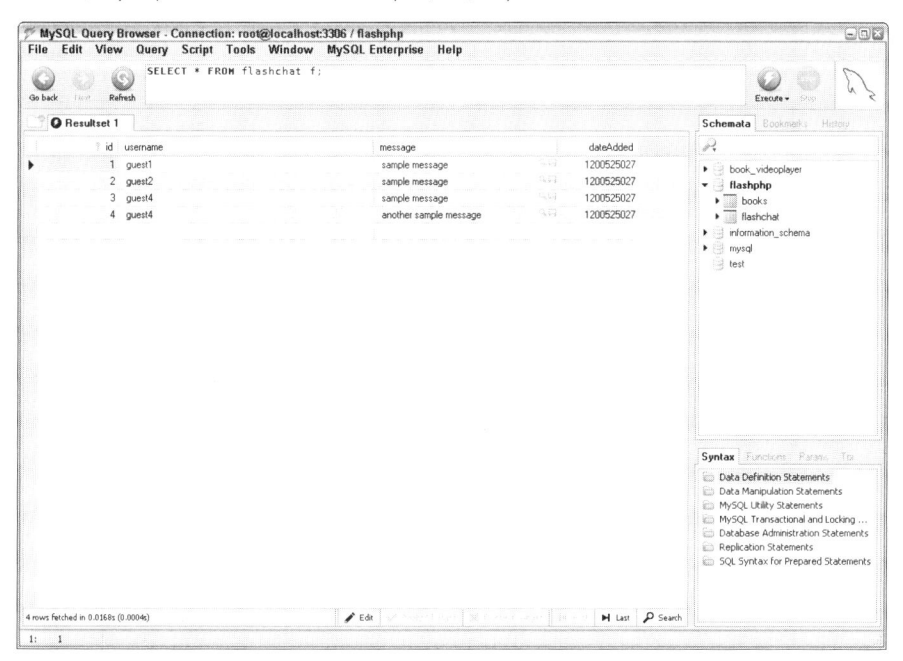

The `mysql_fetch_array()` function grabs a single row from the database table in an associative array format and assigns it to the `$row` variable. The contents of the loop are set up to generate XML nodes that contain the message data, which you looked at earlier in the chapter.

```
while($row = mysql_fetch_array($result))
{
  $xmlData .= "   <message id='" . $row['id'] . "'>\n";
  $xmlData .= "     <name>" . $row['username'] . "</name>\n";
  $xmlData .= "     <msg>" . $row['message'] . "</msg>\n";
  $xmlData .= "   </message>\n";
}
```

At this point, you have a completed SQL call to the server and a loop to generate the message data XML, which is returned to the ActionScript in Flash. Sending the data back to ActionScript is very simple; you just assign the `$xmlData` variable to the print statement.

```
print $xmlData;
```

Part IV Developing Applications

The print statement wraps up your `messages.php` file, which is shown in its entirety here.

```php
<?php

include 'dbconn.php';

$sql = "SELECT * FROM flashChat WHERE dateAdded > " . (time() - (60 * 15));

$result = mysql_query($sql);
$xmlData = "<messages>\n";

while($row = mysql_fetch_array($result))
{
  $xmlData .= "   <message id='" . $row['id'] . "'>\n";
  $xmlData .= "      <name>" . $row['username'] . "</name>\n";
  $xmlData .= "      <msg>" . $row['message'] . "</msg>\n";
  $xmlData .= "   </message>\n";
}

$xmlData .= "</messages>";
print $xmlData;

?>
```

The next PHP file that needs to be developed is `messages.php`, which is responsible for inserting new messages into the MySQL database. The first part of this PHP file starts off the same as the previous one by loading the `dbconn.php` file, which is responsible for handling the login and connection to the MySQL database.

```php
include 'dbconn.php';
```

The next step is to check that the message sent from ActionScript is indeed larger than 0 characters empty string. In PHP, `strlen()` returns the length of a string that is passed in as an argument.

```php
if(strlen($_POST['msg']) > 0)
{
  ...
}
```

Assuming that you have a valid length message, you assign three variables; one is for the username, the second is from the message, and the third is the date in UNIX timestamp format.

```php
$username = $_POST['user'];
$message = $_POST['msg'];
$date = time();
```

The next step in developing this file is take make the actual MySQL call, which is done using `mysql_query()`. This function takes the SQL statement as an argument and either returns a resource `id` or throws an error.

254

Developing Basic Applications   11

The actual SQL statement is fairly similar to others used in previous examples. There is a `flashChat` table within the database that happens to have four columns, but one of those is an `auto_increment` and doesn't need to be defined in an `INSERT` statement.

> **NOTE** In a more robust application, you would want to add a layer of security on data passed in from another source. It doesn't matter if this is Flash, the browser, or a third-party service; it is always important.

```
mysql_query("INSERT INTO flashChat (username, message, dateAdded)
    VALUES (
        '" . $username . "',
        '" . $message . "',
        '" . $date . "'
    )");
```

> **CAUTION** The name `dateAdded` was used because `date` is a reserved word in MySQL and will cause an error in most cases. It is never a good idea to use reserved words for another use in any development language.

The last step in this file is to return a response to Flash notifying that the message has been added and another message can now be added from that user. Overall, the `messages.php` file is pretty simple but it gets the job done.

Here is the completed `messages.php` file for reference.

```
<?php

include 'dbconn.php';

if(strlen($_POST['msg']) > 0)
{
  $username = $_POST['user'];
  $message = $_POST['msg'];
  $date = time();

  mysql_query("INSERT INTO flashChat (username, message,
    dateAdded)
      VALUES (
        '" . $username . "',
        '" . $message . "',
        '" . $date . "'
      )");

  print "resp=MESSAGE_ADDED";
}

?>
```

255

Using PHP to connect to MySQL

The last PHP file in your Flash chat application is the `dbconn.php` file. This file is responsible for connecting to MySQL and providing a link to your tables contained in the database.

> **NOTE** There can only be one connection to a single database at a time. Best practice is to plan your SQL connects to be more efficient. This prevents you from having to jump back and forth.

This file is fairly small but has a very important requirement, which is to honor security measures to the highest extent. A good portion of these sections have noted that security is important. You looked at many examples earlier; in this example security is not excluded for simplicity.

The first part to the file is assigning the database variables that will be passed along for the connection. Oftentimes more advanced applications will have a separate file for configuration variables. That configuration file would be loaded only when the application begins and referenced throughout.

However, because this application is fairly small you will just assign the database connection variables inside the `dbconn.php` connection file.

```
$host = "HOST_NAME";
$user = "SQL_USERNAME";
$pass = "SQL_PASSWORD";
$database = "SQL_DATABASE_NAME";
```

The first variable is often `localhost` or the IP address of the server where MySQL is running if it happens to be running remote from the server where PHP is running. You wouldn't expect to see a remote installation of MySQL in smaller systems, but it is very common in larger applications.

The other three variables are username, password, and the name of the database to which you want to connect. This connection information is provided by your system administrator or host if you don't already know it.

> **NOTE** MySQL creates a default installation with a username of "root" and no password, but it is very insecure this way and should be changed immediately.

Now that the variables are properly defined, you can make the actual connection to MySQL. This is accomplished by the `mysql_connect()` function within PHP. This function accepts three arguments: host, username, and password defined just a moment ago.

```
$link = mysql_connect($host, $user, $pass);
```

The `mysql_connect()` function returns a resource `id` that you store in the `$link` variable. This is referenced when you go to select your database.

Selecting the database is simply a matter of referencing the name of the database to which you want to connect and passing along the link received in the connection step.

```
mysql_select_db($database, $link);
```

The final and most important step is to destroy the variables that contain the MySQL connection information. Destroying or deleting a variable is done by passing the variable reference to the unset() function, which removes the existence of that variable.

```
unset($host);
unset($user);
unset($pass);
unset($database);
unset($link);
```

It is important to have this step to ensure that future aspects of an application can't gain access to these variables. This is especially important when introducing third-party applications into your custom application.

A safer alternative to the previous method is to wrap all of this in a class. This is similar to working with a closed component in Flash. Access is allowed only to what you want others to see; the rest is hidden.

Here is an example of a database connection using a class:

```php
<?php

// simple mysql connection class

class MysqlConnection
{

  public $link;

  private $host = "localhost";
  private $user = "SQL_USERNAME";
  private $pass = "SQL_PASSWORD";
  private $database = "SQL_DB_NAME";

  function MysqlConnection() {}

  public function connect()
  {
    $this->link = mysql_connect(
      $this->host,
      $this->user,
      $this->pass
    );
    mysql_select_db($this->database, $this->link);
  }

  public function setConnectionDetails($h='', $u='', $p='',
   $d='')
  {
```

```
      $this->host = $h;
      $this->user = $u;
      $this->pass = $p;
      $this->database = $d;
    }

    public function getLink()
    {
      return $this->link;
    }
  }

  $sql = new MysqlConnection();
  $sql->connect();

  ?>
```

At first glance it doesn't look very different than the previous connection example; however, the important section is the variable definitions.

```
public $link;

private $host = "localhost";
private $user = "SQL_USERNAME";
private $pass = "SQL_PASSWORD";
private $database = "SQL_DB_NAME";
```

As you learned in Chapter 9, PHP class variables can be given a public and private designation. In this example class, the connection variables are defined as private, locking them tightly within the class. Doing this ensures those variables can't be discovered accidentally, and it also offers another benefit. Say you have a new project and want to connect to a database; doing so would be as simple as the following block of code.

```
<?php

include 'MysqlConnection.php';

$mysqlConn = new MysqlConnection();
$mysqlConn-> setConnectionDetails("host", "user", "pass", "db");
$mysqlConn->connect();

$query = "SELECT * FROM our_table";
$result = mysql_query($query, $mysqlConn->getLink());

?>
```

Notice that you use the custom connection class, give new connection information, and finally pass the database link into the query call. At no point in this code is the connection information accessible or exposed to the general public.

Developing Basic Applications   11

> **NOTE** When connecting to a database on a live server it is a good idea to disable error reporting or at least suppress any connection errors.

Here is the original connection file in its entirety:

```php
<?php
$host = "localhost";
$user = "SQL_USERNAME";
$pass = "SQL_PASSWORD";
$database = "SQL_DB_NAME";

$link = mysql_connect($host, $user, $pass);
mysql_select_db($database, $link);

unset($host);
unset($user);
unset($pass);
unset($database);
unset($link);
?>
```

Creating a database table

At this point, all of the ActionScript and PHP is written. However, if you attempt to test the application it won't run because you haven't defined the SQL table that will interact with the PHP for sending and loading messages.

The SQL syntax is very easy to follow but is important to construct carefully. A poorly built table's performance will suffer more and more as it begins to grow. This SQL creates a `flashChat` table and adds the rows that you use in the PHP. Notice the `id` row, which is not used in the PHP but instead is used internally for indexing and key assignment. Another way to think about the ID is the key that unlocks the mystery to where your data is located within this big table.

The rows that you do use in the PHP are `username`, `message`, and `dateAdded`. The `message` row is most important because it is set as `TEXT`, which gives an open-ended length ability. This basically means a message can be any length. That row also could have been assigned a `varchar()`, which would force the length to a certain predetermined limit, such as:

```
message varchar(150) NOT NULL default ''
```

This new definition for the `message` row would force any chat message longer than 150 characters to be truncated or ended. Setting it as `TEXT` is more convenient but has potential performance concerns as the database and table grow.

```sql
CREATE TABLE flashChat (
  id int(11) not null auto_increment,
  username varchar(20) NOT NULL default '',
  message text NOT NULL,
  dateAdded int(11) NOT NULL default 0,
  PRIMARY KEY (id)
) ENGINE=MyISAM;
```

Part IV **Developing Applications**

It took a lot of code, but your PHP-driven Flash chat application is complete. Take the time to look over the code and extend the example to add more features. Here are a few ideas to get you started.

The first and probably most obvious feature that could be added is some higher level of security between PHP and Flash. You could also add a moderation panel or as a bonus a basic moderation script has been provided in the bonus content available for this book.

At this point, you should have a pretty good understanding of how to build a complete application using Flash, PHP, and MySQL. In the next section, you use Flash and PHP to build a complete photo gallery with categories and navigation controls.

Using PHP to Develop a Photo Gallery

What is better than a Flash gallery? How about a dynamic Flash gallery where PHP feeds auto-updating XML files? This section is a step-by-step guide on how to develop just that. The development will begin with the ActionScript and then move into the PHP side. The last step will be to evaluate the finished application and explain ways to advance it.

As you learned at the beginning of this chapter, every good application is designed and evaluated before any programming begins. Take a moment to look at the finished application, which is available in the source material for this book. Figure 11.4 shows the completed application.

FIGURE 11.4

The completed Flash/PHP photo gallery showing loaded content

The ActionScript for the completed application will automatically populate a category list. Dynamically load in the images and allow previous and next navigation through each category of images.

Developing the ActionScript

Now that you know what the application will do, you can start to place the variables.

```
var phpPath:String = "http://localhost/ch10/photoGallery/";
var phpFile:String = phpPath + "gallery.php";

var images:Array = new Array();

var imageHolder:MovieClip;
var categoryHolder:MovieClip;
```

The first two variables are referencing the PHP file that generates the category and image data. The images variable is used to store the image data sent back from the PHP, which is used for loading the images. The last two variables in this section are holder `MovieClips` for the main image and navigation. Both of these variables are populated at runtime once the image and category data are loaded.

The next set of variables needed is specifically for navigating around the images and categories.

```
var currentID:uint;
var currentImage:Number = 0;
var imageDir:String = "photos/";
var cacheBuster:String = "?cb=1";
```

The `currentID` is used to remember which image is being viewed. This will be used in the previous and next navigation functions. The `imageDir` is a reference to the image directory, which is where the category directories are located. The last variable is a cache buster, which as explained at the beginning of this chapter is used to ensure the loading of data is always fresh and never cached.

Now that you have completed the process of setting all the necessary variables, you can move on to the core of the application, which is functions.

The `init()` function is responsible for creating the two holder `MovieClips`. The `MovieClips` are dynamically created, positioned, and attached to the display list. This is done by making a call to `addChild` and passing along the `movieclip` reference. The `init` function is also where the cache buster is generated. The last step of the `init` function is to make a call to the `loadCategories()` function. It is important that this function is only called at startup because the objects and categories would be undefined or duplicated.

```
function init()
{
   imageHolder = new MovieClip();
   imageHolder.x = 212;
```

261

Part IV   **Developing Applications**

```
    imageHolder.y = 49;
    addChild(imageHolder);

    categoryHolder = new MovieClip();
    categoryHolder.x = 15;
    categoryHolder.y = 50;
    addChild(categoryHolder);

    cacheBuster = getCacheBuster();

    loadCategories();
}
```

Once the initialization `init` phase has been completed the `loadCategories()` function is called. This function calls the PHP file to load in the category list using `URLRequest` and passing along a custom action that tells the script you want the category list. This is important because the `gallery.php` handles both the categories and photo selection. Overall, the `loadCategories` function is pretty similar to other loaders used throughout this book.

```
function loadCategories():void
{
  var action:String = "action=cat";
  var urlRequest:URLRequest = new URLRequest(phpFile +
   getCacheBuster() + "&" + action);

  var urlLoader:URLLoader = new URLLoader();
  urlLoader.addEventListener(Event.COMPLETE, drawCategories);
  urlLoader.load(urlRequest);
}
```

The `drawCategories` function is called once the category list has been sent back from the PHP. The data is loaded into an XML object and parsed using a `for..each` loop. To better understand the loop, look at a sample XML result passed back from the PHP. One of these XML nodes is created for each category in the gallery.

```
<category id="2" name="Landscapes" copyright="Other"/>
```

The category text that is displayed on the stage is a dynamic `TextField` created within the `for..each` loop. You could also attach a movie clip from the library, but doing so results in a more fragmented application and you lose some formatting options.

```
function drawCategories(e:Event):void
{
  ...
  for each(var item in xml..category)
  {
    ...
  }
}
```

Before you continue with the application-specific code look at what exactly is being done to create the `TextField`.

```
var txt:TextField = new TextField();
txt.selectable = false;
txt.width = 200;
txt.text = "Sample Text";
```

The first line is creating a new `TextField` instance and setting a reference to the `txt` variable. The next line is making sure the text can't be selected with the mouse.

> **NOTE** Don't always set the selectable property to `false`. Users often like to copy content, especially blocks of text.

The second-to-last line of code is responsible for setting the width of the `TextField` to 200 pixels to accommodate the text. Then the last line is simply applying the text that will be visible in the textbox.

Once the text field is created, you attach an event listener to load a category of images when the text is clicked.

Anonymous functions

An anonymous function is attached directly to the `addEventListener` call. An anonymous function cannot be called by name because it doesn't have one; it is used as an alternative to a regular function when the task is simple and doesn't require a lot of code. Realistically anonymous functions are used to make code more compact or if you need to access a variable that is scoped locally to the calling method.

Here is an example of an anonymous function similar to the one located within the `drawCategories` function.

```
txtContainer.addEventListener(MouseEvent.CLICK,function(e:Event):
   void
{
   trace("Anonymous function here, I don't have a name.");
});
```

You may notice one potential reason to avoid anonymous functions (aside from not being multi-functional) is they make code a lot harder to read at a glance. This is mostly due to the fact the function definition is buried within the `addEventListener`. Also, an anonymous function cannot be removed, which can cause a potential for memory leaks.

The `drawCategories` function's last task is to attach the text field to the stage using `addChild`, as done for the category.

```
txtContainer.addChild(txt);
categoryHolder.addChild(txtContainer);
```

Part IV Developing Applications

Here is the complete `drawCategories` function for reference.

```
function drawCategories(e:Event):void
{
  var loader:URLLoader = URLLoader(e.target);
  var xml:XML = new XML(loader.data);

  for each(var item in xml..category)
  {
    var txtContainer:MovieClip = new MovieClip();
    var txt:TextField = new TextField();
    txt.selectable = false;
    txt.width = 200;
    txt.text = item.attribute('name');
    txt.y = uint(item.attribute('id') + 4) * 2;
    txt.name = "text_" + item.attribute('id');
    txtContainer.addEventListener(MouseEvent.CLICK,
    function(e:Event):void
    {
      loadImages(e.target.name.substring(5));
    });
    txtContainer.addChild(txt);
    categoryHolder.addChild(txtContainer);
  }
}
```

The next function to focus on is `loadImages`. This is the function that loads the image data from the PHP. The result passed back is nearly identical to the one found in the category function. The action variable is set to photos, and we also add an `id` letting PHP know what photos to load.

```
function loadImages(id:uint):void
{
  var action:String = "action=photos&id=" + id;
  var urlRequest:URLRequest = new URLRequest(phpFile +
   getCacheBuster() + "&" + action);
  var urlLoader:URLLoader = new URLLoader();
  urlLoader.addEventListener(Event.COMPLETE, imagesLoaded);
  urlLoader.load(urlRequest);
  currentID = id;
}
```

A response is sent back when the PHP is loaded, and the `imagesLoaded` function is called. The image data is passed back in XML format and handled with a `for..each` loop.

This loop processes each photo node in the XML data and builds an object, which is added "pushed" to the images array.

```
function imagesLoaded(e:Event):void
{
```

Developing Basic Applications 11

```
    for each(var item in xml..photo)
    {
      images.push({name:'', src:item.attribute('src')});
    }
    ...
}
```

Here is the object by itself and an alternative, more readable method of creating the object.

```
{ name:'', src:item.attribute('src') }
```

Here is the alternative method to define the object.

```
var obj:Object = new Object();
obj.name = '';
obj.src = item.attribute('src');
```

The last task of the `imagesLoaded` function is to set the `currentImage` variable and make a call to the `displayImage` function passing the image source. The image source is loaded from the images array using `currentImage` as the array index.

```
function imagesLoaded(e:Event):void
{
  ...
  currentImage = 0;
  displayImage(images[currentImage].src);
}
```

Here is the complete `imagesLoaded` function:

```
function imagesLoaded(e:Event):void
{
  var loader:URLLoader = URLLoader(e.target);
  var xml:XML = new XML(loader.data);
  images = new Array();
  for each(var item in xml..photo)
  {
    images.push({name:'', src:item.attribute('src')});
  }
  currentImage = 0;
  displayImage(images[currentImage].src);
}
```

With the categories and images loaded, you can display the image. This is done by assigning a `URLRequest` built of the image directory, current category `id`, and the photo's name. The loader class is placed directly into an `addChild` call, which handles the displaying of the image once it is fully loaded. You won't notice any loading time locally, but you might online.

265

Part IV | **Developing Applications**

> **NOTE** It is good practice to place preloaders wherever data is being loaded. This informs the user that something is happening.

```
function displayImage(src:String):void
{
  var loader:Loader = new Loader();
  loader.load(new URLRequest(imageDir + currentID + "/" + src));
  imageHolder.addChild(loader);
}
```

Photo gallery navigation

The navigation portion of the photo gallery is built using two `movieclips` on the Stage. Each of the clips is assigned to an event handler that either loads the next or previous image.

Image navigation

You will notice the `nextImage()` function has some conditional logic. This is checking to see if the `currentImage` variable is a higher number than the total images, which would result in a loading error. The same basic process is done for the `prevImage()` function with the exception that the conditional check is ensuring the value is not less than zero.

> **NOTE** The next and previous image functions will crash if a category has not been chosen.

```
function nextImage(e:MouseEvent):void
{
  currentImage++;
  if(currentImage > images.length-1)
  {
    currentImage = 0;
  }
  displayImage(images[currentImage].src);
}

function prevImage(e:MouseEvent):void
{
  currentImage--;
  if(currentImage <= 0)
  {
    currentImage = images.length-1;
  }
  displayImage(images[currentImage].src);
}
```

The last function in the photo gallery script is used to generate your cache buster, which is used to ensure the calls to the server are never cached. This function is identical to the one used in the Flash chat application you built earlier in this chapter.

Developing Basic Applications 11

The last part of the application is to call `init()` at the start of the application and assign the event handlers used by the navigation buttons.

```
function getCacheBuster():String
{
  var date:Date = new Date();
  cacheBuster = "?cb=" + date.getTime();
  return cacheBuster;
}

init();

prevMC.addEventListener(MouseEvent.CLICK, prevImage);
nextMC.addEventListener(MouseEvent.CLICK, nextImage);
```

Here is the completed ActionScript for the photo gallery application:

```
var phpPath:String = "http://localhost/ch%2010/photoGallery/";
var phpFile:String = phpPath + "gallery.php";

var images:Array = new Array();

var imageHolder:MovieClip;
var categoryHolder:MovieClip;

var currentID:uint;
var imageDir:String = "photos/";

var currentImage:uint = 0;

var cacheBuster:String = "?cb=1";

function init()
{
  imageHolder = new MovieClip();
  imageHolder.x = 212;
  imageHolder.y = 49;
  addChild(imageHolder);

  categoryHolder = new MovieClip();
  categoryHolder.x = 15;
  categoryHolder.y = 50;
  addChild(categoryHolder);

  cacheBuster = getCacheBuster();

  loadCategories();
}

function loadCategories():void
```

267

```
{
  var action:String = "action=cat";
  var urlRequest:URLRequest = new URLRequest(phpFile +
   getCacheBuster() + "&" + action);

  var urlLoader:URLLoader = new URLLoader();
  urlLoader.addEventListener(Event.COMPLETE, drawCategories);
  urlLoader.load(urlRequest);
}

function drawCategories(e:Event):void
{
  var loader:URLLoader = URLLoader(e.target);
  var xml:XML = new XML(loader.data);

  for each(var item in xml..category)
  {
    var txtContainer:MovieClip = new MovieClip();

    var txt:TextField = new TextField();
    txt.selectable = false;
    txt.width = 200;
    txt.text = item.attribute('name');
    txt.y = uint(item.attribute('id') + 4) * 2;
    txt.name = "text_" + item.attribute('id');
    txtContainer.addEventListener(MouseEvent.CLICK,
    function(e:Event):void
    {
      loadImages(e.target.name.substring(5));
    });

    txtContainer.buttonMode = true;

    txtContainer.addChild(txt);
    categoryHolder.addChild(txtContainer);

  }
}

function loadImages(id:uint):void
{
  trace("Load Images: " + id);
  var action:String = "action=photos&id=" + id;
  var urlRequest:URLRequest = new URLRequest(phpFile +
   getCacheBuster() + "&" + action);

  var urlLoader:URLLoader = new URLLoader();
  urlLoader.addEventListener(Event.COMPLETE, imagesLoaded);
  urlLoader.load(urlRequest);
```

Developing Basic Applications 11

```
  currentID = id;
}

function imagesLoaded(e:Event):void
{
  var loader:URLLoader = URLLoader(e.target);
  var xml:XML = new XML(loader.data);
  images = new Array();

  for each(var item in xml..photo)
  {
    images.push({name:'', src:item.attribute('src')});
  }

  currentImage = 0;
  displayImage(images[currentImage].src);
}

function displayImage(src:String):void
{
  trace("Load Image: " + src);

  var loader:Loader = new Loader();
  loader.load(new URLRequest(imageDir + currentID + "/" + src));
  imageHolder.addChild(loader);
}

function nextImage(e:MouseEvent):void
{
  currentImage++;
  if(currentImage > images.length-1)
  {
    currentImage = 0;
  }
  displayImage(images[currentImage].src);
}

function prevImage(e:MouseEvent):void
{
  currentImage--;
  if(currentImage <= 0)
  {
    currentImage = images.length-1;
  }
  displayImage(images[currentImage].src);
}

function getCacheBuster():String
{
```

269

```
        var date:Date = new Date();
        cacheBuster = "?cb=" + date.getTime();
        return cacheBuster;
    }

    init();

    prevMC.addEventListener(MouseEvent.CLICK, prevImage);
    nextMC.addEventListener(MouseEvent.CLICK, nextImage);
```

PHP for the photo gallery

The PHP portion of this photo gallery application is built of three files. The first file is `categories.php`, which is a static representation of categories being sent to ActionScript.

The first part of the code is the category in a multidimensional array format. The category items hold the name, `id`, and copyright information for each category.

```
$categories = array(
  array("Boston", 1, "M. Keefe"),
  array("Landscapes", 2, "Other"),
  array("Las Vegas", 3, "M. Keefe"),
  array("Weddings", 4, "Other"),
);
```

The `getCategories()` function first sets a global reference to the `$categories` variable. The next step is to define a loop that is responsible for building the XML data passed back to ActionScript.

```
function getCategories()
{
  global $categories;

  $xml = "<categories>\n";

  for($i=0; $i < count($categories); $i++)
  {
    $xml .= "  <category id=\"" .
    $categories[$i][1] . "\" name=\"" .
    $categories[$i][0] . "\" copyright=\"" .
    $categories[$i][2] . "\" />\n";
  }

  $xml .= "</categories>";

  return $xml;
}
```

Developing Basic Applications

The loop length is determined by how large the `$categories` array happens to be.

```
count($categories)
```

The body of the loop is nothing more than construction of the XML data, similar to the sample looked at during the ActionScript development portion.

```
$xml .= "  <category id=\"" .
  $categories[$i][1] . "\" name=\"" .
  $categories[$i][0] . "\" copyright=\"" .
  $categories[$i][2] . "\" />\n";
```

The last step of this function is to return the XML data for ActionScript to process.

```
return $xml;
```

Here is the `categories.php` file in its entirety:

```
<?php

$categories = array(
  array("Boston", 1, "M. Keefe"),
  array("Landscapes", 2, "Other"),
  array("Las Vegas", 3, "M. Keefe"),
  array("Weddings", 4, "Other"),
);

function getCategories()
{
  global $categories;

  $xml = "<categories>\n";

  for($i=0; $i < count($categories); $i++)
  {
    $xml .= "  <category id=\"" .
    $categories[$i][1] . "\" name=\"" .
    $categories[$i][0] . "\" copyright=\"" .
    $categories[$i][2] . "\" />\n";
  }

  $xml .= "</categories>";

  return $xml;
}

?>
```

Part IV Developing Applications

The next file to develop is `getPhotos.php`, which opens the photo directory and returns the XML file populated with source information for each of the photos.

The meat of this file is the `getPhotosFromID()` function, which accepts one argument, an `id`. You want to make sure a valid ID is passed before continuing so a simple conditional statement will work in this case. If a valid ID has been found, then you can continue with the opening of the directory and the `while` loop.

```php
<?php

$photo_dir = "photos/";

function getPhotosFromID($id=null)
{
  global $photo_dir;

  if($id == null)
  {
    print "ID Not Provided";
    return false;
  }

  $xml = "<photos id=\"" . $id . "\">";

  $dir = opendir($photo_dir . $id);
  while(false !== ($file = readdir($dir)))
  {
    if($file != "." && $file != "..")
    {
      $xml .= "<photo name=\"" . "" . "\" src=\"" . $file . "\" />\n";
    }
  }
  closedir($dir);

  $xml .= "</photos>";

  return $xml;
}

?>
```

The `while` loop is set up to loop through each file in the directory until the file pointer is `false`, which means no valid file was found.

```php
while(false !== ($file = readdir($dir)))
{
  ...
}
```

Developing Basic Applications 11

You use a conditional `if` statement to exclude .and .. which is directory pointers for current directory and parent directory. If you exclude this check there will be at least two bogus entries in the XML file; or worse, the file can error out all together because it could put the `while` loop into an infinite recursive state.

After all of the images in the directory are gathered, you will want to close the directory to free up valuable resources. This is especially important if the file could be used by someone else at the same time.

```
closedir($dir);
```

The last step in this file is to return the XML for Flash to process.

After have created the category and photo files, you can create the `gallery.php` file, which handles the calls from PHP and returns the proper XML based on what is requested.

```php
<?php

include 'categories.php';
include 'getPhotos.php';

header('Content-type: text/xml');

if($_GET['action'] == 'cat')
{
  print getCategories();
}
else if($_GET['action'] == 'photos')
{
  print getPhotosFromID($_GET['id']);
}

?>
```

This file starts by including the two previous files you created. Then a `header()` call is made to force the output of all content as proper XML. This `header` function can be used for pretty much any content type. You basically set it, and from that point the output follows that format. For example, assume you want to export content as a PNG.

```
header("Content-type: image/png");
```

NOTE Make sure you use the correct content type in your application. Using the wrong one can cause errors and in rare cases cause an application to crash.

The final block of code is used to determine which content you are requesting. The two types of content available in this example are category and photo list. The `$_GET['action']` variable is passed from Flash on the `url` as a query string.

```
http://localhost/photoGallery/gallery.php?cb=1192408716823&action
  =cat
```

273

Part IV — Developing Applications

At this point, the Flash gallery driven by PHP is complete. You can extend this example to add subcategories, transitions, or maybe some titles and descriptions for each image.

That's the cool thing about ActionScript: you can extend from the book's examples or just use them as they ship.

Using PHP to Develop an RSS Reader

RSS readers are a very popular item, and applications can be found for nearly every device that is Web enabled. They can be found on everything from a browser on your desk to the phone in your pocket.

RSS is a group of Web feeds used to publish frequently updated content such as entries, news headlines, podcasts, or entertainment. Another way to think of RSS is someone delivering the daily news directly to you; the only difference is there is no limit to the amount of feeds you can subscribe to.

Following is a look at the RSS application you will develop and how it will function, as shown in Figure 11.5.

FIGURE 11.5

The RSS reader with a PHP delivery system

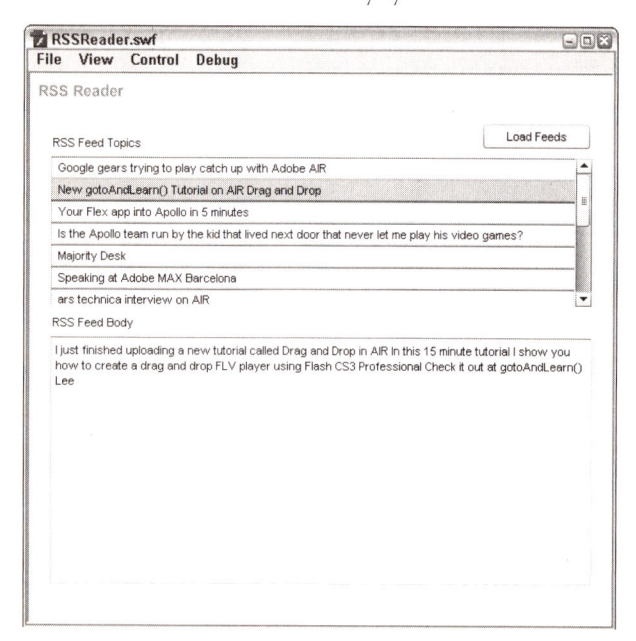

Developing Basic Applications 11

The application is constructed of prebuilt components that have already been placed in the starting file. The three main elements you are interested in are the `List`, `TextArea`, and `Submit` components. Each of these components has been assigned an instance name that is referenced in the ActionScript.

Importing classes

Most of the classes that ship with Flash do not require you to import them. However, there are some exceptions, one of which is the `ListEvent` class.

```
import fl.events.ListEvent;
```

When the event is imported you can assign the variables for your RSS application. The only global variable needed for this application is the php reference.

```
var phpPath:String = "http://locahost/ch10/rssReader/";
var phpFile:String = phpPath + "rss.php";
```

Loading the PHP

The function used to load the PHP, which returns XML is very similar to previous examples. Set up a `URLRequest`, a `URLLoader`, and attach a handler to the `COMPLETE` event.

```
function loadFeeds():void
{
   var urlRequest:URLRequest = new URLRequest(phpFile);
   var urlLoader:URLLoader = new URLLoader();
   urlLoader.addEventListener(Event.COMPLETE, feedHandler);
   urlLoader.load(urlRequest);
}
```

The `feedHandler()` function is responsible for working with the response from the PHP call. In this application, the PHP sends back XML, which is used to populate the `List` component. The RSS entries are placed into the `List` component using the `addItem()` function.

This `feedHandler` function accepts an object as an argument. The object needs at least a `label` property in order to add the item, but you would generally add the `data` property as well.

```
function feedHandler(e:Event):void
{
   ...
   for each(var item in xml..entry)
   {
     topicsList.addItem({label:item..name, data:item..desc});

     topicsList.addEventListener(ListEvent.ITEM_CLICK,
      listClickhandler);
   }
}
```

275

Part IV Developing Applications

The list items load the body text when clicked, so create the function that handles this event. The `ListEvent` is passed from the `ITEM_CLICK` event, which contains the `item` property. The `item` property is where the `data` property is stored. In this example, that data is the RSS body, so you can simply pass that data directly to the `feedBody` TextArea.

```
function listClickhandler(e:ListEvent):void
{
    feedBody.htmlText = e.item.data;
}
```

The last function in the RSS application is the button handler, which is called any time the `Button` component is clicked. This function simply makes a call to the `loadFeeds` function.

```
function submitHandler(e:Event):void
{
    loadFeeds();
}
```

As you can see, the ActionScript is fairly simple for this example. XML really speeds up development of Web-enabled applications, and this is a perfect example of it.

Here is the RSS application code in its entirety for reference:

```
import fl.events.ListEvent;

var phpPath:String = "http://localhost/ch10/rssReader/";
var phpFile:String = phpPath + "rss.php";

function loadFeeds():void
{
  var urlRequest:URLRequest = new URLRequest(phpFile);
  var urlLoader:URLLoader = new URLLoader();
  urlLoader.addEventListener(Event.COMPLETE, feedHandler);
  urlLoader.load(urlRequest);
}

function feedHandler(e:Event):void
{
  var loader:URLLoader = URLLoader(e.target);
  var xml:XML = new XML(loader.data);

  for each(var item in xml..entry)
  {
    topicsList.addItem({label:item..name, data:item..desc});
    topicsList.addEventListener(ListEvent.ITEM_CLICK,
     listClickhandler);
  }
}

function listClickhandler(e:ListEvent):void
```

Developing Basic Applications 11

```
{
    feedBody.htmlText = e.item.data;
}

function submitHandler(e:Event):void
{
    loadFeeds();
}

loadBtn.addEventListener(MouseEvent.CLICK, submitHandler);
```

With the ActionScript portion of the RSS reader finished you can focus on the PHP code.

The RSS feed that is being used for this example, as shown in Figure 11.6, comes from Adobe and is the latest news and information on Adobe AIR.

```
<?php
$rssFeed = "http://weblogs.macromedia.com/mxna/xml/rss.cfm?" .
    "query=bySmartCategory&languages=1&smartCategoryId=28&" .
    "smartCategoryKey=F2DFD9E0-FBB6-4C2D-2AFE6AFD941FDDB1";
?>
```

FIGURE 11.6

How the RSS feed looks in your Web browser, assuming you don't have a reader installed

277

Part IV Developing Applications

The `$feed` variable is a placeholder for the generated XML that is constructed once the RSS feed is successfully loaded. The RSS feed is read in using the `simplexml` library that is shipped with PHP 5. This isn't the only XML parsing library available for PHP, but it is the most efficient and easiest to use.

```
$feed = "";
$xml = simplexml_load_file($rssFeed);
```

At this point, you can begin building the `foreach` loop, which is responsible for constructing the XML document passed back to the ActionScript.

```
$feed .= "<items>\n";

foreach($xml->item as $item)
{
  $desc = $item->description;

  $desc = preg_replace('/[...\[\]]/', '', $desc);

  $feed .= "  <entry>\n";
  $feed .= "    <name>" . $item->title . "</name>\n";
  $feed .= "    <desc><![CDATA[" . $desc ."]]></desc>\n";
  $feed .= "  </entry>\n";
}

$feed .= "</items>\n";
```

The loop takes each element of the XML and loops through the `item` nodes.

You will notice the description is assigned to a `$desc` variable. The reason for this is because the description needs to be cleaned before it is returned. The cleaning process is accomplished using `preg_replace()`, a regular expression function that removes unescaped and improper characters.

```
$desc = preg_replace('/[...\[\]]/', '', $desc);
```

NOTE This book does not provide an in-depth walkthrough on regular expressions (`regex`); however, there is a very good guide found at `http://php.net/manual/en/reference.pcre.pattern.syntax.php`.

The last portion of the PHP code sets the header type and outputs the XML to ActionScript.

```
header('Content-type: text/xml');
print '<?xml version="1.0" encoding="UTF-8"?>' ."\n";
print $feed;
```

You will notice the PHP required to build the RSS application is not in depth; a lot of that is due to `simplexml` being such a great library. This example could be extended to pull in more of the information contained within the RSS feed. For example, you could display the title of the entry, the date, and even the URL where the original entry is located.

Developing Basic Applications   11

Finally, here is the completed PHP for reference:

```php
<?php

$rssFeed = "http://weblogs.macromedia.com/mxna/xml/rss.cfm?" .
  "query=bySmartCategory&languages=1&smartCategoryId=28&" .
  "smartCategoryKey=F2DFD9E0-FBB6-4C2D-2AFE6AFD941FDDB1";

$feed = "";
$xml = simplexml_load_file($rssFeed);

$feed .= "<items>\n";

foreach($xml->item as $item)
{
  $desc = $item->description;

  $desc = preg_replace('/[...\[\]]/', '', $desc);

  $feed .= "  <entry>\n";
  $feed .= "    <name>" . $item->title . "</name>\n";
  $feed .= "    <desc><![CDATA[" . $desc ."]]></desc>\n";
  $feed .= "  </entry>\n";
}

$feed .= "</items>\n";

header('Content-type: text/xml');
print '<?xml version="1.0" encoding="UTF-8"?>' ."\n";
print $feed;

?>
```

Using PHP, Flash, and MySQL to Develop a Dynamic Banner Ad

A lot of designers use Flash to create ads to be placed online. These range from mini ads within a page to full-blown ads that are the page. The most common ad format is the banner ad, which is usually 468 × 60, as shown in Figure 11.7, pixels in size. These banners are usually scripted to load a Web site when clicked. What about tracking those clicks? Even better, why not create a dynamic banner that loads a random ad and doesn't require the owner to update anything more than an XML file and image directory?

This section will be the process of developing a dynamic banner ad in Flash. You then add tracking to this banner using only a few lines of PHP. This example doesn't require any starting files because any image will work for the banner, and the application is going to be developed 100 percent in ActionScript code.

279

Part IV: Developing Applications

FIGURE 11.7

Example of the banner ad application in action

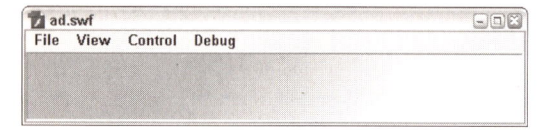

![ad.swf window screenshot]

The first part of the code is responsible for initializing the variables used in the application.

```
var phpPath:String = "http://localhost/ch10/bannerAd/";
var phpFile:String = phpPath + "ads.php";

var imageHolder:MovieClip;
var cacheBuster:String = "?cb=1";
var adURL:String;
```

Once the variables are defined you can build the functions. The first one is responsible for attaching the image holder, adding the event handler, and calling the `loadImage` function.

```
imageHolder = new MovieClip();
imageHolder.x = 0;
imageHolder.y = 0;
imageHolder.addEventListener(MouseEvent.CLICK, loadAdURL);
imageHolder.buttonMode = true;
addChild(imageHolder);

cacheBuster = getCacheBuster();

loadImage();
```

The `loadImage()` function is responsible for loading the XML file that holds the banner ad data. Then assign a handler function that is called after the XML is completely loaded.

```
function loadImage():void
{
  var urlRequest:URLRequest = new URLRequest(phpFile +
   getCacheBuster());
  var urlLoader:URLLoader = new URLLoader();
  urlLoader.addEventListener(Event.COMPLETE, imageLoaded);
  urlLoader.load(urlRequest);
}
```

After the XML is fully loaded, a call to `imageLoaded` is made. This function is responsible for loading the XML data, pulling out the image information, and loading the image. Following is a look at each part, one at a time.

Developing Basic Applications 11

The following is the process of loading the data and creating the XML object:

```
function imageLoaded(e:Event):void
{
  var urlLoader:URLLoader = URLLoader(e.target);
  var xml:XML = new XML(urlLoader.data);
  ...
```

The next part of this function is to pull in the image data and assign it to local variables:

```
var url:String = xml..banner.attribute('url');
var name:String = xml..banner.attribute('name');
var image:String = xml..banner.attribute('src');
var directory:String = xml..banner.attribute('dir');

adURL = url;
```

The last step in this function is to load the image and attach it to the display list:

```
var loader:Loader = new Loader();
loader.load(new URLRequest(directory + image));
imageHolder.addChild(loader);
```

Opening a browser window

The process of loading and displaying the ad is now complete. The next step is to assign the event handler that is called when the banner is clicked. Use `navigateToURL()` to open a new browser window and navigate to the predetermined ad page.

```
function loadAdURL(e:MouseEvent):void
{
  navigateToURL(new URLRequest(adURL));
}
```

The last task of the ActionScript is to call the `init()` function and start the process.

```
init();
```

Here is the completed ActionScript code for reference:

```
var phpPath:String = "http://localhost/ch10/bannerAd/";
var phpFile:String = phpPath + "ads.php";

var imageHolder:MovieClip;
var cacheBuster:String = "?cb=1";
var adURL:String;

function init()
```

281

```
{
  imageHolder = new MovieClip();
  imageHolder.x = 0;
  imageHolder.y = 0;
  imageHolder.addEventListener(MouseEvent.CLICK, loadAdURL);
  imageHolder.buttonMode = true;
  addChild(imageHolder);

  cacheBuster = getCacheBuster();

  loadImage();
}
function loadImage():void
{
  var urlRequest:URLRequest = new URLRequest(phpFile +
   getCacheBuster());
  var urlLoader:URLLoader = new URLLoader();
  urlLoader.addEventListener(Event.COMPLETE, imageLoaded);
  urlLoader.load(urlRequest);
}

function imageLoaded(e:Event):void
{
  var urlLoader:URLLoader = URLLoader(e.target);
  var xml:XML = new XML(urlLoader.data);

  var url:String = xml..banner.attribute('url');
  var name:String = xml..banner.attribute('name');
  var image:String = xml..banner.attribute('src');
  var directory:String = xml..banner.attribute('dir');

  adURL = url;

  var loader:Loader = new Loader();
  loader.load(new URLRequest(directory + image));
  imageHolder.addChild(loader);
}

function loadAdURL(e:MouseEvent):void
{
  navigateToURL(new URLRequest(adURL));
}

function getCacheBuster():String
{
  var date:Date = new Date();
  cacheBuster = "?cb=" + date.getTime();
  return cacheBuster;
}

init();
```

Developing the PHP

At this point the ActionScript code is complete and you can focus on the PHP. The `ads.php` file is made up of two global variables and a function.

The first global variable is the directory where the ad images are located. The second variable is the array containing the ad data.

```
$adImageDir = "./adImages/";
$bannerAds = array(
  array('Banner Name', 'randomimage1.jpg', 'http://localhost/'),
  array('Banner Name', 'randomimage2.jpg', 'http://localhost/'),
);
```

The `getBannerAd` function assigns the two variables as globals so they are accessible within this function.

Random selection

The single banner ad is chosen from the array by using a random key. This random key is generated using the `mt_rand()` function and the length of the `$bannerAds` array.

```
$random  = (mt_rand() % count($bannerAds));
```

The XML file is built by outputting a single line of image data that ActionScript will process.

```
function getBannerAd()
{
  ...

  $xml .= "  <banner id=\"" . 0 .
    "\" dir=\"" . $adImageDir .
    "\" url=\"" . $bannerAds[$random][2] .
    "\" name=\"" . $bannerAds[$random][0] .
    "\" src=\"" . $bannerAds[$random][1] . "\" />\n";

  $xml .= "</banners>";

  return $xml;
}

print getBannerAd();
```

The PHP responsible for loading the banner ad is now complete. As you can see, the amount of code needed to create this application is fairly small. This basic example can easily be extended to add in categories or even multiple images that transition as the movie sits on a browser.

Here is the completed code for reference.

```php
<?php

$adImageDir = "./adImages/";

$bannerAds = array(
  array('Banner 1', 'randomimage1.jpg', 'http://localhost/'),
  array('Banner 2', 'randomimage2.jpg', 'http://localhost/'),
  array('Banner 3', 'randomimage3.jpg', 'http://localhost/'),
  array('Banner 4', 'randomimage4.jpg', 'http://localhost/'),
  array('Banner 5', 'randomimage5.jpg', 'http://localhost/'),
  array('Banner 6', 'randomimage6.jpg', 'http://localhost/'),
  array('Banner 7', 'randomimage7.jpg', 'http://localhost/'),
  array('Banner 8, 'randomimage8.jpg', 'http://localhost/')
);

function getBannerAd()
{
  global $bannerAds, $adImageDir;

  $xml = "<banners>\n";

  $random  = (mt_rand() % count($bannerAds));

  $xml .= "  <banner id=\"" . 0 .
    "\" dir=\"" . $adImageDir .
    "\" url=\"" . $bannerAds[$random][2] .
    "\" name=\"" . $bannerAds[$random][0] .
    "\" src=\"" . $bannerAds[$random][1] . "\" />\n";

  $xml .= "</banners>";

  return $xml;
}

print getBannerAd();

?>
```

You have now successfully created a fully functional PHP and Flash banner ad viewer. The concepts learned in this section can easily be adapted to other projects. In fact, you are encouraged to expand upon the example and create a more robust application.

This application can also be simplified by loading a static XML file; however, this is more difficult to update and doesn't offer the same level of customization. The application as PHP means you can attach a MySQL database layer to it and return the image data from a database, which would most likely be updated from another source.

Using PHP to Develop a Hit Counter

A hit counter is used to determine how many visitors are going to a site. Generally, the hit counter is visible to visitors in the form of text or a graphic. Some sites use other forms of monitoring that are not publicly available, for stats tracking purposes. The major draw and feature of a hit counter is some graphical representation.

You can either use a flat file text or SQL database to store the data for the hit counter. This example uses an SQL database for a couple of reasons: speed (the database can process information much faster) and file permission concerns. In rare cases a server can place a lock on a file, which means that file cannot be opened. This would force the hit counter to fail and is not the ideal result you would be looking for.

Hit counter logic

The logic behind the hit counter is fairly simple. You first make a call to the database to capture the current hit count and increment it by 1.

```
$oldCount = $row['amount'];
$newCount = $oldCount + 1;
```

When you have the new value, send it back into the SQL table. Do this by updating the existing row and setting the amount column to the value of $newCount variable.

```
mysql_query("UPDATE counter SET amount=" . $newCount);
```

The last step in the PHP code is to return the new value to Flash for it to display.

```
return "resp=" . $newCount;
```

That is all the PHP needs for the hit counter logic. Following is the completed file.

```
<?php

include 'dbConn.php';

$query = "SELECT amount from counter";
$result = mysql_query($query);
$row = mysql_fetch_array($result);
$oldCount = $row['amount'];
$newCount = $oldCount + 1;

mysql_query("UPDATE counter SET amount=" . $newCount);

return "resp=" . $newCount;

?>
```

Developing the Flash hit counter

With the PHP done, you can move onto the Flash development, which consists of an all ActionScript application.

The hit counter needs to first call the PHP file, which serves two purposes. The first is calling the PHP file to load and increment the count. The second purpose is to return the new value, which is passed in to a dynamic text field.

The first part is to assign the `phpFile` variable, which is a reference to the hit counter file located on the server.

```
var phpFile:String = " http://localhost/ch10/hitCounter/";
```

The first function to build is the `loadHitCounter()`, which is responsible for calling the server and assigning the response handler.

```
function loadHitCounter():void
{
  var urlRequest:URLRequest = new URLRequest(phpFile);
  var urlLoader:URLLoader = new URLLoader();
  urlLoader.addEventListener(Event.COMPLETE, handleServerResp);
  urlLoader.load(urlRequest);
}
```

After the response is loaded, the `handleServerResp()` is called passing along the loaded data. This data is then sent to the `URLVariables` class to pull out the `resp` property. This property is where the current count is located.

```
function handleServerResp(e:Event):void
{
  var loader:URLLoader = URLLoader(e.target);
  var variables:URLVariables = new URLVariables(loader.data);
  var count:uint = variables.resp;
  ...
}
```

The count is finally placed in the dynamic text field, which is not formatted in this example, but you can easily add this on your own.

```
    var txt:TextField = new TextField();
    txt.selectable = false;
    txt.width = 200;
    txt.text = count + " visitors";
}
```

The absolute last line of code in the ActionScript is the call to the `loadHitCounter` function, which kicks it all off.

```
    loadHitCounter();
```

Summary

In this chapter you learned the elements of developing and designing an application. Then once you understood how the application should be constructed you built a chat client using PHP and Flash.

In the next section you learned how to develop a Flash-based photo gallery with dynamic category and image support using XML.

The last section was devoted to developing other applications using Flash, PHP, and MySQL to better understand the concepts.

You should now have a good idea how to build robust applications that take advantage of dynamic data for updating and functionality.

Chapter 12

Developing Real-World Applications

In this chapter, you learn about developing complete applications from the ground up. The focus is on class-based designs that you can easily update later on. The main aspect of this chapter will be how to use Flash and PHP to develop these applications.

This chapter is broken up into four applications: a PayPal cart, custom shopping cart, Amazon searcher, and a flickr photo gallery searcher. Each application section starts with the PHP code and continues with the ActionScript. Building an application like this makes it easier to test as you build and reduces the amount time in the development process.

The examples in this chapter are built using custom classes, which are covered in Chapter 9. If you haven't read that chapter yet, I strongly recommend you do so before continuing on in this chapter. Of course, if you have used classes in the past, then by all means continue on.

IN THIS CHAPTER

Using PayPal in Flash

Developing a shopping cart

Searching Amazon

Developing a photo gallery

Understanding Real-World Applications

A real-world application is one that has been designed, tested, and deployed with the intention that other users will be using it.

Just like in a real application there will be some sections that use a third-party Application Programming Interface (API) to load in and search data. When working with an API it is common to find a list of the methods and calls allowed as shown in Figure 12.1.

FIGURE 12.1

The flickr API list, which displays which methods and properties are publically available

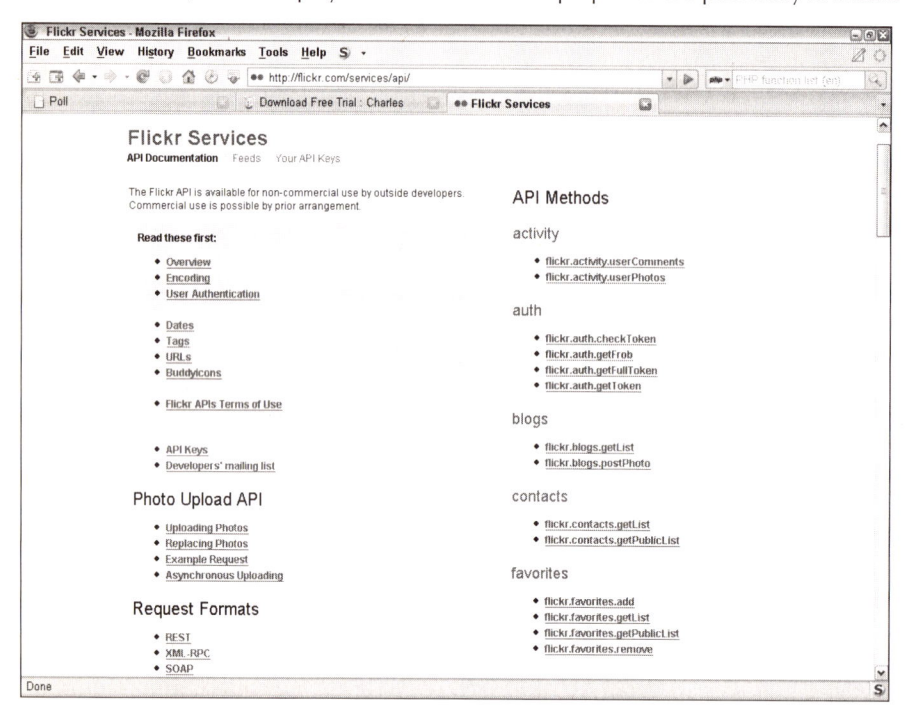

An open API doesn't always mean anyone can gain access. For example, with flickr you are required to pass along a key that authorizes a request. This is not only to lock down certain aspects of an API, but also stops spamming and automated responses that could result in the API being disabled.

The Amazon and flickr examples in this chapter use those APIs, but the first thing to look at are the rules and requirements for the API that you are using.

Using PayPal in Flash

Working with PayPal in Flash is similar to HTML because PayPal offers a common set of connection and access abilities. However, one advantage to developing the solution in Flash is the ability to enhance the user experience as Flash offers more fluid communications with other services because it does not need to reload the entire page or open any additional windows.

Signing up for PayPal Premier

Before you begin to write the code for interfacing with PayPal, create a PayPal Premier account, which you can use to track your sales and authenticate your requests. It only takes a few minutes to set up an account, and it doesn't cost anything.

To set up a PayPal Premier account, follow these steps:

1. In your Web browser, navigate to www.paypal.com. Choose Get Started ⇨ Account Types.
2. On the PayPal Account Types page, click Sign Up Now. The Choose Account Type page appears.
3. Under Premier Account, click Start Now. In the Create a PayPal Account form that appears (see Figure 12.2), type the requested information.
4. After you submit your form, you will received a confirmation e-mail. You must respond to the e-mail to activate your account.
5. Log in and test your new account.

NOTE Remember, you must activate the account via e-mail before you can use it.

FIGURE 12.2

The PayPal account registration screen

Part IV Developing Applications

At this point, you should have a working PayPal login. Using the account you just registered for you can login to PayPal and begin setting up the account specifics.

> **NOTE** The system requires a login and password to generate content. However, in order to submit a data request you only need to provide your e-mail address. This is used to ensure the request is correct. At no time should you place your PayPal password in this form.

Click the Merchant link on the top of the page to visit the Buy Now generator page. The other options on the first screen are not important at this point. Finally, click Create Button, which will move to the next page where the HTML code is for the Buy Now button. Copy the HTML code that is generated by PayPal for the Buy Now buttons.

This code is used to build the Flash example. Following is the sample code copied from PayPal's merchant system generator that you just visited.

```
<form action="https://www.paypal.com/cgi-bin/webscr"
    method="post">
<input type="hidden" name="cmd" value="_xclick">
<input type="hidden" name="business" value="{email_address}">
<input type="hidden" name="item_name" value="{item_name}">
<input type="hidden" name="item_number" value="{item_number}">
<input type="hidden" name="amount" value="{item_amount}">
<input type="hidden" name="currency_code" value="USD">
<input type="hidden" name="weight" value="1">
<input type="hidden" name="weight_unit" value="lbs">
<input type="hidden" name="lc" value="US">
</form>
```

> **NOTE** Ensure that you don't have Button Encryption enabled; doing so makes it impossible to grab the necessary information to build the Flash button.

As you can see, the code generated for the HTML form has all of the necessary variables that will be used to create a Flash button. The next step is to build the Flash code that will make the Buy Now button for the application.

Here is the ActionScript code needed to interface with PayPal, as you can see this code is very similar to the existing HTML code you generated on the PayPal page. The first part to focus on is the `url` variables that are responsible for building the POST data. This POST data is passed along to PayPal when the user clicks Buy Now.

```
// Paypal variables
var pp_cmd:String = "_xclick";
var pp_business:String = "store@example.com";
var pp_item_name:String = "sample product";
var pp_item_number:String = "0001";
var pp_amount:String = "24.99";
var pp_currency:String = "USD";
var pp_weight:String = "1";
var pp_weight_unit:String = "lbs";
var pp_location:String = "US";
```

Developing Real-World Applications

Even though you can clearly see numbers in the block of variables, all of the parameters are set as strings to be compatible with the HTML equivalent. The next piece is to establish the URL, which will be used to interface with PayPal. This is essentially the same variable as `action`, which is found in the original HTML.

```
var paypalURL:String = "https://www.paypal.com/cgi-bin/webscr";
```

When the PayPal variables and data are established, you can create the code that is called when the Buy Now button is clicked.

Here is the function that is used to call PayPal. This method doesn't require the custom variables to be passed in because they are defined outside of the function. Defining a variable outside a function is scoped so any function has access to them. If this variable is defined within the function it would only be visible to the function in which it is defined. The exception is, of course, if the function is global or the variable is returned from the created function.

```
function callPaypal(e:MouseEvent):void
{
  var urlVariables:URLVariables = new URLVariables();
  urlVariables.cmd = pp_cmd;
  urlVariables.business = pp_business;
  urlVariables.item_name = pp_item_name;
  urlVariables.item_number = pp_item_number;
  urlVariables.amount = pp_amount;
  urlVariables.currency_code = pp_currency;
  urlVariables.weight = pp_weight;
  urlVariables.weight_unit = pp_weight_unit;
  urlVariables.lc = pp_location;

  var urlRequest:URLRequest = new URLRequest(paypalURL);
  urlRequest.method = URLRequestMethod.POST;
  urlRequest.data = urlVariables;
  sendToURL(urlRequest);
}
```

Using POST data

The method of the data sent to PayPal is in POST format. This means the variables are included in the call, but not on the URL as seen with GET. Using the POST format holds a few advantages, the first being the URL is clean and can't really be tampered with. The second is the added level of security when passing moderately sensitive data to the server.

If you need to send highly sensitive data, such as billing or credit card information, it is important that you use an HTTPS call. The reason for that is POST really only becomes a Security by Obscurity and isn't the safest result.

Part IV: Developing Applications

This example makes use of the constant `POST` variable that is found in the `URLRequestMethod`. Of course, you can simply use the literal string `POST` because this is what the constant actually has for a variable.

```
urlRequest.method = URLRequestMethod.POST;
```

Using sendToURL

In previous examples, you may have noticed the use of `navigateToURL`, which calls a URL and offers the ability to send `GET` data across the `URL`. This example calls for `POST` data, so the use of `sendToURL` is a better option. It is important to understand that the `sendToURL` method sends the request to the server, but ignores any response that is returned.

```
sendToURL(urlRequest);
```

Setting up PayPal communication

The final step is to assign the button action that is attached to the Buy Now `MovieClip`. Simply place a `MovieClip` on the Stage and give it the instance name `buyNowBtn`. If you choose to have more than one button, I recommend a Class structure that passes the PayPal data to minimize the amount of code needed.

The `callPaypal` function is attached to the button using an event listener. The `CLICK` event is used, which is called when the user clicks the button.

```
buyNowBtn.buttonMode = true;
byNowBtn.useHandCursor = true;
buyNowBtn.addEventListener(MouseEvent.CLICK, callPaypal);
```

The last step is to put all of the code together and test it.

```
// Paypal variables
var pp_cmd:String = "_xclick";
var pp_business:String = "store@example.com";
var pp_item_name:String = "sample product";
var pp_item_number:String = "0001";
var pp_amount:String = "24.99";
var pp_currency:String = "USD";
var pp_weight:String = "1";
var pp_weight_unit:String = "lbs";
var pp_location:String = "US";

var paypalURL:String = "https://www.paypal.com/cgi-bin/webscr";

function callPaypal(e:MouseEvent):void
{
    var urlVariables:URLVariables = new URLVariables();
    urlVariables.cmd = pp_cmd;
```

Developing Real-World Applications 12

```
    urlVariables.business = pp_business;
    urlVariables.item_name = pp_item_name;
    urlVariables.item_number = pp_item_number;
    urlVariables.amount = pp_amount;
    urlVariables.currency_code = pp_currency;
    urlVariables.weight = pp_weight;
    urlVariables.weight_unit = pp_weight_unit;
    urlVariables.lc = pp_location;

    var urlRequest:URLRequest = new URLRequest(paypalURL);
    urlRequest.method = URLRequestMethod.POST;
    urlRequest.data = urlVariables;
    sendToURL(urlRequest);
}

buyNowBtn.buttonMode = true;
byNowBtn.useHandCursor = true;
buyNowBtn.addEventListener(MouseEvent.CLICK, callPaypal);
```

At this point, you have a working example of a Buy Now button for PayPal. It is just a matter of adding the specific item information. You can also create a class to make this creation process easier, as mentioned earlier.

PayPal also offers a shopping cart–based system where you can allow the user to choose multiple items and quantities. This item info is stored in the same basic format POST data, but keeps track of each individual item. Whether you use the cart option or a one-item Buy Now solution you only need to send one request.

This example didn't actually require the use of any PHP. You can easily extend the example by first sending the order information to PHP and storing the purchases for your own order tracking system. PayPal even offers solutions for developers to directly connect to their payment system and get confirmation if an order goes through. This service is beyond the scope of the book, but PayPal provides adequate documentation to get started.

Using Flash and PHP to Build a Cart

The previous section focused on building a Buy Now button in Flash using PayPal as the payment system. That system works pretty well, but it doesn't really offer the developer complete control of the cart, payment, and storage components. Most of the time when you choose to build a custom solution you will end up with better results. This is not to say everyone can develop the next PayPal interface, but how much of that site do you use? Building a custom solution is where you get to focus on the features you will use and exclude the ones you won't.

This shopping cart is broken into four parts: design, MySQL, PHP, and the ActionScript that brings it all together.

295

Part IV Developing Applications

Designing the shopping cart

The shopping cart application will be built using classes for reusability. This also makes it easier to modify later on.

CROSS-REF For more information on ActionScript classes, see Chapter 9.

Developing the StoreItem class

The first portion of code to focus on will be the individual product items that will be displayed to the left of the shopping cart. The store items `MovieClip` will be dynamically added to the Stage and will be assigned to a custom class `StoreItem`.

The class is responsible for assigning the store item variables and displaying the necessary values. Just like the class chapter, these classes are built up of stand-alone packages for simplicity, so there is no need to provide a package structure.

The first part of the code imports the `MovieClip` and `TextField` classes. This custom class extends the `MovieClip` class and the `TextField` needs to be loaded because there are text boxes in the `movieclip`.

```
import flash.display.MovieClip;
import flash.text.TextField;
```

There are five private variables that are used to hold the item specific data. This data is later shared with the shopping cart, but for now the data just needs to be stored.

```
private var albumName:String;
private var albumDesc:String;
private var albumThumb:String;
private var albumPrice:String;
private var storeItemID:uint;
```

The `StoreItem` method is left empty and actually isn't required because the ActionScript compiler will place it automatically, but for completeness it is a good idea to have it.

```
function StoreItem() {}
```

The first custom method is responsible for saving the item data to the private variables that were just defined. The five arguments defined in this function are passed from the caller and will hold the item data that is used later.

```
public function setStoreData(
  id:uint,
  n:String,
  d:String,
  t:String,
  p:String):void
{
```

Developing Real-World Applications   12

```
  storeItemID = id;
  albumName = n;
  albumDesc = d;
  albumThumb = t;
  albumPrice = p;

  ...
}
```

The two text boxes that hold the name and description for each item are the last part of this custom class. The data that was passed in is assigned to each text box. Normally, you would probably check for valid data, but because you are controlling the PHP that is returned you can be sure the data will be valid.

```
nameTxt.text = albumName;
descTxt.text = albumDesc;
```

The final method in this class is used to send the data back to whoever calls it. The return action sends back a custom object that is filled with the item data in the previous method.

```
public function getItem():Object
{
  return
  {
    target:this,
    id:storeItemID,
    name:albumName,
    price:albumPrice
  };
}
```

The above method has a special type of return defined. This return value is an inline Object which is used to simplify code by excluding unnecessary variable names.

Each of the types: `Array`, `Object`, and `String` have a shorthand way to define them. For example, the `Object` type can be defined simply with:

```
var sampleObj:Object = {name:value};
```

Table 12.1 shows the type and the shorthand equivalent for it. Using the shorthand values can save development time because you have to type less.

> **WARNING** The shorthand can create problems because you create a "weakly" typed object. Therefore you cannot benefit from compile time type checking. You may access the dynamic object improperly and you will not know until runtime. This means that you should use caution when creating your properties and variables in shorthand.

Part IV Developing Applications

TABLE 12.1

Types and Shorthand Equivalents

Array	new Array()	[]
Object	new Object()	{}
String	new String()	""

Both application methods that were created are public because they are called from external classes. You could also build an intermediate function that offers a higher level of security, which would be responsible for calling the private methods.

With the `StoreItem` class built, you can move to the `ShoppingCartItem`, which is attached to the shopping cart item `MovieClip`.

Developing the ShoppingCartItem class

This class is basically responsible for holding the item `id`, which will be used in the `ShoppingCart` class. Just like the previous class, this one also needs to import the `MovieClip` and `TextField` classes to accommodate the components located in this `MovieClip`.

```
package
{

  import flash.display.MovieClip;
  import flash.text.TextField;

  public class ShoppingCartItem extends MovieClip
  {
    private var cartItemID:uint;
    function ShoppingCartItem() { }

    public function getID():uint
    {
      return cartItemID;
    }

    public function setID(id:uint):void
    {
      cartItemID = id;
    }
  }

}
```

The last portion of this class is responsible for getting and setting the `cartItemID`. This value is used to link the products with the cart items.

298

Developing Real-World Applications   12

The last custom ActionScript class is the `ShoppingCart`. This class is fairly large, so it will be broken up into pieces to better understand it. The best place to start is to first look at a class skeleton, which shows the methods that are used in this application. I often build this skeleton first, which can double as an outline.

```
package
{
  public class ShoppingCart extends MovieClip
  {
    function ShoppingCart() {}

    public function addProduct(product:Object):void {}
    public function removeProduct(e:MouseEvent):void {}
    public function updateList():void {}
    public function updateTotal():void {}
    public function checkout():void {}
    public function setGatewayURL(url:String):void {}
    private function round2D(n:Number):Number {}
  }
}
```

The most logical place to begin on this class is by assigning the `Class` imports that will be needed.

```
import flash.display.MovieClip;
import flash.text.TextField;
import flash.events.MouseEvent;
import flash.net.*;
```

The properties for this class consist of all private variables so they can't be accessed by other classes.

```
private var cartItemCount:uint = 0;
private var cartContents:Array;

private var cartItemHeight:uint = 20;
private var lineSpacing:uint = 30;
private var gateway:String;
```

The constructor is responsible for setting up the Checkout button and initializing the cart item array.

```
function ShoppingCart()
{
  cartContents = new Array();
  cont = cartContents;
  checkoutBtn.addEventListener(MouseEvent.CLICK, function():void
  {
    var xml:String = "<?xml version='1.0' ?>\n\r";
    xml += "<products total=\"" + totalTxt.text + "\">";
    for(var i in cont)
```

299

```
      {
        xml += "<product>";
        xml += "\t<quantity>" +
          cont[i].cartItem.quantityTxt.text
          + "</quantity>";

        xml += "\t<name>" + cont[i].name + "</name>";
        xml += "\t<price>" + cont[i].price + "</price>";
        xml += "</product>";
      }
      xml += "</products>";

      var variables:URLVariables = new URLVariables();
          variables.action = "checkout";
          variables.xml = xml;

      var urlRequest:URLRequest = new URLRequest(gateway);
      urlRequest.data = variables;
      urlRequest.method = "GET";

      navigateToURL(urlRequest);
    })
  }
```

The contents of the Checkout button may seem overwhelming, but it is simply building a custom XML document that will be passed to the PHP. The `xml` variable starts off by assigning the proper XML heading. Without this heading, PHP would assume the file is incomplete and not load it.

```
var xml:String = "<?xml version='1.0' ?>\n\r";
```

The `for..` loop is responsible for going through the `cartContents` array and pulling out each cart item. Once inside the loop, the `cartItem` is a reference to the custom `ShoppingCartItem` that was created in the previous section. These items hold the quantity and item `id`, which will be placed in this custom XML document.

```
cont = cartContents;
for(var i in cont)
{
  ...
  xml += "\t<name>" + cont[i].name + "</name>";
  ...
}
```

Once the `for..` loop completes the process of building the XML, the PHP file located on the server can be called. The request is a basic `GET`, passing along the XML data.

```
var variables:URLVariables = new URLVariables();
variables.action = "checkout";
variables.xml = xml;

var urlRequest:URLRequest = new URLRequest(gateway);
```

Developing Real-World Applications   12

```
urlRequest.data = variables;
urlRequest.method = "GET";

navigateToURL(urlRequest);
```

The PHP code expects two variables to be passed along. The action in this case is checkout, and the xml data that was generated by the selected shopping cart items in the shopping cart code.

The next step is to build the methods. The first method is responsible for adding a product to the shopping cart. The shopping cart is built up of ShoppingCartItem class instances, but this class is actually a movieclip in the library. The first step is to create a new instance of this movieclip. After creating a new instance, an event listener is added to the removeProduct button, which is located within the movieclip. The default quantity of a new item is set to 1; this can then be updated, which you learn in the next section.

```
public function addProduct(product:Object):void
{
  ...
  var cartItem:ShoppingCartItem = new ShoppingCartItem();
  cartItem.removeItemBtn.addEventListener(MouseEvent.CLICK,
   removeProduct);
  cartItem.quantityTxt.text = "1";
  cartItem.nameTxt.text = product.name;
  ...
}
```

The next step is to create a fake ID that you can use to add and remove the instance later.

```
cartItem.setID(cartItemCount); // faux id for removal system
```

The placement of a new shopping cart item instance is determined by first multiplying the cartItemCount by the height and then adding a spacing to that.

```
cartItem.y = (cartItemCount * cartItemHeight) + lineSpacing;
```

Once the new instance is positioned, it is temporarily added to the product object so that future pieces of code can access it without hunting for it. Then it is added to the cartContents array.

```
product.cartItem = cartItem;
cartContents.push(product);
```

The next portion of the addProduct method is responsible for adding the instance to the display list, incrementing the count and finally making a call to the price updater.

```
addChild(cartItem);
cartItemCount++;
updateTotal();
```

At this moment, if you were to add an item to the shopping cart it would allow duplicates to be added. When the desired result is to increment the quantity a for.. loop is placed at the beginning of the method to take care of this.

301

```
public function addProduct(product:Object):void
{
  // Look for product in list
  for(var i in cartContents)
  {
    if(cartContents[i].id == product.id)
    {
    var q:Number = cartContents[i].cartItem.quantityTxt.text;
      cartContents[i].cartItem.quantityTxt.text = q + 1;
      updateTotal();
      return;
    }
  }
  ...
}
```

The loop is set up to first check for a valid cart item ID. If a valid ID is found, the quantity is assigned to the q variable. This is then appended to the value of the quantity text box and a call to the price updater is made to ensure that it is always correct. A return is used to halt any further execution of code located within this function.

This method was probably the largest, as it is responsible for a lot of the functionality in this application. The completed code is provided in one final display at the end of this section, and of course, is also available on the book's Web site.

The next method is used to remove an item from the shopping cart. The `getID` method that was created in the `ShoppingCartItem` class is used in this function to retrieve the `id`. The `parent` reference is used to take the target (Delete button) and inform the code what the parent or upper object is. This provides a solid link to the `ShoppingCartItem` class instance and ultimately the method to retrieve the `id`.

```
public function removeProduct(e:MouseEvent):void
{
  var id:uint = e.target.parent.getID();
  ...
}
```

After the `id` is known it can be used to remove the item from the array of cart items and from the display list. The splice method is used to delete the cart item using the `id`, which is actually the position the item can be found in the array. The second argument in the splice method is to ensure only one element is deleted.

```
cartContents.splice(id, 1);
removeChild(e.target.parent);
cartItemCount--;
```

NOTE If the second argument is not provided, the splice method will remove all of the items from that point.

Developing Real-World Applications

The Flash file has a note automatically added that is displayed to inform the user that no items exist in the cart. However, this is removed when an item is added. The problem is, if the user removes all of the items from the cart it needs to be displayed again, so a simple `if` statement is added to the end of the `remove` method to handle this.

```
if(cartItemCount == 0)
{
  noItemsTxt.visible = true;
}
```

Finally, a call to the `updateTotal` and `updateList` methods is made to ensure the data stays consistent and the price is updated.

```
updateList();
updateTotal();
```

The cart items are added to the array as the user clicks the Add to Cart button; however, you may remember in the previous section that the cart item can be found in the array using the cart `id`. The problem is if an item is removed the list is now mixed and an incorrect item can be added or removed. The solution is to provide new `id`'s as an item is removed. This is accomplished by looping through all the remaining cart items and making a call to set a new `id`.

```
public function updateList():void
{
  for(var i:uint=0; i < cartItemCount; i++)
  {
    cartContents[i].cartItem.setID(i);
  }
}
```

The other side effect to removing an item freely is it can create a gap in the list. This doesn't change how the application functions, but visually it isn't the cleanest. The way around this little issue is to realign the list as an item is removed.

```
public function updateList():void
{
  for(var i:uint=0; i < cartItemCount; i++)
  {
    cartContents[i].cartItem.setID(i);
  }
  cartContents[i].cartItem.y = (i * cartItemHeight) +
    lineSpacing;
}
```

In the previous methods there has been a call to `updateTotal`. This method is responsible for keeping the price total updated as items are added and edited. The process is to loop through the cart items, multiply the price by the quantity, and display the final result. The result is then tested for valid numbers and a decimal (.) is provided if needed.

Part IV Developing Applications

```
public function updateTotal():void
{
  var total:Number = 0;

  for(var i:uint=0; i < cartItemCount; i++)
  {
    total += Number(cartContents[i].price) *
    Number(cartContents[i].cartItem.quantityTxt.text);
  }

  totalTxt.text = "$" + String(round2D(total));

  // tack on extra 0 if needed or two 0's
  if(totalTxt.text.indexOf('.') == -1)
  {
    totalTxt.appendText(".00");
  }
  else if(totalTxt.text.indexOf('.') + 2 == totalTxt.text.length)
  {
    totalTxt.appendText("0");
  }
}
```

The setGatewayURL method set the gateway property which refers to the url that is called when the Checkout button is clicked.

```
public function setGatewayURL(url:String):void
{
  gateway = url;
}
```

At this point the ShoppingCart class has been created. The last portion of code that is needed will be placed on the Timeline. This code will be responsible for setting everything up and ultimately controlling the individual elements.

The Timeline ActionScript could also be placed in a Document class, which is explained in Chapter 9. However, for simplicity, it will be included directly in the Flash file.

The first part is to assign the php file, which will be built in the next section.

```
var phpFile:String = "http://localhost/ch11/store/flashCart.php";
```

The shopping cart is already on the stage with an instance name and is simply assigned to the cart variable to be used in the rest of the code. The next step is to create an empty movieclip that holds the store items.

```
var cart:MovieClip = shoppingCart;
cart.setGatewayURL(phpFile);

var storeItems:MovieClip = new MovieClip();
```

Developing Real-World Applications 12

```
storeItems.x = 25;
storeItems.y = 80;
```

The request to the server is pretty much the same process that has been used in the past. The only unique portion is the action that is attached to the end of the `url`.

```
var urlRequest:URLRequest = new URLRequest(phpFile
  + "?action=getproducts");
var urlLoader:URLLoader = new URLLoader();
urlLoader.addEventListener(Event.COMPLETE, productsLoaded);
urlLoader.load(urlRequest);
```

After the server loads the data, the response function is called. This function is responsible for parsing the XML and adding the store item to the shopping cart. Here is a sample of the XML that is returned and parsed.

```
<products>
  <product id="1"
    name="Cool Tracks"
    desc="Another hot release"
    thumbnail="" />
</products>
```

This function is also responsible for loading a new instance of the `StoreItem` movieclip, which contains the information for each product. The button in this instance also gets an event attached to it that is responsible for adding a new item to the shopping cart.

```
function productsLoaded(e:Event):void
{
  ...
  var id:uint = 0;
  for each(var xmlItem in xml..product)
  {
    var item:StoreItem = new StoreItem();
    item.y = 85 * id;
    item.setStoreData(
      id,
      xmlItem.attribute('name'),
      xmlItem.attribute('desc'),
      xmlItem.attribute('thumbnail'));
      xmlItem.attribute('price'));
    item.addToCartBtn.addEventListener(MouseEvent.CLICK,
      addItemHandler);
    storeItems.addChild(item);
    id++;
  }
  addChild(storeItems);
}
```

305

The `addItemHandler` function first grabs the unique object and adds the product to the cart. The object is found by loading the object from the parent container, similar to the code that was used in the previous section. The to `trace()` statements are simply for testing and are never seen by the final user of the application.

```
function addItemHandler(e:MouseEvent):void
{
  var prod:Object = e.target.parent.getItem();

  trace("Add Item: " + e.target.parent);
  trace("Item ID: " +  prod.id);

  cart.addProduct(prod);
}
```

It took a while and resulted in a lot of new code, but all of the ActionScript needed for this example is complete. The next part to focus on is the PHP code that is called by the Checkout button.

Actually, the PHP and MySQL go hand in hand, so it is better to build the required SQL table before the PHP is written. This makes it easier to debug in the long run.

```
CREATE TABLE flashStore_products (
   `id` int NOT NULL AUTO_INCREMENT,
   `name` varchar(25),
   `category` int(3) NOT NULL DEFAULT 0,
   `description` TEXT,
   `thumbnail` varchar(200) NOT NULL DEFAULT "",
   `price` varchar(10) NOT NULL,
   `active` int(1) NOT NULL DEFAULT 1,
   PRIMARY KEY (`id`)
)
```

The SQL is responsible for holding all of the information for each item in the store. In a complete application, this would probably be populated by a content management system. For this example, the `INSERT` code is provided so that you can quickly test the example.

```
INSERT INTO flashStore_products (name, description,price)
   VALUES ('Cooler Music', 'Another new one');
```

Building the PHP

When the SQL is set up the PHP can be written. The PHP is responsible for loading the store items and handling a checkout request. These two tasks can be broken up into multiple files and are probably better off as classes, but for simplicity it will all be located within this one php file.

Before the database can be used, a connection needs to be established. This is accomplished by loading an external file that holds the database connection information.

```
include 'dbconn.php';
```

Developing Real-World Applications

The contents of that `dbconn.php` file are seen here.

```php
<?php

$host = "localhost";
$user = "username";
$pass = "password";
$database = "database name";

$link = mysql_connect($host, $user, $pass);
mysql_select_db($database, $link);

unset($host);
unset($user);
unset($pass);
unset($database);

?>
```

Now you can determine which action is being requested. There are two possible options: `getproducts`, which returns an `xml` document of store items, or `checkout`, which loads the `xml` from Flash and displays it.

```php
if($_GET['action'] == 'getproducts')
{
  print getProducts();
}
else if($_GET['action'] == 'checkout')
{
  $xml = new SimpleXMLElement($_GET['xml']);

  $nodeCount = count($xml->product);

  print "<table border=\"1\" width=\"500\">";
  print "<tr><td><strong>Quantity</strong></td>";
  print "<td><strong>Product</strong></td>";
  print "<td><strong>Price</strong></td></tr>";

  for($x=0; $x < $nodeCount; $x++)
  {
    print "<tr style=\"background-color:#eeeeee;\">";
    print "<td style=\"width:60px;text-align:center;\">"
      . $xml->product[$x]->quantity . "</td>";
    print "<td>" . $xml->product[$x]->name . "</td>";
    print "<td>" . $xml->product[$x]->price . "</td></tr>";
  }

  print "<tr>";
  print "<td colspan=\"3\">Total: <strong>"
```

Part IV Developing Applications

```
                . getAttribute($xml, 'total') . "</strong></td></tr>";

        print "</table>";
        print "<br />Checkout code goes here<br />";
    }
```

The `getproducts` action simply makes a call to another function that returns the `xml` generated from the database entries. The checkout action, as shown in Figure 12.3, is a little more involved. It starts off by grabbing the XML data passed from Flash. This XML is loaded into the `SimpleXML` library where it is parsed and each of the store items is retrieved.

FIGURE 12.3

Here is a sample of the checkout page, loaded from Flash. This page is visible when the Checkout button is clicked.

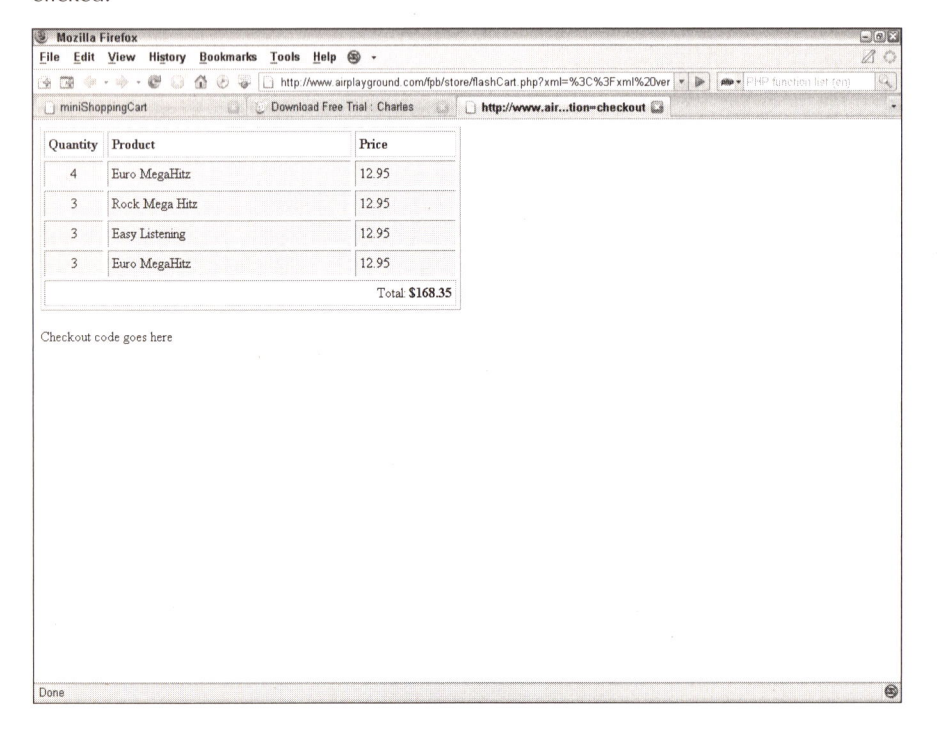

This function is called from the first action and is responsible for building an XML document from the data in the database. The store items are broken down by `id`, name, `desc`, and thumbnail, which are all visible in the Flash file.

The result set from MySQL returns any item that is currently active. This result is then passed into a `while` loop, which is where the XML data is built. Finally, the XML is returned to the caller and, in this example, is printed to the screen for Flash to load.

308

Developing Real-World Applications

```
function getProducts()
{
  global $link;

  $result = mysql_query("SELECT * FROM flashStore_products
    WHERE active=1", $link);

  $xml = "<products>\n";
  while($row = mysql_fetch_array($result))
  {
    $xml .= "<product id=\"" . $row['id'] .
      "\" name=\"" . $row['name'] .
      "\" desc=\"" . $row['description'] .
      "\" thumbnail=\"" . $row['thumbnail'] . "\" />\n";
"\" price=\"" . $row['price'] ."\" />\n";

  }
  $xml .= "</products>";

  return $xml;
}
```

The last function is actually a forgotten feature of `SimpleXML`. This function takes two arguments, the `xml` and the attribute name you are looking for. It first loops through all of the arguments and matches those arguments against the passed-in variable. It returns either the value of the attribute or `false`, depending on what the result is.

```
function getAttribute($xml, $name)
{
  foreach($xml->attributes() as $key=>$val)
  {
    if($key == $name)
    {
      return (string)$val;
    }
  }
  return false;
}
```

Now that all of the code is complete, here are the three classes and Timeline code provided in one place for easier viewing and comparison with your code.

ShoppingCart

```
package
{

  import flash.display.MovieClip;
  import flash.text.TextField;
  import flash.events.MouseEvent;
```

Part IV Developing Applications

```
import flash.net.*;

public class ShoppingCart extends MovieClip
{
  private var cartItemCount:uint = 0;
  private var cartContents:Array;

  private var cartItemHeight:uint = 20;
  private var lineSpacing:uint = 30;
  private var gateway:String;

  function ShoppingCart()
  {
    cartContents = new Array();

    checkoutBtn.addEventListener(MouseEvent.CLICK,
function():void
    {
      var xml:String = "<?xml version='1.0' ?>\n\r";
      xml += "<products total=\"" + totalTxt.text + "\">";

      for(var i in cartContents)
      {
        xml += "<product>";
        xml += "<quantity>" +
        cartContents[i].cartItem.quantityTxt.text
        + "</quantity>";
        xml += "<name>" + cartContents[i].name
        + "</name>";
        xml += "<price>" + cartContents[i].price
        + "</price>";
        xml += "</product>";
      }
      xml += "</products>";

      var variables:URLVariables = new URLVariables();
      variables.action = "checkout";
      variables.xml = xml;

      var urlRequest:URLRequest = new URLRequest(gateway);
      urlRequest.data = variables;
            urlRequest.method = "GET";

      navigateToURL(urlRequest);
    })
  }

  public function addProduct(product:Object):void
  {
    // Look for product in list
```

```
   for(var i in cartContents)
   {
     if(cartContents[i].id == product.id)
     {
     var quantity:Number =
     cartContents[i].cartItem.quantityTxt.text;

     cartContents[i].cartItem.quantityTxt.text =
quantity + 1;

     updateTotal();
     return;
     }
   }

   if(cartItemCount == 0)
   {
     noItemsTxt.visible = false;
   }

   var cartItem:ShoppingCartItem =
     new ShoppingCartItem();

   cartItem.removeItemBtn.addEventListener(
     MouseEvent.CLICK, removeProduct);

   cartItem.quantityTxt.text = String(1);
   cartItem.nameTxt.text = product.name;
   cartItem.setID(cartItemCount);

   cartItem.y =
   (cartItemCount * cartItemHeight) + lineSpacing;

   product.cartItem = cartItem;

   cartContents.push(product);

   addChild(cartItem);

   cartItemCount++;

   updateTotal();
 }

 public function removeProduct(e:MouseEvent):void
 {
   var id:uint = e.target.parent.getID();

   cartContents.splice(id, 1);
   removeChild(e.target.parent);
```

Part IV Developing Applications

```
    cartItemCount--;

    if(cartItemCount == 0)
    {
      noItemsTxt.visible = true;
    }

    updateList();
    updateTotal();
}

public function updateList():void
{
  for(var i:uint=0; i < cartItemCount; i++)
  {
    cartContents[i].cartItem.setID(i);
    cartContents[i].cartItem.y =
    (i * cartItemHeight) + lineSpacing;
  }
}

public function updateTotal():void
{
  var total:Number = 0;
  for(var i:uint=0; i < cartItemCount; i++)
  {
  total += Number(cartContents[i].price) *
  Number(cartContents[i].cartItem.quantityTxt.text);
  }

  totalTxt.text = "$" + String(round2D(total));

  // tack on extra 0 if needed or two 0's
  if(totalTxt.text.indexOf('.') == -1)
  {
    totalTxt.appendText(".00");
  }
  else if(totalTxt.text.indexOf('.') + 2 ==
totalTxt.text.length)
  {
    totalTxt.appendText("0");
  }

}

public function setGatewayURL(url:String):void
{
  gateway = url;
}

private function round2D(n:Number):Number
```

Developing Real-World Applications

```
      {
        return Math.round(n * Math.pow(10, 2)) / Math.pow(10, 2);
      }
    }
  }
```

ShoppingCartItem

```
package
{

  import flash.display.MovieClip;
  import flash.text.TextField;

  public class ShoppingCartItem extends MovieClip
  {
    private var cartItemID:uint;

    function ShoppingCartItem() { }
    public function getID():uint
    {
      return cartItemID;
    }

    public function setID(id:uint):void
    {
      cartItemID = id;
    }
  }

}
```

StoreItem

```
package
{
  import flash.display.MovieClip;
  import flash.text.TextField;

  public class StoreItem extends MovieClip
  {
    private var albumName:String;
    private var albumDesc:String;
    private var albumThumb:String;
    private var albumPrice:String;
    private var storeItemID:uint;

    function StoreItem() {}

    public function setStoreData(
      id:uint, n:String,
```

Part IV Developing Applications

```
      d:String, t:String, p:String):void
    {
      storeItemID = id;
      albumName = n;
      albumDesc = d;
      albumThumb = t;
      albumPrice = p;

      nameTxt.text = albumName;
      descTxt.text = albumDesc;
    }

    public function getItem():Object
    {
      return {
        target:this,
        id:storeItemID,
        name:albumName,
        price:albumPrice
      };
    }
  }
}
```

Timeline code

```
var phpFile:String = "http://localhost/ch11/store/flashCart.php";

var cart:MovieClip = shoppingCart;
cart.setGatewayURL(phpFile);

var storeItems:MovieClip = new MovieClip();
storeItems.x = 25;
storeItems.y = 80;

var urlRequest:URLRequest = new URLRequest(phpFile +
    "?action=getproducts");
var urlLoader:URLLoader = new URLLoader();
urlLoader.addEventListener(Event.COMPLETE, productsLoaded);
urlLoader.load(urlRequest);

function productsLoaded(e:Event):void
{
  var urlLoader:URLLoader = URLLoader(e.target);
  var xml:XML = new XML(urlLoader.data);

  trace("XML: " + xml);

  var id:uint = 0;
  for each(var xmlItem in xml..product)
  {
```

Developing Real-World Applications

```
    var item:StoreItem = new StoreItem();
    item.y = 85 * id;
    item.setStoreData(id,
      xmlItem.attribute('name'),
      xmlItem.attribute('desc'),
      xmlItem.attribute('thumbnail'));
      xmlItem.attribute('price'));
    item.addToCartBtn.addEventListener(
      MouseEvent.CLICK, addItemHandler);
    storeItems.addChild(item);
    id++;
  }
  addChild(storeItems);
}

function addItemHandler(e:MouseEvent):void
{
  var prod:Object = e.target.parent.getItem();

  trace("Add Item: " + e.target.parent);
  trace("Item ID: " +  prod.id);

  cart.addProduct(prod);
}
```

PHP code

```php
<?php

$host = "localhost";
$user = "username";
$pass = "password";
$database = "database name";

$link = mysql_connect($host, $user, $pass);
mysql_select_db($database, $link);

unset($host);
unset($user);
unset($pass);
unset($database);

?>

<?php

include 'dbconn.php';

function getProducts()
{
```

315

Part IV Developing Applications

```php
  global $link;

  $result = mysql_query("SELECT * FROM flashStore_products
    WHERE active=1", $link);

  $xml = "<products>\n";

  while($row = mysql_fetch_array($result))
  {
    $xml .= "<product id=\"" . $row['id'] .
      "\" name=\"" . $row['name'] .
      "\" desc=\"" . $row['description'] .
      "\" thumbnail=\"" . $row['thumbnail'] . "\" />\n";
"\" price=\"" . $row['price'] ."\" />\n";

  }

  $xml .= "</products>";

  return $xml;
}

if($_GET['action'] == 'getproducts')
{
  print getProducts();
}
else if($_GET['action'] == 'checkout')
{
  $xml = new SimpleXMLElement($_GET['xml']);

  $nodeCount = count($xml->product);

  print "<table border=\"1\" width=\"500\">";
  print "<tr><td><strong>Quantity</strong></td>";
  print "<td><strong>Product</strong></td>";
  print "<td><strong>Price</strong></td></tr>";

  for($x=0; $x < $nodeCount; $x++)
  {
    print "<tr style=\"background-color:#eeeeee;\">";
    print "<td style=\"width:60px;text-align:center;\">"
      . $xml->product[$x]->quantity . "</td>";
    print "<td>" . $xml->product[$x]->name . "</td>";
    print "<td>" . $xml->product[$x]->price . "</td></tr>";
  }

  print "<tr><td style=\"text-align:right;\" colspan=\"3\">Total:
    <strong>" . getAttribute($xml, 'total') .
    "</strong></td></tr>";

  print "</table>";
```

```
      print "<br />Checkout code goes here<br />";
   }

   function getAttribute($xml, $name)
   {
      foreach($xml->attributes() as $key=>$val)
      {
         if($key == $name)
         {
            return (string)$val;
         }
      }
      return false;
   }

   ?>
```

The example is now complete; it is just a matter of placing the PHP on an active Web server. From this point you can extend the example to have multiple categories, products, and images. Realistically, building the application in a class format offers greater expandability, but don't just take my word for it. Experiment and extend the example.

Using PHP and Flash to Build an Amazon Search Application

Amazon offers a very powerful set of tools designed to work with its site data. This section covers the building of a search application using Amazon.com as the data source. This example uses the ECS (Amazon E-Commerce Service), which provides direct access to Amazon's amazing searching and inventory system.

In order to use the ECS you need to have a valid Amazon access ID, which is provided when you create a developer's account. This registration process is quick and free; all you need is a valid e-mail address and an active account.

Using the Amazon Web Service

To get started with creating a developers account, visit the Amazon Web Service (AWS) page at www.amazon.com/gp/aws/landing.html.

NOTE Be sure to activate the account via e-mail before you begin to use it.

The AWS is set up to be accessed from different mediums. The format used for this example is Representational State Transfer (REST), which is basically a formatted URL with all of the necessary information provided in GET format.

Part IV Developing Applications

Here is a sample request sent to Amazon, as shown in Figure 12.4, to return information about possible book matches for a keyword or series of keywords.

```
http://ecs.amazonaws.com/onca/xml?Service=AWSECommerceService&AWS
    AccessKeyId={AWS_ACCESS_KEY}&Operation=ItemSearch&SearchIndex=
    Books&ResponseGroup=Medium&Keywords={SEARCH_TERMS}
```

The `AWS_ACCESS_KEY` is the access `id` that is provided by Amazon, and the `SEARCH_TERMS` would be the keyword(s) that are passed along for searching.

As you may have noticed, the XML response from Amazon is fairly complex. However, for this example the focus will be on the book title, author, and thumbnail path. Amazon is actually very nice to provide the amount of detail it does. You can build some pretty interesting applications with the AWS system.

FIGURE 12.4

Here is the XML response from Amazon, after a search for "PHP".

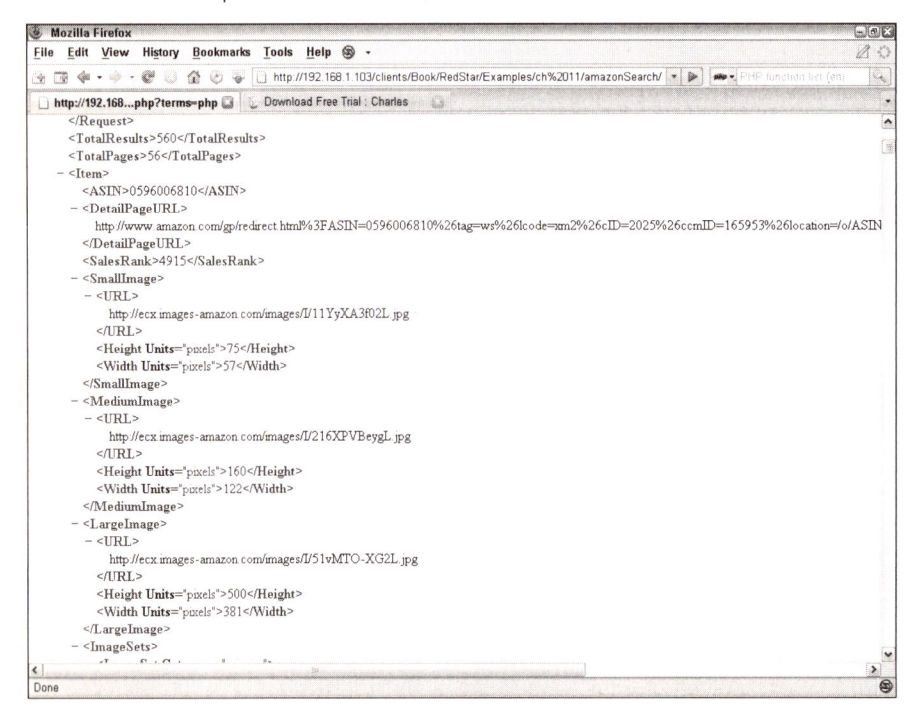

318

Developing Real-World Applications

In fact, the URL sent to Amazon can be modified to search for different items or subjects all together. The AWS is set up to even return valid error messages similar to this one if you don't provide an operation parameter.

```
AWS.InvalidOperationParameterThe Operation parameter is invalid.
    Please modify the Operation parameter and retry. Valid values
    for the Operation parameter include TagLookup, ListLookup,
    CartGet, SellerListingLookup, CustomerContentLookup,
    ItemLookup, SimilarityLookup, SellerLookup, ItemSearch,
    VehiclePartLookup, BrowseNodeLookup, CartModify, ListSearch,
    CartClear...
```

The search system offers a lot of types and modifiers, and you don't have to rely on this "create an error" concept to see what is available. Amazon happens to provide very robust documentation in the developer's center. Log in for access.

Simplifying the XML response

When the XML response was loaded in the previous section, the result was overwhelming. There are many XML nodes and data that just aren't applicable to this application. You could pass this raw data into Flash, but what if you want to cache the results? You would have a bunch of unused information clogging up your database.

The idea is to build a custom XML response that only contains the data necessary for this application.

```
<?php

$terms = "";

define("AWS_ACCESS_KEY", "{AWS_KEY_GOES_HERE}");
```

It is important to check for valid tags before a response is sent to Amazon. It really doesn't harm anything, but it could be considered a fraudulent request.

```
if(!empty($_GET['terms']))
{
    ...
}
```

Assuming valid tags where found, build the request that will be sent to the AWS.

```
if(!empty($_GET['terms']))
{
    $terms = $_GET['terms'];
    $request = 'http://ecs.amazonaws.com/onca/xml' .
        '?Service=AWSECommerceService&' .
        'AWSAccessKeyId=' . AWS_ACCESS_KEY .
        '&Operation=ItemSearch' .
```

Part IV Developing Applications

```
    '&SearchIndex=Books' .
    '&ResponseGroup=Medium' .
    '&Keywords=' . $terms;
}
```

Now call the AWS, passing along the search parameters.

```
$rawXml = file_get_contents($request);
```

The response from the AWS is loaded using `file_get_contents`, which reads in the entire file requested into a string. In this example, the string is saved to the `$rawXML` variable. A call to the `simplexml` library is made to build a properly formatted XML object.

```
$xmlResponse = simplexml_load_string($rawXml);
```

The next step is to build the custom XML document that will be sent back to Flash when it is requested. The `nodeCount` variable is hard-coded to 4 so that only four book results are saved. Even if Amazon returns thousands, Flash only sees four.

```
$nodeCount = 4;

$xml = "<?xml version=\"1.0\" ?>\n<books>";

for($i=0; $i < $nodeCount; $i++)
{
    ...
}

$xml .= "</books>";
```

The contents of the `for..` loop is where the majority of the XML building process occurs. For example, to load the current book title, you first access the `Items` node. Once inside that node, the selected `Item` node is accessed using the `$i` variable to determine which child should be referenced. Inside the current child node, there is another child with the node name `ItemAttributes`, which contains a `title` node and ultimately becomes the name of the book for this selected child.

```
$xmlResponse->Items->Item[$i]->ItemAttributes->Title
```

As you can see, Amazon packs this XML file full of information, which in this instance makes it sort of difficult to load the desired information. The process of loading the author and thumbnail data is pretty much the same — just access each child and reference the desired node.

```
$xml .= "\t<book>";
$xml .= "\t\t<title><![CDATA[" . $xmlResponse->Items
    ->Item[$i]->ItemAttributes->Title . "]]></title>";
$xml .= "\t\t<author><![CDATA[" . $xmlResponse->Items
    ->Item[$i]->ItemAttributes->Author . "]]></author>";
$xml .= "\t\t<price><![CDATA[" . $xmlResponse->Items
```

Developing Real-World Applications

```
    ->Item[$i]->ItemAttributes->ListPrice
    ->FormattedPrice . "]]></price>";
$xml .= "\t\t<thumb>" . $xmlResponse->Items->Item[$i]
    ->SmallImage->URL . "</thumb>";
$xml .= "\t</book>";
```

CAUTION The data to generate the XML is one line per $xml variable; the wrapping is to fit this page and can potentially break your code.

The last portion of the PHP for this example creates a header type so XML readers know the format that is being sent. Then it finally outputs it to the screen.

```
header("content-type: text/xml");
print $xml;
```

The Flash (ActionScript) required for the application is all in external classes. This is done because it is easier to manage and maintain moving forward.

CROSS-REF If you need a more in-depth explanation of classes, I strongly recommend you read Chapter 9.

The Flash File (FLA) for this application consists of a simple design with a search box and button. The main class, BookSearch, is assigned as the document class and is responsible for managing the overall application. Here is the class skeleton, which gives you an idea of what methods and properties are used to create this application.

```
package
{
  import flash.display.MovieClip;
  import flash.events.*;
  import flash.net.*;

  public class BookSearch extends MovieClip
  {
    public var webServiceURL:String;
    private var bookItems:Array;
    private var bookItemsContainer:MovieClip;

    public function BookSearch() {}

    public function searchHandler(e:MouseEvent):void  {}

    public function loadSearchResults(terms:String):void {}

    public function loadedResultsHandler(e:Event):void {}

    private function removeOldResults():void {}
  }
}
```

321

Part IV Developing Applications

The constructor method is used to initialize the array, create a container `movieclip`, and add the event listener to the Search button.

```
public function BookSearch()
{
  bookItems = new Array();
  bookItemsContainer = new MovieClip();
  bookItemsContainer.y = 100;
  searchBtn.addEventListener(MouseEvent.CLICK, searchHandler);
}
```

The final step of the constructor method is to add the new book container to the display list, which ultimately makes it visible.

```
public function BookSearch()
{
  bookItems = new Array();
  bookItemsContainer = new MovieClip();
  bookItemsContainer.y = 100;
  searchBtn.addEventListener(MouseEvent.CLICK, searchHandler);
  addChild(bookItemsContainer);
}
```

The next method to focus on is the `searchHandler()`. This method is called when the user clicks the Search button. When this method is called it first checks the length of the data from the search box to ensure a valid search will happen. If the value is of valid length, a call to remove the old search results is made.

```
public function searchHandler(e:MouseEvent):void
{
  if(searchTxt.text.length > 0)
  {
    removeOldResults();
    loadSearchResults(searchTxt.text);
  }
}
```

Once a valid search term is found, the next step is to set up and make the call to the PHP, which is responsible for interfacing with the AWS. The call used in this example is very similar to previous examples. You first set up the variables object, assign that to the `URLRequest`, create a new `loader` instance, and finally assign an event listener.

```
public function loadSearchResults(terms:String):void
{
  var urlVariables:URLVariables = new URLVariables();
  urlVariables.terms = terms;

  var urlRequest:URLRequest = new URLRequest(webServiceURL);
```

Developing Real-World Applications 12

```
    urlRequest.data = urlVariables;

    var urlLoader:URLLoader = new URLLoader();
    urlLoader.addEventListener(Event.COMPLETE,
      loadedResultsHandler);
    urlLoader.load(urlRequest);
}
```

You might have noticed this method has been made public. This is done so other applications can use the searching ability, because that is what reusability is all about. Of course, if you allow others to call this method directly, you would most likely want to place another term check to make sure bad data isn't going to be sent.

Once the Web server returns the data, it is sent to the `loadedResultsHandler()` method. The response is sent in XML format and, using a `for..each` loop each element is pulled out and sent to a unique `BookItem` class instance.

```
    var xml:XML = new XML(urlLoader.data);

    for each(var item in xml..book)
    ...
```

The `BookItem` is referencing a `movieclip` in the library. This `movieclip` is prefilled with dummy entries that are populated with the real data before they are displayed on the Stage.

```
    var bookItem:BookItem = new BookItem();
    bookItem.setValues(
      item..title,
      item..author,
      item..price,
      item..thumb
    );
    bookItem.y = (bookItems.length * (bookItem.height + 30));
    bookItems.push(bookItem);
    bookItemsContainer.addChild(bookItem);
```

The completed event handler follows:

```
    public function loadedResultsHandler(e:Event):void
    {
      var urlLoader:URLLoader = URLLoader(e.target);
      var xml:XML = new XML(urlLoader.data);

      for each(var item in xml..book)
      {
        var bookItem:BookItem = new BookItem();
        bookItem.setValues(
          item..title,
          item..author,
```

323

```
            item..price,
            item..thumb
        );

        bookItem.y = (bookItems.length * (bookItem.height + 30));
        bookItems.push(bookItem);
        bookItemsContainer.addChild(bookItem);          }
    }
```

The last method for the document class is used to remove the existing book item instances. This method is called each time a new search begins, to ensure the data doesn't accidentally stack up.

```
    private function removeOldResults():void
    {
      if(bookItems.length > 0)
      {
        bookItems = new Array();
        removeChild(bookItemsContainer);
        bookItemsContainer = new MovieClip();
        bookItemsContainer.y = 100;
        addChild(bookItemsContainer);
      }
    }
```

The first part of the method checks for valid entries because the first time the application runs there would be no existing products on the Stage.

```
    if(bookItems.length > 0)
    {
        ...
       }
```

If there are existing items, a new array is created that clears the existing objects. Then, using `removeChild`, the old container is cleared and a new one is created. This is done to free up resources and remove the existing products.

```
        bookItems = new Array();
        removeChild(bookItemsContainer);
        bookItemsContainer = new MovieClip();
```

The last step is to add the new book container to the display list, which is done by calling `addChild()` and passing the new instance of the container as an argument.

```
        addChild(bookItemsContainer);
```

Now you can move on and create the `BookItem` class, which is used for each product that is added to the Stage. It is responsible for storing off the product data and loading in the book thumbnail.

Developing Real-World Applications   12

Before any development of the class begins it is a good idea to look at the skeleton, such as in the previous example. Doing so allows you to better understand how it is intended to work.

```
package
{
  import flash.display.MovieClip;
  import flash.text.TextField;
  import flash.display.Loader;
  import flash.net.URLRequest;

  public class BookItem extends MovieClip
  {
    public function BookItem() {  }
    public function setValues(t:String, a:String, p:String,
      i:String):void {}
    public function loadThumb():void {}
    public function getValues():Object {}
  }
}
```

The first method in most classes is the constructor, and this one is no exception, except for the fact that this constructor is empty. The next method is `setValues`, which is responsible for storing the passed values. These values will be the book data that is retrieved from Amazon. You can also pass this information in as an object but for this example it is easier to understand using stand-alone variables.

```
public function
    setValues(t:String,a:String,p:String,i:String):void
{
  title = t;
  author = a;
  price = p;
  thumb = i;

  titleTxt.text = title;
  authorTxt.text = author;
  priceTxt.text = price;

  loadThumb();
}
```

Once all the variables are stored off, a call to `loadThumb` is made, which is responsible for retrieving the thumbnail of the book cover. When using the `Loader` class, you can pass it into the `addChild`, which removes the need for an event listener, but even more importantly, it loads on its own because the book cover isn't required. You can also create a visual loader to inform the user that something is actually loading. The remainder of the method is just a standard `URLRequest`, which you should be familiar with from previous examples.

```
public function loadThumb():void
{
  var thumbLoader:Loader = new Loader();
  var thumbURL:String = thumb;
  var thumbURLRequest:URLRequest = new URLRequest(thumbURL);
  thumbLoader.load(thumbURLRequest);
  thumbLoader.x = 10;
  addChild(thumbLoader);
}
```

The last method is for returning the `BookItem` data that was populated in the previous methods.

```
public function getValues():Object
{
  return {title:title, author:author, price:price};
}
```

At this point, you have completed an Amazon search application with PHP and Flash. You have also obtained a wealth of information regarding the AWS system and should be pumped up to build your own Web service-enabled applications.

A few potential projects to build are CD search application, genre matching system, or even a gallery that uses your local iTunes or similar music player's library to build a visual cloud of music you have listened to. Check the Web site for this book to see other examples of applications built using the Amazon AWS system.

Developing a Photo Gallery Using flickr

The photo gallery is a very popular application that is often built using Flash. It offers a very unique way to showcase your work or in some cases is used as an information delivery application, such as on gaming and news sites.

In this section, you learn to develop a photo gallery using the flickr photo service provided by Yahoo. The Flash application will make a call to PHP, which will interact with the flickr Web services and finally return that data back to Flash for displaying.

Before you begin developing the application, sign up for a flickr API key, which is a two-step process. The first step is to create a flickr account by visiting the registration page at www.flickr.com/signup/.

Once you have a flickr account, apply for an API by visiting www.flickr.com/services/api/keys/apply/.

NOTE If you select the Non-commercial option it authorizes your request almost instantly.

Developing Real-World Applications 12

This example uses a `Document` class to handle the majority of the loading and displaying process. In fact, the bulk of this class is similar to the previous example. If you completed that example you can copy those class files and make the changes as needed.

Here is the class skeleton, which will give you a better idea of how the class will work.

```
package
{
  import flash.display.MovieClip;
  import flash.events.*;
  import flash.net.*;

  public class PhotoGallery extends MovieClip
  {
    public var webServiceURL:String;
    private var photos:Array;
    private var photosContainer:MovieClip;

    public function PhotoGallery() {}
    public function searchHandler(e:MouseEvent):void  {}
    public function loadSearchResults(terms:String):void {}
    public function loadedResultsHandler(e:Event):void {}

    private function removeOldPhotos():void {}
  }
}
```

The first method is actually the constructor, which in this application handles the creation of a new container and also initializes the element array.

```
public function PhotoGallery()
{
  photos = new Array();
  photosContainer = new MovieClip();
  photosContainer.y = 75;
}
```

After the new `movieclip` is created, it needs to be added to the display list, and an event handler needs to be assigned to the Search button located on the Stage.

```
searchBtn.addEventListener(MouseEvent.CLICK, searchHandler);
addChild(photosContainer);
```

The next method to focus on is the `searchHandler()`. When this method is called it first checks for a valid search term. If the value is valid, a call to remove the old images is made.

```
public function searchHandler(e:MouseEvent):void
{
  if(searchTxt.text.length > 0)
```

327

Part IV Developing Applications

```
    {
      removeOldPhotos();
      loadSearchResults(searchTxt.text);
    }
  }
```

The next method is for calling the PHP, which is responsible for interfacing with flickr. The `tags` variable is passed in from the search handler and is sent to the PHP via a `GET` request.

```
  public function loadSearchResults(tags:String):void
  {
    var urlVariables:URLVariables = new URLVariables();
    urlVariables.tags = tags;

    var urlRequest:URLRequest = new URLRequest(webServiceURL);
    urlRequest.data = urlVariables;

    var urlLoader:URLLoader = new URLLoader();
    urlLoader.addEventListener(Event.COMPLETE,
      loadedResultsHandler);
    urlLoader.load(urlRequest);
  }
```

The PHP is set up to return an XML result set, which is a stripped-down version of what is returned from flickr. This is very similar to the Amazon example, because Web services tend to return a lot of information that isn't needed for an application such as this one.

The XML data is first loaded into an `XML` object for proper parsing to be possible. Once the `XML` object is created, it runs through a `for..each` loop to pull out each photo node.

```
  public function loadedResultsHandler(e:Event):void
  {
    var urlLoader:URLLoader = URLLoader(e.target);
    var xml:XML = new XML(urlLoader.data);

    for each(var item in xml..photo)
    {
      ...
    }
  }
```

Using each photo node you need to create a `PhotoItem` instance, which is where the flickr image is loaded. Think of this instance as a container for each image. This instance also is where the image data is stored for future use.

```
  var photoItem:PhotoItem = new PhotoItem();
  photoItem.setValues(item..title, item..thumb);
```

Developing Real-World Applications — 12

When a new instance of the `PhotoItem` is created, it needs to be aligned in the container. This position is determined by taking the length of the photos array and multiplying it by the height of the new `photoItem`. That value is then increased by 50 pixels to allow spacing for the thumbnail.

```
photoItem.y = (photos.length * (photoItem.height + 50));
```

Another more elegant solution is to create an event handler that would align the photos once it is loaded. This offers the ability to have multiple-sized images and be more dynamic.

The last task of this method is to add the new instance to the photos array and to finally display it.

```
photos.push(photoItem);
photosContainer.addChild(photoItem);
```

Each time a new search is performed, a call to the `removeOldPhotos` method is made. This method is responsible for removing the existing images and ensuring the data isn't crossed.

```
private function removeOldPhotos():void
{
  if(photos.length > 0)
  {
    photos = new Array();
    removeChild(photosContainer);
    photosContainer = new MovieClip();
    photosContainer.y = 75;
    addChild(photosContainer);
  }
}
```

This method is set to private so other code can't accidentally remove the images. If you want to allow external removal of the images you can create a delegator method that checks some authorization level. If the request is valid, the images are allowed to be removed.

The next class to create, now that the `Document` class is completed, is the `PhotoItem`. This class holds the information for each image that is loaded from flickr. It is also responsible for loading the thumbnail positioning the instance on the stage.

```
package
{
  import flash.display.MovieClip;
  import flash.text.TextField;
  import flash.display.Loader;
  import flash.net.URLRequest;

  public class PhotoItem extends MovieClip
  {
    private var title:String;
    private var thumb:String;

    public function BookItem() {  }
```

329

Part IV Developing Applications

```
    public function setValues(t:String, i:String):void {}
    public function loadThumb():void {}
    public function getValues():Object {}
  }
}
```

When a new instance of this class is created, a call to the `setValues` is made to store the image data. This method accepts two arguments: `title` and `thumbnail path`. Both of these variables are stored in private variables so they can't accidentally be accessed and modified.

```
title = t;
thumb = i;
```

Once the data is loaded, the title is appended to the `titleTxt` component located in the `movieclip`. The title is also moved out to make room for the thumbnail.

```
titleTxt.text = title;
titleTxt.x = 100;
```

The final piece is to make a call to the `loadThumb` method.

```
loadThumb();
```

The `loadThumb` method is responsible for loading the image that is found in the XML document.

```
public function loadThumb():void
{
  var thumbLoader:Loader = new Loader();
  var thumbURL:String = thumb;
  var thumbURLRequest:URLRequest = new URLRequest(thumbURL);
  thumbLoader.load(thumbURLRequest);
  thumbLoader.x = 10;
  addChild(thumbLoader);
}
```

The last method is responsible for passing back the image information.

```
public function getValues():Object
{
  return {title:title};
}
```

You might have noticed the thumbnail loader is the same code that was used in the book searching example. You may also have noticed that loader code across this entire book is very similar. What this should tell you is a class should have been built to handle this one task, and a simple import would replace that ten lines of code that have been duplicated across the applications.

This isn't really noticeable for a smaller application but it would be if you were developing a larger-scale project. Class reusability is explained in greater detail in Chapter 9. But basically, what it comes down to is when you are able to make something modular, it is probably a good idea to do so.

Interfacing with the Web service

The next step in the photo gallery is to build the PHP code that will be responsible for connecting to flickr and parsing the XML response.

The first step is to define the flickr API key that is provided from flickr.

```
<?php

define("FLICKR_ACCESS_KEY", "{FLICKR_API_KEY}");
```

Flickr has a partially unique way of building image URLs. The easiest way to work with this format is by using the `sprintf` function. This function accepts a string with placeholder variables that are then filled in with real variables using values provided in the other arguments.

```
$flickrURLTemplate= "http://farm%s.static.flickr.com/
    %s/%s_%s_s.jpg";
```

To avoid erroneous requests, a simple `if` statement is used to make sure the `tags` variable that comes from Flash in fact has a search term. If for some reason the variable is empty, the script exits and no more code is run from that point.

```
if(empty($_GET['tags']))
{
  exit();
}
```

If a valid `tag` value is found, the next step is to pull in the `tag` data and make the call to flickr to start the search process.

```
$apiMethod = "flickr.photos.search";
$request = "http://api.flickr.com/services/rest/" .
  "?method=" . $apiMethod .
  "&tags=" . $searchTags .
  "&api_key=" . FLICKR_ACCESS_KEY.
  "&per_page=5";

$rawXml = file_get_contents($request);
```

The photo service returns an XML document that is stored in the `$rawXml` variable. After the XML is loaded, it is passed along to the `simplexml_load_string()` method, which creates a proper object that PHP can then parse.

```
$xmlResponse = simplexml_load_string($rawXml);
```

How many images to display are determined by loading the value that is located in the XML document.

```
$nodeCount = getAttribute($xmlResponse->photos, "perpage");
```

Building the custom XML document

The process of building the custom XML document is done using a `for` loop that grabs each photo node and pulls in the required information.

```
$xml = "<?xml version=\"1.0\" ?>\n<photos>";

for($i=0; $i < $nodeCount; $i++)
{
  $farmID= getAttribute($xmlResponse->photos->photo[$i], "farm");
  $serverID= getAttribute($xmlResponse->photos->photo[$i],
    "server");
  $photoID= getAttribute($xmlResponse->photos->photo[$i], "id");
  $secret= getAttribute($xmlResponse->photos->photo[$i],
    "secret");

  $xml .= "\t<photo>";
  $xml .= "\t\t<title><![CDATA[" . getAttribute($xmlResponse-
    >photos
    ->photo[$i], "title") . "]]></title>";
  $xml .= "\t\t<thumb>" .
    sprintf($flickrURLTemplate,
      $farmID,
      $serverID,
      $photoID,
      $secret) .
    "</thumb>";
  $xml .= "  </photo>";
}
```

The first part of the loop is for building the image path, which is passed into the `sprintf` function. After the overall XML document is created, the last step is to output to the caller, which in this case would be Flash.

```
header("content-type: text/xml");
print $xml;
```

Now that the PHP is completed and the overall application has been developed, you can test it, as shown in Figure 12.5.

Developing Real-World Applications   12

FIGURE 12.5

Here is the final application displaying the images from a search using the tag `orange`.

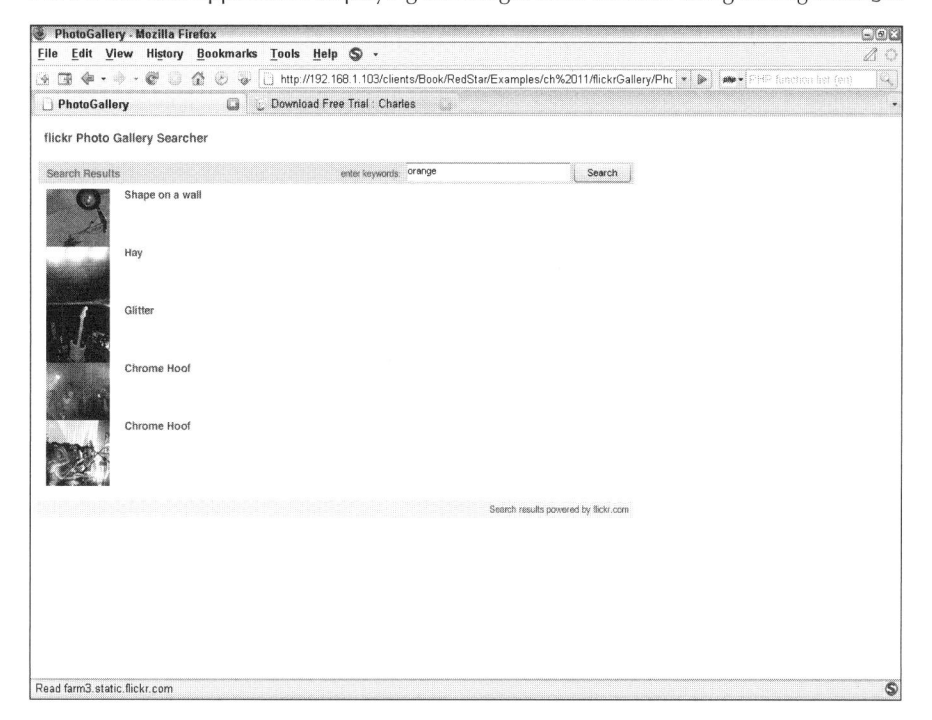

Summary

In this chapter you learned how to connect Flash to the PayPal Web services to develop a custom shopping cart. Once you completed the PayPal development portion you learned how to develop a custom shopping cart in Flash using Classes to simplify the development process.

You then learned how to develop a searching system that utilized the Amazon.com searching API and gained an understanding of how third-party services return data.

In the last part of the chapter you developed an image application using the flickr API. In the process, you learned some of the more robust features of PHP to drill down the data and build the requests using `sprintf`.

The next step is to expand on this example and possibly build a photo gallery script with categories and the ability to add/edit photos. You could even integrate this little portion into a bigger application while using flickr as the graphical frontend or photo storage point.

Chapter 13

Using Advanced Real-World Applications

IN THIS CHAPTER

Drawing application in Flash

Using GD library in PHP

Develop site monitor

Develop Video Player with Flash

Develop a poll application

Develop a simple file editor

Real-world applications are meant to be complete products that have been tested and are ready to be deployed for the general public to enjoy them. This chapter focuses on building a series of applications that do just that. The starting files have been provided so you can focus on the core of the applications, which would be the development process.

Each example is broken into its individual classes, files, and packages depending on what is required. If you have never worked with classes, I strongly recommend that you read Chapter 10. This will ensure the examples and coding styles are easy to follow.

Building a Drawing Application in Flash

This application takes the drawing (see Figure 13.1) and uses PHP to create an exportable image format. The first portion of the code is responsible for the drawing portion of the application.

Part IV Developing Applications

FIGURE 13.1

Here is the completed drawing application.

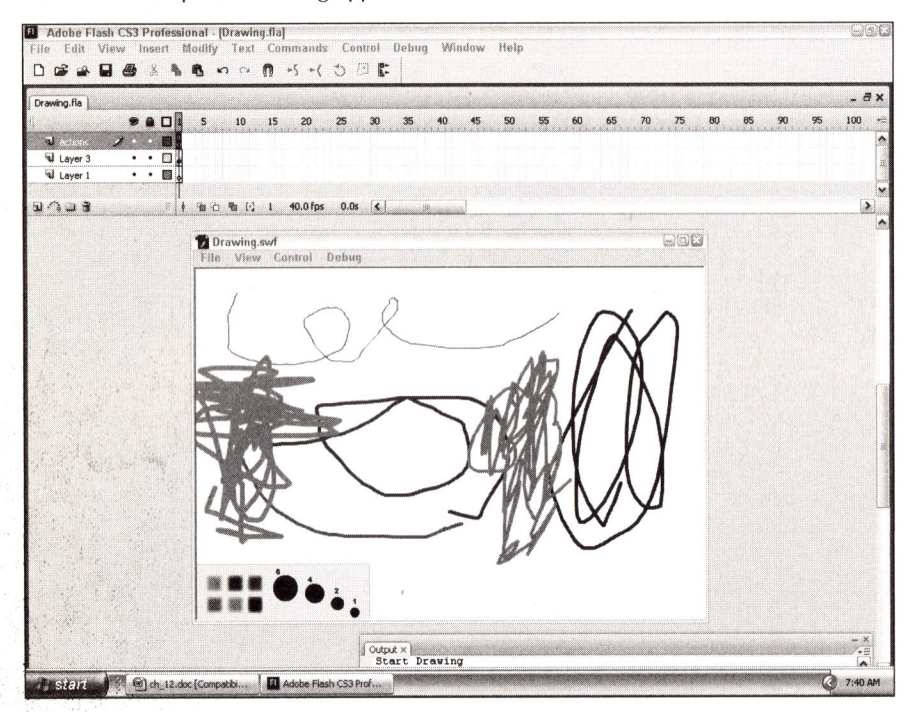

Drawing API in Flash

The drawing API that is included with Flash offers a wide range of tools, such as lines, circles, squares, and gradients. This example focuses on the line to create a Flash-based drawing tool.

Once the starting file is opened {START_FILE}, you can begin to set up the initialization variables that hold the default pen color and size, as well as the container reference.

```
var penMC:MovieClip;
var isDrawing:Boolean = false;

var penTipSize:uint = 1;
var penColor:Number = 0x000000;
```

The drawing application will be set up to draw the line when the mouse button is held down and stop when the mouse button is released. During the time the mouse button is down a persistent call to a mouse move function occurs to place the pen point at a different location. The pen is programmed to draw the line wherever the mouse pointer is located.

Using Advanced Real-World Applications

The next step is to build the event handlers that will be used to determine the pen state and enable or disable the drawing ability. The `isDrawing` variable is toggled to define the current state of the application. This `startDrawing()` method is only called when the mouse is clicked. It is important that a new line is created in case the color or size variables have changed.

```
function startDrawing(e:MouseEvent):void
{
  trace("Start Drawing");
  isDrawing = true;
  penMC.graphics.lineStyle(penTipSize, penColor, 1.0);
  penMC.graphics.moveTo(mouseX, mouseY);
}
```

After the drawing flag is set you can start drawing the actual pen stroke(s). The position of the pen is determined by the current location of the mouse pointer.

```
function drawing(e:MouseEvent):void
{
  if(isDrawing)
  {
    penMC.graphics.lineTo(mouseX, mouseY);
  }
}
```

Now that the line is properly being drawn, it is a good idea to stop it once the mouse button is released. That is done by attaching a handler to the mouse up event.

```
function stopDrawing(e:MouseEvent):void
{
  trace("Stop Drawing");
  isDrawing = false;
}
```

The last method in this example is fairly complex. It is responsible for building the Toolbox and initializing the mouse event handlers.

```
function init():void
{
  penMC = new MovieClip();
  stage.addEventListener(MouseEvent.MOUSE_DOWN, startDrawing);
  stage.addEventListener(MouseEvent.MOUSE_UP, stopDrawing);
  stage.addEventListener(MouseEvent.MOUSE_MOVE, drawing);
  addChild(penMC);
  ...
```

The Toolbox is built up of `movieclips` that are already on the Stage and conveniently found within a container `movieclip`.

337

Part IV Developing Applications

```
toolsMC.swatchPurpleMC.addEventListener(MouseEvent.CLICK,
 function():void
{
  penColor = 0x9999CC;
});
toolsMC.swatchBlueMC.addEventListener(MouseEvent.CLICK,
 function():void
{
  penColor = 0x0000FF;
});
toolsMC.swatchRedMC.addEventListener(MouseEvent.CLICK,
 function():void
{
  penColor = 0xFF0000;
});
toolsMC.swatchGreenMC.addEventListener(MouseEvent.CLICK,
 function():void
{
  penColor = 0x00FF00;
});
toolsMC.swatchOrangeMC.addEventListener(MouseEvent.CLICK,
 function():void
{
  penColor = 0xFF9900;
});
toolsMC.swatchBlackMC.addEventListener(MouseEvent.CLICK,
 function():void
{
  penColor = 0x000000;
});

toolsMC.brushSize1MC.addEventListener(MouseEvent.CLICK,
 function():void
{
  penTipSize = 1;
});
toolsMC.brushSize2MC.addEventListener(MouseEvent.CLICK,
 function():void
{
  penTipSize = 2;
});
toolsMC.brushSize4MC.addEventListener(MouseEvent.CLICK,
 function():void
{
  penTipSize = 4;
});

toolsMC.brushSize6MC.addEventListener(MouseEvent.CLICK,
 function():void
```

```
{
  penTipSize = 6;
});
```

When all of the tools are in place, the container swaps depths with the pen `movieclip` to ensure you can't accidentally draw on the tool interface.

```
  swapChildren(toolsMC, penMC);
}
```

Now that the ActionScript for the drawing application is set, here is the completed code.

```
var penMC:MovieClip;
var isDrawing:Boolean = false;

var penTipSize:uint = 1;
var penColor:Number = 0x000000;

function init():void
{
  penMC = new MovieClip();
  stage.addEventListener(MouseEvent.MOUSE_DOWN, startDrawing);
  stage.addEventListener(MouseEvent.MOUSE_UP, stopDrawing);
  stage.addEventListener(MouseEvent.MOUSE_MOVE, drawing);
  addChild(penMC);

  toolsMC.swatchPurpleMC.addEventListener(MouseEvent.CLICK,
   function():void
  {
    penColor = 0x9999CC;
  });
  toolsMC.swatchBlueMC.addEventListener(MouseEvent.CLICK,
   function():void
  {
    penColor = 0x0000FF;
  });
  toolsMC.swatchRedMC.addEventListener(MouseEvent.CLICK,
   function():void
  {
    penColor = 0xFF0000;
  });
  toolsMC.swatchGreenMC.addEventListener(MouseEvent.CLICK,
   function():void
  {
    penColor = 0x00FF00;
  });
  toolsMC.swatchOrangeMC.addEventListener(MouseEvent.CLICK,
   function():void
  {
    penColor = 0xFF9900;
  });
```

Part IV Developing Applications

```
  toolsMC.swatchBlackMC.addEventListener(MouseEvent.CLICK,
   function():void
  {
    penColor = 0x000000;
  });

  toolsMC.brushSize1MC.addEventListener(MouseEvent.CLICK,
   function():void
  {
    penTipSize = 1;
  });
  toolsMC.brushSize2MC.addEventListener(MouseEvent.CLICK,
   function():void
  {
    penTipSize = 2;
  });

  toolsMC.brushSize4MC.addEventListener(MouseEvent.CLICK,
   function():void
  {
    penTipSize = 4;
  });

  toolsMC.brushSize6MC.addEventListener(MouseEvent.CLICK,
   function():void
  {
    penTipSize = 6;
  });
  swapChildren(toolsMC, penMC);
}

function startDrawing(e:MouseEvent):void
{
  trace("Start Drawing");
  isDrawing = true;
  penMC.graphics.lineStyle(penTipSize, penColor, 1.0);
  penMC.graphics.moveTo(mouseX, mouseY);
}

function drawing(e:MouseEvent):void
{
  if(isDrawing)
  {
    penMC.graphics.lineTo(mouseX, mouseY);
  }
}

function stopDrawing(e:MouseEvent):void
{
  trace("Stop Drawing");
```

Using Advanced Real-World Applications

```
    isDrawing = false;
}

init();
```

That is all there is to a basic drawing application in Flash. You can expand upon this example by providing different pen tips or maybe some varying colors to allow for shading and other painting styles.

The next section builds from this example and uses PHP to render and save the image to the server.

Using GD Library in PHP

The GD library in PHP is a collection of functions that give you the ability to manipulate and create images. GD also has text support provided you have the correct libraries installed. Working with the GD library is fairly straightforward; you either create an image or open an existing image as a base and modify that as needed.

One of the more common uses of the GD library includes the automatic creation of watermarks that are applied to a gallery of images. Some use it to create dynamic thumbnails, similar to how your local image editor would do.

```
http://www.php.net/manual/en/ref.image.php
```

The GD library offers a huge list of functions, but some of them require additional libraries. In fact, it is a good idea to run some code, such as the following, to determine what is installed.

```
<?php var_dump(gd_info()); ?>
```

That code prints what the status of the different components of GD are, such as what is and isn't installed. This is a sample result from that `var_dump` call.

```
array(9)
{
  ["GD Version"] => string(24) "bundled (2.0 compatible)"
  ["FreeType Support"] => bool(false)
  ["T1Lib Support"] => bool(false)
  ["GIF Read Support"] => bool(true)
  ["GIF Create Support"] => bool(false)
  ["JPG Support"] => bool(false)
  ["PNG Support"] => bool(true)
  ["WBMP Support"] => bool(true)
  ["XBM Support"] => bool(false)
}
```

The previous code lets you know that you don't have FreeType (font) and JPG (image) support enabled or installed. With this information, you can continue and install the necessary libraries. Keep in mind that installing applications in a command-line environment isn't as simple as a

341

Part IV Developing Applications

double-click. It involves extensive building of tools and sometimes requires other libraries, which means it can take a lot of work to get the complete GD kit working.

If you are pressed for time and are working locally you can take a look at the Quick Start options available in Chapter 1, which come with a complete version of PHP and GD. If you're running from a remote system it may be best to contact your Web host for installation requests.

> **CAUTION** The GD library (core) doesn't come with every version of PHP. Check with your Web host or install it as needed.

From this point moving forward you should have GD installed with at least JPG support in order to complete the examples. Before building the final application, it is best to get familiar with the GD library by looking at a few examples.

Here is a simple GD example that creates a pink rectangle and outputs it to the browser as a JPG (see Figure 13.2).

```
$image = imagecreate(250, 80);
$bgColor = imagecolorallocate($image, 255, 0, 120);
header("Content-Type: image/jpeg");
imagejpeg($image);
```

FIGURE 13.2

Here is the image that was generated by the GD library using the simple code.

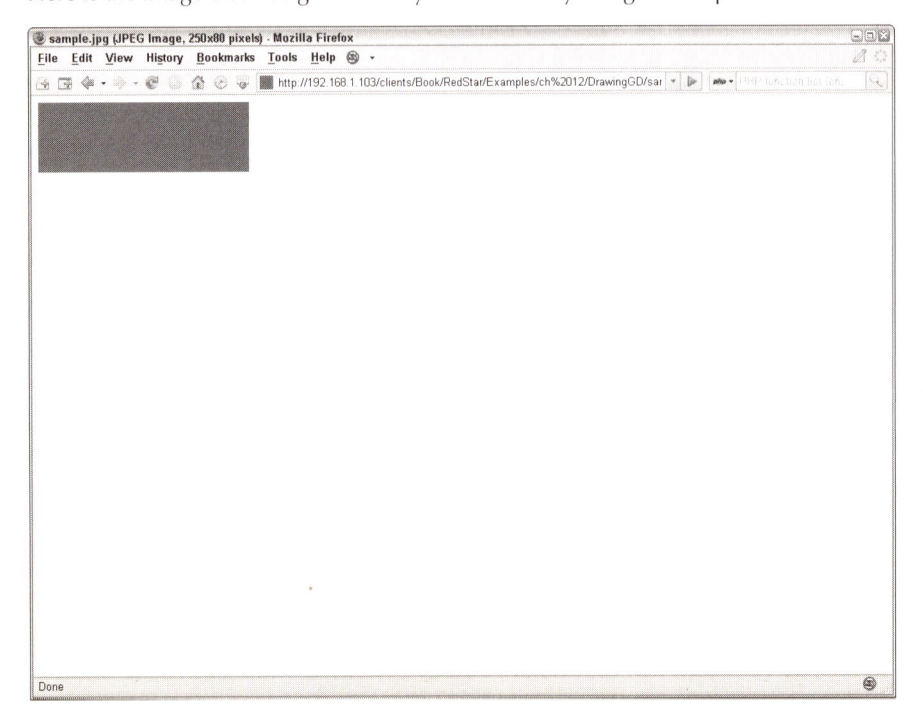

Using Advanced Real-World Applications

Here is a continuation of the previous example, but this time it saves the JPG file to the Web server. By adding a second argument to the `imagejpeg()` function, which is a filename, the image is saved with the filename `sample.jpg` instead of being output to the browser.

```
$image = imagecreate(250, 80);
$bgColor = imagecolorallocate($image, 255, 0, 120);
header("Content-Type: image/jpeg");
imagejpeg($image, './sample.jpg');
```

While these examples are fairly simple they should give you an idea of how to work with the GD library. If you have the other libraries installed, you can render text on those images among many other very interesting results. The GD library is a great feature of PHP and really has come in handy for many tasks, no matter how large.

Now, let's move on to the real application that was started in the previous section. The ActionScript is letting the user draw an image and change settings, and it all works seamlessly; however, the user is not able to save the image unless he prints it. The idea is to inspect the image and send that data to PHP, which will be responsible for creating an image pixel by pixel and saving it to the Web server.

Generating an image in the GD library

This section focuses on using PHP to render the image that is drawn in the Flash application. Normally, you start with the PHP code first, but in this application the PHP is only used as a renderer so it makes sense to start with the Flash portion.

The majority of the application was written in the previous section; you simply take that code and expand upon it to add the necessary actions.

The PHP code is responsible for loading the passed-in XML into an object that is then used to generate, or render, the final image. The width, height, and XML are all passed using POST data because a GET request would fail.

```
$width = $_POST['width'];
$height = $_POST['height'];

$points = simplexml_load_string($_POST['pointData']);
```

When the data is properly loaded, you can set up the base for the rendered image. This is done using the `imagecreatetruecolor()` function, which is part of the GD library.

```
$img = imagecreatetruecolor($width, $height);
```

The actual image is generated by looping through all of the XML data that is pulling out the color values that were captured in Flash.

```
$limit = count($points->point);

for($j=0; $j < $limit; $j++)
```

Part IV Developing Applications

```
  {
    $x = $points->point[$j]->x;
    $y = $points->point[$j]->y;

    $color = $points->point[$j]->c;
    $color = hexdec($color);

    imagesetpixel($img, $x, $y, $color);
  }
```

The pixel data is placed in a grid pattern one line at a time; the $x and $y are the point each color is to be placed. All of this data is passed to the `imagesetpixel` function on each pass of the inner loop.

The last step of the PHP once the image is created is to render the image as a PNG, such as shown in Figure 13.3, and save it to the file system.

```
header('Content-Type: image/png');
imagepng($img, 'render_' . time() . '.png');
```

FIGURE 13.3

A sample image rendered as a PNG

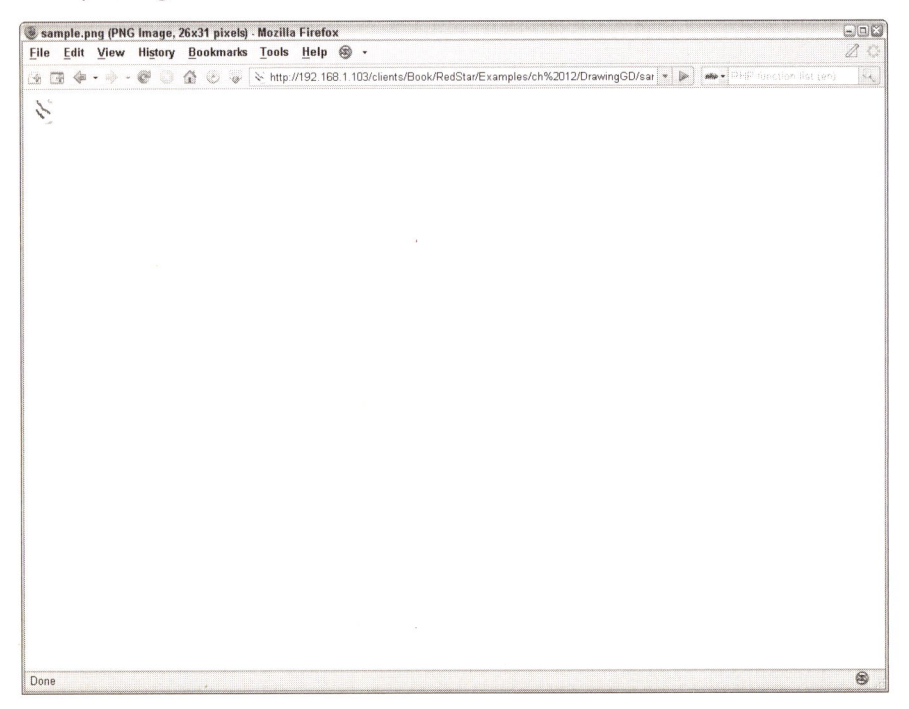

Using Advanced Real-World Applications

> **CAUTION** The process of building an image pixel by pixel is processor intensive and can take a long time, depending on the size of the image.

Here is the completed PHP code:

```
<?php

$width = $_POST['width'];
$height = $_POST['height'];

$points = simplexml_load_string($_POST['pointData']);

$img = imagecreatetruecolor($width, $height);

$limit = count($points->point);

for($j=0; $j < $limit; $j++)
{
  $x = $points->point[$j]->x;
  $y = $points->point[$j]->y;

  $color = $points->point[$j]->c;
  $color = hexdec($color);

  imagesetpixel($img, $x, $y, $color);
}

header('Content-Type: image/png');
imagepng($img, 'render_' . time() . '.png');

?>
```

Gathering the pixel data in Flash

There are only a few updates necessary to the Flash code from the previous section, but for now focus on gathering the image data using the `BitmapData` class.

The first step in this function is to determine the dimensions of the image.

```
var width:uint = penMC.width;
var height:uint = penMC.height;
```

The next variable to define is the PHP file reference.

```
var phpFile:String =
    "http://localhost/ch12/DrawingGD/ImageGenerator.php";
```

The next step is to build a new bitmap using the `draw()` method of the `BitmapData` class. The draw method takes one argument, which is the target. This method takes the argument and copies the pixel data to the new bitmap.

345

Part IV Developing Applications

```
var bmp:BitmapData = new BitmapData(width, height, true,
   0xFFFFFF);
bmp.draw(penMC);
```

After the new bitmap is created, you can build a loop that will scan the bitmap and grab the color of each pixel.

```
var xml:String = "<points>";

for(var i:uint=0; i < width; i++)
{
  for(var j:uint=0; j < height; j++)
  {
    var color:String = bmp.getPixel(i, j).toString(16);

    if(color == "0")
    {
      color = "FFFFFF";
    }

    xml += "<point>";
    xml += "\t<x>" + i + "</x>";
    xml += "\t<y>" + j + "</y>";
    xml += "\t<c>" +  color + "</c>";
    xml += "</point>";
  }
}

xml += "</points>";
```

The color data is stored in a custom XML document that is sent off to PHP once the entire image is scanned. The variables are stored in a new instance of the `URLVariables` object and are passed to PHP in POST data format.

```
var urlVariables:URLVariables = new URLVariables();
urlVariables.width = width;
urlVariables.height = height;
urlVariables.pointData = xml;

var urlRequest:URLRequest = new URLRequest(phpFile);
urlRequest.method = URLRequestMethod.POST;
urlRequest.data = urlVariables;
sendToURL(urlRequest);
```

The response is sent to PHP using the `sendToURL` method. This silently calls the Web server and does not expect any response. The reason for using this method is because the request will be fairly large if the rendered image has a lot of pixel data.

Using Flash to Develop a Site Monitor

When you own or operate a Web site it can sometimes go offline, but most likely you will never know if it is down for just a brief moment unless you happen to be checking the site. What happens if you operate many Web sites and are busy working while your site goes down? Most likely your site goes offline and you are not aware of it.

This section contains the explanation and development of a Flash-based site monitor that logs failed attempts to reach the server. It can even be set up to e-mail the administrator if the system encounters a site that has not responded after a certain point (configurable by the operator).

The MySQL table schema (outline) is as follows:

```
CREATE TABLE siteMonitor (
  id INT NOT NULL AUTO_INCREMENT,
  name VARCHAR(100) DEFAULT "" NOT NULL,
  uri TEXT NOT NULL,
  active VARCHAR(1) DEFAULT 1 NOT NULL,
  PRIMARY KEY (id)
);
```

CROSS-REF There are many ways that you can load the MySQL schema into your database. For an explanation, see Chapter 2.

Developing the PHP for the site monitor

The first part of the PHP is loading in the connection information for the database. This is placed in an external file, so it can be shared across projects. In fact, if you are using the same database as previous examples in this book, you can reuse the old `dbconn.php` because it will not be changed for this application.

If you haven't already created the `dbconn.php`, here are the contents. You fill in the real information for your server, which can be obtained from the Web server administrator if you are not the owner, or your hosting provider if you do own your server.

```
<?php

$host = "localhost";
$user = "USERNAME";
$pass = "PASSWORD";
$database = "DATABASE_NAME";

$link = mysql_connect($host, $user, $pass);
mysql_select_db($database, $link);

unset($host);
unset($user);
```

```
unset($pass);
unset($database);

?>
```

After the database connection is set you can continue the development of the `monitor.php` file. The `$action` is passed along the URL, but needs to be valid in order for the script to know which state it should be running in.

```
$action = (isset($_GET['action'])) ? $_GET['action'] : "";
```

Assuming the action is valid and the value is `getsites`, which is set up to return a listing of the sites that are being monitored. The process of retrieving the site list is accomplished using a loop that loads in the information from the MySQL database. The site list is returned to Flash as an XML object defining each of the sites and where they are located.

The SQL to retrieve the list is set up to load all entries where the active value is equal to 1.

```
SELECT * FROM siteMonitor WHERE active=1
```

After the SQL data is retrieved, it is passed to a `while` loop, which is responsible for grabbing each row and building a line of XML defining the site information.

```
$result = mysql_query("SELECT * FROM siteMonitor WHERE
   active=1");

$xml = "<?xml version=\"1.0\" ?>\n";
$xml .= "<sites>\n";
  while($row = mysql_fetch_array($result))
  {
    ...
  }
  $xml .= "</sites>";
```

The line of XML is built using the `$row` data, which is passed into the `sprint()` function. The `sprintf` is used to automatically fill in the necessary XML attributes using the SQL row data.

```
  $xml .= sprintf("\t<site name=\"%s\" uri=\"%s\" />\n",
$row['name'],
    $row['uri']);
```

Now that the XML data is built, it is sent out to the browser and returned to Flash. This is done by setting the `content-type` of the response to `text/xml`, which is the MIME type of XML. Then the last step is to use a print statement to actually output the data.

```
header("Content-type: text/xml");
print $xml;
```

Using Advanced Real-World Applications

Here is a sample of the response that would be returned to Flash:

```xml
<?xml version="1.0" ?>
<sites>
  <site name="Adobe" uri="http://www.adobe.com" />
  <site name="AIRPlayground" uri="http://www.airplayground.com"
   />
  <site name="mkeefeDESIGN" uri="http://www.mkeefedesign.com" />
  <site name="Google" uri="http://www.google.com" />
</sites>
```

Using PHP to e-mail the administrator

When a site has been unreachable for a certain amount of time, it is probably a good idea to notify someone. The notification is sent using the built-in `mail()` function. The e-mail alerts the admin of a server as to what site is experiencing the outage and at what time the report was sent, in the rare case the e-mail is delayed or is just not noticed right away.

The first step is to verify the previous action is set to e-mail the admin. Otherwise, this entire block of code would be ignored.

```php
else if($action == "emailadmin")
{
    ...
}
```

If the action is valid, the next step is to construct the e-mail message and retrieve the values passed from Flash that define the site experiencing the outage.

```php
$from = "sitemonitor@yoursite.com";
$to = "admin@yoursite.com";
$site = $_GET['site'];
$siteURI = $_GET['siteURI'];

$date = date("F j, Y \\a\\t h:i a", time()); // today's date
```

The body of the e-mail is defined as a series of `$emailInfo` variables concatenated together using the dot (.), which is used to let PHP know this variable is a continuation.

```php
$emailInfo  = "";
$emailInfo .= "**This is an automated response**.\n\n";
$emailInfo .= "The site status monitor has been informed\n";
$emailInfo .= " the following site is not responding:\n";
$emailInfo .= "----------------------------------------\n";
$emailInfo .= "Site:        " . $site . " [" . $siteURI . "]\n";
$emailInfo .= "Date Sent:   " . $date . "\n\n";
$emailInfo .= "----------------------------------------\n";
```

349

Part IV Developing Applications

The header of the e-mail needs to follow the specification that defines how e-mail is to be constructed and the `$from` value needs to be valid, even though the actual e-mail address used doesn't.

```
// Mail headers, do not alter
$mailHeaders = "From: " . $from . " <> \n\n";
```

When all of the variables and e-mail information have been created, the actual e-mail can be sent. This is done by making a call to the `mail()` function, passing along the information that was built in the previous steps.

```
if(mail(
  $to,
  "Automated response from Site Monitor",
  $emailInfo,
  $mailHeaders))
{
  print "result=success";
}
```

> **NOTE** The `mail()` function returns a success message if the function is properly called. The function does not know the status of the actual sending of the e-mail.

Here is the completed PHP code for `monitor.php`:

```
<?php

require('dbconn.php');

$action = (isset($_GET['action'])) ? $_GET['action'] : "";

if($action == "getsites")
{
  $result = mysql_query("SELECT * FROM siteMonitor WHERE
    active=1");

  $xml = "<?xml version=\"1.0\" ?>\n";
  $xml .= "<sites>\n";
  while($row = mysql_fetch_array($result))
  {
    $xml .= sprintf("\t<site name=\"%s\" uri=\"%s\" />\n",
   $row['name'],
      $row['uri']);
  }
  $xml .= "</sites>";

  header("Content-type: text/xml");
```

350

```
    print $xml;
}
else if($action == "emailadmin")
{
  $from = "sitemonitor@yoursite.com";
  $to = "admin@yoursite.com";
  $site = $_GET['site'];
  $siteURI = $_GET['siteURI'];

  $date = date("F j, Y \\a\\t h:i a", time()); // today's date

  $emailInfo   = "";
  $emailInfo .= "**This is an automated response**.\n\n";
  $emailInfo .= "The site status monitor has been informed\n";
  $emailInfo .= " the following site is not responding:\n";
  $emailInfo .= "----------------------------------------\n";
  $emailInfo .= "Site:     " . $site . " [" . $siteURI . "]\n";
  $emailInfo .= "Date Sent:    " . $date . "\n\n";
  $emailInfo .= "----------------------------------------\n";

  // Mail headers, do not alter
  $mailHeaders = "From: " . $from . " <> \n\n";

  print $emailInfo;
  if(mail(
    $to,
    "Automated response from Site Monitor",
    $emailInfo,
    $mailHeaders
  ))
  {
    print "result=success";
  }
}

?>
```

Developing the ActionScript for the site monitor

At this point, the PHP code has been completed, and the next section focuses on the ActionScript development process. The Flash file has been provided for this example on the book's Web site, which has all of the design elements in place, as shown in Figure 13.4, so you can focus on the development.

Part IV Developing Applications

FIGURE 13.4

Here is the completed application with one of the sites indicating a failure.

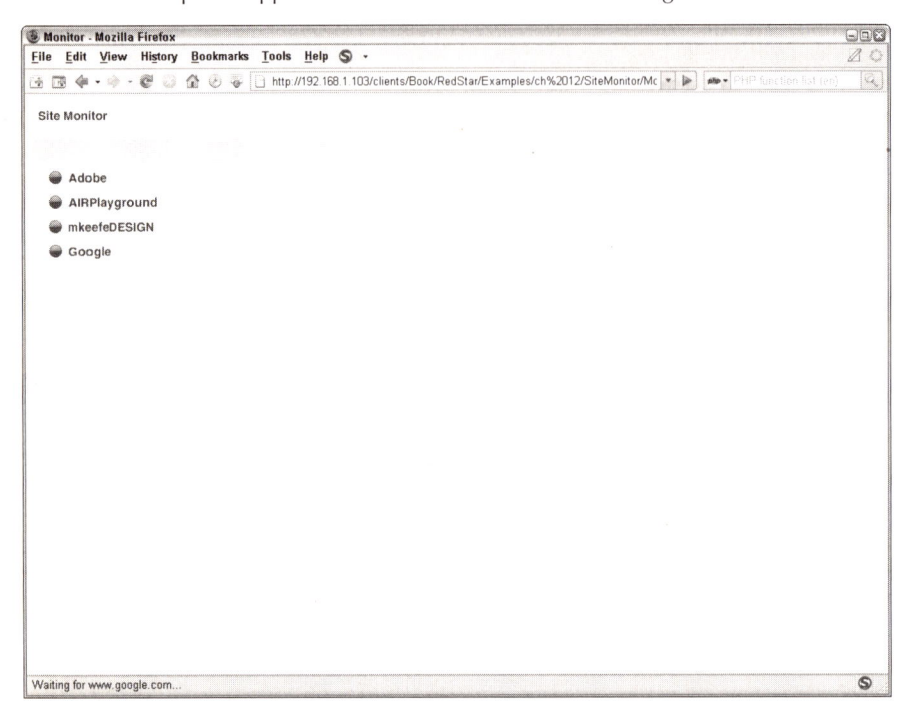

Here is the class skeleton for the `Document` class.

```
package
{
   import flash.display.MovieClip;
   import flash.net.*;
   import flash.events.*;

   public class SiteMonitor extends MovieClip
   {
      public function SiteMonitor() {}
      private function loadSites():void {}
      private function loadSiteHandler(e:Event):void {}
   }
}
```

The constructor in the `Document` class is responsible for assigning the `siteContainer` `movieclip`, adding that `movieclip` to the display list and finally making a call to the `loadSites()` method.

Using Advanced Real-World Applications   13

```
siteContainer = new MovieClip();
siteContainer.y = 80;
siteContainer.x = 20;
addChild(siteContainer);

loadSites();
```

The `loadSites()` method is responsible for loading the list of sites to watch. An event is attached to the loading sequence, which is called when the site data is successfully retrieved.

```
var variables:URLVariables = new URLVariables();
variables.action = "getsites";

var urlRequest:URLRequest = new URLRequest(phpFile);
urlRequest.data = variables;

var urlLoader:URLLoader = new URLLoader();
urlLoader.addEventListener(Event.COMPLETE, loadSiteHandler);
urlLoader.load(urlRequest);
```

The next method is called when the site data is successfully loaded. An event is passed as an argument that contains the response from PHP.

```
private function loadSiteHandler(e:Event):void
{
   ...
}
```

The response is XML, so you need to first create an XML object that will be looped through using a `for..each` loop.

```
var urlLoader:URLLoader = URLLoader(e.target);
var xml:XML = new XML(urlLoader.data);

var i:uint = 0;
for each(var item in xml..site)
{
   ...
}
```

The contents of the `for..each` loop creates a new instance of the `SiteMonitorItem` class that is attached to a `movieclip` in the Timeline of the same name.

```
var siteItem:SiteMonitorItem = new SiteMonitorItem();
siteItem.phpFile = phpFile;
siteItem.siteURI = item..attribute('uri');
siteItem.siteNameTxt.text = item..attribute('name');
```

Part IV Developing Applications

```
        siteItem.statusMC.gotoAndStop(2);

        siteItem.y = (i * (siteItem.height + 10));

        siteContainer.addChild(siteItem);
        i++;
```

The `siteItem` variable holds the newly created class instance, which is used to assign the `phpFile`, `siteURI`, and site name. The `uri` and site name are parsed from the XML object using the `attribute()` method, which takes an argument that is the attribute name you are looking for. The placement of the `siteItem` object is determined by a simple equation using the height of the object and the value of the `i` variable, then taking that sum and adding a 10px padding.

At this point the document class is finished. Here is the completed code:

```
        package
        {
          import flash.display.MovieClip;
          import flash.net.*;
          import flash.events.*;

          public class SiteMonitor extends MovieClip
          {

            public var siteContainer:MovieClip;
            public var phpFile:String =
              "http://localhost/SiteMonitor/monitor.php";

            public function SiteMonitor()
            {
              siteContainer = new MovieClip();
              siteContainer.y = 80;
              siteContainer.x = 20;
              addChild(siteContainer);

              loadSites();
            }

            private function loadSites():void
            {
              var variables:URLVariables = new URLVariables();
              variables.action = "getsites";

              var urlRequest:URLRequest = new URLRequest(phpFile);
              urlRequest.data = variables;

              var urlLoader:URLLoader = new URLLoader();
              urlLoader.addEventListener(Event.COMPLETE,
                loadSiteHandler);
```

Using Advanced Real-World Applications

```
      urlLoader.load(urlRequest);
    }

    private function loadSiteHandler(e:Event):void
    {
      var urlLoader:URLLoader = URLLoader(e.target);
      var xml:XML = new XML(urlLoader.data);

      var i:uint = 0;
      for each(var item in xml..site)
      {
        var siteItem:SiteMonitorItem = new
   SiteMonitorItem();
        siteItem.phpFile = phpFile;
        siteItem.siteURI = item..attribute('uri');
        siteItem.siteNameTxt.text =
          item..attribute('name');
        siteItem.statusMC.gotoAndStop(2);
        siteContainer.addChild(siteItem);

        siteItem.y = (i * (siteItem.height + 10));

        siteItem.checkSite();

        i++;
      }
    }
  }
}
```

The next class to focus on is the `SiteMonitorItem`, which is assigned to the `movieclip` in the library of the same name. Here is the class skeleton for that class:

```
package
{
  public class SiteMonitorItem extends MovieClip
  {
    public function SiteMonitorItem() {}
    public function checkSite():void {}

    private function noResponse(event:IOErrorEvent):void {}
    private function siteResponsedHandler(e:Event):void {}
    private function stopChecking():void {}

    public function get attempts():uint {}
    public function set attempts(num:uint):void {}
  }
}
```

The constructor of this class is empty, so you can leave it out and continue to the next method, which is `checkSite()`. This method is called by the `Document` class when the wait timer expires. The purpose of this method is to begin the action of checking the site and the correct handler depending on the response received.

```
public function checkSite():void
{
  var urlRequest:URLRequest = new URLRequest(siteURI);
  var urlLoader:URLLoader = new URLLoader();
  urlLoader.addEventListener(Event.COMPLETE,
    siteResponsedHandler);
  urlLoader.addEventListener(IOErrorEvent.IO_ERROR, noResponse);
  urlLoader.load(urlRequest);
}
```

The majority of that method is the same as previous examples, with the exception of the second event listener. This event listener is assigned to the `IO_ERROR`, which occurs when a file is not properly loaded or called. The `noResponse()` method will be called when the site cannot be loaded, as shown here:

```
urlLoader.addEventListener(IOErrorEvent.IO_ERROR, noResponse);
```

The `noResponse()` method is responsible for incrementing the `failedAttempts` variable, but using a setter method instead of accessing the variable directly.

```
private function noResponse(event:IOErrorEvent):void
{
  attempts = attempts + 1;
}
```

If the site is loaded, a call to `siteResponsedHandler()` is made to clear the previous failed attempts and basically reset the error count.

```
private function siteResponsedHandler(e:Event):void
{
  failedAttempts = 0;
}
```

A call to `stopChecking()` occurs when a site fails to respond after a predetermined number of times, set by the `MAX_ATTEMPTS` constant.

```
private function stopChecking():void
{
  stopCheck = true;
}
```

The last two methods in this class are the getter and setters for the `failedAttempts` variable. The getter simply returns the current value of the `failedAttempts` value. The setter not only

Using Advanced Real-World Applications   13

increments the `failedAttempts` variable, but also determines if all future checks should be stopped based on the current failure count.

```
public function get attempts():uint
{
  return failedAttempts;
}

public function set attempts(num:uint):void
{
  if(num == undefined)
  {
    failedAttempts++;
  }
  else
  {
    failedAttempts = num;
  }

  if(failedAttempts == MAX_ATTEMPTS)
  {
    statusMC.gotoAndStop(1);
    stopChecking();
  }
}
```

If `failedAttempts` equals the `MAX_ATTEMPTS` constant, a call to `stopChecking()` is made and the status indicator moves to the first frame displaying a red circle.

At this point the `SiteMonitorItem` class is now complete and the Flash movie can be tested to ensure it works properly with the PHP code written before.

Following is the completed class file `SiteMonitorItem` that is attached to the `movieclip` of the same name:

```
package
{
  import flash.display.MovieClip;
  import flash.net.*;
  import flash.events.*;
  import flash.text.TextField;

  public class SiteMonitorItem extends MovieClip
  {
    public var phpFile:String;
    public var siteURI:String;

    private var stopCheck:Boolean = false;
```

357

Part IV Developing Applications

```
private var failedAttempts:uint = 0;

private const MAX_ATTEMPTS:uint = 3;

public function SiteMonitorItem() { }

public function checkSite():void
{
  var urlRequest:URLRequest = new URLRequest(siteURI);
  var urlLoader:URLLoader = new URLLoader();
  urlLoader.addEventListener(Event.COMPLETE,
    siteResponsedHandler);
  urlLoader.addEventListener(IOErrorEvent.IO_ERROR,
    noResponse);
  urlLoader.load(urlRequest);
}

private function noResponse(event:IOErrorEvent):void
{
  attempts = attempts + 1;
}

private function siteResponsedHandler(e:Event):void
{
  failedAttempts = 0;
}

private function stopChecking():void
{
  stopCheck = true;
}

public function get attempts():uint
{
  return failedAttempts;
}

public function set attempts(num:uint):void
{
  if(num == undefined)
  {
    failedAttempts++;
  }
  else
  {
    failedAttempts = num;
  }

  if(failedAttempts == MAX_ATTEMPTS)
  {
    statusMC.gotoAndStop(1);
```

```
            stopChecking();
        }
    }

    }
}
```

Using Flash to Develop a Video Player

Video players, such as the one illustrated in Figure 13.5, are becoming more and more popular as the Internet continues to get faster. The idea behind this section is to develop a video player that is interfaced with PHP to load in the video list, as well as keep track of the play count.

Flash already ships with a pretty versatile video player component, but you can still expand upon it, which is exactly what this section will help you achieve.

The application is constructed of a `VideoPlayer` and `ComboBox` component that has already been placed on the Stage. The start file `{START_FILE}` is provided so you can focus on the development and can quickly test as you go.

FIGURE 13.5

A video player with a video loaded and playing

Part IV Developing Applications

> **NOTE** You need an FLV video file in order to test this application. One is included with the source material found on the book's Web site.

Many of the applications you develop in Flash will consist of some ActionScript. The complexity of the ActionScript will be determined based on what the application will be. In this example you will be using an external class to develop the video player.

The first part of the application to be developed is the ActionScript code, which is broken up in classes for greater scalability. The main ActionScript will be attached to the application using the `Document` class.

To start, look at the class skeleton, which will give you a better idea of how the application will flow.

```
package
{
  public class VideoPlayer extends MovieClip
  {
    public function VideoPlayer(){}
    public function loadData():void {}

    private function dataLoaded(e:Event):void {}
    private function comboHandler(e:Event):void {}
  }
}
```

The constructor method of the `Document` class is responsible for assigning the `VideoPlayer` instance. It is also the point where the necessary event listeners are defined.

```
_player = this['player'];
this['videoListCombo'].addEventListener(Event.CHANGE,
    comboHandler);
```

The last part of the constructor method is to call the `loadData` method and gather the XML data.

```
loadData();
```

The `loadData()` method is for loading the video data, which is returned in XML format.

```
public function loadData():void
{
  var urlVariables:URLVariables = new URLVariables;
  urlVariables.a = "getvideos";

  var urlRequest:URLRequest = new URLRequest(phpFile);
  urlRequest.data = urlVariables;

  var urlLoader:URLLoader = new URLLoader();
  urlLoader.addEventListener(Event.COMPLETE, dataLoaded);
  urlLoader.load(urlRequest);
}
```

Using Advanced Real-World Applications   13

Here is a sample of the XML response, which has the attributes populated instead of nodes.

```
<videos>
  <video name="Sample Video 1" src="color1.flv" playCount="7" />
  <video name="Sample Video 2" src="color2.flv" playCount="3" />
  <video name="Sample Video 3" src="color3.flv" playCount="5" />
  <video name="Sample Video 4" src="color4.flv" playCount="4" />
  <video name="Sample Video 5" src="color5.flv" playCount="1" />
  <video name="Sample Video 6" src="color6.flv" playCount="2" />
</videos>
```

After the XML data object is loaded, a call to `dataLoaded()` is made, which is responsible for populating the `ComboBox`. A `for..each` loop is used to parse the video data, which is then added to the `ComboBox` component.

```
this['videoListCombo'].addItem({label:'Choose Video...', data:-
    1});
for each(var item in xml..video)
{
  var name:String = item..attribute('name');
  var src:String = item..attribute('src');

  this['videoListCombo'].addItem({label:name, data:src});
}
```

The last method of the `Document` class is an event handler for the `ComboBox` component.

```
private function comboHandler(e:Event):void
{
  if(e.target.selectedItem.data == -1) return;
  trace("Load Video: " + e.target.selectedItem.data);
  _player.source = 'videos/' + e.target.selectedItem.data;
}
```

This event handler method is used to load the video file, but only if a valid data value is found. A simple `if` statement is used to determine if the label is selected.

```
if(e.target.selectedItem.data == -1) return;
```

That is all there is to this class. Here is the completed `Document` class:

```
package
{
  import flash.display.MovieClip;
  import flash.events.*;
  import flash.net.URLVariables;
  import flash.net.URLRequest;
  import flash.net.URLLoader;
  import flash.media.Video;
  public class VideoPlayer extends MovieClip
  {
```

361

Part IV   **Developing Applications**

```
public var phpFile:String =
"http://localhost/ ch12/VideoPlayer/videoManager.php";

private var _player:FLVPlayback;

public function VideoPlayer()
{
  _player = this['player'];
  this['videoListCombo'].addEventListener(
    Event.CHANGE, comboHandler);
  loadData();
}

public function loadData():void
{
  var urlVariables:URLVariables = new URLVariables;
  urlVariables.a = "getvideos";

  var urlRequest:URLRequest = new URLRequest(phpFile);
  urlRequest.data = urlVariables;

  var urlLoader:URLLoader = new URLLoader();
  urlLoader.addEventListener(Event.COMPLETE,
    dataLoaded);
  urlLoader.load(urlRequest);
}

private function dataLoaded(e:Event):void
{
  var urlLoader:URLLoader = URLLoader(e.target);
  var xml:XML = new XML(urlLoader.data);

  this['videoListCombo'].addItem({
    label:'Choose Video...', data:-1});
  for each(var item in xml..video)
  {
    var name:String = item..attribute('name');
    var src:String = item..attribute('src');

    this['videoListCombo'].addItem({
       label:name, data:src});
  }
}

private function comboHandler(e:Event):void
{
```

Using Advanced Real-World Applications

```
        if(e.target.selectedItem.data == -1) return;
        trace("Load Video: " + e.target.selectedItem.data);
        _player.source = 'videos/' +
          e.target.selectedItem.data;
      }
    }
  }
```

The next step is to develop the PHP code that is used to return an XML object. For this example, the video data is a static array, but you can easily update it to use a MySQL database similar to the previous examples.

```
$videos = array(
  array("Sample Video 1", "color.flv", 0),
  array("Sample Video 2", "color.flv", 0),
  array("Sample Video 3", "color.flv", 0),
  array("Sample Video 4", "color.flv", 0),
  array("Sample Video 5", "color.flv", 0),
  array("Sample Video 6", "color.flv", 0)
);
```

This example only has one action, which is to retrieve the video list and build an XML object to be passed back to Flash.

```
if($action == "getvideos")
{
  $xml = "<videos>";
  for($i=0; $i < count($videos); $i++)
  {
    $xml .= "\t<video";
    $xml .= " name=\"" . $videos[$i][0] . "\"";
    $xml .= " src=\"" . $videos[$i][1] . "\"";
    $xml .= " playCount=\"" . $videos[$i][2] . "\"";
    $xml .= " />\n";
  }
  $xml .= "</videos>";
```

After the XML object is created, a header type of XML is outputted; the last step is to output the actual XML code.

```
header("Content-type: text/xml");
print $xml;
```

That is all the PHP code that is needed to develop this video application. Here is the completed PHP:

```php
<?php

$action = (isset($_GET['a'])) ? $_GET['a'] : "";

$videos = array(
  array("Sample Video 1", "color.flv", 0),
  array("Sample Video 2", "color.flv", 0),
  array("Sample Video 3", "color.flv", 0),
  array("Sample Video 4", "color.flv", 0),
  array("Sample Video 5", "color.flv", 0),
  array("Sample Video 6", "color.flv", 0)
);

if($action == "getvideos")
{
  $xml = "<videos>";
  for($i=0; $i < count($videos); $i++)
  {
    $xml .= "\t<video";
    $xml .= " name=\"" . $videos[$i][0] . "\"";
    $xml .= " src=\"" . $videos[$i][1] . "\"";
    $xml .= " playCount=\"" . $videos[$i][2] . "\"";
    $xml .= " />\n";
  }
  $xml .= "</videos>";

  header("Content-type: text/xml");
  print $xml;
}

?>
```

Developing a Poll Application

A poll is a very common feature of any Web site, but a person will often use a service that manages the poll instead of creating his or her own. The main problem with that approach is your data is on someone else's server. A less common issue is the lack of freedom with the design of the poll application.

Building the PHP and MySQL

This application consists of the design, PHP development, and ActionScript to develop a full functional polling application, such as the one shown in Figure 13.6. The initial focus is on the SQL code that stores the poll data.

Using Advanced Real-World Applications 13

FIGURE 13.6

A completed poll application displaying some sample data

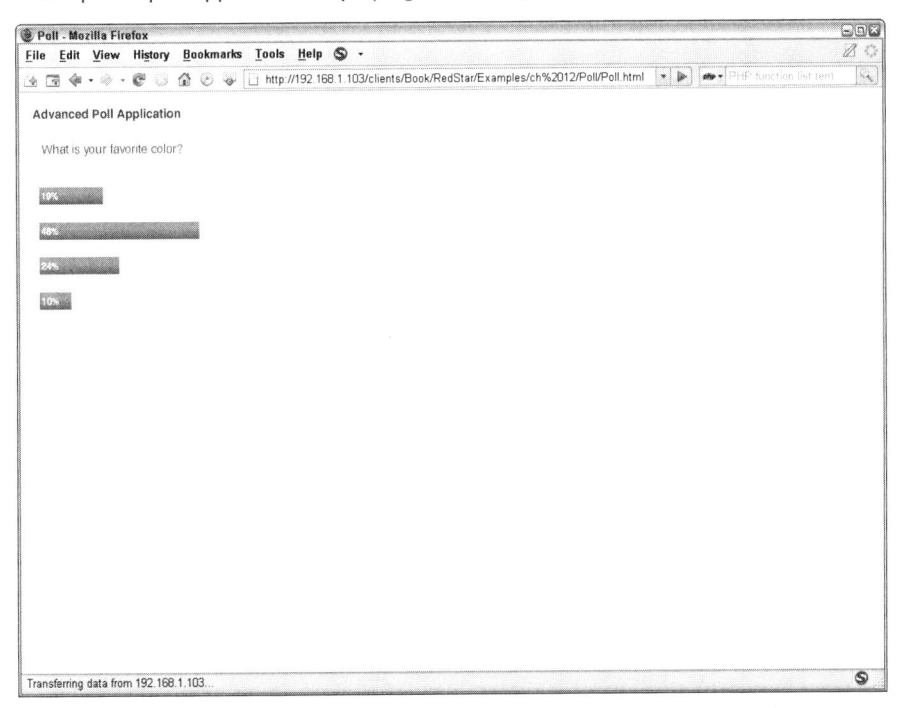

To offer more than one poll, a unique ID is assigned to each answer that determines which question it is associated with.

```
CREATE TABLE poll (
   id INT NOT NULL DEFAULT 0,
   pollValue TEXT NOT NULL,
   pollType VARCHAR(20) DEFAULT "" NOT NULL,
   pollVotes INT(11) NOT NULL,
   active VARCHAR(1) DEFAULT 1 NOT NULL
);
```

This table schema is placing the questions and answers in one table for simplicity. However, in a more robust application you would want to place the question and answers in two separate tables for better scalability. This is how you make a database more efficient.

After the SQL is written, you can move on to developing the PHP code. This application has two actions: the ability to get poll data and to vote. In a more advanced application you would most likely have an editor and removal system.

Part IV Developing Applications

The action and poll ID are passed by the URL, so the first part of the code is responsible for storing that information.

```
$action = (isset($_GET['a'])) ? $_GET['a'] : "";
$pollID = (isset($_GET['id'])) ? $_GET['id'] : "";
```

The next step is to load the poll data from the database using a simple `SELECT` statement.

```
$sql = "SELECT * FROM poll WHERE id=" . $pollID;
$query = mysql_query($sql);
```

When the SQL data is loaded, it is passed into a `while` loop that is responsible for constructing the XML data. An `if` statement is used to determine if a valid vote is available; if it is, the `xml` attribute is added.

```
$xml = "<poll id=\"" . $pollID . "\">\n";

while($row = mysql_fetch_array($query))
{
  $xml .= "\t<element";
  $xml .= " type=\"" . $row['pollType'] . "\"";
  $xml .= " value=\"" . $row['pollValue'] . "\"";

  if($row['pollType'] == "answer")
  {
    $xml .= " votes=\"" . $row['pollVotes'] . "\"";
  }

  $xml .= " />\n";
```

The second action is to cast a vote using the poll ID and question value as a unique way to determine the correct poll value to update.

```
else if($action == "vote")
{
  $votes = (isset($_GET['v'])) ? $_GET['v'] : "";
  $question = (isset($_GET['q'])) ? $_GET['q'] : "";

  $votes = $votes + 1;

  $sql = "UPDATE poll SET pollValue=" . $votes . " WHERE id=" .
    $pollID . " AND pollValue=" . $question;
  mysql_query($sql);
}
```

The last step of the PHP is to generate an XML header and output the created XML object to the browser, where Flash will load it.

```
header("Content-type: text/xml");

print $xml;
```

Using Advanced Real-World Applications

Here is the completed PHP file that will be used in the poll application:

```php
<?php

require 'dbconn.php';

$action = (isset($_GET['a'])) ? $_GET['a'] : "";
$pollID = (isset($_GET['id'])) ? $_GET['id'] : "";

if($action == "getpolldata")
{
  $sql = "SELECT * FROM poll WHERE id=" . $pollID;
  $query = mysql_query($sql);

  $xml = "<poll id=\"" . $pollID . "\">\n";

  while($row = mysql_fetch_array($query))
  {
    $xml .= "\t<element";
    $xml .= " type=\"" . $row['pollType'] . "\"";
    $xml .= " value=\"" . $row['pollValue'] . "\"";

    if($row['pollType'] == "answer")
    {
      $xml .= " votes=\"" . $row['pollVotes'] . "\"";
    }

    $xml .= " />\n";
  }

  $xml .= "</poll>";

  header("Content-type: text/xml");

  print $xml;

}
else if($action == "vote")
{
  $votes = (isset($_GET['v'])) ? $_GET['v'] : "";
  $question = (isset($_GET['q'])) ? $_GET['q'] : "";

  $votes = $votes + 1;

  $sql = "UPDATE poll SET pollValue=" . $votes . " WHERE id=" .
    $pollID . " AND pollValue=" . $question;
  mysql_query($sql);
}

?>
```

Part IV Developing Applications

Developing the ActionScript for the poll

The ActionScript for the poll application is broken into two pieces. The first piece is a `Document` class that controls the majority of the polling application. The second is a `PollItem` that is duplicated for each answer in the loaded poll.

The data that was loaded from PHP is returned in XML format. Here is a sample of that response:

```xml
<poll>
  <element type="question" value="What is your favorite color?" />

  <element type="answer" value="Black" votes="0" />

  <element type="answer" value="Blue" votes="0" />

  <element type="answer" value="Orange" votes="0" />

  <element type="answer" value="Red" votes="0" />
</poll>
```

The first class to focus on is the `PollItem` because it will be loaded by the `Document` class, and it is the next step to work in a logical order. Here is the class skeleton for the `PollItem`:

```
package
{
  public class PollItem extends MovieClip
  {
    public function PollItem() {}
    public function get data():Object {}
    public function setData(i:uint, a:String, v:uint):void {}
  }
}
```

The first portion of the class is the variables, which in this class are the `id`, `answer`, and `vote` value for each poll item instance.

```
private var ID:uint;
private var answer:String;
private var votes:uint;
```

This class actually only had two methods. The first method is a getter that returns an object filled with the item data.

```
public function get data():Object
{
  return {id:ID, answer:"", votes:votes};
}
```

368

Using Advanced Real-World Applications

The second method is responsible for assigning the data to each poll item. The stored variables are all set to `private`, which allows the developer to control the access and keep consistent throughout the entire application process.

```
public function setData(i:uint, a:String, v:uint):void
{
  ID = i;
  answer = a;
  votes = v;
}
```

That is all there is to the `PollItem` class, which is shown here complete:

```
package
{
  import flash.display.MovieClip;
  import flash.text.TextField;

  public class PollItem extends MovieClip
  {
    private var ID:uint;
    private var answer:String;
    private var votes:uint;
    public function PollItem() {}

    public function get data():Object
    {
      return {id:ID, answer:"", votes:votes};
    }

    public function setData(i:uint, a:String, v:uint):void
    {
      ID = i;
      answer = a;
      votes = v;
    }
  }
}
```

The final class is the `Document` class, which is attached to the Stage by setting the value in the Property inspector. Here is the class skeleton:

```
package
{
  public class Poll extends MovieClip
  {
    public function Poll() {}
    public function loadPollData():void {}
    public function dataLoaded(e:Event):void {}
  }
}
```

369

The first method is called from the constructor and is responsible for loading the poll data in XML format based on the poll id that is passed in a GET request.

```
public function loadPollData():void
{
  var urlVariables:URLVariables = new URLVariables;
  urlVariables.a = "getpolldata";
  urlVariables.id = POLL_ID;

  var urlRequest:URLRequest = new URLRequest(phpFile);
  urlRequest.data = urlVariables;

  var urlLoader:URLLoader = new URLLoader();
  urlLoader.addEventListener(Event.COMPLETE, dataLoaded);
  urlLoader.load(urlRequest);
}
```

After the data is loaded, a call to the `dataLoaded()` method is made, which is responsible for displaying the poll data using the `PollItem` instances.

The response from the server is sent in XML format, which is parsed and used to build the poll graphics. Each element of the poll data is stored as an attribute rather than a node in an attempt to keep the code lightweight.

```
var type:String = item..attribute('type');
var value:String = item..attribute('value');
var total:uint = uint(xml..attribute('total'));
```

The `type` variable is used to determine whether an element is a question or an answer.

```
if(type == "question")
{
  this['questionTxt'].text = value;
  continue;
}

if(type == "answer")
{
  var votes:uint = uint(item..attribute('votes'));
}
```

The `pollItem` variable stores the instance of the `PollItem` class, which contains the graphics for each poll element. The percentage is determined with some very basic math, which divides the vote count by the total and multiplies that by 100 to generate a percentage.

```
var pollItem:PollItem = new PollItem();
pollItem['percentTxt'].text = Math.round(votes / total * 100) +
    "%";
pollItem['barMC'].width = (votes / total * 100) * 4;
```

Using Advanced Real-World Applications 13

The last step in the method is for aligning each `pollItem`, attaching the `pollItem` to the display list, and finally adding it to the `pollItems` array.

```
pollItem.y = (pollItems.length * (pollItem.height + 20));

container.addChild(pollItem);
pollItems.push(pollItem);
```

At this point, the `Document` class is built, and is shown in its entirety here:

```
package
{
  import flash.display.MovieClip;
  import flash.events.*;
  import flash.net.URLVariables;
  import flash.net.URLRequest;
  import flash.net.URLLoader;
  import flash.text.TextField;

  public class Poll extends MovieClip
  {
    public var POLL_ID:uint = 1;
    public var phpFile:String =
      "http://localhost/ch12/Poll/poll.php";

    public var container:MovieClip;
    public var pollItems:Array;

    public function Poll()
    {
      pollItems = new Array();
      container = new MovieClip();
      container.x = 15;
      container.y = 100;

      addChild(container);

      loadPollData();
    }

    public function loadPollData():void
    {
      var urlVariables:URLVariables = new URLVariables;
      urlVariables.a = "getpolldata";
      urlVariables.id = POLL_ID;

      var urlRequest:URLRequest = new URLRequest(phpFile);
```

371

Part IV **Developing Applications**

```
      urlRequest.data = urlVariables;

      var urlLoader:URLLoader = new URLLoader();
      urlLoader.addEventListener(Event.COMPLETE,
        dataLoaded);
      urlLoader.load(urlRequest);
    }

    public function dataLoaded(e:Event):void
    {
      var urlLoader:URLLoader = URLLoader(e.target);
      var xml:XML = new XML(urlLoader.data);

      for each(var item in xml..element)
      {
        var type:String = item..attribute('type');
        var value:String = item..attribute('value');
        var total:uint =
          uint(xml..attribute('total'));

        if(type == "question")
        {
          this['questionTxt'].text = value;
          continue;
        }

        if(type == "answer")
        {
          var votes:uint =
            uint(item..attribute('votes'));
        }

        var pollItem:PollItem = new PollItem();
        pollItem['percentTxt'].text =
          Math.round(votes / total * 100) + "%";
        pollItem['barMC'].width =
          (votes / total * 100) * 4;

        pollItem.y =
          (pollItems.length *
          (pollItem.height + 20));

        container.addChild(pollItem);
        pollItems.push(pollItem);
      }
    }
  }
}
```

372

Building a Simple File Editor

At this point you have seen a wide selection of real-world applications, but there is still one that hasn't been talked about. That of course would be a content management system. A complete content management system would be a massive project, but this section focuses on one aspect of the application.

The file editor, which is used to add and edit files, is a crucial piece to any content management system. It is likely that at some point the admin is going to need updates made. Rather than download the source material, it is much more efficient to use a dynamic file editor.

The application for this section is just that — a dynamic file editor that is connected to PHP to actually save and load the files. Normally you can use Flash to load the files, but PHP offers the ability to load files that are not stored in the Web root. This is a good idea for template files, because they never need to be directly accessed by a guest.

The design of the file editor is a basic `TextArea`, `Submit` button, `TextField`, and `ComboBox`. Nothing that exciting for designing the file editor; instead, the real meat of the application is within the ActionScript and PHP code.

Starting with the PHP code allows you to test the Flash portion as you begin to develop it. The PHP is actually very simple for this example. First, check for a valid file because whether you are saving or loading, you need a valid file.

```
if(!empty($_GET['file']))
{
  $file = './files/' . $_GET['file'];
  ...
}
```

After you determine there is a valid file, the next step is to check whether the action is blank. If the action is blank, the code will automatically load the action; if the action contains a value it gets compared using an inner `if` statement.

```
if($_GET['action'] == 'save')
{
  ...
}
else
{
  ...
}
```

This example only allows loading and saving the files. In a more robust application you would most likely want to have a delete or move action as well.

373

Part IV Developing Applications

The `save` action is responsible for loading the requested file, replacing the existing text, and finally resaving the file. It is important to note that the example is overlooking a crucial piece to any real-world application, which is escaping the data that is sent from Flash. You may also want to add an access key so arbitrary code can't be run on from the browser via a GET request.

The variable `$fileContents` is retrieved from the GET data sent by Flash.

```
$fileContents = $_GET['fileContents'];
```

The file is loaded using `fopen` with write access set to overwrite. This means the original content is removed and only the new version is saved.

```
$handle = fopen($file, 'w+');
```

Once the file is loaded, a call to `fwrite()` is made, which actually writes the contents to the file and saves the file. The last step of the `save` action is to close the file resource and free up the memory.

```
fwrite($handle, $fileContents);
fclose($handle);
```

The loading of a file is much easier. Basically, you reference the file and load the contents using `file_get_contents()`, which returns the entire file as a string, as shown in Figure 13.7.

```
$loadedFile = file_get_contents($file);
print "fileContents=" . $loadedFile;
```

Here is the completed php file, which should be saved with the name `fileManager.php`:

```
<?php

error_reporting(0);

if(!empty($_GET['file']))
{
  $file = './files/' . $_GET['file'];
  if($_GET['action'] == 'save')
  {
    $fileContents = $_GET['fileContents'];

    $handle = fopen($file, 'w+');
    fwrite($handle, $fileContents);
    fclose($handle);
  }
  else
  {
    $loadedFile = file_get_contents($file);
    print "fileContents=" . $loadedFile;
  }
```

Using Advanced Real-World Applications

```
    }
?>
```

The next step is to develop the ActionScript. The design portion has been previously created so you can move right to the code.

The first step is to define the variables used for this example.

```
var
    phpFile:String="http://localhost/ch12/FileEditor/fileEditor.ph
    p";
var files:Array = ['sample.txt', 'anotherfile.txt',
    'readme.txt'];
var storedFileData:String;
```

FIGURE 13.7

The raw file contents passed from PHP as seen from a Web browser

fileContents=The contents of the sample file, more Lets add some whitespace and newlines how about some more

After the variables are defined, you can move on to the functions. The first function is responsible for populating the file list combo box.

```
function populateFileList():void
{
...
}
```

The `addItem` method of the combo box accepts an Object as an argument, which defines the data for the label and data. For this application, the filename is used for both the label and data value.

```
for(var i:uint=0; i < files.length; i++)
{
   fileListCombo.addItem({label:files[i], data:files[i]});
}
```

The method `loadFile` is called when the `loadbtn` is clicked. This handler sets up a file request with a file variable that PHP uses to load the actual file.

```
function loadFile(e:MouseEvent):void
{
  var variables:URLVariables = new URLVariables();
  variables.file = fileListCombo.selectedItem.data;

  var urlRequest:URLRequest = new URLRequest(phpFile);
  urlRequest.data = variables;

  var urlLoader:URLLoader = new URLLoader();
  urlLoader.addEventListener(Event.COMPLETE, fileLoaded);
  urlLoader.load(urlRequest);
}
```

After the requested file is loaded and PHP returns the contents, it is sent into the `bodyTxt` TextArea and also to the `storedFileData` variable. This variable is used to cache the unmodified results. You can revert to these results later by clicking the Reset button.

```
function fileLoaded(e:Event):void
{
  var urlLoader:URLLoader = URLLoader(e.target);
  var variables:URLVariables = new URLVariables(urlLoader.data);

  bodyTxt.text = unescape(variables.fileContents);
  storedFileData = bodyTxt.text;
}
```

The reset method simply replaces the body content with the unmodified data that is stored as the original file is loaded.

Using Advanced Real-World Applications

```
function resetHandler(e:MouseEvent):void
{
  bodyTxt.text = storedFileData;
}
```

The last method needed in this application is responsible for saving the edited content. Before the data is saved, it is cached, which eliminates the need to reload the data.

```
function saveHandler(e:MouseEvent):void
{
  var body:String = bodyTxt.text;
  storedFileData = body;
  ...
}
```

The variables passed to the PHP define the action, the name of the file, and raw contents that will replace the existing file data. The name of the file is gathered from the `ComboBox` by accessing the `selectedItem` object.

```
var variables:URLVariables = new URLVariables();
variables.file = fileListCombo.selectedItem.data;
variables.action = "save";
variables.fileContents = body;
```

This particular `URLRequest` does not require an event listener because the saving process happens on its own and is completed once PHP receives all of the `fileContents`.

> **NOTE** In a remote application it is a good idea to notify the user of the saving process because a large file may take time to save.

```
var urlRequest:URLRequest = new URLRequest(phpFile);
urlRequest.data = variables;

var urlLoader:URLLoader = new URLLoader();
urlLoader.load(urlRequest);
```

The last task of the ActionScript is to register the events for the buttons and make a call to the `populateFileList()` function to prefill the file `ComboBox`.

```
// Register Events
loadFileBtn.addEventListener(MouseEvent.CLICK, loadFile);
saveBtn.addEventListener(MouseEvent.CLICK, saveHandler);
resetBtn.addEventListener(MouseEvent.CLICK, resetHandler);
populateFileList();
```

Part IV   Developing Applications

FIGURE 13.8

The completed file editor with a sample file loaded

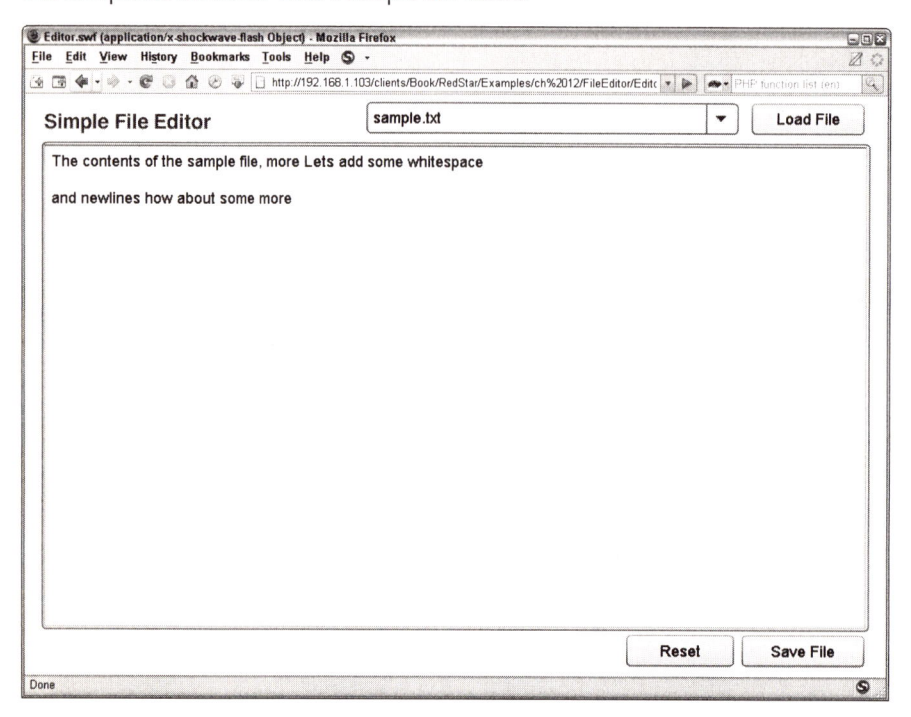

[screenshot of Simple File Editor application with sample.txt loaded, showing text "The contents of the sample file, more Lets add some whitespace" and "and newlines how about some more", with Load File, Reset, and Save File buttons]

The application, as shown in Figure 13.8, is now completed. The following is the full ActionScript source code:

```
var
   phpFile:String="http://localhost/ch12/FileEditor/fileEditor.ph
   p";
var files:Array = ['sample.txt', 'anotherfile.txt',
   'readme.txt'];
var storedFileData:String;

function populateFileList():void
{
  for(var i:uint=0; i < files.length; i++)
  {
    fileListCombo.addItem({label:files[i], data:files[i]});
  }
}

function loadFile(e:MouseEvent):void
```

Using Advanced Real-World Applications 13

```
{
  var variables:URLVariables = new URLVariables();
  variables.file = fileListCombo.selectedItem.data;

  var urlRequest:URLRequest = new URLRequest(phpFile);
  urlRequest.data = variables;

  var urlLoader:URLLoader = new URLLoader();
  urlLoader.addEventListener(Event.COMPLETE, fileLoaded);
  urlLoader.load(urlRequest);
}

function fileLoaded(e:Event):void
{
  var urlLoader:URLLoader = URLLoader(e.target);
  var variables:URLVariables = new URLVariables(urlLoader.data);

  bodyTxt.text = unescape(variables.fileContents);
  storedFileData = bodyTxt.text;
}

function resetHandler(e:MouseEvent):void
{
  bodyTxt.text = storedFileData;
}

function saveHandler(e:MouseEvent):void
{
  var body:String = bodyTxt.text;
  storedFileData = body;

  var variables:URLVariables = new URLVariables();
  variables.file = fileListCombo.selectedItem.data;
  variables.action = "save";
  variables.fileContents = body;

  var urlRequest:URLRequest = new URLRequest(phpFile);
  urlRequest.data = variables;

  var urlLoader:URLLoader = new URLLoader();
  urlLoader.load(urlRequest);
}

// Register Events
loadFileBtn.addEventListener(MouseEvent.CLICK, loadFile);
saveBtn.addEventListener(MouseEvent.CLICK, saveHandler);
resetBtn.addEventListener(MouseEvent.CLICK, resetHandler);

populateFileList();
```

379

Part IV | **Developing Applications**

Summary

In this chapter you learned how to develop advanced real-world applications, such as using Flash and PHP to build a file editor, video player, and site monitor.

While developing the site monitor you learned new events that make it easier to work with bad data, as well as tying PHP, MySQL, and Flash together. The application was enhanced by adding custom actions, such as the process of e-mailing the administrator when a site doesn't respond.

In the polling application you learned how to develop a complete application using Flash as the display medium. The overall application was written to be very scalable and, in fact, changing the one ID variable in the document class will load a totally different poll question (provided one exists).

At this point you should fully understand how to develop real-world applications that are easy to update and maintain. In fact, the majority of this chapter can be added together to create a management system or other module-based applications.

Chapter 14

Debugging Applications

IN THIS CHAPTER

Using error reporting in PHP

Using trace in Flash

Alternative debugging apps

When building an application, it is almost certain that some element will stop working or maybe never work from the beginning. This can be a point when any bonus time a development cycle may have disappears. The idea is to create your application with debugging in mind. Adding comments actually can speed up debugging down the line.

Of course, adding debugging as you go is similar to writing an outline. You think about it just as you realize it's too late. The key is not to let a project get to this point. This chapter focuses on the best way to debug applications. You start with the built-in tools and then progress to some external applications and practices that make it less painful.

Using Error Reporting in PHP

Let's start with looking at debugging a PHP application. By default, PHP ships with a certain level of debugging enabled. It is set up to report fatal errors (program crashes) and warnings (missing files and arguments). This level of error reporting is okay for a development server, but a major issue with the default install is that the errors are printed to the screen and every user can see them.

The alternative and safer option is to enable error logging to an error log file similar to how Apache is set up. Enabling error logging is done by editing the `php.ini` file. If you do not have administrator access available on your server, you need to contact someone that has this access. The `php.ini` file is usually located in the `/etc/` directory on UNIX and `C:\WINDOWS\`, which is generally only accessible by the server administrator.

Part IV Developing Applications

The `php.ini` file is stored in various locations depending on the server configuration. However, the nice thing is, PHP can tell you where it is stored. Simply create a new file, name it `info.php`, and add the following code:

```
<?php
phpinfo();
?>
```

When you run this file in a browser you are presented with a wealth of information specific to your current version of PHP. One of the first blocks of information is the `ini` path, which looks something like this:

```
Configuration File (php.ini) Path   /usr/local/php5/lib/php.ini
```

CAUTION Incorrectly altering the `php.ini` file can result in your server not functioning. Use caution when editing this file.

After you successfully find the `php.ini` file, open it in your favorite text editor or use `vi` if you're using command line. Using `vi`, a command to open a file, looks like this:

```
vi /usr/local/php5/lib/php.ini
```

With the file open, scroll through until you reach a section that looks like this:

```
; Log errors to specified file.
;error_log = filename
```

The lines that start with `;` (semicolon) are comments in the `ini` files. As you can see, the `error_log` is not defined and thus is not saving to any file. The method to enable this option is to remove the semicolon (`;`) and replace `filename` with an actual file path and name, such as

```
error_log = /usr/local/debug/php_errors
```

After you make the changes and save the `php.ini` file, you need to restart your Web server in order to allow PHP to read the `ini` file. This is necessary because the PHP only reads the `ini` file(s) at startup to maximize performance.

After you start to generate errors the log file begins to fill. If you read the log file you should see strings such as the following. Most likely, the errors you receive will actually tell you what is wrong, because an error that provides incorrect information is really not that useful.

```
[18-Jul-2007 20:51:17] PHP Fatal error:   file.php on line 30
[09-Aug-2007 21:23:37] PHP Fatal error:   file.php on line 13
[03-Nov-2007 23:10:21] PHP Fatal error:   file.php on line 56
...
```

A production server should only log errors, which means outputting errors should also be disabled in the `php.ini` file. Open the `ini` file and change the `output_errors` value to `Off` and restart Apache again.

```
display_errors = Off
```

Displaying errors for debugging

With the server securely logging errors without displaying them to general users, you can look at what error reporting in PHP can offer the developer. From the standpoint of debugging, error reporting in PHP is very robust. There are the standard errors such as fatal errors, missing files, warnings, and so on. Even more important is the ability to create your own error.

In order to create a custom error you simply call `trigger_error()`, which takes two arguments. The first argument is the error string to display and the second (optional) argument is what error level the error should be reported as. Here is a simple `trigger_error` call:

```
trigger_error("Cannot load non-existent user data",
   E_USER_WARNING);
```

Debugging variables

Debugging code isn't always about syntax errors; in fact, most times it isn't. Oftentimes you find a variable out of scope or not initialized, which will not cause an error. Of course, PHP does have many functions and methods that are tailored to debugging.

You have probably used `print` or `echo` before, but believe it or not those functions are actually very useful for debugging an application. Basically, you can trace out variables and get a better idea of how a program is functioning.

Debugging arrays

Working with an array is a little different because a simple print will display `Array`. However, you can use the `print_r()` function to view an array. It will even display an array within an array and so on, also known as a multidimensional array. Here is a sample result displayed from the `print_r` call:

```
Array
(
  [0] => Array
  (
    [one] => 1
  )

  [1] => Array
  (
    [two] => 2
  )
)
```

Understanding the error levels

While using `trigger_error` you may notice that the second parameter is a constant. This constant defines a certain error level. PHP offers a wide range of error levels and even allows the developer to change the level as the code progresses.

383

Part IV Developing Applications

Here is how to pragmatically change the error level, in this case making even NOTICES get reported:

```
error_reporting(E_ALL);
```

Table 14.1 shows the error levels and a description of what the error level covers.

TABLE 14.1

Error Levels and Descriptions

Error	Description
`E_ERROR`	Fatal runtime errors. These indicate errors that cannot be recovered from, such as a memory allocation problem. Execution of the script is halted.
`E_WARNING`	Runtime warnings (nonfatal errors). Execution of the script is not halted.
`E_PARSE`	Compile-time parse errors. Parse errors should only be generated by the parser.
`E_NOTICE`	Runtime notices. Indicates that the script encountered something that could indicate an error, but could also happen in the normal course of running a script.
`E_CORE_ERROR`	Fatal errors that occur during PHP's initial startup. This is like an `E_ERROR`, except it is generated by the core of PHP.
`E_CORE_WARNING`	Warnings or nonfatal errors that occur during PHP's initial startup. This is like an `E_WARNING`, except it is generated by the core of PHP.
`E_COMPILE_ERROR`	Fatal compile-time errors. This is like an `E_ERROR`, except it is generated by the Zend Scripting Engine.
`E_COMPILE_WARNING`	Compile-time warnings or nonfatal errors. This is like an `E_WARNING`, except it is generated by the Zend Scripting Engine.
`E_USER_ERROR`	User-generated error message. This is like an `E_ERROR`, except it is generated in PHP code by using the PHP function `trigger_error()`.
`E_USER_WARNING`	User-generated warning message. This is like an `E_WARNING`, except it is generated in PHP code by using the PHP function `trigger_error()`.
`E_USER_NOTICE`	User-generated notice message. This is like an `E_NOTICE`, except it is generated in PHP code by using the PHP function `trigger_error()`.
`E_STRICT`	Runtime notices. Enable to have PHP suggest changes to your code that will ensure the best interoperability and forward compatibility of your code.
`E_ALL`	All errors and warnings, as supported, except of level `E_STRICT` in PHP < 6.

As you can see, PHP offers a lot of debugging options beyond the basic outputting and logging. In fact, you can customize a lot of the error handling found in the `php.ini` file to further debug your various applications.

Debugging Applications   14

If you want to get a serious level of debugging and code watching tools, then you might want to take a look at the Zend Studio IDE (see Figure 14.1) built on top of the Eclipse framework. This application is not freeware; however, it is the most robust PHP editor and debugger/profiler on the market at the time of this writing. A license for Zend studio ranges from $150 to $300 depending on the version you purchase.

> **NOTE** Zend Studio is not the only PHP editor; however it has the most robust debugger. Additionally you can use PHPEclipse which has similar features to Zend. However the setup process is a little more involved.

FIGURE 14.1

The Zend Studio IDE with the debugging panels visible

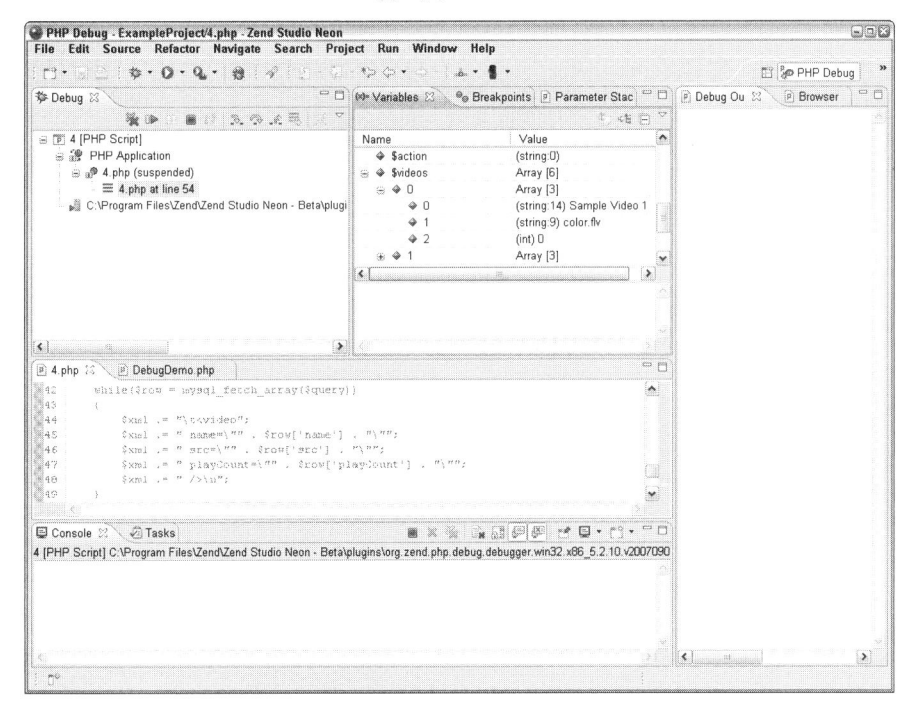

Debugging in Flash

Similar to PHP, Flash offers a pretty useful set of tools for debugging. In fact, the Flash IDE has a complete debugging system built right in where you can quickly inspect your code (see Figure 14.2), apply breakpoints, and step around a block of code to drill down and find a bug.

385

Part IV: Developing Applications

FIGURE 14.2

Here is the panel that is used to inspect an application.

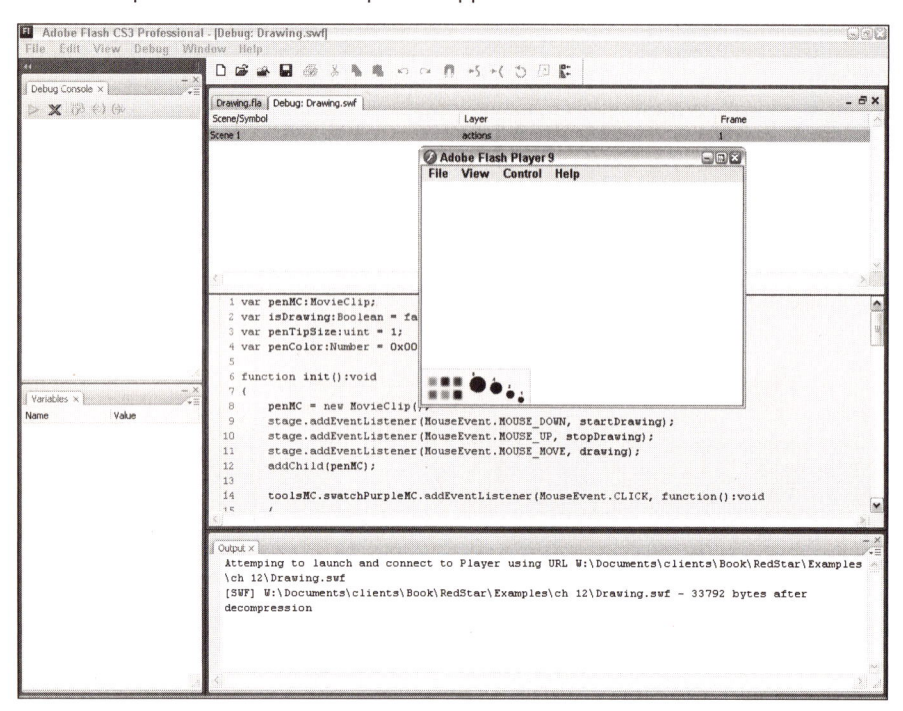

Flash also has an Output panel (see Figure 14.3) that is used to view `trace()` statements called from the code. A `trace` statement is a basic function that accepts a string as an argument. This is then sent to the output panel and offers the ability to display elements of an application as it is running.

```
trace("Here is a very basic debug message");
```

A common question with using trace statements is will they continue to output in a compiled movie? They will, but you can select the "Omit trace actions" option in the Publish Settings dialog box to disable it.

The simple trace method can be useful when debugging basic code examples. However, for more complete applications, you will most likely want to build your own debug manager. This can be done fairly simply.

Debugging Applications 14

FIGURE 14.3

This is an example of the Output panel as seen in Flash.

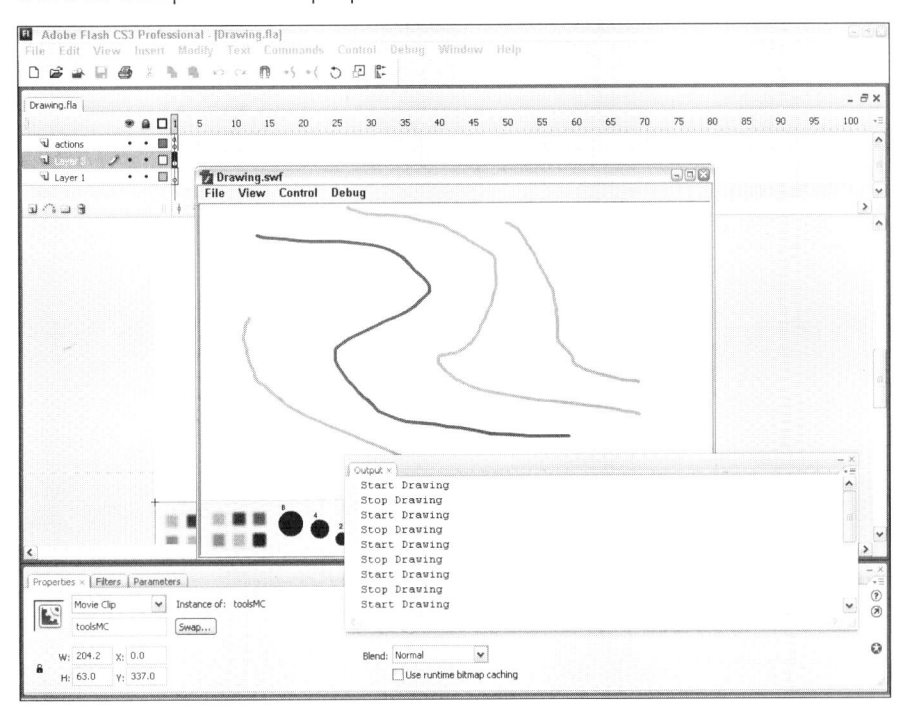

First, create a `TextArea` component on the stage with an instance name of `debugTxt`. Then create a custom trace function that will populate that `TextArea`. Using the `appendText` method will add to the existing text, rather than deleting it.

```
function tracer(debug:String):void
{
    debugTxt.text.appendText(debug);
}
```

You could also create a custom class that any portion of your code is able to call. However, you will quickly find that the standard trace isn't perfect. For example, you can't pragmatically clear the display or place priority on certain events.

In fact, debugging in Flash isn't as advanced as the possibilities in PHP, but it still gets the job done.

Part IV Developing Applications

At this point, you have seen how Flash can be used to debug an application and how PHP can be used for the same task. Now look at a few third-party options and libraries to make this process even easier.

The majority of data passed back and forth in Flash is done so using remote calls, also known as remoting or Flash remoting. This method of sharing data has become fairly popular but doesn't lend itself to being debugged or watched. Part of this is due to the fact an object is self-contained and also the way Flash interacts with a remoting source.

Using a third-party tool named Charles or Charles Web Debugging Proxy, which can be downloaded from `http://xk72.com/charles/`, makes it very simple to look at this data as it is passed around. Charles is not freeware, but does offer a full demo. At the time of this writing, a license was $50. To me, it is worth it.

Figures 14.4 and 14.5 show remoting data and how it looks to Charles.

FIGURE 14.4

Here is the request that is sent out to the remoting service.

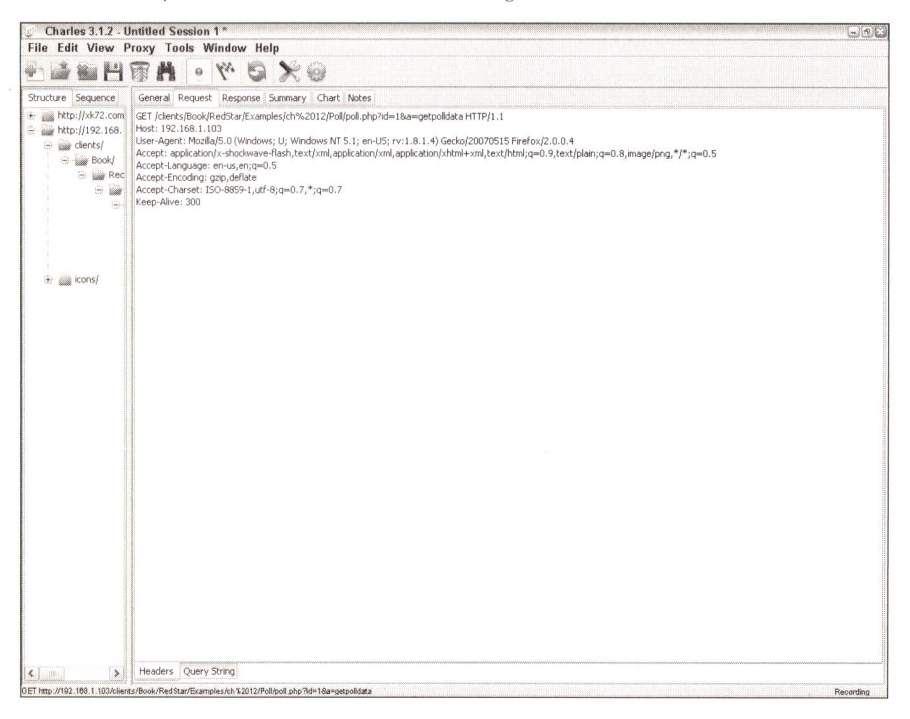

FIGURE 14.5

Here is the standard Charles interface showing an XML response from a remoting system.

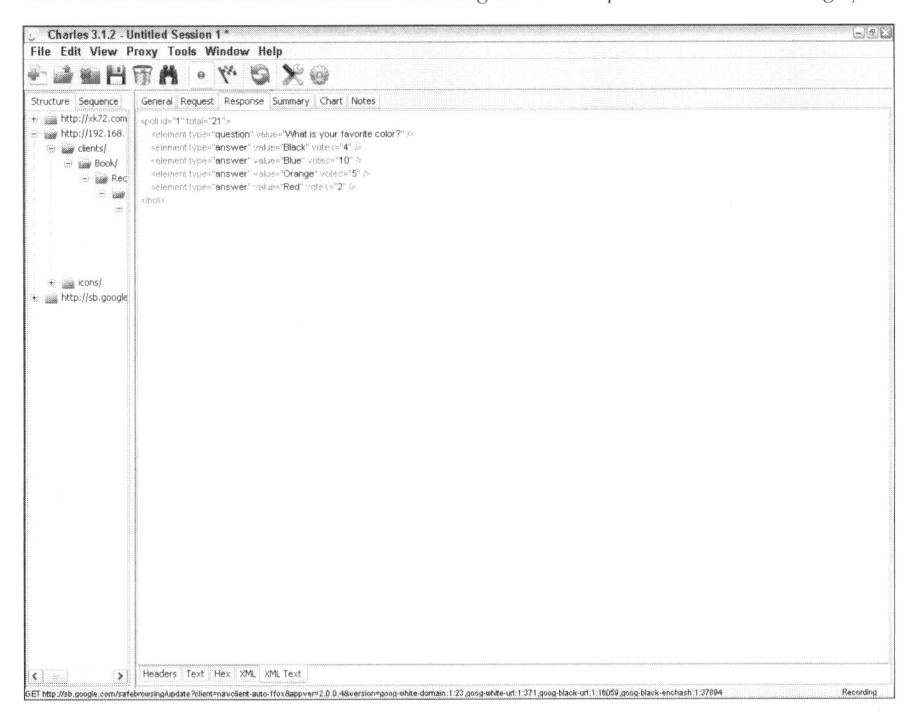

Another great tool is a plug-in for the Firefox Web browser called LiveHTTPHeaders that watches the network traffic. The partial downside to this application is it only watches browser traffic. If you're testing or debugging the application locally it will not see those calls.

More info about LiveHTTPHeaders can be found at `http://livehttpheaders.mozdev.org/`.

Using an Alternative Trace

The last topic in this chapter will be building a new trace that allows colors as well as other features. This trace alternative is built as a stand-alone SWF and can be called by any other SWF in the same domain (local is your machine). The code behind this trace alternative is based upon the `LocalConnection` class, which is a prebuilt class that allows multiple movies to share communications as long as they are in the same domain. The first part of the code is responsible for building the local connection object and registering the `callback` function.

Part IV Developing Applications

```
var receivingLC:LocalConnection = new LocalConnection();
receivingLC.client = this;

function debug(str:String, level:String):void
{
  var debugLevel:String =
    ((typeof(level) == 'undefined') ? 'NORMAL' : level);
  var color:String = null;

  switch(debugLevel)
  {
    case 'NORMAL':
      color = '#000000';
      break;
    case 'ERROR':
      color = '#E60000';
      break;
    case 'NOTE':
      color = '#77C0FD';
      break;
    case 'WARNING':
      color = '#FBF400';
      break;
    case 'RESPONSE':
      color = '#27C201';
      break;
    case 'REGISTER':
      color = '#FC8AFF';
      break;
    case 'CLASS':
      color = '#FD779F';
      break;
    case 'ATTENTION':
      color = '#FF6600';
      break;
    case 'URGENT':
      color = '#FF0000';
      break;
    case 'STATUS':
      color = '#CCFF00';
      break;
  }

  if(color == null)
  {
    color = '#000000';
```

Debugging Applications

```
    }

    debugTxt.htmlText += ("<font color=\"" + color + "\">" + str +
     "</font>" + "\n");

    var scrollPos:uint = debugTxt.verticalScrollPosition
    var maxScroll:uint = debugTxt.maxVerticalScrollPosition;
    if(scrollPos + 5 > maxScroll)
    {
      debugTxt.verticalScrollPosition = maxScroll;
      //debugTxt.scroll = max_scroll;
    }

};
```

After the callback and local connection object are all built, it is time to start the connection. This is done by calling the `connect()` method of the local connection object instance.

```
receivingLC.connect("remoteDebug");
```

The remainder of the code is purely for display of the debugging window and is not required for functionality purposes.

```
function clearHandler(e:MouseEvent):void
{
  debugTxt.htmlText = "";
}

clearBtn.addEventListener(MouseEvent.CLICK, clearHandler);

// Resize Code
stage.scaleMode = StageScaleMode.NO_SCALE;
stage.align = StageAlign.TOP_LEFT;
stage.addEventListener(Event.RESIZE, function():void
{
  debugTxt.width = stage.stageWidth - 25;
  debugTxt.height = stage.stageHeight - 75;
  clearBtn.x = (stage.stageWidth - 12) - clearBtn.width;
  clearBtn.y = (stage.stageHeight - 12) - clearBtn.height;
});
```

That is all the code required to build a trace alternative, and using it requires very little code. The call to the custom trace looks a little like this. The `send()` method requires four arguments, which are the following. The first is the local connection object, the second is the method to call, the third is string to trace, and the fourth is the error level.

```
var sendingLC:LocalConnection = new LocalConnection();
sendingLC.send("remoteDebug", "debug", "Object Not Found!",
   "ERROR");
```

Part IV | **Developing Applications**

Summary

You should now have a pretty solid knowledge of the tools and practices available to successfully debug your applications in Flash and PHP. These are not the only tools and practices available to debug an application. Developers are coming up with better ways all the time, partially because it is an important task and also because it is the most dreaded in the development cycle.

In this chapter you learned how to create your own custom errors and how to work with the standard error types found in PHP. You also learned how to debug code within Flash using the Output panel and `trace` statements.

The last section of the chapter focused on the development of a custom debug handler in ActionScript, which displays the messages in a color-coded scrollbox to better identify your debug messages.

Part V
Server, Application, and Database Maintenance

IN THIS PART

Chapter 15
Maintaining an Application

Chapter 16
Maintaining a Scalable and More Efficient Server

Chapter 17
Building Complete Advanced Applications

Chapter 15

Maintaining an Application

The process of maintaining an application is accomplished by simply following some rules. These rules have been established over time as applications continue to be developed daily.

This chapter focuses on these individual rules. By the end of the chapter, you will understand not only how to follow them, but also how they can make your job easier.

The last section focuses on working in a team environment, using common note taking, commenting, and version control from the perspective of a single developer. Even after an application is written, it isn't uncommon to come back and make changes. If you plan this during the original writing process and follow some simple steps, it makes the updates a lot easier to manage and implement moving forward.

Often, an attempted rewrite is made rather than correcting a few small issues. This usually is due to poor planning in the beginning and results in additional development time that can't always be accounted for.

IN THIS CHAPTER

Commenting code

Managing a ChangeLog

Managing multiple versions

Using custom libraries

Commenting Code

Code commenting is more important as a project continues to grow, or as additional developers are brought on to a project. The process of commenting code is not a required part of writing an application, but it is helpful when looking at a project that has been in development for some time.

Oftentimes the commenting style is either defined in a project outline or set by the project lead.

Commenting can even be beneficial when you write you own code because you can leave notes to return to a piece of code at a later date. This is especially important if you ever intend to distribute the code as an open source project or sell the application.

Commenting code also makes it easier to write or generate documentation with little or no additional modification needed by the developer.

Understanding styles for commenting code

Each language has its own style of code commenting. For example, a very common form of commenting is seen in HTML documents, which looks like this:

```
<!-- This is an HTML comment -->
```

HTML only offers one style of commenting, where other complete scripting languages have various commenting styles. Here are some examples of the more common commenting styles found in Flash, PHP, and MySQL.

Block comments

PHP, ActionScript (Flash), and MySQL allow block comments.

```
/*
 *
 * This is a block style comment,
    * which can have any number of lines.
 *
 */
```

Line comments in MySQL

MySQL allows line comments using a -- at the start of a line.

```
-- This is a MySQL comment; the database will not read this.
```

Inline comments

You can also use an inline comment to remove a certain section of code. This allows you to quickly test a section of code and locate bugs more quickly. Here is an inline comment that removes the WHERE clause section of an SQL query.

```
SELECT name, status FROM users/* WHERE id=1004 AND
   status='active'*/;
```

The previous comment results in the query returning all of the users in the database because the conditional portion has been commented out.

> **NOTE** Malformed line and inline comments can sometimes create hard-to-trace bugs unless your code editor uses colored syntax highlighting.

Maintaining an Application

Compiler comments
Some development languages and applications use compiler comments. These specialized comments tell an application compiler how to handle certain types of data. These comments should not be removed by hand unless you intend to remove that functionality.

Comments in XML
Some of the various applications that have been developed in previous chapters deal with XML. It is important to realize that XML can act in an unknown way when comments are used improperly.

This only becomes an issue when a `--` is used within a comment such as the following:

```xml
<!-- Person, contains all info -- globally used -->
<person>
  <name>Alex</name>
  <age>27</age>
  <gender>Male</gender>
</person>
```

As you can see, the `--` mimics the ending tag and will confuse the XML parser to the point where it thinks the XML is malformed and in some rare cases won't load it.

Comments in Apache
Using comments in Apache is generally limited to the `.htaccess` files to determine site settings. It is important to note that comments in Apache's files can cause rendering issues. If for some reason a directive is not working properly, look for comments as the first culprit of the issue.

Here is an example of a comment in an Apache `.htaccess` file.

```
# Force PHP to render .html files
AddType application/x-httpd-php .html .htm
```

Mixing comments
You can mix various styles of comments as necessary. This is common when explaining a section of code, such as a function or method definition. As you can see, a block comment is used to describe the function and a line comment explains the code in the function.

```
/*

@num1: first number
   @num2: second number
   @return: sum of two arguments

@author: developer's name
@description: static function that multiplies two numbers

*/
```

Part V — Server, Application, and Database Maintenance

```
static function multiplyBy(num1:Number, num2:Number):Number
{
  // return the sum of num1 & num2
  return (num1 * num2);
}
```

Properly commenting your code can have obvious advantages. More popular code editors offer features that can hide or collapse comments so they only are in the way when you want them to be.

You will even find some editors that syntax highlighted comments. Some professional editors use your comments to create inline help files called *code hints* (see Figure 15.1).

These code hints are inline boxes that pop up as you begin to type. They provide the possible items available based on the code entered so far.

A more advanced ActionScript editor, such as FDT by PowerFlasher, has the ability to learn your code and displays your custom comments within its version of code hints.

FIGURE 15.1

Example of a code hint displayed in Flash CS3 for the `MovieClip` properties

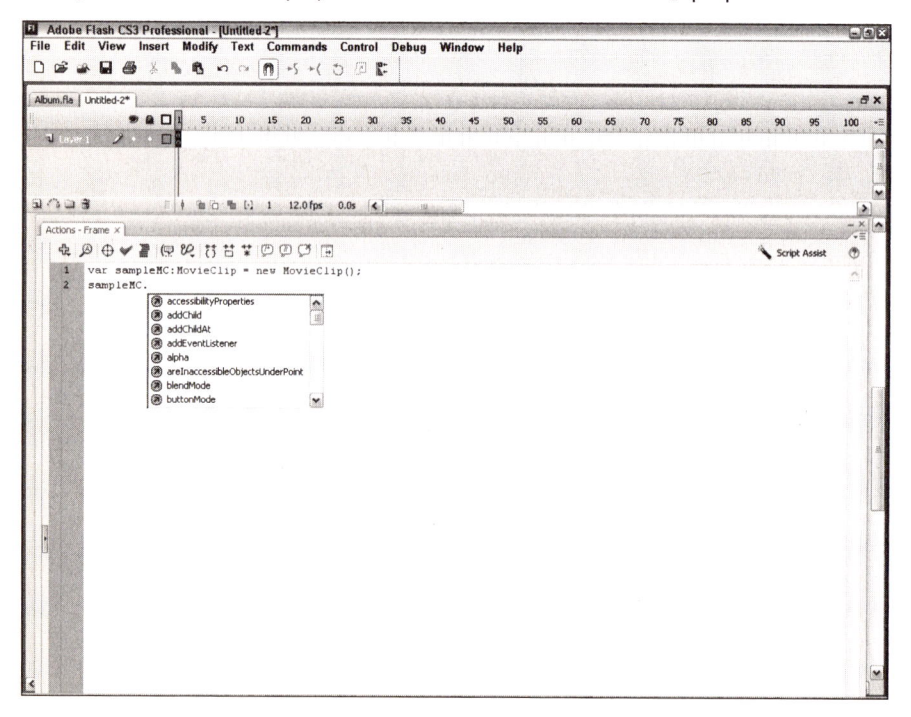

Removing comments and debug helpers

Comments are often removed due to file size, which can be a valid concern on a large program. However, most of the time, comments are automatically removed when an application is compiled or built.

Depending on the application you use, debug statements should also be removed. For example, the native Flash IDE that ships with CS3 has a configuration option in the Publish Settings dialog box. If you select Omit Trace Actions, which is located on the Flash tab of the Publish Settings, trace calls are removed from the application.

NOTE If Omit Trace Actions is enabled during debugging you will not see any trace calls displayed in the Output window.

If you decide to use a custom Class or package for debugging, then you could use Find and Replace to remove those instances. However, be careful to not accidentally remove application-specific code.

As you can see, comments can be beneficial from the standpoint of code readability. You also now know that properly commenting your code has additional advantages when using some of the more robust code editors available today.

Managing a ChangeLog

A `ChangeLog` is a formatted block of records or log entries placed in a custom file. These files generally have the name `CHANGES` or `UPDATES`. This section is used to take notes on the features of an application or to communicate progress with the rest of a development team.

An advantage to using a `ChangeLog` is that some applications can read this formatted log and automatically display it, as shown in Figure 15.2. This, of course, depends on the application you are using but can be very beneficial as an application begins to grow.

Bug tracking

Many developers use this dynamic `ChangeLog` format to track bugs. This is a process that many commercial and freeware applications, such as Jira and Bugzilla, use to create a more graphical alternative to the basic text file.

Using bug tracking with teams

Bug tracking becomes especially important when teams are involved. For instance, many open source technologies consist of developers around the world. Imagine how tedious it would be to track bugs in e-mails or phone calls across all these developers. This is where bug tracking becomes especially important. That doesn't mean a single developer can't benefit from the same system.

FIGURE 15.2

Here is a Web page displaying a `ChangeLog` that was dynamically generated.

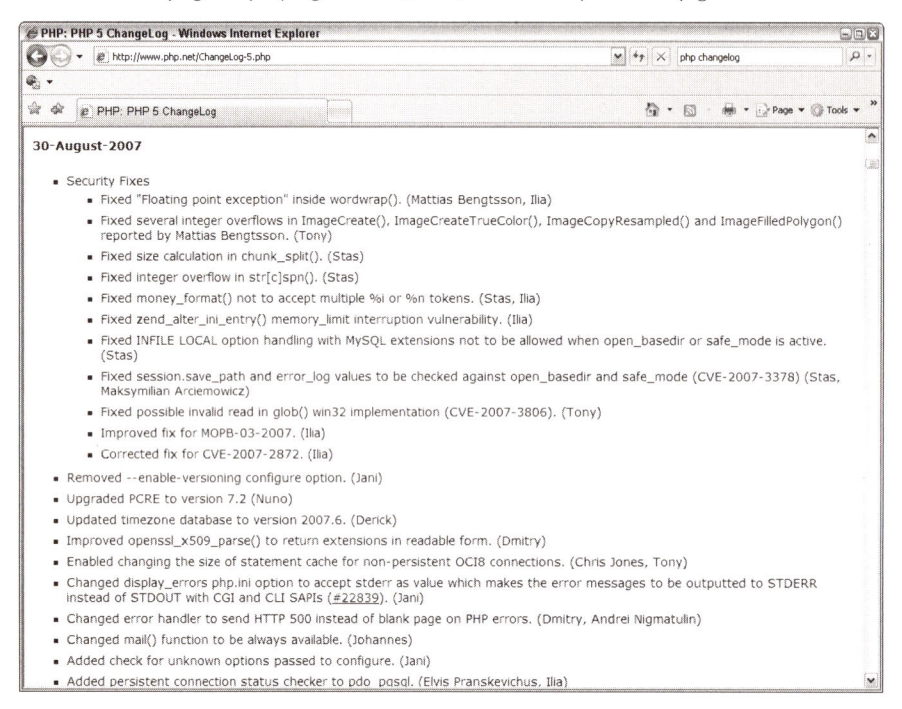

Additional uses

A `ChangeLog` isn't limited to a few lines of text. Realistically, as you can see, it can contain bug fixes, notes to other developers, and information regarding a specific element. For example, if you decide to use a bug tracking application, it is a good idea to include the bug ID within the `ChangeLog` entry or let the application for tracking handle this.

Properly documenting bug IDs makes it easier to follow up on a bug later during application development, or if you return to a project once it is completed.

Dynamic creation of changes

Version control applications, which are discussed in the following section, even have the ability to automatically generate a `ChangeLog`. The advantage to this approach is the developer doesn't have to spend project time editing or updating the log. However, a disadvantage to this is the file becomes less personalized and sometimes makes it harder to fully understand.

Managing Multiple Versions

Version control is the management of multiple versions of code or files for an application. These applications often are used in development teams, but can easily be used by a single developer.

The advantage to using version control is the tracking and backup code that is stored as you develop or maintain an application. This added level of security on a project can allow the developer to experiment with an idea and still have the ability to revert to a stable version.

It also allows a developer to keep code consistent across development platforms. This feature is a very common use for solo developers who travel and code on a mobile system. They simply connect to the development server, download the latest version, and are ready to go. When they return, a simple update is made to the same server and the application is back in sync.

Version control applications

There are various version control applications available for your development environments today. Selecting which version control application to use is determined by looking at the features and requirements of your development process.

The more common version control application is SVN (SubVersion). Another popular application is CVS (Concurrent Versions System). Support for version control is often built directly into a code editor, such as the open source Eclipse editor.

Version control support in CS3

New to Adobe Flash CS3 is the ability to use Version Cue directly within Flash. Version Cue (see Figure 15.3) is Adobe's version control application that was found within its other applications.

Using Version Cue in Flash CS3

You will find a menu item "Check In..." under the File menu. This item is used to bring up the Version Cue management dialog and is where you are able to save versions of your application.

You will find an entry of Check In... located in the File menu.

The advantage to using Version Cue is it ships with CS3 and is integrated into the suite of applications. This is especially important if you are developing assets in one application, code in another, and managing the site in a third.

You can even allow your team to log in to the Version Cue server remotely and make changes. This means, for instance, your developer can be virtually in the same office as the rest of your team.

FIGURE 15.3

Screenshot of Version Cue, which ships with the Creative Suite 3 programs

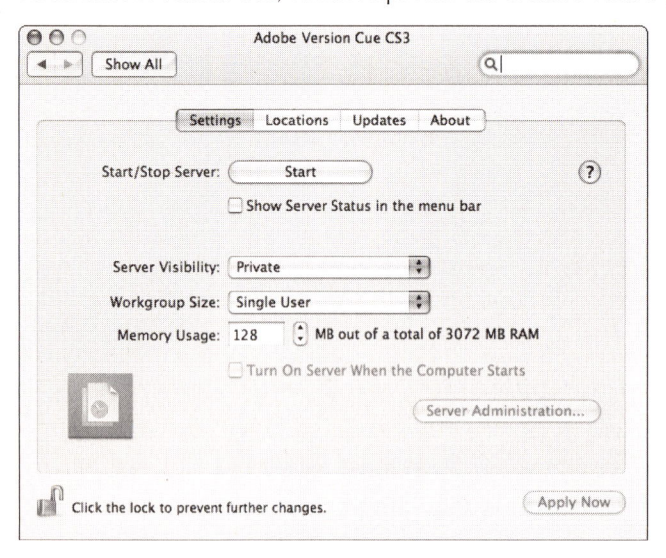

Setting up version control

The process of setting up version control depends on the system your development environment runs. A more complete installation guide would be included with the application that you decide to use. Basic installation would include unpacking the contents of the version control application, modifying the configuration file, and alerting Apache to the existence of that application.

Using version control

Normally, the process of using version control is integrated into your code editor. However, there are applications available to use version control directly within your operating system.

Two version control managers for Windows and Mac OS X are shown in Table 15.1.

TABLE 15.1

Version Control Managers for Windows and Mac OS X

Name	URL	OS
TortoiseSVN	http://tortoisesvn.tigris.org/	Windows
SCPlugin	http://scplugin.tigris.org/	Mac OS X

> **NOTE** For a more secure and final development setup, it is best to install your version control application on a separate machine.

Backing up version control

The more popular version control systems offer integrated backup solutions, but oftentimes you will find that backing up the application you are writing will include the version control data. Normally, these files are set as hidden and should never be edited manually if for some reason they do become accessible.

> **CAUTION** Editing a version control file manually can result in corrupt backups and even harm the integrity of the code of your application.

Additional use of version control

Additional use of version control is the ability to publish the file structure to the Web for sharing. This isn't always the intended result, but you will find companies such as Adobe, Google, and Microsoft that take this approach.

Using version control cuts down on the amount of extra work necessary to publish your application's source code and allows others to keep code updated just by connecting to your version control system remotely.

Using Custom Libraries

Custom libraries can make your code easy to maintain. In older versions of ActionScript (before AS3), packages didn't really exist, so it was hard to properly maintain and share an application's source code.

ActionScript 3 introduced a more common coding practice called packages. This offers the ability to create one instance of your class and share it across projects all contained within a single folder or file.

> **CROSS-REF** A more thorough look into custom libraries can be found in Chapter 9.

Using custom libraries with version control

If you create a separate install for your version control system you can use this same machine to store your custom libraries and then include them remotely in your Flash file(s).

The advantage to this approach is the ability to update a package and have all applications that use that package update as well.

Publishing an SWC

You can create an SWC in Flash, which allows you to distribute components and ActionScript classes. To publish an SWC, select the Export SWC option in the Publish Settings dialog box.

The SWC file contains a compiled clip and the ActionScript class files that support it.

> **NOTE** It is a good idea to document class and package changes because existing applications could stop working.

The process of using custom libraries may not seem like a very important aspect of application development. However, once you begin to develop larger-scale applications that share common attributes you will notice how much time is saved by not having to rewrite code.

Summary

In this chapter you learned how to comment your code and why it makes for a better application overall. You also learned how this becomes especially important when developing an application with others.

You got an introduction on how to incorporate a ChangeLog into your development and how some third-party applications can use this information to display more detailed bug tracking.

In the last section you learned how to use version control and were introduced to Version Cue, which is a new addition to Flash CS3.

Chapter 16

Maintaining a Scalable and More Efficient Server

This chapter focuses on the best practices for maintaining your server while also introducing more advanced application improvement techniques such as caching, efficient databases, backups, and scalable code.

After you learn and apply this information to your applications, you will quickly notice that they run more efficiently. If you keep these steps in mind at the beginning of the application development process, you will not have to rework the application later.

> **IN THIS CHAPTER**
>
> Keeping the server updated
>
> Caching and optimizing
>
> Handling backups

Running an Updated Server

One of the simplest but most ignored methods for maintaining a more efficient server is keeping your libraries and core server-side code updated. Oftentimes these programs that are responsible for running your applications are updated as the developers continue to find ways to speed them up or make them more efficient. This updating process is not referring to your personal code, but the libraries and services your code depends on.

Updating your server not only provides performance enhancements, but also can ensure your Web server is more secure. PHP, for example, is updated frequently as more enhancements and coding changes are introduced. This is due to new security concerns being discovered, which results in a stronger application overall.

Before updating your system, ensure your applications will be compatible. For example, applications developed in PHP 4 are not always compatible with PHP 5. You will find some instances where another piece of software on your server may require a specific version. A good example of this is mail clients, such as a specific version of Horde (a popular e-mail application) requires PHP 4 and will simply fail on a newer version.

This doesn't mean you should never update; quite the opposite actually. It just takes a little homework and research prior to installing new versions.

Using automatic updates

As you know, installing new versions of applications on your server is not always the best option. You need to be more aware of this with automatic updaters. For example, you will find automatic updates are more likely to provide brand-new functionality but at the same time they also provide code that hasn't been tested as thoroughly.

You will find that not all of your server-side applications offer automatic updates, but it is best to check beforehand and ensure that those options are disabled.

Some hosting providers perform periodic security updates, sometimes without your permission or even informing you of the update. This is one of the many reasons I prefer to run a self-managed, dedicated server as opposed to paying a little less and letting the hosting provider handle security and version updates.

Zend Platform

The exception to not installing automatic updates is when you use the Zend Platform. This toolkit ensures your system is properly up to date with all the latest security enhancements, while making sure your existing script will still work properly.

The cost of Zend Platform can cause a dilemma for smaller organizations and single developers, but the overall time saved in the long term is a valid reason to purchase it.

Working with Development Installs

Installing new applications or libraries is not good practice when working with a live server. However, this doesn't mean you can't experiment with new code by installing a development system.

You can build or purchase hosting on a new server to get a development system setup, but this may not be the most cost-effective solution, especially if you are a one-man shop.

Building another version of Apache on the same system

The alternative is to install a separate version of Apache on your live server. By default, Apache can only have one version running because every version tries to share the same server port.

However, you can modify this setting by editing the `httpd.conf` file. You will find this configuration file in the `conf/` directory of your new Apache install.

Open this file in your favorite text editor or vi, if you are running a remote server, and modify the following block:

```
# Change this to Listen on specific IP addresses as shown below
  to
# prevent Apache from glomming onto all bound IP addresses
  (0.0.0.0)
#
#Listen 12.34.56.78:80
Listen 80
```

The majority of that block of code is a comment explaining what this parameter is responsible for. You can modify the port on which your development system can be found by changing this number to something similar to the following:

```
...
#
#Listen 12.34.56.78:80
Listen 9004
```

After you save and restart Apache, you can access this new install by visiting `http://localhost:9004`.

> **NOTE** Applications on your machine use different ports, so it is best to check the port before choosing a new one.

Working with bleeding-edge technology

When you have the new system installed, you can begin to experiment with new bleeding-edge technology without harming your live setup. Bleeding-edge software as shown in Figure 16.1 is newly released versions that have not been tested as much as stable releases would be. This allows you to work with more advanced and newer features, but also means you could run into bugs and development issues when using these versions. As you continue to test this new technology you can determine whether it should be used in a live environment and move it over when it is ready.

Dependencies

Many libraries and tools that you will use on your Web server depend on other libraries. For example, PHP's GD library for image manipulation requires the `libjpeg` library in order to properly edit images.

When you update your server, you need to be aware of these dependencies because updating one portion can result in broken or incomplete installations. Oftentimes you will find information on the developer's site regarding specific update information or you can consult `php.net` in the comments section. There you will find other developers reporting their results in various development situations.

Part V   Server, Application, and Database Maintenance

FIGURE 16.1

An example of bleeding-edge releases from `php.net`

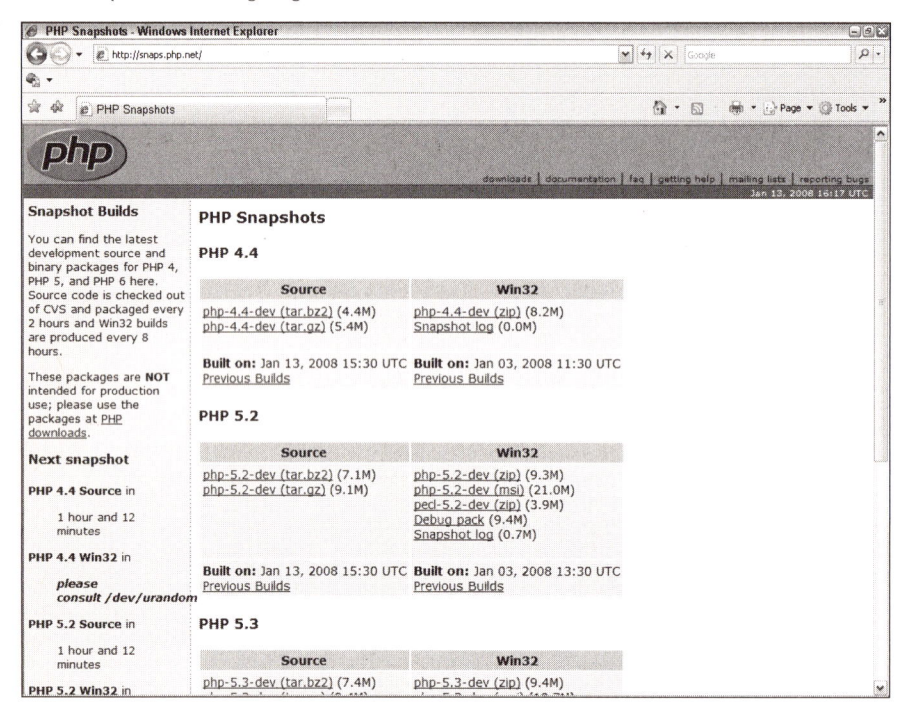

Caching and Optimizing

Keeping your server up to date is only one way to run an efficient server. In fact, there are much more important practices to follow first. One of these more important practices is optimizing your server-side code and the system it runs on. Not only should you follow best practices when developing your applications, you should also maintain your server to be optimized based on your specific needs.

Optimizing PHP

Following the steps to optimizing your installation of PHP will allow you to run a better server overall. These optimization steps are fairly simple to follow and can easily be repeated as you work on more servers.

Processor versus RAM

Unlike most applications that require more memory, PHP relies more heavily on the processor in your server. This means a dual-processor system is more efficient than a single processor with more memory. That does not mean memory is not important, because certain portions of PHP use a considerable amount of memory.

The output buffer and database plug-ins require more memory as they are accessed because they tend to store a majority of the information for quicker access next time. This means the first request is slow but requests following that are faster if you have enough memory to properly handle the requests to be stored.

This doesn't mean you should run out and immediately purchase more memory or even more processors because there are ways to optimize your server without spending any money on additional software or hardware.

Ten tips for optimizing your code

The following is a list of ten tips to follow that will produce better performance in your code, as well as limit the strain on the Web server. They appear here in order from least important to most important.

1. Limit the amount of error handling your applications manage. Less error handling means better overall performance, unless you are experiencing bottlenecks already. Then error handling may be important.

2. Use the included functions; don't create your own. Whenever possible, try to use the provided functions in PHP because they are precompiled and are optimized to run more efficiently. They have also been tested over and over to ensure they work.

3. Use a select instead of multiple `if/else` statements. Not only will using a select produce cleaner code, it will also result in better performance when PHP executes that portion of your code.

4. Avoid myths like `echo` is faster than `print`. As with most programming languages, PHP has various myths, such as all code should be on one line. One of the most common myths is that `echo` is faster than `print` when sending code to the output buffer or screen. This is simply not true. You can use either statement. I personally prefer `print` because it is printing to the display or buffer.

5. Close database connections using functions such as `mysql_close` (for mysql) when not being used. Database connections end when the script completes, but this is not always the best way. For example, if you have a program that makes database calls and modifies these results, the database connection stays active (unless you close it) the entire time your script is working on the result set.

6. Use `unset()` to remove variables when they are no longer being used. Deleting variables, especially large arrays and objects when no longer in use, results in better performance overall.

7. Try to limit regular expressions and use standard string functions whenever possible. Regular expressions, while more robust, can consume a considerable amount of memory. Oftentimes you will find a simple string function (for example, `strstr`) produces the same result and with a significant performance increase in most cases.

8. Be smart about class usage. Simple tasks will suffer from unnecessary OOP code. You will find simpler tasks consume more memory when developed using OOP practices. It is important to not only know which techniques exist, but also when they should be used.

9. Monitor your applications to determine bottlenecks. Slowdowns in code performance can be traced back to one specific location, known as a bottleneck. Think of an actual bottle, where the neck slows down the flow of liquid as it groups to pass through the narrow top of the bottle. The same is true for code as most libraries and scripts have one point where they all meet.

   A bottleneck in your application may exist in your code, but could also be in a database call or file system interaction. Monitoring your application will expose the issues and allow you to fix the performance problem.

10. Cache your PHP code, whenever possible.

After you optimize your code, but still need to improve more, caching may be an option. You can develop a custom solution or use an existing system, such as `memcached`, which is examined in the next section. You can also cache the actual PHP script by precompiling it, which speeds up subsequent requests.

PHP by default compiles your `.php` files every time they are requested. Caching avoids this by storing the precompiled code. This is much more efficient and means faster performance.

These ten tips are not the only ways to optimize your code, but provide a list of common slowdowns and myths when developing your applications. As you can now see, with a few code modifications and attention to how the Web server handles your scripts, you can ensure better performance while maintaining ultimate functionality.

I have seen some applications remove features when the program begins to expand, and this is simply the wrong approach. Removing features from a slow application is similar to throwing wild amounts of new hardware to solve a performance problem.

Zend Optimizer

The Zend Optimizer is one product that is used to optimize and cache your code, but also provides a secure result because your code is compiled and encrypted. The encryption is achieved by running your source code through the Zend Guard, as shown in Figure 16.2, which obfuscates your open code.

Maintaining a Scalable and More Efficient Server

This tool is not free, but as you continue to develop more robust applications, you will learn that the cost is outweighed by the increase in performance you achieve.

FIGURE 16.2

Zend Guard with an active project loaded

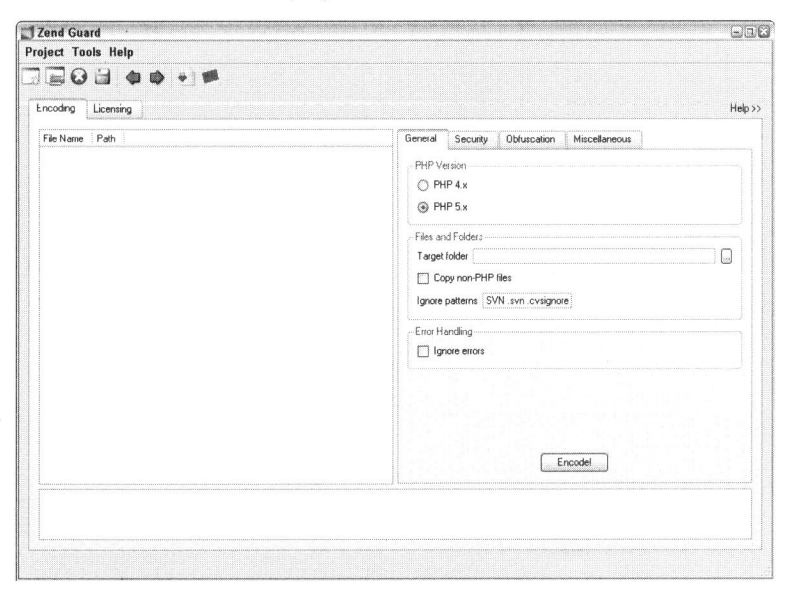

Zend Studio

A more optimized server can be traced back to the application development process. Zend offers a development studio that can profile and debug your code, allowing you to locate bottlenecks before you deploy your code.

The Zend Studio, as shown in Figure 16.3, even allows remote debugging, which allows you to test your applications on the live server while still being able to monitor and debug when needed.

You can find more information about these tools on the Zend Web site at www.zend.com/en/products/guard/optimizer/ and www.zend.com/en/products/studio/.

Part V Server, Application, and Database Maintenance

FIGURE 16.3

Code editor found in the Zend Studio IDE

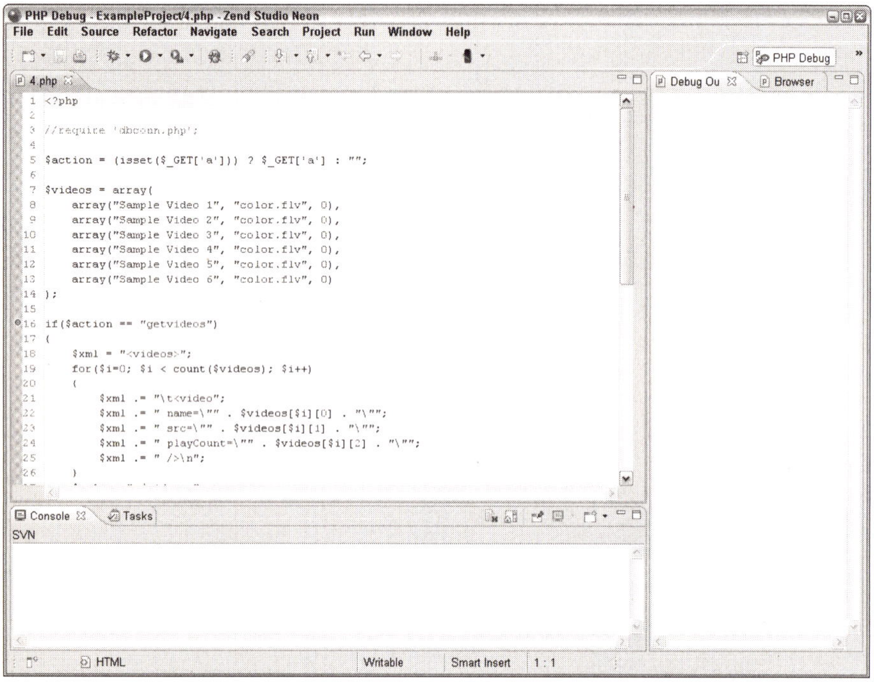

Optimizing Apache

The process of optimizing Apache is broken up into four pieces. This allows the developer to focus on each specific step rather than forcing them to modify every aspect of the server. In rare cases you will only see minimal performance updates, but will notice it more as the application and demand continue to grow.

Hardware

The first place to look when attempting to optimize Apache is the hardware it runs on. For example, Apache consumes a lot of memory over time. More memory can be a benefit here because it will be able to properly maintain itself.

Dedicated server

Make sure Apache is running on a dedicated server. This technically includes the development install that you learned about in the previous section. It is important to understand the development install version of Apache doesn't consume that many resources, being a single-user product. It is best to let Apache have the entire server to run more efficiently. Enterprise (large) applications will oftentimes run a stand-alone server to handle the Web traffic.

Maintaining a Scalable and More Efficient Server — 16

Configuration files

Modifying the configuration files (`*.conf`) can produce a performance increase if you remove directives that are not being used. As you learn the configuration layout, you can remove the comments, which will make it easier to look at in the long run.

Apache provides a series of configuration starter files, but try to avoid the high-performance version because it actually becomes less efficient in the long run. The reason is because this version overly optimizes Apache, which forces it to run less efficiently unless you are experiencing very high traffic.

Logging and errors

Whenever possible try to limit the amount of log usage. You can either disable logging altogether or limit the amount of information that is written to the logs. Errors are harder to trace because Apache does not inform you of these issues. In most cases, however, when a server is functioning properly this is not a problem.

If you choose to enable logging, make sure you edit those files on a different machine because the process of opening and parsing these sometimes large files can have a performance impact.

MaxClients

You can modify the `MaxClients` directive in the `httpd.conf` configuration file to increase performance, but be aware that any client attempting to connect after the limit is hit will be unable to view your site. In rare cases, this may not be a bad thing because it will preserve the performance for the existing users.

```
<IfModule prefork.c>
StartServers         8
MinSpareServers      5
MaxSpareServers     20
MaxClients         150
MaxRequestsPerChild 1000
</IfModule>
```

NOTE The `MaxClients` directive only applies when the `prefork` module is configured and enabled.

There are other ways to optimize Apache, but short of adding additional hardware and cost to your organization, this list will have your server running much more efficiently.

Optimizing MySQL

Now that you have optimized PHP and the Apache Web server, the next logical place to optimize is MySQL. You can optimize MySQL after it is installed, but there are some good practices to keep in mind prior to installing it, when possible.

Part V: Server, Application, and Database Maintenance

Better performance from installation

Choosing the best compiler for your system when you build MySQL can usually get you 10 to 30 percent better performance. Compile MySQL with only the character sets and options you intend to use. Oftentimes a quick evaluation of your intended use can result in better performance, because at a glance you can determine which features you will and will not use.

The MySQL documentation has various tips on better performance, and as you continue to implement more of them you will want to run the compiled binary using the MySQL benchmark test to truly determine if the modifications will result in better performance.

MySQL is a long road application. This means you want better performance overall and not just for very quick actions. For example, assume you have a table with 100,000 rows, which is not that uncommon in large applications. Performing a search on this table will take some time, so a tuned MySQL with fast access in mind will actually be the bottleneck. It is better to have MySQL tuned with long-term processes in mind to work with data in these volumes.

Logging slow queries

One of the best ways to locate bottlenecks in your MySQL database is to enable logging when needed. It is important to understand that logging in itself is a performance killer, but sometimes is necessary to fix other issues.

MySQL logs slow queries to a log file. If you tail this file, which is used to actively watch the flow, you will be informed of slow queries. You can also let this log fill and then test it later, depending on how active your system is.

```
tail -f /var/lib/mysql/192-168-1-107-slow.log
```

The path of this slow query log file will be different depending on your environment.

NOTE Windows does not offer a "tail" command by default, but you can install the Server Tools available from Microsoft.

NOTE You may need to enable "slow query logging" in the configuration files of MySQL.

Checking tables

Another way to ensure a database is running properly is to check the table health, by issuing the following command in the prompt. Replace `table_name` with the actual name of the table that you want to check.

```
CHECK TABLE table_name
```

For example:

```
mysql> check table poll;
+-----------+-------+----------+----------+
| Table     | Op    | Msg_type | Msg_text |
```

Maintaining a Scalable and More Efficient Server

```
+-----------+-------+----------+----------+
| book.poll | check | status   | OK       |
+-----------+-------+----------+----------+
1 row in set (0.00 sec)
```

Limit startup options

Another way to get better performance out of MySQL is to limit the options that load when started. MySQL ships with various options for each and every use case, but it is safe to say you will not use all of them. Similar to Apache, if you modify the configuration files in MySQL, you will notice better performance.

Additional tools

The MySQL development group provides many free profiling and administration tools. These tools can be downloaded from the main MySQL Web site and will help you optimize and monitor your databases remotely. The advantage to using these tools is not having to monitor your server using basic command-line tools. These GUI-enabled tools allow you to understand what your Web server is doing from a visual perspective, as shown in Figure 16.4.

FIGURE 16.4

The MySQL Query Browser

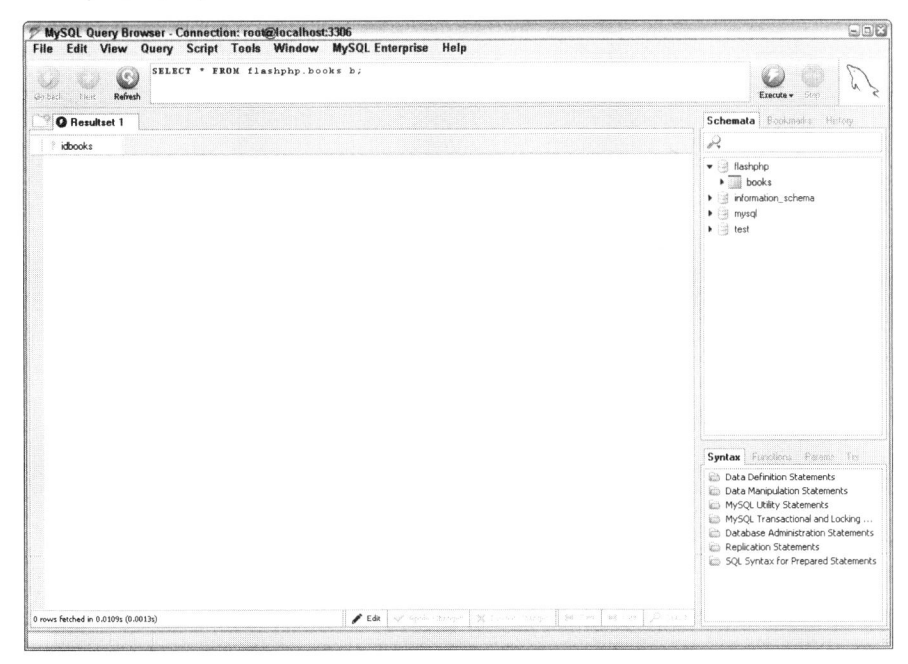

415

Caching

The topic of caching is normally looked at once you experience bottlenecks in an application, but you can install caching solutions before a problem occurs.

Working with memcached

One of the bottlenecks in server-side scripts is the database. You have the ability to tweak the configuration, which you did in the previous section. Sometimes this can only go so far as a system continues to grow.

The answer to this problem is to install software to help deal with database slowdowns, such as memcached, which is a high-performance memory object caching system. This system is built with the intent to speed up dynamic Web applications by removing database load, which is encountered more often as the system continues to grow. You can download the latest version of memcached from danga.com at www.danga.com/memcached/.

Installing memcached on Linux

The following section will cover the installation process of memcached on a Linux Web server. This version requires another library to be installed, which will also be covered.

Installing libevent

Before you install memcached, you need to install a dependency library. This is libevent, which can be downloaded at www.monkey.org/~provos/libevent/.

Unpack the archive and perform the same installation steps you have seen in the previous examples when installing applications.

```
$ tar -xvf libevent-1.3b.tar.gz
```

Change the current directory to the newly created libevent to continue the installation process.

```
$ cd libevent-1.3b
```

The last step to setting up the dependency is to configure and build the necessary install files and install the libevent library.

```
$ ./configure
$ make
$ make install
```

Installing memcached

Once libevent is installed, you can continue with the installation of memcached.

```
$ gunzip memcached-x.x.x.tar.gz
```

Start by unpacking the archive that you just downloaded.

```
$ tar -xvf memcached-x.x.x.tar
```

Next, change the current directory to continue the installation.

```
$ cd memcached-x.x.x
```

The last step of the installation process is to create the installer script and install the application.

```
$ ./configure
$ make
$ make install
```

With `memcached` installed, start it up and move on to the PHP extension.

```
$ ./memcached -d -m 2048 -l 127.0.0.1 -p 11211
```

Downloading the memcached extension for PHP

At this point, the next step is to install the PHP extension that is used to interact with `memcached`.

The first step is to download `memcached` from the PECL package repository.

```
$ wget http://pecl.php.net/get/memcache-x.x.x.tgz
```

NOTE The version number has been removed to ensure you download the correct version, rather than force a version on the reader. It is best to read the documentation before downloading a version.

Installing the memcached PHP extension

Once the file is downloaded, unzip and untar the archive file.

```
$ gzip -df memcache-x.x.x.tgz
$ tar -xvf memcache-x.x.x.tar
```

Change to the directory that the `memcached` archive has created.

```
$ cd memcache-x.x.x
```

A call to `phpize` is made to build the unpacked files into a compatible PHP extension.

```
$ phpize
```

The next step is to configure the install, make the install files, and finally install the application using the following three commands:

```
$ ./configure
$ make
$ make install
```

When the installation is complete, you need to modify the php.ini file and add the new extension.

```
extension=memcache.so
```

Installing memcached on Windows

The first step to installing memcached is to download the binary version directly from `http://jehiah.cz/projects/memcached-win32/`.

1. Unzip the binaries in your desired directory (e.g., `c:\memcached`).
2. Install the service: `'c:\memcached\memcached.exe -d install'` from the command prompt.
3. Start the server from the Microsoft Management Console.
4. Use the server, by default listening to port 11211.

Now that you have memcached installed and started, the next step is to configure PHP. Start by checking the PHP extensions directory (`C:\php\ext`) for the `memcached` extension (`php_memcache.dll`).

If you do not see the extension in that directory you can visit the PECL repository and download it from there: `http://pecl4win.php.net/ext.php/php_memcache.dll`

The next step is to open the php.ini file and add the `memcached` extension to the existing list of extensions.

```
extension=php_memcache.dll
```

The last step is to restart Apache.

Wrapping up installation for Linux and Windows

The last step is to restart PHP by restarting Apache and running the `phpinfo` function to see if `memcached` has been successfully added.

Saving data to the cache

The power of `memcached` cannot be explained in a little section, but the following is a good overview of how to load and save data into the caching system.

The first step is to create a new instance of the `Memcache` library object.

```
$cache = new Memcache;
```

After you create the object, create a new connection. For this example, everything is running on the same server, but memcached really shines when installed on multiple servers. The second argument in the `connect` method is the port number on which `memcached` is running.

```
$cache->connect("localhost", 11211);
```

Maintaining a Scalable and More Efficient Server

After you make the new connection, you can create some sample data, which would probably be a more advanced block of data in a real-world application.

```
$sampleData = array("apples", "oranges" "bananas", "waffles");
```

After you create the sample data, which in this example is a basic array, you need to send the data to the caching system. This is done by making a call to the `set` method of the `Memcached` class.

The first argument is the name of the key, which should be unique because this is the way you will retrieve this information.

```
$cache->set("uniquekey", $sampleData, false, 86400);
```

The second argument is the sample data to store in the cache.

```
$cache->set("uniquekey", $sampleData, false, 86400);
```

`Memcached` has the ability to store the data in a compressed form, which is set by the third argument. This option is a `true` or `false` flag.

```
$cache->set("uniquekey", $sampleData, false, 86400);
```

The fourth and final argument determines how long the cached data should stay alive in seconds. In this example, the data would stay alive for 24 hours.

```
$cache->set("uniquekey", $sampleData, false, 86400);
```

NOTE The expire option of memcached data cannot exceed 2592000 (30 days).

```
$cache->set("uniquekey", $sampleData, false, 86400);
```

As you can see, the code required to save data to the cache is fairly simple and makes it very easy to adapt into existing applications.

Here is the complete example script for saving data to the cache.

```php
<?php

$cache = new Memcache;
$cache->connect("localhost", 11211);

$sampleData = array("apples", "oranges" "bananas", "waffles");

$cache->set("uniquekey", $sampleData, false, 86400);

?>
```

419

Loading cached data

Once you store information in the cache, the process for retrieving that information is a matter of calling one method of the `Memcache` class. This method accepts one argument, which is the key that you used to save the data in the cache.

```
$result = $memcache->get("uniquekey");
```

That is all there is to loading the cached information. As you can see, loading data from the cache is very similar to the overall process of working with the database. This means it is not hard to seamlessly integrate into your existing code.

Managing servers

The `memcached` caching system can be installed on the same machine your Web server runs on. However, it performs better if it is added to an array of other machines. These additional machines do not have to be on the same domain, location, or even be all that powerful from a hardware perspective.

Adding new servers

You can use `connect()` to add new servers but there is a better function, `addServer()`, which does not use as many resources and only establishes a network connection when required. You can add as many servers as you want, but they will only be used when required by the system.

Closing a connection

The process of closing a cached server connection is done by making a call to the `close()` method. This method will not close persistent connections. These connections are closed only when the Web server is shut down or restarted.

```
$cache = new Memcache;
$cache->close();
```

Deleting an item in the cache

Items will automatically be deleted from the cache when they expire, but it is not uncommon that you may want to remove data immediately. The delete() method accepts two arguments. The first argument is the key to match and delete. The second argument is a timeout delay where the caching service will wait this amount of time before removing the value.

You can use this method to speed up the deletion process of certain elements by setting the timeout to a few minutes or hours in the future.

Moving forward with memcached

Now that you have an understanding of how to install, modify, and use `memcached` you should see a substantial performance increase. The advantage to working with `memcached` is you can add more servers as the load becomes more demanding. This continues to remove the stress from the database and makes your applications more responsive.

Maintaining a Scalable and More Efficient Server

The `Memcached` class offers a few other methods that you may find useful, depending on your intended use. You can also use this `memcached` caching system with multiple programming languages, but the focus in this section has been PHP 5.

Handling Backups

Backing up your data is not only a best practice to ensure your data is stored securely; backups can also be used to periodically clean your system and limit the files that are available on the system. Oftentimes you will have many `Oldfilename.php` or `test.php` files throughout your server as you test more code concepts. The problem with these extra files is it slows down directory scans and makes it harder to manage the files that matter.

File management

Running a more efficient server can include minimizing what is installed on your server. In the next section you will learn how to exclude non-used files to limit overhead.

Managing necessary files

If you limit your server to only have active code and leave the experimentation for a development server or section, you will notice a directory scanning and searching performance increase.

This doesn't mean those unneeded files should be deleted. In fact, that is the exact opposite of what you should do. The best practice is to set up timed backups that look for these files or simply have a backup system that backs up the entire server and moves it to a remote location.

Limit larger files

Try to limit the use of larger files whenever possible. These files take longer to open and require more memory when opened. If not excluded, they also slow down the backup process, which gets a more in-depth look in the following section.

> **NOTE** Don't store backup data on the same drive because you will have an even larger resource issue.

Backup management

Running backups on your system will ensure you don't lose necessary files. This can include user uploaded files or core server configurations.

Timed backups

UNIX Web servers offer a service called `cron`, which can be set up to run at a predetermined time based on the setup information. You can find more information about the `cron` service by looking up the manual page for it.

```
man cron
```

Here is the format of a `crontab` file, where you repeat the last line for each new command.

```
# +--------------- minute (0 - 59)
# | +------------ hour (0 - 23)
# | | +---------- day of month (1 - 31)
# | | | +-------- month (1 - 12)
# | | | | +---- day of week (0 - 6) (Sunday=0 or 7)
# | | | | |
  * * * * *  command to run
```

All `cron` jobs are located in the same file, which is normally loaded by typing the following command:

```
crontab -e
```

In Windows, you can use the Task Scheduler, which can provide the same basic functionality.

Backup directories using PHP

With the `cron` system, which can run a command at a given time, at your disposal you can build an automated backup system that is called by the `cron`. These backups can be run at any time, but unless you have a special requirement, it is best to run them when your server encounters the least amount of stress.

The first part to the backup script is defining the directory to backup. This portion is built as an array, which is used to allow more than one directory to be backed up.

```
$dirs = array("/var/www/vhosts/example.org/myfiles");
```

The `backupDir` defines where the archive file is saved after it is created.

```
$backupDir = "/var/www/vhosts/example.org/backups";
```

A date is stored that is used as the archive filename. You can modify the archive name to include the hours and minutes if you decide to create more than one backup per day.

```
$date = date('m-d-y');
```

The core of the backup script is within a `foreach` loop. This loop is responsible for backing up each directory defined in the array. For this example, there is only one directory defined, so this loop will only run once.

```
foreach($dirs as $dir)
{
...
}
```

Continuing with the script, the next section is located all within the `foreach` loop. The first part is to use `preg_replace` to remove all but the directory name from the `$dir` variable. This is passed through another `preg_replace` to define the archive name.

Maintaining a Scalable and More Efficient Server   16

```
$dir = preg_replace('/\/$/', '', $dir);
$archiveName = preg_replace('/^(.*)\/.*?/', '', $dir);
```

After you define the archive name, the next step is to build the command that will create the archive file.

```
$tgzName = "{$archiveName}-{$date}.tgz";
$tgzFile = "{$backupDir}/{$tgzName}";
$backupCmd = "tar czf {$tgzFile} {$archiveName}";
```

The $backupCmd variable is passed into the system command, which informs PHP to run the passed-in command at the system level of your Web server. This would be the same as executing the command in the command prompt or terminal.

```
$result = system($backupCmd . " 2>&1");
```

For debugging purposes you may want to output the command in case an error occurs, as well as the original command to ensure the structure is properly defined.

```
print "Command: " . $backupCmd . "<br />";
print "Result: " . $result;
```

That is the end of the file backup script. As you can see, the structure of this script is straightforward and the only important aspect is the system function, which could be disabled in some environments.

Here is the completed script, which you reference in the `crontab` file to automate the process.

```
<?php

// File Backup

$dirs = array("/var/www/vhosts/example.org/myfiles");
$backupDir = "/var/www/vhosts/example.org/backups";

$date = date('m-d-y');

foreach($dirs as $dir)
{
  $dir = preg_replace('/\/$/', '', $dir);
  $archiveName = preg_replace('/^(.*)\/.*?/', '', $dir);

  $tgzName = "{$archiveName}-{$date}.tgz";
  $tgzFile = "{$backupDir}/{$tgzName}";

  $backupCmd = "tar czf {$tgzFile} {$archiveName}";

  $result = system($backupCmd . " 2>&1");

  print "Command: " . $backupCmd . "<br />";
```

```
    print "Result: " . $result;
}

?>
```

Backing up your important files is one way to maintain an efficient system. However, the database is another aspect that should be periodically cleaned. You never want to accidentally remove important information so it is a good idea to set up a backup system for this as well.

With the exception of a few commands, the database backup script is very similar to the file backup script and can be combined into one backup script which is explained in the next section. If you choose to combine the two scripts you may want to limit the backup directories. Otherwise, the backups could result in slower performance.

Using PHP to back up databases

As you learned in the previous section, you can assign automated backup scripts to the `crontab` file. Another common backup script is one that handles your databases. Just like the file backup, you should then move them to a remote directory to ensure the added file size doesn't affect your live server.

You will find that as your system begins to grow you may want to invest in a backup server that doesn't need many resources because it would be used purely for storage. This isn't a required element, but it gives you an added level of protection with your data, as well as makes your live server more efficient.

The first part of the database backup script is to define the MySQL connection details.

```
$dbHost = "localhost";
$dbUsername = "root";
$dbPassword = "pass";
```

The database for this example is a book store application, but you could modify the database to match any of the many databases you will mostly likely have in your system.

```
$dbName = "bookStore";
```

If you have defined these variables in another part of your application, you can simply load that configuration file to ensure the values only need to be updated once. You replace the previous four lines with a simple `include` or `require` call.

```
require "/path/to/configuration/dbConnection.php";
```

The backup storage directory `$backupDir` is defined as a string in this example, but you could modify it to an array as you did in the file backup script. This is important if you have more than one database, as most systems do.

```
$backupdir = '/var/www/vhosts/example.org/dbBackups';
```

Maintaining a Scalable and More Efficient Server   16

> **NOTE** Define the backup directory outside of the public path whenever possible to ensure the Web browser cannot access the backups.

The filename of the archive needs to be unique to ensure the archives do not overwrite each other. You can create a random hash using the time, which would be unique, but it would make it impossible to determine which archive you created.

A much more elegant solution is to append pieces of the date to the archive name, which creates a readable and unique filename. Rather than make multiple calls to date you can use the `getdate()` function, which returns an array of date information that you can then reference by the key names.

```
$today = getdate();
```

To ensure the date is readable in the best way possible, a series of `if` statements is used to ensure the date values are always two digits. This is not a programming requirement, but more importantly a consistency that makes it easier to read the date in the filename.

```
$month = $today[mon];

if($month < 10)
{
   $month = "0" . $month;
}

$day = $today[mday];

if($day < 10)
{
   $day = "0" . $day;
}

$year = $today[year];
```

The actual archive creation is broken into three parts, but all in the same command. The first part makes a call to the database by passing in the necessary login information.

```
$mysqlCommand = "mysqldump --opt -h %s -u %s -p%s %s";
```

The second part of the command accepts the MySQL data and pushes it into the `gzip` function, which is where the actual archive is created.

```
$gzipCommand ="gzip > %s/%s-%s-%s-%s.gz";
```

The third and final part of the command takes the variables defined in the previous sections and creates the command string using `sprintf` to cleanly create the command. The `sprintf` function uses placeholders and accepts additional arguments to fill those placeholders. This is the same as creating an inline string, but it creates a cleaner and easier string.

425

```
$run_command = sprintf($mysqlCommand . " | " . $gzipCommand,
    $host, $user, $pass, $db,
    $backupdir, $db, $month, $day, $year);
```

The pipe | character is a special command that tells the system to capture the output of the command to the left of the pipe and pass it into the function defined on the right side of the pipe.

In this example, the MySQL data is captured and passed into the `gzip` call.

The last step in the database backup script is to actually make the system call, which gathers the MySQL data and creates the archive file.

```
system($run_command);
```

> **NOTE** The `system()` command is not available if disabled in the `php.ini` file or if `safe_mode` is enabled.

Here is the complete script, which you can quickly modify and add to your existing `crontab`. You can even combine the two backup scripts and add in more functionality. The previous examples are meant to get you started.

```
<?php

#!/usr/bin/php

//require 'connectfile.php';

$dbHost = "localhost";
$dbUsername = "root";
$dbPassword = "pass";
$dbName = "bookStore";

$backupdir = '/var/www/vhosts/example.org/dbBackups';

$month = $today[mon];

if($month < 10)
{
   $month = "0" . $month;
}

$day = $today[mday];

if($day < 10)
{
   $day = "0" . $day;
```

```
    }

    $year = $today[year];

    $mysqlCommand = "mysqldump --opt -h %s -u %s -p%s %s";

    $gzipCommand ="gzip > %s/%s-%s-%s-%s.gz";

    $run_command = sprintf($mysqlCommand . " | " . $gzipCommand,
       $host, $user, $pass, $db,
       $backupdir, $db, $month, $day, $year);

    system($run_command);

    ?>
```

Summary

In this chapter, you learned various techniques on how to maintain a scalable and more efficient Web server. This covered the topics of modifying the Apache configuration files, limiting what gets loaded, and disabling error logging to improve overall performance.

You then learned how to optimize MySQL, which can account for a large majority of bottlenecks in an application and can even bubble up to consume the resources of the Web server.

In the final part of the chapter, you were introduced to memcached, which was used to build a high-performance caching system that eliminated the majority of the overhead from the database.

Using each of these techniques on any of your development projects will result in better performance. New hardware doesn't need to be the only solution if you properly optimize your Web server using these techniques.

You also learned about new tools that can assist you in optimizing your system using a graphical approach instead of the traditional command prompt.

Chapter 17

Building Complete Advanced Applications

Rather than have the book end with a basic overview, I thought a fully developed video player application would allow you to fully understand the process of building an application.

This chapter utilizes various concepts and technologies learned in the previous chapters. I recommend reading those first unless you are just curious about the types of applications you can develop using Flash and PHP or already have some familiarity with Flash and PHP.

This chapter is divided into five parts, each building on the previous section and resulting in a complete, PHP-driven video player. You can also take the concepts and components developed in this chapter and use them in your own projects. For example, the login component will be developed as a stand-alone module, which allows you to drop it into another application with very little modification.

IN THIS CHAPTER

Using a basic video player

Building a video player in Flash and PHP

Working with video tracking

Building a user login component in Flash

Finalizing the video player

Building a Basic Video Player

Flash offers a large array of functionality. The possibilities of what you can develop using Flash are only limited by your time and imagination.

Video is a very valuable asset on the Internet with the advancement of high-speed broadband connections. Flash is the best way to deliver video because of the wide availability of the Flash Player for all of the most popular Web browsers.

Flash allows developers to build a video player and be assured that the widest audience possible will be able to view it. It also doesn't hurt that

Part V | **Server, Application, and Database Maintenance**

Adobe has developed a fully functional single video player that allows developers to easily incorporate it in an existing project.

In fact, building a basic video player in Flash, as shown in Figure 17.1. requires very few lines of code.

Start by dragging a `FLVPlayback` component from the Components pane to the Stage. Give this new player an instance name of `myPlayer` and open the Actions pane.

For simplicity, use one of the sample video files that Adobe provides for testing:

```
www.helpexamples.com/flash/video/water.flv
```

FIGURE 17.1

`FLVPlayback` video component displayed on the Stage

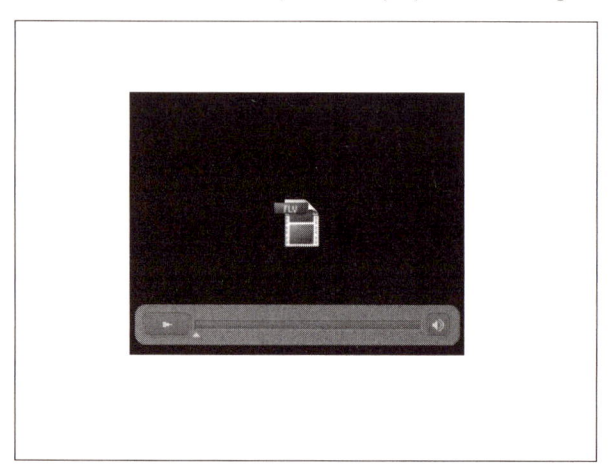

The next step is to set the source property of the video player by pointing it to the sample FLV file:

```
myPlayer.source = "http://helpexamples.com/flash/video/
    water.flv";
```

Test the movie and you should see the sample video load, then automatically start playing. Congratulations, you have played an FLV in Flash, using the prebuilt video player component.

The video player has a fairly large collection of methods and properties, but some of the more common are related to playback control. For example, remember how the video played once it was loaded? This may not be the desired result all the time, so the video player allows you to modify this behavior by setting the `autoPlay` property to `false`.

Building Complete Advanced Applications

```
myPlayer.source = "http://helpexamples.com/flash/video/
   water.flv";
myPlayer.autoPlay = false;
```

Now when the video loads, it waits for a call to the `play` method before it starts playing. This functionality is most commonly used on interactive Web sites to ensure the video or sound doesn't get anyone in trouble while viewing a site. Normally started by the user clicking a button or something similar, let's enhance the functionality and add a simple mouse event to start the video.

You can start by adding a button to the Stage and giving it an instance name of `myPlayBtn`. Then modify the code and add the mouse handler function:

```
myPlayer.source = "http://helpexamples.com/flash/video/
   water.flv";
myPlayer.autoPlay = false;

myPlayBtn.addEventListener(MouseEvent.CLICK,
   beginPlaybackHandler);

function beginPlaybackHandler(e:MouseEvent):void
{
  myPlayer.play();
}
```

You also want your users to be able to stop the playback of a video. This is nearly identical to the process of playing a video.

Start by adding another button to the Stage, with the instance name `myStopBtn`. Then add the new event handler and assign it to the Stop button, such as:

```
myPlayer.source =
    "http://helpexamples.com/flash/video/water.flv";
myPlayer.autoPlay = false;

myPlayBtn.addEventListener(MouseEvent.CLICK,
   beginPlaybackHandler);

function beginPlaybackHandler(e:MouseEvent):void
{
  myPlayer.play();
}

myStopBtn.addEventListener(MouseEvent.CLICK,
   stopPlaybackHandler);

function stopPlaybackHandler(e:MouseEvent):void
{
  myPlayer.stop();
}
```

Part V: Server, Application, and Database Maintenance

For simplicity, the video player component has the ability to be skinned, which means you don't have to design a custom interface. This custom skin loads in a default set of playback controls.

In fact, Adobe offers a large list of skins, each in different colors or with various selections of buttons and functionality. For example, here is the most common example used. This skin is a full set of controls that is placed underneath the video player component. Seeing as this skin has basic playback controls, you can replace the existing mouse handler and use the internal version:

```
myPlayer.source = "http://helpexamples.com/flash/video/
   water.flv";
myPlayer.autoPlay = false;
myPlayer.skin = "SkinUnderPlayStopSeekMuteVol.swf";
```

> **NOTE** The video player skin must be in the same directory as your SWF. You can also set the skin using the Component Inspector.

The skin can be found in the same directory as your Flash movie once you select at least one skin from the Property inspector.

As you can see, the functionality of the video player component allows you to build a basic player fairly quickly. The problem with this component is encountered when you want to play more than one video or even add categories of videos.

Fortunately, Adobe developed a wonderful component and even made it easy to use on you own custom development projects, which you learn to do later in this chapter. You will create and add the additional functionality you want.

Building a Video Player in Flash and PHP

In the previous section you learned how to develop a basic video player, with a hard-coded source file, and it worked well enough. The problem is, this result is not scalable and really doesn't offer any re-usability, which is crucial when building an application.

Getting started

The video player application that you develop in this section has already been designed, as shown in Figure 17.2, so that you can focus on the development portion.

The prebuilt video player is available on the book's Web site, where you can also find the completed application to get an idea of what you will be building as a finished product.

This video player is broken up into three parts. The first part is the MySQL component that stores the video references and the categories.

Building Complete Advanced Applications 17

FIGURE 17.2

Example of the video player design you will be working with in this chapter

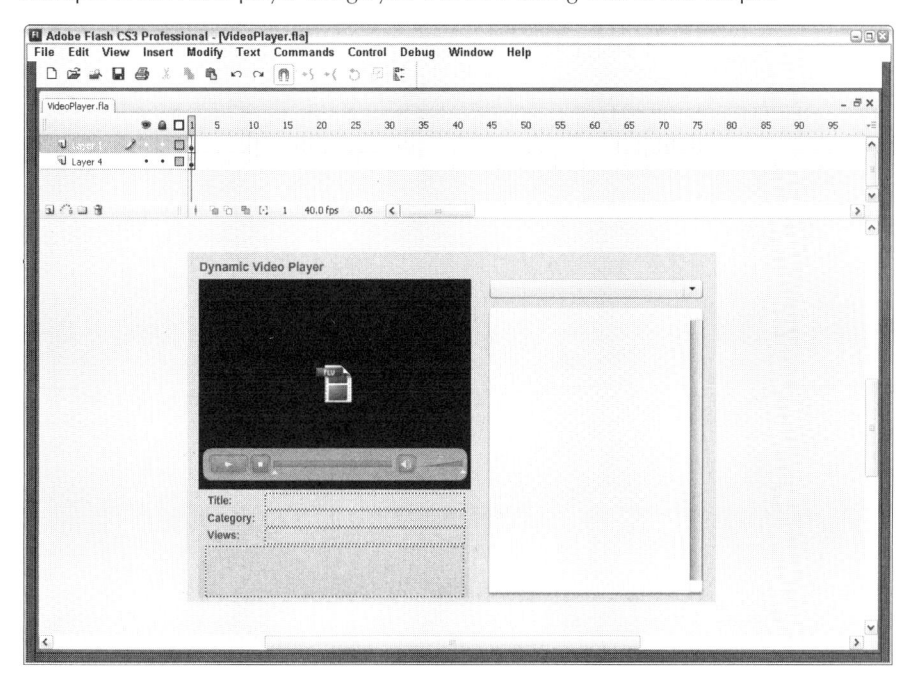

Building the database and MySQL tables

Start by opening your favorite database editor and create a new database for this project. You can name this database anything you prefer. I used `book_videoplayer`, but that is only a suggestion.

After the database is created, you can start adding the table schema structure for the videos and categories data. For this application the tables have already been defined, but feel free to look them over to gain a better understanding of what they are responsible for.

The tables in this application are split up to ensure they are optimized and to easily understand which table is responsible for each task. It is best to split functionality in multiple tables, also referred to as normalizing. Doing so ensures your database will be the most efficient and allows it to expand.

The table structure in this application is straightforward. For example, the video name, description, and source references are found in the videos table, which is constructed similar to the following:

433

```
CREATE TABLE `videos` (
  `id` int(11) NOT NULL auto_increment,
  `catId` int(11) default NULL,
  `name` varchar(200) default NULL,
  `src` varchar(200) default NULL,
  `description` text,
  `count` int(11) default 0,
  `active` varchar(1) default '1',
  PRIMARY KEY  (`id`)
) ENGINE=MyISAM;
```

As you can see, this table is nothing special, but it handles the core of the application management. You can add more columns if you decide you want to expand on the original application.

A database is not the only storage option. You can use an XML file or even hardcode the video paths in Flash, but the idea is to develop an expandable application. This means that the database is the most logical option to store the video and category data. The database also offers the ability to expand and grow as you add more features to your application.

The second table you need to add is the categories table, which stores an id used in the PHP in the next section and the name of the category that is displayed in the Flash application.

```
CREATE TABLE `categories` (
  `id` int(11) NOT NULL auto_increment,
  `name` varchar(100) default NULL,
  `active` varchar(1) default '1',
  PRIMARY KEY  (`id`)
) ENGINE=MyISAM;
```

Adding sample data to the tables

You can now prefill the tables to test it all, as shown in Figure 17.3. You can use your favorite database editor and add the sample data by hand, or use the following sample INSERT statements that add a few categories and videos:

```
INSERT INTO categories (name) VALUES ('Category 1');
INSERT INTO categories (name) VALUES ('Category 2');

INSERT INTO videos (catId, name, src, description)
  VALUES (1, 'Sample Video 0:1', 'sample.flv', 'Cool Video
    Here');
INSERT INTO videos (catId, name, src, description)
  VALUES (2, 'Sample Video 0:2', 'sample.flv', 'Cool Video
    Here');
```

FIGURE 17.3

Sample table data displayed in the MySQL query browser

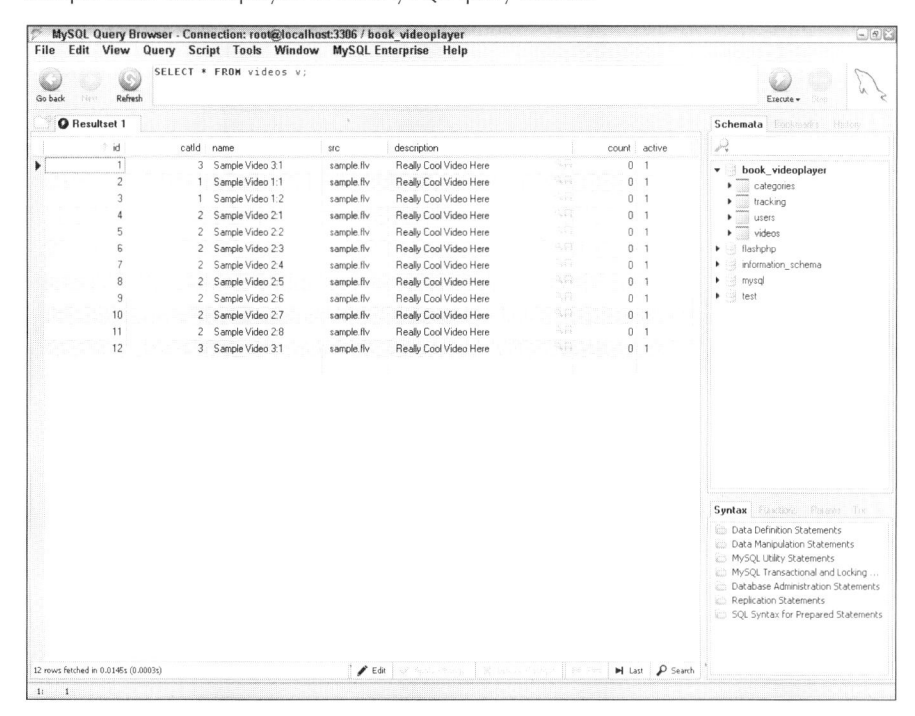

Testing the database

After you load the data into the database you can test it. This can be done by building a simple PHP file that connects to the database and runs a very simple query. You have learned how to connect to the database in the previous chapters. For this example, you need to define the connection details and make a call to the `mysql_connect` function.

```php
<?php

$link = mysql_connect('localhost', 'root', 'password');
mysql_select_db('book_videoplayer', $link);

?>
```

When the connection is established, the next step is to build the SQL query.

```php
<?php

$link = mysql_connect('localhost', 'root', 'password');
```

```php
mysql_select_db('book_videoplayer', $link);

$catID = 1;
$query = sprintf("SELECT * FROM categories where id=%d", $catID);

?>
```

The last step is to return something. For simplicity, let's display one of the category names.

```php
<?php

$link = mysql_connect('localhost', 'root', 'password');
mysql_select_db('book_videoplayer', $link);

$catID = 1;
$query = sprintf("SELECT * FROM categories where id=%d", $catID);

$result = mysql_query($query, $link);
$row = mysql_fetch_array($result);

print "Category Name: <strong>" . $row['name'] . "</strong>";

?>
```

Save this file as `sqltest.php` in your Web server home directory and call it up using your favorite Web browser. When you execute the PHP file, you should see output similar to the following:

```
Category Name: Category 1
```

If you see anything else, make sure you check the connection details. If for some reason you get a blank page, place the following line at the top of your file to force PHP to display all potential errors:

```
error_reporting(E_ALL);
```

Now that you have seen a simple MySQL query run using the date for this application, try calling two tables and testing the functionality the final application will have. The only two lines of code that need to be modified are the SQL query and the output.

```php
<?php

$link = mysql_connect('localhost', 'root', 'password');
mysql_select_db('book_videoplayer', $link);

$catID = 1;
$query = sprintf("SELECT v.name FROM videos v, categories c WHERE
    v.catId=c.id AND c.id=%d", $catID);

$result = mysql_query($query, $link);

while($row = mysql_fetch_array($result))
```

Building Complete Advanced Applications

```
{
  print "Video Name: " . "<strong>" . $row['name'] . "</strong>";
}

?>
```

When you run this code, you should be presented a list of videos for that specific category. This code searches the category and video tables and returns all videos that share the same `ids`. This is the most basic join of MySQL tables, but it works perfectly for this application.

Remoting integration

The next step is to build the actual PHP that will be called by Flash using remoting. In fact, this section is similar in the fact you will be using AMFPHP. But the actual development portion beyond this is different.

CROSS-REF More information on remoting can be found in Chapter 8.

The advantage to building this application using remoting is it gives you the ability to test it more easily. This is because you can build the AMFPHP classes and then test them using standard PHP code or the included browser viewer that ships with AMFPHP.

You also have the ability to reuse these classes in other projects or with HTML portions of the same project. For example, assume you want to build a user panel that can display the latest movies from a specific category. You can do this by building a very basic HTML page and calling the remoting class to return the necessary data, just like you would in Flash.

Database connector class

The classes in this application are dependent on the database. Rather than define the connection details in every class, it is better to build a database connector class that is responsible for making the initial connection and storing the connection credentials.

The connector class has five private variables. The first four define the connection information.

```
<?php

class DatabaseConnector
{

  private $host   = "localhost";
  private $user   = "root";
  private $pass   = "password";
  private $dbName = "book_videoplayer";

}

?>
```

437

Part V Server, Application, and Database Maintenance

The fifth variable is used to store the database link resource `id`.

```
private $link = null;
```

The constructor for this class is empty because the private variables are defined previously.

```
function DatabaseConnector() { }
```

The private `connect` method is only called when an existing connection is not found. This method passes in the private connection details and stores the resource `id` in the `$this->link` property, which is only visible to this class.

```
private function connect()
{
  $this->link = mysql_connect($this->host, $this->user, $this-
    >pass);
  mysql_select_db($this->dbName, $this->link);
}
```

The second method, `getConnection`, is set as public so other classes have access to it. However, the comments define it as private to ensure remoting classes cannot access it. This method first checks for an existing connection resource and if one isn't found, a call to the `connect` method is made.

The last step of this function is to return the active connection resource, which is used in other classes.

```
/**
 * Get database connection
 * @access private
 * @returns database link, to be used in other sql calls
 */
public function getConnection()
{
  if($this->link == null)
  {
    $this->connect();
  }

  return $this->link;
}
```

As you can see, this class is very handy because it takes care of storing the database connection. Additionally, if one isn't found, it creates one.

Here is the completed class, which should be saved as `DatabaseConnector.php` in your project directory so it can be accessed by the other classes.

Building Complete Advanced Applications

```php
<?php

class DatabaseConnector
{
  private $host  = "localhost";
  private $user  = "root";
  private $pass  = "password";
  private $dbName = "book_videoplayer";

  private $link = null;

  function DatabaseConnector() { }

  private function connect()
  {
    $this->link = mysql_connect(
      $this->host,
      $this->user,
      $this->pass
    );
    mysql_select_db($this->dbName, $this->link);
  }

  /**
  * Get database connection
  * @access private
  * @returns database link, to be used in other sql calls
  */
  public function getConnection()
  {
    if($this->link == null)
    {
      $this->connect();
    }

    return $this->link;
  }

}
?>
```

Video class

Now that the database connector class is completed, the next class to develop is for managing the videos. This class returns the video list based on video or category id.

Part V: Server, Application, and Database Maintenance

The first part of this class is to load in the database connector file, which this Videos class will extend.

```php
<?php

require_once 'DatabaseConnector.php';

?>
```

You may remember `extends` from the ActionScript classes you developed in previous examples. The syntax in PHP is identical. Basically, define the class and whichever class it will extend, similar to the following:

```php
<?php

require_once 'DatabaseConnector.php';

class Videos extends DatabaseConnector
{

}

?>
```

The Video class has one method, `getVideos`. This method accepts a video and category `id` as separate arguments to determine which videos to return.

```php
/**
 * get videos
 * @access remote
 * @returns array of videos
 */
function getVideos($categoryID=-1, $videoID=-1)
{
   ...
}
```

The first part of this method needs to check for valid `id`s to ensure the SQL will not be compromised. This step is not required, but ensures your application is more secure.

```php
if($categoryID == -1 || strlen($categoryID) == 0)
{
   trigger_error("Category ID required to return video list");
}
```

This statement calls `trigger_error` if an invalid or missing category `id` is passed in. The reason for using the `trigger_error` is because AMFPHP gracefully halts all further process and returns the desired error to the calling script, in this case that will be ActionScript.

Building Complete Advanced Applications

The next step is to assign the variables for this method and create an array that will hold the video data that is passed back to ActionScript.

```
$vidSQL = "";
$rows = array();
```

Once the basics have been defined, the next step is to determine if the script should be looking for one single video or a list of them. This assigns the correct SQL if the code should only be looking for one video.

```
// look for specific video?
if($videoID != -1 && strlen($videoID) != 0)
{
  $vidSQL = " AND v.id=" . $videoID;
}
```

The database link can be defined by simply making a call to the `getConnection` method of the `DatabaseConnector` class because the `Video` class is extending that. The local `$link` variable is assigned the active connection to be used in the remainder of the MySQL interaction within this function.

```
$link = $this->getConnection();
```

The database query is fairly complex because it checks two tables for data and returns one video list based on that check. This query is similar to the one you built when testing out the database at the beginning of this section. This query uses the `$vidSQL`, which will either be a valid addition to the SQL or a blank string when not looking for a specific video.

```
$query = sprintf("SELECT
  v.name,
  v.src,
  v.id as 'vid',
  c.name as 'cat',
  v.description,
  v.count
FROM categories c, videos v
WHERE v.catId=c.id
AND v.catId=%d
AND v.active=1 " . $vidSQL, $categoryID);
```

The special portion of this SQL query is the modification of the column names, such as

```
v.id as 'vid'
```

This is done because the result set has the name `id` in both tables and only one name can be returned. If you keep the standard naming you will only have access to one table of `id` info. Knowing which one will be returned is a matter of which order they are called in. The renaming only modifies the `resultset`, so you don't have to worry about the original data being affected.

Part V Server, Application, and Database Maintenance

The next step is to run the MySQL query and retrieve the results, which are then looped through and passed out of the function as a multidimensional array.

```
$result = mysql_query($query, $link);
```

Before the loop is run, it is a good idea to ensure some rows were returned from the query. Failure to do this simple check could result in an endless loop. This can harm the Web server because you will most likely not realize it is occurring.

This simple check is done by checking the number of rows returned using the `mysql_num_rows` function. This function returns a numerical value representing the number of rows returned in the query.

```
if(mysql_num_rows($result) == 0)
{
  trigger_error("No videos found");
  return false;
}
```

Assuming that a valid `resultset` was found, the next step is to loop through the results and fill the array variable that was previously defined.

```
while($row = mysql_fetch_array($result, MYSQL_ASSOC))
{
  array_push($rows, $row);
}
```

The last step of this function is to return the array of video data. This method will not get to this point unless valid video data is ready to be passed back.

```
return $rows;
```

That is all there is to the `Video` class. This file should be saved as `Videos.php`. Here is the completed class, which can also be found in the book's code on the Web site.

```
<?php

require_once 'DatabaseConnector.php';

class Videos extends DatabaseConnector
{

  /**
  * get videos
  * @access remote
  * @returns array of videos
  */
  function getVideos($categoryID=-1, $videoID=-1)
  {
```

Building Complete Advanced Applications

```php
        if($categoryID == -1 || strlen($categoryID) == 0)
        {
        trigger_error("Category ID required to return video list");
        }

        $vidSQL = "";
        $rows = array();

        // look for specific video?
        if($videoID != -1 && strlen($videoID) != 0)
        {
          $vidSQL = " AND v.id=" . $videoID;
        }

        $link = $this->getConnection();

        $query = sprintf("SELECT
            v.name,
            v.src,
            v.id as 'vid',
            c.name as 'cat',
            v.description,
            v.count
          FROM categories c, videos v
          WHERE v.catId=c.id
          AND v.catId=%d
          AND v.active=1 " . $vidSQL, $categoryID);

        $result = mysql_query($query, $link);

        if(mysql_num_rows($result) == 0)
        {
          trigger_error("No videos found");
          return false;
        }

        while($row = mysql_fetch_array($result, MYSQL_ASSOC))
        {
          array_push($rows, $row);
        }

        return $rows;
    }

}

?>
```

The second class for this example is the Category class, which also has one method. This method is responsible for returning all of the active categories to the video player.

443

Part V — Server, Application, and Database Maintenance

Before the method is created, you must load in the Database connection, exactly like you did in the Video class.

```
require_once 'DatabaseConnector.php';
```

The first part of the `getCategories` method is responsible for creating a new `$rows` variable that will hold the categories returned from the database. The link variable is filled with an active database connection, which will be used in the following SQL calls.

```
$rows = array();
$link = $this->getConnection();
```

The SQL query basically pulls in all the categories that are active, meaning the active column is set to a value of 1. This SQL query is then passed into `mysql_query` which is responsible for actually executing the SQL call.

```
$query = "SELECT id, name FROM categories WHERE active=1";
$result = mysql_query($query, $link);
```

The `if` statement checks for at least one valid row before continuing and will throw an error if no valid rows are found. Assuming valid rows are found, a `while` loop is used to fill the `$rows` variable and once the loop is complete the `$rows` variable is returned.

```
if(mysql_num_rows($result) == 0)
{
  trigger_error("No categories found");
  return false;
}

while($row = mysql_fetch_array($result, MYSQL_ASSOC))
{
  array_push($rows, $row);
}

return $rows;
```

That is all there is to the Category class, and as you can see the structure of the Category class is fairly similar to the Video class in the previous section.

Here is the completed Category class:

```
<?php

require_once 'DatabaseConnector.php';

class Categories extends DatabaseConnector
{

  /**
   * get categories
```

Building Complete Advanced Applications

```
 * @access remote
 * @returns array of categories
 */
 function getCategories()
 {
   $rows = array();

   $link = $this->getConnection();

   $query = "SELECT id, name FROM categories WHERE active=1";

   $result = mysql_query($query, $link);

   if(mysql_num_rows($result) == 0)
   {
     trigger_error("No categories found");
     return false;
   }

   while($row = mysql_fetch_array($result, MYSQL_ASSOC))
   {
     array_push($rows, $row);
   }

   return $rows;
 }
}

?>
```

Testing the classes

At this point both AMFPHP service classes have been written. You can quickly test the usage of them or move on to the ActionScript development portion of this application. Testing the class is very simple: you basically create a new PHP file, call the `video` or `category` method, and print the result.

For example, here is a simple test, also referred to as unit testing:

```
<?php

include 'amfphp/services/Videos.php';

$videos = new Videos();

$list = $videos->getVideos(1);

print_r($list);

?>
```

445

If you run this example in your browser you should see output similar to the following example:

```
Array
(
  [0] => Array
  (
    [name] => Sample Video 1:1
    [src] => sample.flv
    [vid] => 1
    [cat] => Category A
    [description] => Really Cool Video Here
    [count] => 0
  )

  ...
)
```

You should now have two complete classes that can be used in your ActionScript to interact with the database contents. The next step is to build the ActionScript portion of the application, which is handled by external classes for reusability.

Advanced video player development

In the previous sections of this example you developed the database and tables. Then you built the PHP services that interact with the database tables. The next step is to develop the ActionScript that is responsible for displaying and managing the video player.

If you look at the video player, as shown in Figure 17.4, on the Flash Stage you will notice there are four parts: the main video player component, info box, video list, and drop-down menu that will store the video categories. If you deselect everything by clicking on the Stage or pressing Esc, a `document` class with the name `VideoPlayer` appears.

This class is where most of the video player is managed from, rather than having code directly on the Timeline. This also gives you the option to develop in an external editor such as FDT, or you can use the stand-alone editor that ships with Flash.

Creating the document class

Start by creating a new ActionScript file using the ActionScript editor in Flash and name it `VideoPlayer.as`. Save this file in the application directory where your FLA is located to ensure the file will be loaded. You can also use the ActionScript file that is provided in the book's source on the Web site.

Building Complete Advanced Applications · 17

FIGURE 17.4

A video player that has already been designed for you

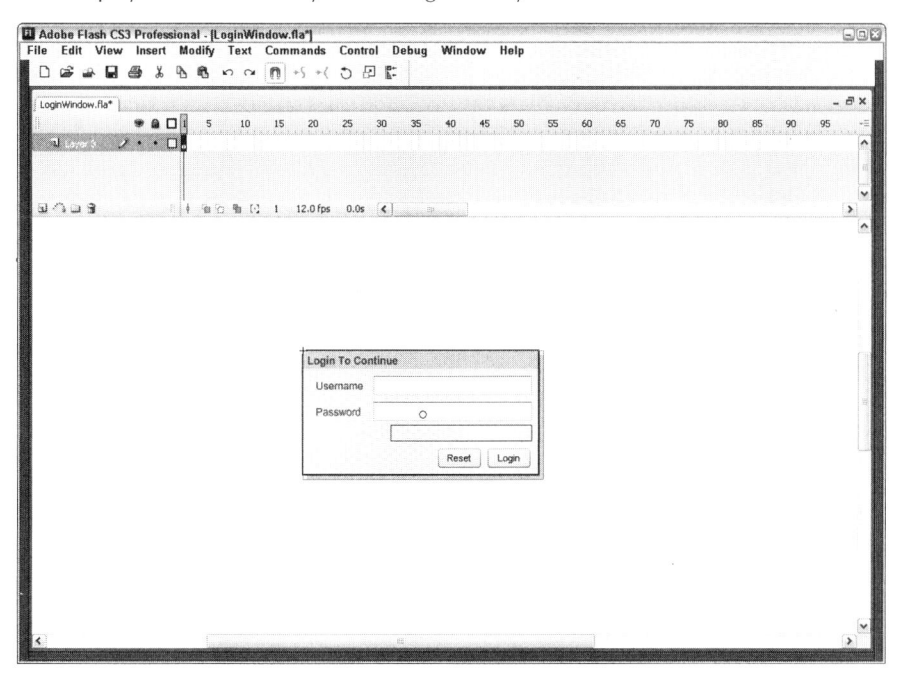

After this new ActionScript file is created and saved, it is time to begin developing the core scripting that handles the video player. Start by building the class outline and extend the class by the `MovieClip` class, which is required for a document class.

```
package
{
  import flash.display.MovieClip;

  public class VideoPlayer extends MovieClip
  {
  }
}
```

Now that the core class outline is constructed, you can begin to build the actual functionality. In addition to the `MovieClip` class, you need to `import` two more classes. The `Event` class will be used for all basic event handling, and the `net.*` package will contain all of the classes necessary for communicating with the remoting service.

```
import flash.events.Event;
import flash.net.*;
```

447

Part V Server, Application, and Database Maintenance

This `VideoPlayer` class will need to have a few properties defined, which will be stored as private to ensure they are protected and cannot accidentally be modified by external classes. The second property will store the active `NetConnection`, which is used to interact with the remoting service. You will work with this in the next section of code.

```
private var gatewayURL:String;
private var gateway:NetConnection;
private var selectedCatID:Number;
```

VideoPlayer constructor

The constructor function is responsible for initializing a few properties, modifying the visual portion of the video player display, and calling the `category` method.

```
function VideoPlayer()
{
  gatewayURL = "http://localhost/amfphp/gateway.php";
  getCategories();

  videoPlayer.visible = false;
  videoListCombo.enabled = false;
}
```

getCategories method

The next method in the `VideoPlayer` class is `getCategories()`, which is called from the constructor when the application initializes. This method starts by creating a new instance of the `Responder`, which handles the response from the remoting service.

```
public function getCategories():void
{
  var responder:Responder = new Responder(
    categoryResponseHandler,
    onFault
  );
}
```

Once the responder is defined, the next step is to assign the gateway to a new instance of the `NetConnection` class. This is where the actual call to remoting service begins.

```
public function getCategories():void
{
  var responder:Responder = new Responder(
    categoryResponseHandler,
    onFault
  );

  gateway = new NetConnection();
}
```

Building Complete Advanced Applications

After the gateway has been properly assigned, the next step is to connect to the remoting service, passing the gateway path as the single argument.

```
public function getCategories():void
{
  var responder:Responder = new Responder(
    categoryResponseHandler,
    onFault
  );

  gateway = new NetConnection();
  gateway.connect(gatewayURL);
}
```

The last step in the `getCategories` method is to make the remoting call. This defines the service you want to connect to, as well as passes along the responder to handle both success and failure responses.

```
public function getCategories():void
{
  var responder:Responder = new Responder(
    categoryResponseHandler,
    onFault
  );

  gateway = new NetConnection();
  gateway.connect(gatewayURL);
  gateway.call("Categories.getCategories", responder);
}
```

categoryResponseHandler method

Now that the `getCategories` method is completed, the next method to develop is the `categoryResponseHandler`, which was defined in the `Responder` instance. This method is called when a valid `recordset` is returned from the remoting service.

```
private function categoryResponseHandler(response:Object):void
{
  ...
}
```

The contents of this class handle the data response from the remoting service and populate the `ComboBox` using this video reference data. The first step is to enable the `ComboBox`, otherwise you won't be able to add new contents to it.

```
videoListCombo.enabled = true;
```

449

Once the `ComboBox` is enabled, the next step is to add the first item, which informs the user to select an option. This default option will have a value of −1 to alert that it is not a valid `id`. You could use 0, aside from the fact that is a valid ID in the database.

```
videoListCombo.addItem({label:'Choose a Category...', data:-1});
```

A `for each` loop is constructed to handle all of the response items. This will handle any number of video items, which is essential because the remoting service does not return the same number each time, as not every category has the same amount of videos.

```
for each(var item in response)
{
   videoListCombo.addItem({label:item.name, data:item.id});
}
```

This loop takes each item in the response object and assigns the name and `id` to the `ComboBox` values. This populates the `ComboBox` and allows the user to select a video category.

The last step of the `categoryResponseHandler` method is to assign the event listener to the `ComboBox`. This event fires whenever the selected item of the `ComboBox` component changes.

```
videoListCombo.addEventListener(Event.CHANGE, categoryHandler);
```

categoryHandler method

The `categoryHandler` method is called whenever the user selects a different item in the `ComboBox` component instance.

```
private function categoryHandler(e:Event):void { ... }
```

This method handles the process of validating the selected category `id`. The actual category `id` is found in the `selectedItem` property of the passed-in event.

```
var id:Number = e.currentTarget.selectedItem.data;
```

This category `id` is validated using a basic conditional statement that checks for a value of −1, which was assigned to the default item.

```
if(id == -1) return;
```

If that value is not found, then you know the `id` is valid, and the category `id` is assigned to the `selectedCatID` property allowing easy access to the current category `id`.

```
selectedCatID = id;
```

Last, a call to the `getVideos` method is made to load in the video list based on the current `id`.

```
getVideos();
```

Building Complete Advanced Applications

getVideos method

The `getVideos` method is called when a valid category is found. This method is used to make the initial call to the remoting service, which will load the correct list of videos based on the category stored in the previous method.

The only part of this method that is different from the `getCategories` method is the parameters passed in to the `call` method and the success function assigned to the `Responder`.

```
public function getVideos():void
{
  var responder:Responder = new Responder(
    videosResponseHandler,
    onFault
  );

  gateway = new NetConnection();
  gateway.connect(gatewayURL);
  gateway.call("Videos.getVideos", responder, selectedCatID, '');
}
```

You could create a master connection handler and pass in these different properties, but for simplicity, multiple methods are used.

videosResponseHandler method

One of the largest methods in this application would have to be the `videosResponseHandler`.

```
private function videosResponseHandler(response:Object):void
{
  ...
}
```

This is because that method is responsible for loading the video list and populating the `ScrollPane` component with the custom `VideoListItem` assets. These assets can be found in the Flash library for this project as they have been completed for you. Later in this project you develop the ActionScript that is attached to those assets.

The first part of this method is to define the `nextY` variable that offsets each video list item and creates an empty `MovieClip`, which is assigned to the `source` property of the `ScrollPane` instance.

```
var nextY:uint = 5;

var listItem:MovieClip = new MovieClip();
videoList.source = listItem;
```

The majority of this method is found within the `for..each` loop. This loop runs through each item in the video list response.

```
for each(var item in response)
{
  ...
}
```

Each pass of the loop creates a new `VideoListItem` instance. These instances get an event handler assigned to them and a unique placement in the list using the `nextY` variable previously defined.

```
var videoListItem:MovieClip = new VideoListItem();
videoListItem.y = nextY;
videoListItem.x = 2;

videoListItem.addEventListener(VideoListItem.ITEM_CLICK,
    listItemHandler);
```

The next portion of the loop sets custom properties of the `videoListItem` that defines the title, description, and video to load when the item is clicked on.

```
videoListItem.title = item.name;
videoListItem.desc = item.description;
videoListItem.videoObj = item;
videoListItem.setItem(item.vid, '', item.src);
```

Now that the `VideoListItem` instance has been completed, the next step is to add it to the `listItem` display list, which makes it visible in the `ScrollPane`.

```
listItem.addChild(videoListItem);
```

Each pass of the loop increments the `nextY` variable to ensure each video item is placed at a unique position. This value is determined by adding the height of the current video item plus a slight padding to the existing `nextY` variable.

```
nextY += videoListItem.height + 2;
```

The last step of the `videosResponseHandler` method is to refresh the `ScrollPane` component by calling the `update` method. If you do not call this method, the scrollbar in the `ScrollPane` would not reflect the added video items.

```
videoList.update();
```

As you can see, the `videosResponseHandler` method is responsible for a lot of the functionality in the video listing even though it is only part of the overall application. It did require a lot of custom code to properly create.

listItemHandler method

The `listItemHandler` method is called whenever one of the video items in the `ScrollPane` is clicked.

```
private function listItemHandler(e:Event):void
{
  ...
}
```

This method updates the current video information in the `videoMetaInfo MovieClip` found below the video player.

```
videoMetaInfo.titleTxt.text = e.currentTarget.videoObj.name;
videoMetaInfo.categoryTxt.text = e.currentTarget.videoObj.cat;
videoMetaInfo.viewsTxt.text = e.currentTarget.videoObj.count;
videoMetaInfo.descTxt.text =
   e.currentTarget.videoObj.description;
```

It is also responsible for replacing the source of the video player and playing the new video.

```
videoPlayer.visible = true;
videoPlayer.source = e.currentTarget.source;
videoPlayer.play();
```

Handling errors in remoting responses

The last method of the `VideoPlayer` class is a handler for errors in the remoting service. This method does not need to be unique unless you prefer to handle each error differently. I prefer to display the contents of the error during development because, as you may remember, the `trigger_error` calls in the PHP, which returns a user error message.

```
private function onFault(responds:Object):void
{
  trace("Debug::Error");
  for(var i in responds)
  {
    trace("  " + responds[i]);
  }
}
```

For this application, the error message is traced during development and completely ignored when running the real world. Later in this chapter, you create a realistic error handler that is similar to those found on popular video-sharing Web sites.

You have now completed the entire `VideoPlayer` class, which is the majority of the video application, at least for the ActionScript portion of the project.

Here is the `VideoPlayer` class in its entirety so you can easily look over how each of the methods interacts with each other. This source code is also available on the book's Web site for you to cut and paste.

Part V   Server, Application, and Database Maintenance

```
package
{
  import flash.display.MovieClip;
  import flash.events.Event;
  import flash.net.*;

  public class VideoPlayer extends MovieClip
  {
    private var gatewayURL:String;
    private var gateway:NetConnection;
    private var selectedCatID:Number;

    function VideoPlayer()
    {
      gatewayURL = "http://localhost/amfphp/gateway.php";
      getCategories();

      videoPlayer.visible = false;
      videoListCombo.enabled = false;
    }

    public function getCategories():void
    {
      var responder:Responder =
        new Responder(categoryRespHandler, onFault);

      gateway = new NetConnection();
      gateway.connect(gatewayURL);
      gateway.call("Categories.getCategories", responder);
    }

    private function categoryRespHandler(response:Object):void
    {
      videoListCombo.enabled = true;
      videoListCombo.addItem(
        {label:'Choose a Category...', data:-1}
      );
      for each(var item in response)
      {
        videoListCombo.addItem(
          {label:item.name, data:item.id}
        );
      }
      videoListCombo.addEventListener(Event.CHANGE,
        categoryHandler);
    }

    private function categoryHandler(e:Event):void
    {
      var id:Number = e.currentTarget.selectedItem.data;
```

Building Complete Advanced Applications   17

```
  if(id == -1) return;

  selectedCatID = id;

  trace("Load Category ID: " + id);
  getVideos();
}

public function getVideos():void
{
  var responder:Responder =
    new Responder(videosResHandler, onFault);

  gateway = new NetConnection();
  gateway.connect(gatewayURL);
  gateway.call("Videos.getVideos",
    responder,
    selectedCatID,
    ''
  );
}

private function videosRespHandler(response:Object):void
{
  var nextY:uint = 5;

  var listItem:MovieClip = new MovieClip();
  videoList.source = listItem;

  for each(var item in response)
  {
    var videoListItem:MovieClip =
      new VideoListItem();
    videoListItem.addEventListener(
      VideoListItem.ITEM_CLICK,
      listItemHandler
    );
    videoListItem.y = nextY;
    videoListItem.x = 2;

    videoListItem.title = item.name;
    videoListItem.desc = item.description;
    videoListItem.videoObj = item;
    videoListItem.setItem(item.vid,'', item.src);

    listItem.addChild(videoListItem);

    nextY += videoListItem.height + 2;

    videoList.update();
```

455

```
        }
      }
      private function listItemHandler(e:Event):void
      {
        var info:Object = e.currentTarget.videoObj;
        videoMetaInfo.titleTxt.text = info.name;
        videoMetaInfo.categoryTxt.text = info.cat;
        videoMetaInfo.viewsTxt.text = info.count;
        videoMetaInfo.descTxt.text = info.description;

        videoPlayer.visible = true;
        videoPlayer.source = e.currentTarget.source;
        videoPlayer.play();
      }

      // Error Handler
      private function onFault(responds:Object):void
      {
        trace("Debug::Error");
        for(var i in responds)
        {
          trace("   " + responds[i]);
        }
      }
    }
  }
```

Building the VideoListItem class

The next step before you can test the application is to build the `VideoListItem` class. If you attempt to run the application in its current form you would not only get errors, but you would also not be able to load any videos because the items are not clickable at the moment.

The first step is to create a new ActionScript file in your favorite editor. Save this file as `VideoListItem.as` to the same directory where your FLA is located. After the file is created, you need to build the skeleton of the class file, which needs to extend the `MovieClip` class because it is attached to a `MovieClip` instance in the library.

```
package
{
  import flash.display.MovieClip;
  public class VideoListItem extends MovieClip
  {
  }
}
```

In addition to the `MovieClip` class being imported, you must also import a few other classes in order to properly develop this class. These other classes handle the text, events, and mouse portions of the video item instances.

Building Complete Advanced Applications   17

```
import flash.display.MovieClip;
import flash.text.TextField;
import flash.events.Event;
import flash.events.MouseEvent;
```

The class also needs to have some default properties defined, which will be modified later in the class. Most of the properties are basic string definitions. However, the last property, ITEM_CLICK, is a special public constant that is used in the event handler. This is made public so that the variable can be accessed outside of the class.

```
public var videoObj:Object;

private var _id:uint;
private var _title:String;
private var _desc:String;
private var _thumb:String;
private var _src:String;

public static const ITEM_CLICK:String = "onItemClick";
```

VideoListItem constructor

The constructor in this class simply sets the alpha of the item to 50 percent, but because alpha is a 0 to 1 value, the 50 percent is actually 0.5.

```
function VideoListItem()
{
  alpha = 0.5;
}
```

setItem method

The first custom method in this class is setItem. This method is called on the creation of a new instance and sets the id, thumb, and video source parameters. For this example, the thumb option is not used, but you can expand the example because it has already been added.

```
function setItem(id:uint, thumb:String, src:String)
{
  _id = id;
  _thumb = thumb;
  _src = src;
}
```

The second part of the setItem method assigns the event listeners for the mouse object. This is also where you enable the mouse pointer icon when the user rolls the mouse over the video item.

```
function setItem(id:uint, thumb:String, src:String)
{
  _id = id;
  _thumb = thumb;
```

```
        _src = src;

       buttonMode = true;
       useHandCursor = true;
       addEventListener(MouseEvent.ROLL_OVER, overHandler);
       addEventListener(MouseEvent.ROLL_OUT, outHandler);
       addEventListener(MouseEvent.CLICK, clickHandler);
    }
```

Mouse handler methods

The mouse handler methods are used to modify the `alpha` value of the video item. In this example, they basically set the `alpha` to fully visible or partially visible. You could easily add a tween to this property and have the `alpha` property smoothly change.

```
        private function overHandler(e:MouseEvent):void
        {
          e.currentTarget.alpha = 1.0;
        }

        private function outHandler(e:MouseEvent):void
        {
          e.currentTarget.alpha = 0.5;
        }
```

The `clickHandler` method fires the `ITEM_CLICK` event that alerts any listening objects of the click. In this case, the event would notify the `VideoPlayer` and that specific video would be loaded.

```
        private function clickHandler(e:MouseEvent):void
        {
          dispatchEvent(new Event(ITEM_CLICK));
        }
```

The remaining methods in the `VideoListItem` class are for getting and setting the properties previously defined. For example, the title can be retrieved by calling `get title`, such as:

```
        public function get title():String
        {
         return _title;
        }
```

You can also set the `title` property by calling `set title` and passing in the title of the video.

```
        public function set title(val:String):void
        {
          _title = val;
          titleTxt.text = val;
        }
```

Building Complete Advanced Applications

Defining the getter and setter methods

The remaining getter/setter methods appear in the following code and also are in the completed class available in the book's source code:

```
public function get id():uint
{
  return _id;
}

public function get source():String
{
  return _src;
}

public function get desc():String
{
  return _desc;
}
public function set desc(val:String):void
{
  _desc = val;
  descTxt.text = val;
}
```

That is all there is to the `VideoListItem` class. As you can see, it is mostly self-contained, which makes this little object reusable in other applications. In this example, you are building a video player, but you could easily change that to a product viewer, document viewer, or anything else you can think of.

Here is the completed `VideoListItem` class, which you can study or simply copy and paste it from the book's Web site.

```
package
{
  import flash.display.MovieClip;
  import flash.text.TextField;
  import flash.events.Event;
  import flash.events.MouseEvent;

  public class VideoListItem extends MovieClip
  {
    public var videoObj:Object;

    private var _id:uint;
    private var _title:String;
    private var _desc:String;
    private var _thumb:String;
```

459

Part V Server, Application, and Database Maintenance

```
private var _src:String;

public static const ITEM_CLICK:String = "onItemClick";

function VideoListItem()
{
  alpha = 0.5;
}

function setItem(id:uint, thumb:String, src:String)
{
  _id = id;
  _thumb = thumb;
  _src = src;

  buttonMode = true;
  useHandCursor = true;
  addEventListener(MouseEvent.ROLL_OVER, overHandler);
  addEventListener(MouseEvent.ROLL_OUT, outHandler);
  addEventListener(MouseEvent.CLICK, clickHandler);
}

private function overHandler(e:MouseEvent):void
{
  e.currentTarget.alpha = 1.0;
}

private function outHandler(e:MouseEvent):void
{
  e.currentTarget.alpha = 0.5;
}

private function clickHandler(e:MouseEvent):void
{
  dispatchEvent(new Event(ITEM_CLICK));
}

public function get id():uint
{
  return _id;
}

public function get source():String
{
  return _src;
}

public function get title():String
{
```

Building Complete Advanced Applications   17

```
      return _title;
    }
    public function set title(val:String):void
    {
      _title = val;
      titleTxt.text = val;
    }

    public function get desc():String
    {
      return _desc;
    }
    public function set desc(val:String):void
    {
      _desc = val;
      descTxt.text = val;
    }
  }
}
```

At this point you have completed the Flash and PHP video player. You can now test the application, and you will see the same interface you started with. The difference is, if you select a category, the `ScrollPane` will be populated with the videos from that category.

You can then click on a video item and that video will begin to play. As it stands, the video player is a pretty robust application that can be expanded.

In the next section you will do just that by adding some basic tracking. Then, in a later section, you add a user login component that results in a truly real-world application while maintaining the original functionality the player has now.

Working with Video Tracking

In the previous section, you built a complete Flash-based video player that has PHP allowing for a dynamic result. This application allows the owner to simply update the database, and the Flash application reflects those updates the next time it loads.

A problem comes in when the owner wants to know which videos are popular. You want the project to help him determine which video content is popular so he can add more of that similar content.

The solution is to develop video tracking that logs how many times a video has been viewed. This is done by having a column in the database that holds the active count. You then add the necessary support to the PHP classes and finally update the Flash to display the count.

The database does not need to be updated because the count column was added in the previous section even though it wasn't used. Adding more columns than you will use to start is common so the application has the ability to grow. Extra columns may also be a result of temporarily removing a feature from an application after the database schema is created.

Updating the video class

The videos service class was created in the previous section. All you have to do now is add the new method used to modify the video count:

```
public function updatePlayCount($vid)
{
  $link = $this->getConnection();
  ...
}
```

This method accepts one parameter, which is an `id` referencing the video that should be updated. The first part of this method creates a link to the database using the existing database class you built in the previous section. This `$link` variable is passed into all future SQL actions in this method.

The second part of the method is to create an SQL query that grabs the current play count of the desired video.

```
public function updatePlayCount($vid)
{
  $link = $this->getConnection();

  $query = sprintf("SELECT count FROM videos WHERE id=%d", $vid);
  $result = mysql_query($query, $link);
}
```

Checking for valid records

After the value is loaded, the next step is to check for a valid record using the familiar `mysql_num_rows` function.

```
public function updatePlayCount($vid)
{
  $link = $this->getConnection();

  $query = sprintf("SELECT count FROM videos WHERE id=%d", $vid);
  $result = mysql_query($query, $link);

  if(mysql_num_rows($result) > 0)
  {
    ...
  }
}
```

Building Complete Advanced Applications

The contents of that conditional statement are where the value is updated, based on the count determined in the previous SQL query.

```
$row = mysql_fetch_row($result);
$count = $row[0];
$count++;
$queryUpdate = sprintf("UPDATE videos SET count=%d WHERE id=%d",
   $count, $vid);
mysql_query($queryUpdate, $link);
```

The SQL query that updates the database is built using `sprintf` to cleanly pass in the count and video `id`, rather than building a hard-to-read string, which is more common. The use of `sprintf` is all the more important when you come back to a project later.

At this point, you have made all of the changes to the `Videos.php` file and can continue with the modifications necessary to the ActionScript classes.

Adding video tracking to ActionScript

The video tracking feature can be added in one of two places. You can add the update so that it runs when the video starts to play, or you can add it so the count is only updated after the video has been fully viewed.

Each option has advantages. For this example, the tracking call is made when a new video is requested, rather than waiting for the video to complete. This action is similar to a hit counter on a Web site, with the exception that it will not be unique in this application. However, you can add the necessary code from the previous examples to ensure the update is unique.

updateVideoTracking method

The new tracking methods can be added at any point in the `VideoPlayer` class, but a logical place is above the `onFault` method. The first part of this new method is to create a new instance of the `Responder` class, passing the response handler method as the first parameter.

```
private function updateVideoTracking(vid:uint):void
{
   var responder:Responder = new Responder(
     updateTrackingHandler,
     onFault
   );
   ...
}
```

After the new `Responder` instance is created, the next step is to create the gateway connection using a new instance of the `NetConnection` class. This process is identical to the other remoting calls you made in the previous section.

```
private function updateVideoTracking(vid:uint):void
{
```

463

```
      var responder:Responder = new Responder(
        updateTrackingHandler,
        onFault
      );
      gateway = new NetConnection();
      gateway.connect(gatewayURL);
    }
```

The final update to the `updateVideoTracking` method is where the call to the remoting service is made. This call passes along the video `id` to update and the response should be the new count or an error if something goes wrong.

```
    private function updateVideoTracking(vid:uint):void
    {
      var responder:Responder = new Responder(
        updateTrackingHandler,
        onFault
      );
      gateway = new NetConnection();
      gateway.connect(gatewayURL);
      gateway.call("Videos.updatePlayCount", responder, vid);
    }
```

Once the count is updated, the new count is returned to Flash. Just like the previous remoting calls, a response handler is needed in order to capture this response. In this example, the new count is sent to the `TextField` located within the `videoMetaInfo` `MovieClip` to reflect the current count.

```
    private function updateTrackingHandler(response:Object):void
    {
      videoMetaInfo.viewsTxt.text = response.count;
    }
```

The last step to adding the tracking feature is to modify the existing `listItemHandler` method and add in the call to the update method, such as the following:

```
    private function listItemHandler(e:Event):void
    {
      ...
      updateVideoTracking(e.currentTarget.videoObj.vid);
    }
```

At this point the tracking addition is complete. As you can see, the original creation process in the first section really allows the ability to introduce new functionality with minimal updates.

Now your video player can properly track the videos and inform you as to which videos are more popular than others. You could easily develop an admin panel where all of this data could be viewed, or you can log in to your SQL editor and look at the videos table for the active count on each video.

Building a User Login Component in Flash

Now that the video player is pretty much packed full of features, it is pretty safe to assume the Web site should require registration in order to use the player. Adding the registration is a matter of creating a basic form and updating a database table, nothing that a few lines of code can't accomplish.

The more advanced portion of this feature is Flash's need to interact with the user login. To start, the Flash application needs to display a login pane when the application starts and also needs to disable the interface until the user successfully logs in.

Keeping with the idea of making the code reusable, let's develop the login component in a new Flash file and then simply drop it in place when it is completed.

Start by opening the login component starter file, which already has the design completed for you, as shown in Figure 17.5. All you need to be concerned with is the code behind the login component.

FIGURE 17.5

The login component that has been previously designed

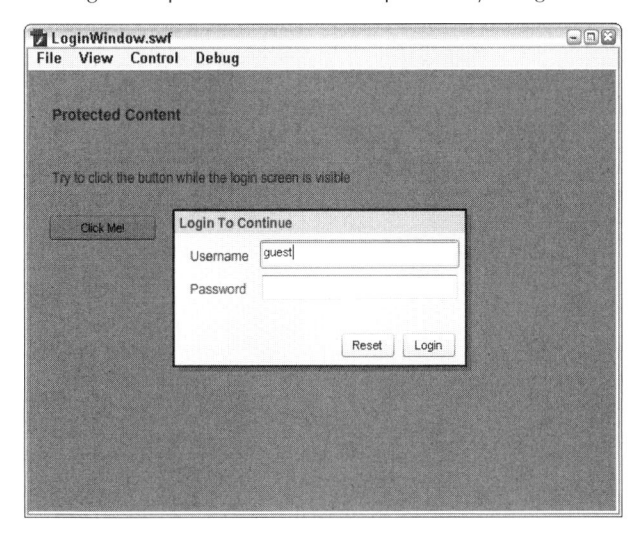

When the component is open you will notice the `MovieClip` in the library is assigned to a class with a name of `LoginWindow`. You cannot customize that class so you need to create a new ActionScript file and save it in the project folder with the FLA.

Developing the LoginWindow class

Now that the file is created you can begin to build the login code. The first step is to construct the class skeleton and extend the `MovieClip`, which is the same process you have been following in the previous sections.

This class not only needs to import the standard `MovieClip` class, but also is going to require some new ones. These new classes will be used to create the actions for disabling the interface and handling the mouse interaction.

```
package
{
  import flash.display.MovieClip;
  import flash.geom.Rectangle;
  import flash.events.Event;
  import flash.events.MouseEvent;
  import flash.net.*;

  public class LoginWindow extends MovieClip
  {
    function LoginWindow()
    {
      ...
    }
  }
}
```

The properties for this class are responsible for event handling and creating references to the `MovieClips` created at runtime.

```
public var data:Object;

private var _visible:Boolean = false;
private var container:MovieClip;
private var blocker:MovieClip = null;

public static var LOGIN_ATTEMPT:String = "onLoginAttempt";
```

LoginWindow constructor

The constructor of the `LoginWindow` class is where the `container` property is set. This is also where the event handlers for the buttons are placed. This is done to ensure the buttons are assigned once visible to ensure the code is stable.

```
function LoginWindow()
{
  container = this;

  loginMC.resetBtn.addEventListener(MouseEvent.CLICK,
   resetHandler);
```

Building Complete Advanced Applications 17

```
loginMC.loginBtn.addEventListener(MouseEvent.CLICK,
  loginHandler);
}
```

redraw method

The `redraw` method is called whenever the interface changes. This is mostly a concern when the user has the ability to resize the Stage, although most Web site applications have a fixed size. This method needs to have some logic regarding the blocking clip to ensure it isn't drawn more than once. The blocking clip is a movieclip that removes interaction from the application which forces the user to log in by "blocking" the mouse clicks.

```
public function redraw():void
{
  if(blocker == null)
  {
    ...
  }
  else
  {
    ...
  }
  ...
}
```

The contents of the conditional for when the blocker clip is null draws the actual blocking `MovieClip` using the built-in drawing API.

```
blocker = new MovieClip();
blocker.alpha = 0.5;
blocker.graphics.beginFill(0x000000);
blocker.graphics.drawRect(0, 0, stage.stageWidth,
   stage.stageHeight);
```

Once the clip has been drawn, the next step is to assign fake event handlers to the blocking clip. Flash doesn't have a native interface that you can disable because the code could be customized. The way around this is to build a pseudo-disabler. This is nothing more than a `MovieClip` placed on the stage that traps all the mouse interaction and cancels it. This prevents the underlying interface and application from being used until this blocking clip is removed.

```
blocker.addEventListener(MouseEvent.ROLL_OVER, dummyHandler);
blocker.addEventListener(MouseEvent.ROLL_OUT, dummyHandler);
blocker.addEventListener(MouseEvent.CLICK, dummyHandler);
```

After the first time the display is redrawn, the blocker will have already been created. A simple width and height adjustment is the only necessary update. In fact, if you call the standard `redraw` method without the conditional, each time you would see another blocking clip as they begin to stack up.

```
blocker.width = stage.stageWidth;
blocker.height = stage.stageHeight;
```

467

Regardless of whether this is the first pass of the `redraw` method or not, the blocking clip needs to be repositioned. The login window is placed dead center, which means you can calculate the padding around it, multiply this to create a negative number, and place the blocking clip using that calculation.

```
// reverse the offset to position blocker
blocker.y = y * -1;
blocker.x = x * -1;
```

When all the calculations are complete, you can add the blocker `MovieClip` to the `DisplayList`, which makes it visible in the application.

```
addChild(blocker);
```

NOTE Making all the position-based calculations before the clip is added to the display list minimizes flickering and jumping objects in your application.

Swapping placement of two MovieClips

ActionScript 3 does not have any depth management like what is found in ActionScript 2 and its predecessors. The equivalent is taking the `id` of a clip and swapping it with another clip. This appears to be depth management, except for the very important fact that ActionScript takes care of the reordering when the children are swapped.

In this example, you want to make sure the login box is above the blocking clip because if it is placed below it, the user is not able to interact or log in to the application:

```
container.swapChildren(loginMC, blocker);
```

Centering a MovieClip

The last step of the redraw `method` is to center the login box on the Stage to ensure it is always in the middle. This is constantly updated when the `redraw` method is called because resizing the stage would make the login box sit at a noncentered position.

```
loginMC.x = (stage.stageWidth / 2) - (loginMC.width / 2);
loginMC.y = (stage.stageHeight / 2) - (loginMC.height / 2);
```

The calculation uses the stage dimensions and login box dimensions to determine the middle point. This is where the `loginMC MovieClip` is placed when the calculation is completed.

close method

The `close` method has one task: to remove the current login box and allow the application to be used once again. The removal process is achieved by removing the `container` child, which contains the login box and blocking `MovieClip`.

```
public function close():void
{
  container.parent.removeChild(container);
}
```

resetHandler method

The `resetHandler` method is called whenever the Reset button is clicked. This method clears all of the status messages and empties the login and password fields.

```
private function resetHandler(e:MouseEvent):void
{
  loginMC.username.text = "";
  loginMC.password.text = "";
  loginMC.responseTxt.text = "";
}
```

loginHandler method

The `loginHandler` method is attached to the CLICK event of the `loginBtn`. This method is called whenever the `loginBtn` is clicked by the mouse.

```
private function loginHandler(e:MouseEvent):void
{
  ...
}
```

This method is responsible for checking the username and password fields for valid data. If one of these fields is empty, the function is exited and a response message is displayed below the password field.

```
loginMC.responseTxt.text = "";

if(loginMC.username.text == "" || loginMC.password.text == "")
{
  loginMC.responseTxt.text = "username & password required";
  return;
}
```

If the username and password fields are found to have acceptable values, those values are stored in the `data` property, which will be read by the calling script in a custom event handler.

```
data = {
  username:loginMC.username.text,
  password:loginMC.password.text
};
```

The last part of this method is to fire off a custom event, alerting the calling script that a username and password have been captured and need to be validated.

```
dispatchEvent(new Event(LOGIN_ATTEMPT));
```

This component has been developed to separate the display and security logic, which means the component can be reused because nothing is hardcoded into the actual login logic.

Part V — Server, Application, and Database Maintenance

The last real method is a setter, which is used to externally set the response string. This would be called from the `loginHandler` if the validation failed and you want to show the user so that he or she can attempt another password or username.

```
public function set responseString(s:String):void
{
   loginMC.responseTxt.text = s;
}
```

The `dummyHandler` method does not have any functionality. It is used to block any mouse events that occur on the blocking `MovieClip`. This method is required because an event handler needs a valid function, and if you define an anonymous one, it creates a slow memory leak.

```
private function dummyHandler(e:MouseEvent):void
{
   // no action
}
```

At this point you have completed the `LoginWindow` class and can move to the next step, which is to create some simple ActionScript to test the component. When that is properly tested you can create the PHP service and make the login component interact with the database to actually look for real users attempting to log in.

Here is the complete `LoginWindow` class.

```
package
{
   import flash.display.MovieClip;
   import flash.geom.Rectangle;
   import flash.events.Event;
   import flash.events.MouseEvent;
   import flash.net.*;

   public class LoginWindow extends MovieClip
   {
     public var data:Object;

     private var _visible:Boolean = false;
     private var container:MovieClip;
     private var blocker:MovieClip = null;

     public static var LOGIN_ATTEMPT:String = "onLoginAttempt";

     function LoginWindow()
     {
       container = this;

       loginMC.resetBtn.addEventListener(MouseEvent.CLICK,
         resetHandler);
```

Building Complete Advanced Applications 17

```
    loginMC.loginBtn.addEventListener(MouseEvent.CLICK,
      loginHandler);
}

public function redraw():void
{
  if(blocker == null)
  {
    blocker = new MovieClip();
    blocker.alpha = 0.5;
    blocker.graphics.beginFill(0x000000);
    blocker.graphics.drawRect(
      0,
      0,
      stage.stageWidth,
      stage.stageHeight
    );
    blocker.addEventListener(
      MouseEvent.ROLL_OVER,
      dummyHandler
    );
    blocker.addEventListener(
      MouseEvent.ROLL_OUT,
      dummyHandler
    );
    blocker.addEventListener(
      MouseEvent.CLICK,
      dummyHandler
    );
  }
  else
  {
    blocker.width = stage.stageWidth;
    blocker.height = stage.stageHeight;
  }

  // reverse the offset to position blocker
  blocker.y = y * -1;
  blocker.x = x * -1;

  addChild(blocker);

  container.swapChildren(loginMC, blocker);

  loginMC.x = (stage.stageWidth / 2) -
  (loginMC.width / 2);

  loginMC.y = (stage.stageHeight / 2) -
```

471

Part V Server, Application, and Database Maintenance

```
      (loginMC.height / 2);

    _visible = true;
  }

  public function close():void
  {
    container.parent.removeChild(container);
  }

  private function resetHandler(e:MouseEvent):void
  {
    loginMC.username.text = "";
    loginMC.password.text = "";
    loginMC.responseTxt.text = "";
  }
  private function loginHandler(e:MouseEvent):void
  {
    loginMC.responseTxt.text = "";

    if(
      loginMC.username.text == "" ||
      loginMC.password.text == "")
    {
      loginMC.responseTxt.text =
        "username & password required";
      return;
    }

    data = {
      username:loginMC.username.text,
   password:loginMC.password.text
    };
    dispatchEvent(new Event(LOGIN_ATTEMPT));
  }

  public function set responseString(s:String):void
  {
    loginMC.responseTxt.text = s;
  }

  private function dummyHandler(e:MouseEvent):void
  {
    //
  }
 }
}
```

Testing the login component

The next step is to test the login component to make sure everything is working properly. The first step is to create a new instance of the `LoginWindow` component in a stand-alone FLA, or you can use the sample file found with the book's source code.

```
var login:LoginWindow = new LoginWindow();
```

Once the instance is created, the next step is to assign an event handler for the custom `LOGIN_ATTMEPT` event that is called when the user types data into both the username and password fields and then clicks the Login button.

```
login.addEventListener(LoginWindow.LOGIN_ATTEMPT, loginHandler);
```

After the Login window component loads and the proper event handler is assigned, the next step is to add it to the display list, which makes it visible.

```
addChild(login);
```

Assigning a stage event handler

You want to make sure any modification to the stage redraws the login component, or items that are being blocked can accidentally reposition themselves beyond the blocking `MovieClip`.

```
stage.align = StageAlign.TOP_LEFT;
stage.scaleMode = StageScaleMode.NO_SCALE;
stage.addEventListener(Event.RESIZE, stageResizeHandler);
```

After the event is assigned to the `stage` object, you need to create the function that is being referenced in the event listener. For this application, the handler simply makes a call to the `redraw` method of the `login` component. In a real-world application you may have more functionality in this event, but for now this is fine for testing.

```
function stageResizeHandler(e:Event):void
{
   login.redraw();
}
```

Handling the login attempt

The next function is used to handle login attempts. For simplicity, this function has a predefined username and password that is later replaced with a remoting service in the next section.

If a valid login is reached, the `close` method of the `login` component is called. This removes the Login box and enables the application for that session.

```
function loginHandler(e:Event):void
{
   if(login.data.username == "guest" && login.data.password ==
    "pass")
```

```
      {
        login.close();
      }
    }
```

> **NOTE** This application does not store logins, which means the valid login is only for the active session. Users will have to log in each time they visit the application.

The `loginHandler` function is handling successful logins, but does not notify the user of an incorrect login attempt. This can be fixed by adding an `else` statement that updates the response box in the Login box.

```
function loginHandler(e:Event):void
{
  if(login.data.username == "guest" && login.data.password ==
  "pass")
  {
    login.close();
  }
  else
  {
    login.responseString = "username and password incorrect";
  }
}
```

The last step is to make the initial call to the `resize` event to draw the login component for the first time. You can also call the `redraw` method directly, rather than going through the `resize` event.

```
stage.dispatchEvent(new Event(Event.RESIZE));
```

Here is the completed code for this test. The majority of the login component is handled internally but it still offers ultimate usability.

```
var login:LoginWindow = new LoginWindow();
login.addEventListener(LoginWindow.LOGIN_ATTEMPT, loginHandler);

addChild(login);

stage.align = StageAlign.TOP_LEFT;
stage.scaleMode = StageScaleMode.NO_SCALE;
stage.addEventListener(Event.RESIZE, stageResizeHandler);

function stageResizeHandler(e:Event):void
{
  login.redraw();
}

function loginHandler(e:Event):void
{
  trace("Do Login");
```

Building Complete Advanced Applications

```
    trace("Username: " + login.data.username);
    trace("Password: " + login.data.password);

    if(login.data.username == "guest" && login.data.password ==
     "pass")
    {
      trace("user logged in");
      login.close();
    }
    else
    {
      login.responseString = "username and password incorrect";
    }

  }

    stage.dispatchEvent(new Event(Event.RESIZE));
```

Now that you have completed the ActionScript necessary for the sample, you can test the login component. You should be presented with the login screen immediately and not be able to interact with any portion of the movie, excluding the login screen, as shown in Figure 17.6, until you type the correct login.

FIGURE 17.6

Sample application displaying the login component

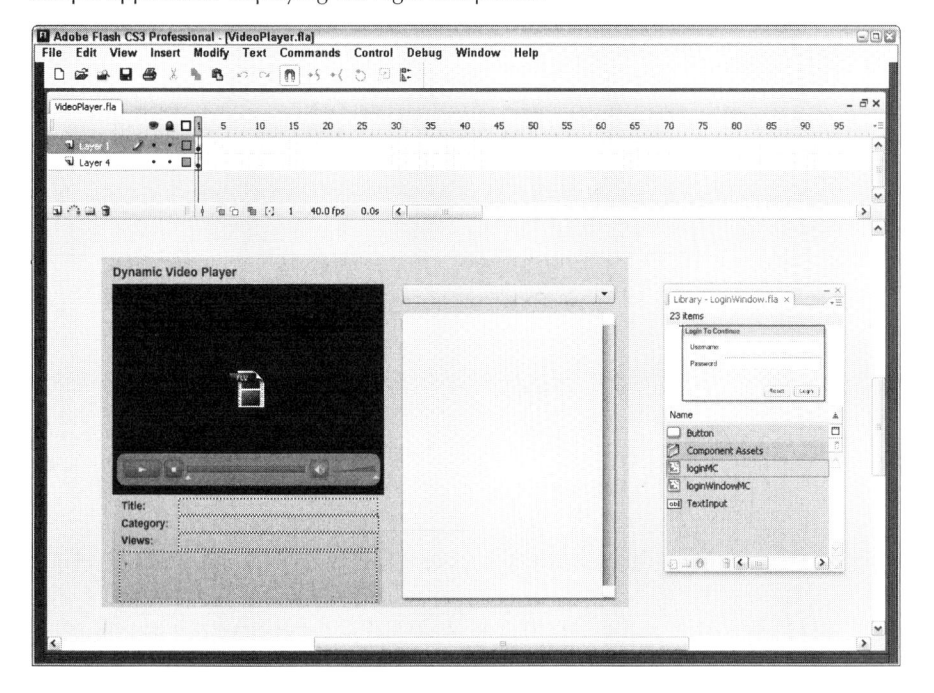

Building the PHP login manager class

The next step in building the login system is to connect it to the database of users, because a hard-coded login and password is not very practical and certainly not secure.

Creating the user's MySQL table

The first step is to create the user's table in the existing database:

```
CREATE TABLE `users` (
  `id` int(11) NOT NULL auto_increment,
  `username` varchar(25) default NULL,
  `password` varchar(40) default NULL,
  `active` varchar(1) default '1',
  PRIMARY KEY  (`id`)
) ENGINE=MyISAM;
```

Then you can prefill the table with some sample logins for testing purposes:

```
INSERT INTO users (username, password) VALUES ('guest',
   MD5('pass'));
INSERT INTO users (username, password) VALUES ('timmy',
   MD5('bird'));
```

A distinct difference from the predefined logins in Flash is that these logins have encrypted passwords as an added level of security.

Before you can add the logic for connecting to the service, you need to create the PHP class. This class will check for valid users, and if one is found, it will return a `true`, which means the user is valid and the Login box can be removed.

Building the user class

The `User.php` class is just like the other service classes in that it extends the `DatabaseConnector` class for all database communication. Here is the skeleton of `user` class:

```
<?php

require_once 'DatabaseConnector.php';

class User extends DatabaseConnector
{
  function User()
  {
    ...
  }
}

?>
```

Building Complete Advanced Applications

login method

The first and only method in this class is `login`. This method accepts two arguments: the username and password to validate. The first part of this method is to create a new connection to the database:

```
/**
 * Check user auth
 * @access remote
 * @returns status of user login attempt
 */
function login($user, $pass)
{
  $link = $this->getConnection();
}
```

When the database connection is established, you can mark the user as not logged in. This prevents any possible hacking attempts that could accidentally make a user log in.

```
$loggedIn = false;
```

Next is the SQL query that attempts to validate the username and password combo. The password is passed into the `md5` function because Flash sends the password in clear text, but the database stores the `md5` result.

```
$query = sprintf("SELECT * FROM users WHERE
  username='%s' AND
  password=MD5('%s')", $user, ($pass));
```

The next step is to make the database call and store the response in the `$result` variable, as shown in the following code:

```
$result = mysql_query($query, $link);
```

Once the response is stored, a conditional statement is used to determine if any rows were returned. If a row is returned, it means the data is valid and the user has been authenticated based on the credentials he or she passed along.

When a valid response is found, the `$loggedIn` variable is set as `true` to inform Flash that the user is, in fact, valid and has now successfully logged in.

```
if(mysql_num_rows($result) > 0)
{
  $loggedIn = true;
}
```

The last step is to return the result so Flash can act accordingly.

```
return array('response' => $loggedIn);
```

477

Part V Server, Application, and Database Maintenance

Now that you have completed the PHP class, the next step is to test it. For this test you can use the service browser that is included with AMFPHP. You will find that browser at a URL similar to the following, depending on where you installed the source:

```
http://localhost/flashphp/amfphp/browser/
```

Last, here is the complete `User` class, which should be saved as `User.php` in the services directory of your AMFPHP installation if you haven't already done so:

```php
<?php

require_once 'DatabaseConnector.php';

class User extends DatabaseConnector
{

  /**
  * Check user auth
  * @access remote
  * @returns status of user login attempt
  */
  function login($user, $pass)
  {
    $link = $this->getConnection();

    $loggedIn = false;

    $query = sprintf("SELECT * FROM users WHERE
      username='%s' AND
      password=MD5('%s')", $user, ($pass));
    $result = mysql_query($query, $link);

    if(mysql_num_rows($result) > 0)
    {
      $loggedIn = true;
    }

    return array('response' => $loggedIn);
  }
}

?>
```

Adding remoting to the login component

Now that you have completed the PHP User class, the next step is to modify the existing login component to use this new service class.

The first step is to add the `gateway` variable and URL where the `gateway.php` file can be found on your development server.

```
var gateway:NetConnection;
var gatewayURL:String = "http://localhost/amfphp/gateway.php";
```

The original example did the username validation directly within the Flash file. While this was functional, it wasn't very practical because only one login or password can be used.

loginHandler method

This new system modifies the existing `loginHandler` function by adding a remoting service call, sending the username and password that was captured by the login window component.

```
function loginHandler(e:Event):void
{
  trace("Do Login");
  trace("Username: " + login.data.username);
  trace("Password: " + login.data.password);

  var responder:Responder = new Responder(loginRespHandler,
    onFault);
  gateway = new NetConnection();
  gateway.connect(gatewayURL);
  gateway.call("User.login", responder,
    login.data.username,
    login.data.password
  );
}
```

The `Responder` class needs a response handler defined, so the next function handles this service response. For this example, the service will either return a Boolean for whether the user is logged in or not, or an error if something goes wrong.

```
function loginRespHandler(o:Object):void
{
  ...
}
```

A simple conditional statement is used to determine if the user is logged in based on the response from the remoting service.

Handling the login response

If the user is logged in, a call to the `close` method of the login component is made to hide the login window and enable the application interface.

```
function loginRespHandler(o:Object):void
{
  if(o.response == true)
  {
    login.close();
  }
}
```

Part V — Server, Application, and Database Maintenance

An `else` option is added to handle the incorrect login attempts by updating the response message of the login component.

```
function loginRespHandler(o:Object):void
{
  if(o.response == true)
  {
    login.close();
  }
  else
  {
    login.responseString = "username and password incorrect";
  }
}
```

Handling response errors

The last function required for the login system is the `onFault`, which handles errors in the service calls. For example, if the script managed to attempt a login check with no username or password, the SQL would fail. This error will be raised by the PHP class and sent back to Flash, assuming it is properly handled.

```
function onFault(responds:Object):void
{
  trace("Debug::Error");
  for(var i in responds)
  {
    trace("  " + responds[i]);
  }
}
```

Now that the remoting code has been added to the previous example login component, you can test it, and you really shouldn't notice any difference. The only change would be the ability to use more than one username, as long as it is found in the users table that you created at the beginning of this section.

Here is the login component example with the proper remoting code included:

```
var gateway:NetConnection;
var gatewayURL:String = "http://localhost/amfphp/gateway.php";

var login:LoginWindow = new LoginWindow();
login.addEventListener(LoginWindow.LOGIN_ATTEMPT, loginHandler);

addChild(login);

stage.align = StageAlign.TOP_LEFT;
stage.scaleMode = StageScaleMode.NO_SCALE;
stage.addEventListener(Event.RESIZE, stageResizeHandler);

function stageResizeHandler(e:Event):void
```

Building Complete Advanced Applications

```
  {
    login.redraw();
  }

  function loginHandler(e:Event):void
  {
    trace("Do Login");
    trace("Username: " + login.data.username);
    trace("Password: " + login.data.password);

    var responder:Responder = new Responder(loginRespHandler, onFault);
    gateway = new NetConnection();
    gateway.connect(gatewayURL);
    gateway.call("User.login", responder,
      login.data.username,
      login.data.password
    );
  }

  function loginRespHandler(o:Object):void
  {
    trace("Response: " + o.response);

    if(o.response == true)
    {
      trace("user logged in");
      login.close();
    }
    else
    {
      login.responseString = "username and password incorrect";
    }
  }

  function onFault(responds:Object):void
  {
    trace("Debug::Error");
    for(var i in responds)
    {
      trace("   " + responds[i]);
    }
  }

  stage.dispatchEvent(new Event(Event.RESIZE));
```

Finalizing the Video Player

The last section of this chapter is finalizing the video player. You will implement the login component you built in the previous section and learn how to use an external library.

Using an external library

The advantage to using an external library is you only have to update one location and all instances of that library usage are also updated.

For example, imagine you have a logo with a specific color on it and suddenly the company decides that it wants to recolor the logo. Rather than opening every instance of that logo and editing it, you can open the master FLA, edit that, and then update the instances, which automatically reflect the changes.

You can use this concept for much more than a simple logo, because you will be loading the login component from the example file you built in the previous section.

Adding the login component

Start by opening the `VideoPlayer.fla` file if it isn't already opened. Then choose File ➪ Import ➪ Open External Library.

In this dialog box, you can navigate to the directory where the login component is stored and select that file. With the file selected, click Open.

Drag the `LoginWindowMC` from this library into the library of the `VideoPlayer` FLA. You should now see two new `MovieClips` in the library of your `VideoPlayer` file. This is because the `LoginWindowMC` has a supporting file that contains all of the design, which is automatically copied when you drag the parent.

Now that the login component is added, you can modify the existing `VideoPlayer` class file to add this new functionality. To start, add the component creation, but forget about the login logic.

The new code should be added to the constructor function, similar to the following:

```
function VideoPlayer()
{
  gatewayURL = "http://localhost/amfphp/gateway.php";
  getCategories();

  videoPlayer.visible = false;
  videoListCombo.enabled = false;

  var login:LoginWindow = new LoginWindow();
  login.addEventListener(LoginWindow.LOGIN_ATTEMPT,
   loginHandler);

  addChild(login);
  login.redraw();
}
```

Building Complete Advanced Applications   17

Before you test the code, add the `loginHandler` method to avoid any runtime errors. You can add this method at any point in the code. I recommend somewhere toward the bottom of the class to maintain the overall flow of the file.

```
private function updateTrackingHandler(response:Object):void
{
  ...
}

private function loginHandler(response:Object):void
{
  ...
}
```

The last step is to import the `LoginWindow` class so the static property can be loaded for the event handler.

```
package
{
  import flash.display.MovieClip;
  import flash.events.Event;
  import flash.net.*;
  import LoginWindow;

  public class VideoPlayer extends MovieClip
  {
    ...
  }
}
```

When you test the application you should immediately see the login window. Because you didn't add any logic at this point, there is no way to close the login window, but you can see it is working, so you can continue.

The logic, which is responsible for calling the remoting service, needs to be added to the existing `loginHandler` method.

```
function loginHandler(e:Event):void
{
  var responder:Responder = new Responder(loginRespHandler,
    onFault);
  gateway = new NetConnection();
  gateway.connect(gatewayURL);
  gateway.call("User.login", responder,
      login.data.username,
      login.data.password
  );
}
```

483

Part V Server, Application, and Database Maintenance

The next step is to copy the `loginRespHandler` and add it below the `loginHandler` in the `VideoPlayer` class.

```
function loginRespHandler(o:Object):void
{
  trace("Response: " + o.response);

  if(o.response == true)
  {
    trace("user logged in");
    login.close();
  }
  else
  {
    login.responseString = "username and password incorrect";
  }
}
```

The proper code has now been added to the `VideoPlayer` class; however, there is one final modification needed before the login component will function properly.

The `login` variable that is defined in the constructor needs to be a global property, because as it stands right now, no other method in this class has access to it.

```
package
{

  ...
  public class VideoPlayer extends MovieClip
  {
    ...
    private var selectedCatID:Number;
    private var login:LoginWindow;

    function VideoPlayer()
    {
      ...
      login = new LoginWindow();
    }
  }

}
```

Now that the `login` variable is properly defined, you can test the application, as shown in Figure 17.7. You should be able to type a valid username and password, and the login component should disappear when you do so.

Building Complete Advanced Applications 17

FIGURE 17.7

Final video player with login box visible

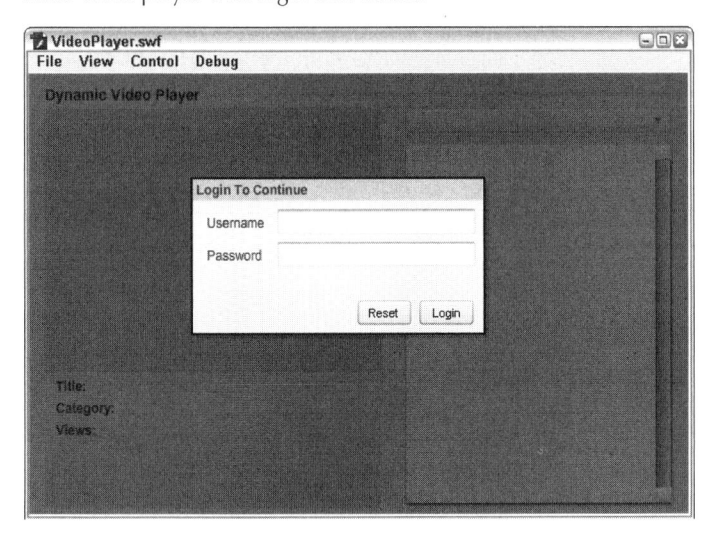

As you can see, the login component being built this way really makes it possible to add it to any existing project. To extend on this example, you could add a shared object that would preserve the session and make it so the user doesn't need to log in each time.

You should now have a great understanding of building and working with advanced, real-world applications. I am sure you are thinking of many various applications to build after seeing how they function in depth.

The following is a table outlining the names of files and where they should be stored for this complete application. The path is based on the project directory which should be in your Apache home directory in order for the application to run properly.

Application Source File Locations

File Name	Save Path
LoginWindow.swf	/
LoginWindow.fla	/
LoginWindow.as	/
VideoListItem.as	/
VideoPlayer.as	/
SkinOverPlayStopSeekMuteVol.swf	/

continued

Application Source File Locations *(continued)*

File Name	Save Path
color.flv	/videos
Categories.php	/amfphp/services
DatabaseConnector.php	/amfphp/services
Videos.php	/amfphp/services
Tracking.php	/amfphp/services
User.php	/amfphp/services

Summary

In this chapter, you started by building a very basic video player and expanded upon that concept to build a multicategory video player. Using PHP to handle the data between Flash and the database made the application more dynamic.

Once you had the video player completed, you began to expand on that by adding video tracking. You learned how easy it was to implement new features into the existing code based on the way the original video player application was developed in the previous section.

The fourth part of the chapter introduced the process of developing custom components that could be reused in your future projects. For this example, you developed a login component that would disable an application until the user logged in.

The fifth and final part was bringing all of these techniques together to develop a final real-world video player application with a login module and video tracking from the previous sections. All you have to do now is populate the database with real data and you will have a fully expandable, multicategory, tracking, secure video player application.

Index

Symbols and Numerics

* wildcard, 145
; (semicolon), 382
| (pipe), 426
' (single quote), 133

A

absolute global classpath, 195
act variable, 123
Action Message Format (AMF), 198
_action variable, 234
action variable, 293
$action variable, 348
ActionScript
    adding video tracking to, 463
    and AMFPHP, 195, 216–218
    chat client applications
        handling XML response, 248–251
        overview, 242–245
        stop caching with dynamic data, 245–248
    dynamic banner ad
        developing PHP, 283
        opening browser window, 281–282
        overview, 279–281
        random selection, 283–284
    dynamic data, 85
    hit counter, 286
    photo gallery, 261–266
    and PHP cookies, 121
    poll applications, 368–372
    site monitors, 351–359
    static data, 85
    video player applications
        basic, 360–364
        categoryHandler method, 450
        categoryResponseHandler method, 449–450
        constructor function, 448
        creating document class, 446–448
        getCategories method, 448–449
        getVideos method, 451
        handling errors in remoting responses, 453–456
        listItemHandler method, 452–453
        overview, 446
        videosResponseHandler method, 451–452
ActionScript editors, 60–61
ActionScript panel, 60, 81–83
ActionsScript 3 (AS3), 198–201
active sandbox
    running applications in local sandbox, 147–150
    unloading application, 150–151
Add to Cart button, 303
addChild function, 233, 265, 324
addDataToObject function, 121
addEventListener call, 263
addItem( ) function, 217, 275, 376
addItemHandler function, 306
addProduct method, 301
addServer( ) function, 420
addslashes( ) function, 133, 134, 137
administrators, e-mailing site, 349–351
ads.php file, 283
advertisements, dynamic banner
    developing PHP, 283
    opening browser window, 281–282
    overview, 279–281
    random selection, 283–284
Album class, 214
allFields variable, 108
allowDomain( ) function, 145, 164
alpha values, 457–458
alternative traces, 389–391
Amazon search applications
    overview, 317
    simplifying XML response, 319–326
    using AWS, 317–319
AMF (Action Message Format), 198
AMFPHP
    ActionScript for integration, 216–218
    AS3 and PHP developers
        debug gateway, 200–201
        debugging tools, 199
        installing, 198–199
        service browser, 200

A Index

AMFPHP *(continued)*
    in Flash, 205–210
    real-world application, 210–218
    testing with custom service, 201–205
Anchor tag, 247
`AND` condition, 58
anonymous functions, 263–266
`answer` variable, 368
Apache
    adding to Web servers
        UNIX, 9–13
        Windows, 4–9, 13
    building another version of on same system, 406–407
    comments in, 397
    default Welcome Screen, 8
    determining modules installed, 40–42
    determining version, 40
    modifying custom error documents, 43
    optimizing, 412–413
    starting and stopping, 40
Apache Configuration Directory, 29–31
apachect1 application, 11
`appendText` method, 208, 387
Application Programming Interface (API), 289
applications
    Amazon search
        overview, 317
        simplifying XML response, 319–326
        using AWS, 317–319
    chat client
        Flash portion, 242–251
        overview, 242
        PHP code, 252–260
        PHP socket server for, 168–175
    debugging
        alternative trace, 389–391
        error reporting in PHP, 381–385
        in Flash, 385–389
        overview, 381
    drawing
        in Flash, 336–341
        overview, 335–336
    dynamic banner ads
        developing PHP, 283
        opening browser window, 281–282
        overview, 279–281
        random selection, 283–284
    elements of, 239–242
    ensuring exlusive use, 151–152
    hit counters, 285–286
    maintenance
        `ChangeLog`, 399–400
        commenting code, 395–399
        custom libraries, 403–404
        overview, 395
        version control, 401–403
    overview, 239
    PayPal cart
        overview, 290–291
        `POST` data, 293–294
        `sendToURL` method, 294
        setting up communication, 294–295
        signing up for PayPal Premier, 291–293
    photo gallery
        developing ActionScript, 261–266
        developing using flickr, 326–333
        navigation, 266–270
        overview, 260–261
        PHP for, 270–274
    poll
        building PHP and MySQL, 364–368
        developing ActionScript, 368–372
        overview, 364
    real-world
        Amazon search application, 317–326
        developing photo gallery using flickr, 326–333
        drawing application, 335–341
        GD library, 341–346
        overview, 289–290, 335
        PayPal cart, 290–295
        poll application, 364–372
        simple file editor, 373–379
        site monitors, 347–359
        video player, 359–364
    RSS readers
        importing classes, 275
        loading PHP, 275–279
        overview, 274–275
    running in local sandbox, 147–150
    scalable, 219, 242
    shopping cart
        building PHP, 298–315
        developing `ShoppingCartItem` class, 298–306
        developing `StoreItem` class, 296–298
        overview, 295–296
    unloading, 150–151
    video player
        adding sample data to tables, 434–435
        advanced development, 446–456
        basic, 429–432

Index

building database and MySQL tables, 433–434
building `VideoListItem` class, 456–461
finalizing, 481–486
overview, 429, 432
testing database, 435–437
user login component, 465–481
using Flash to develop, 359–364
video tracking, 461–464
arguments, 50, 130
`Array` type, 297
arrays, 48, 383
`array_search` function, 175
`array_shift` function, 171
AS3 (ActionsScript 3), 198–201
as3CoreLib library, 192, 196
`attribute( )` method, 354
attributes, 118
auto play option, 430–431
`auto_increment` function, 255
automatic updates, 406
`AWS_ACCESS_KEY` access id, 318

B

`$backupCmd` variable, 423
`$backupDir` directory, 424
`backupDir` file, 422
backups
    server
        backup management, 421–424
        file management, 421
        using PHP, 424–427
    version control, 403
banner ads, dynamic
    developing PHP, 283
    opening browser window, 281–282
    overview, 279–281
    random selection, 283–284
`$bannerAds` array, 283
basic authentication, 38–39
binding, socket, 154
`BitmapData` class, 345
bleeding-edge technology, 407
block comments, 396–397
`bodyTxt TextArea` function, 376
Bold tag, 247
`BookItem` class, 323–324
`BookSearch` class, 321
booleans, 48
`break` control, 53

Break tag, 247
breaks, 54
browser windows, opening, 281–282
bug tracking, 399–400
Button component, 242–243
Button Encryption, 292
Buy Now button, 295

C

cache busters, 244–246, 249
caching
    with memcached system
        installing on Linux, 416–418
        installing on Windows, 418–420
        managing servers, 420–421
        overview, 416
    PHP codes, 410
    saving data, 418–419
Call button, 202
`call` method, 451
`callback` function, 87, 141, 389
`callDatabase` method, 221
`callPaypal` function, 294
`callServer` method, 234
camel-case, 91
cart applications
    PayPal
        overview, 290–291
        `POST` data, 293–294
        `sendToURL` method, 294
        setting up communication, 294–295
        signing up for PayPal Premier, 291–293
    shopping cart
        building PHP, 298–315
        developing `ShoppingCartItem` class, 298–306
        developing `StoreItem` class, 296–298
        overview, 295–296
cartContents array, 301
`cartItemCount` class, 301
`categories.php` file, 270
`$categories` variable, 270
Category class, 443–444
`category` method, 445, 448
`categoryHandler` method, 450
`categoryResponseHandler` method, 449–450
CHANGE event, 180
`ChangeLogs`, 399–400
Charles Web Debugging Proxy, 133, 388

489

Index

chat client applications
    Flash portion, 242–251
        handling XML response, 248–251
        overview, 242–245
        stop caching with dynamic data, 245–248
    overview, 242
    PHP code, 252–260
        connecting to MySQL, 256–259
        creating database table, 259–260
        overview, 252–255
    PHP socket server for, 168–175
        ending connection, 175
        excluding master server from communication, 171
        handling errors, 174–175
        master client connection, 172–173
        notifying all clients, 174
        notifying specific client, 173–174
        properties, 168–171
        server monitoring, 175
        special parameters, 171–172
`ChatServer` class, 176
Checkout button, 300
`checkSite( )` method, 356
child socket resource id, 157
`$childSocket` variable, 157–158
Class imports, 299
class variables, 258
classes. *See also individual classes by name*
    basic socket, 165–166
    custom, 231–235
    defined, 220–221
    in Flash, 229–231
    for loading data in Flash, 86–87
    in PHP, 225–228
    remoting, 205–210
    RSS reader applications, 275
    securely writing to file, 137–138
`Class.method`, 223
clean URLs, 38
`clear( )` method, 119
`clearButtonHandler` function, 180
`clearIndicators` function, 108
CLI (command-line version), 155–156
`CLICK` event, 294
`clickHandler` method, 458
client connections, 154, 157–158
`close( )` method, 420, 468, 473, 479
`closeHandler` function, 182
closing
    cached server connections, 420
    MySQL connections, 75–76
CMSs (content management systems), 373–379
code commenting, 395–399
code editor, 60. *See also* ActionScript panel
code fragments, 51
code hints, 398
code skeleton, 106–107
`ComboBox` component, 359, 361, 373, 377, 449
command-line version (CLI), 155–156
commenting code, 395–399
commercial Flash libraries, 192–193
communication, PayPal, 294–295
`communicator` class, 233
compiler comments, 397
`COMPLETE` event, 275
Component Inspector, 432
Components pane, 430
concatenating data, 71
Concurrent Versions System (CVS), 401
conditions, MySQL
    `AND`, 58
    `OR`, 59
    `WHERE`, 58
`conf/` directory, 407
configuration files, 256, 413
configuration variables, 256
`connect( )` method, 206, 213, 391, 420, 438
`connectHandler` function, 163
connecting
    in Flash
        connection types, 65–69
        determining status of PHP, 64–65
    Flash to PHP
        concatenating data, 71
        multiple pieces of data, 71–73
    PHP to MySQL
        bringing all together, 77–84
        closing connection, 75–76
        determining status of MySQL, 73–74
        persistent connection, 75
        selecting database, 74, 76
`connection` method, 212
`_connection` private variable, 212
connections
    client, 157–158
    closing cached server, 420

490

Index

database, 257
master, 154
master client, 172–173
MySQL, 75–76
parameter, 213
persistent, 75
remote socket, 163–164
constructor method
chat properties, 169
defined, 221
developing ActionScript, 360
`LoginWindow` class, 466–467
static method, 223
`VideoListItem`, 457
`VideoPlayer` class, 448
XML response, 322
constructors. *See* constructor method
contact form
calling PHP, 103
event handlers, 103–105
mailing in PHP, 105–106
container child, 468
`container` property, 466
content management systems (CMSs), 373–379
`continue` control, 53–54
control structures, PHP
`break` control, 53
`continue` control, 53–54
`else` statements, 51–52
`elseif` statements, 52
`foreach` loop, 53
`if` statements, 51
`include` statement, 55
`include_once` statement, 56
`for` loop, 52–53
`require` statement, 54–55
`require_once` statement, 55
`switch` control, 54
`while` loop, 52
$_COOKIE variable, 114
cookieName variable, 123
cookies
Flash
bringing all together, 119–122
deleting shared objects, 119
loading shared objects, 118
saving shared objects, 118–119
overview, 113

PHP
assigning multiple, 117–118
deleting, 116
expiring, 116
loading, 114–115
saving, 115
sharing, 114
`createMasterClient` method, 172–173
`createNewTextField` method, 233
cron service, 421
crontab file, 422–424
crossdomain.xml file, 164
crypto package, 196
CS3, 401–402
`currentID` variable, 261
`currentImage` variable, 265–266
custom authentication system, 38–39
custom classes, 231–235
custom error documents
dynamic error documents, 43–46
modifying Apache, 43
overview, 42
custom file extensions, 38
custom libraries, 403–404
Custom option, 6–7
custom playback handlers, 431
custom URLs, 38
custom variable definitions, 71
custom XML documents, 332–333
CVS (Concurrent Versions System), 401

D

data
loading
in Flash, 85–87
one-way, 88
two-way, 88–89
XML in Flash, 89–92
XML in PHP, 92–93
PHP, 95–97
returning, 143–144
sending to server, 67–68
storing
passwords, using PHP, 141–142
securely writing to file, 137–141
user
HTML data, 136
sanitizing, 133–135
XML in PHP, 93–95

491

D Index

`data` object, 118
`data` property, 275, 469
database connection, 257
database editor, 434
database plug-ins, 409
database slowdowns, 416
`DatabaseConnector` class, 437–439, 441, 476
`DatabaseConnector.php` file, 438
databases
    backing up with PHP, 424–427
    video player applications, 433–434
DataGrid component, 216–217
`dataLoaded( )` method, 370
date table, 255
`dateAdded` row, 255, 259
`$daysBeforeExpiration` variable, 116
`dbconn.php` file, 252, 254, 256, 307, 347
Debug Gateway, 200
`debuggateway.php` file, 200
debugging applications
    alternative trace, 389–391
    error reporting in PHP, 381–385
    in Flash, 385–389
    overview, 381
    removing helpers, 399
debugging tools, 199
`debugTxt` instance, 387
dedicated servers, 412
`delete( )` method, 420
`DELETE` statement, 58
deleting items in caches, 420
dependencies, server, 407–408
`$desc` variable, 278
descendant accessor, 91–92
design, application, 240–241
development systems, 4, 406–408
`$dir` variable, 422
directories, backup, 422–424
`disable` function, 182
`disableInterface` function, 182
disabling auto play option, 430–431
`dispatchEvent` function, 180
`display_errors` directive, 129
`displayImage` function, 265
`DisplayObject` class, 222
Document class
    class skeleton for, 352
    constructor method of, 360
    in Flash, 229–230
    main discussion, 446–448

    photo gallery, 327–329
    `PollItem` class, 368
    Timeline ActionScript, 304
Dom XML, 92–93
domain, 114
double slash, 138
downloading, 417
`draw( )` method, 345
`drawCategories` function, 262, 263
drawing applications
    in Flash, 336–341
    overview, 335–336
Dreamweaver CS3 program, 31–32
`dummyHandler` method, 470
dynamic banner ads
    developing PHP, 283
    opening browser window, 281–282
    overview, 279–281
    random selection, 283–284
dynamic data, 85, 162
dynamic error documents, 43–46
dynamic objects, 121
dynamic text field, 286
dynamic XML
    from database, 94–95
    printing, 93–94

E

`E_ALL` message, 384
`echo` function, 383
`E_COMPILE_ERROR` message, 384
`E_COMPILE_WARNING` message, 384
`E_CORE_ERROR` message, 384
`E_CORE_WARNING` message, 384
editors, file, 373–379
`E_ERROR` message, 384
E4X, 89–92
element array, 327
`else` option, 480
`else` statements, 51–52, 474
`elseif` statements, 52
`$emailInfo` variable, 349
e-mailing site administrators, 349–351
empty password, 134
`empty` string, 254
`enable` function, 182
encapsulation, 225
encrypted string, 141
`E_NOTICE` message, 384

Index F

ENT_COMPAT constant, 136
ENT_NOQUOTES constant, 136
ENT_QUOTES constant, 136
E_PARSE message, 384
error documents, custom
    dynamic error documents, 43–46
    modifying Apache, 43
    overview, 42
error_log function, 382
errors
    importing classes in PHP, 226
    levels of, 383–385
    messages, 319
    optimizing Apache, 413
    in remoting responses, 453–456
    reporting, 259, 381–385
    video player user login component, 480–481
E_STRICT message, 384
E_USER_ERROR message, 384
E_USER_NOTICE message, 384
E_USER_WARNING message, 384
evaluation stage, 239–240
Event class, 447
event handlers
    contact form, 103–105
    login module, 107–110
    sandbox, 149
    sockets, 162–163
    stage, 473
event listeners, 68, 87–88, 162, 178
E_WARNING message, 384
example.org domain, 152
exit parameters, 175
exit request, 171–172
extends method, 440
Extension Manager, 194
extensions, memcached PHP, 417–418
external classes, 298
external libraries, 192, 482

F

-f option, 158
failedAttempts variable, 356, 357
false flag, 419
Fatal Error: function, 197
$feed variable, 278
feedBody TextArea function, 276
feedHandler( ) function, 275
file editors, 373–379

file locking, 63
file upload box, 130
file uploads, 128–130
file_get_contents function, 320, 374
fileContents object, 377
$fileContents variable, 374
fileManager.php file, 374
fileNameTxt variable, 131
files
    flat, 57, 63
    limiting, 421
    securely writing to
        classes, 137–138
        magic_quotes options, 138–139
        shared objects, 139–141
    untarring, 10
Firefox Web browser, 389
FLA (Flash File), 321
Flash
    alternative editors, 61
    connecting to PHP, 71–73
    connection types, 65–69
    deleting shared objects, 119
    determining status of PHP, 64–65
    Flash-enabled devices, 62
    form development, 99–100
    loading data in, 85–87
    loading shared objects, 118
    loading XML in, 89–92
    login module
        code skeleton, 106–107
        event handlers, 107–110
        server integration for, 110–111
    saving shared objects, 118–119
    sockets, 161–167
Flash client, 177–188
Flash CS3, 194–196
Flash File (FLA), 321
Flash IDE, 59–61
Flash Security Sandbox
    active
        running applications in local sandbox, 147–150
        unloading application, 150–151
    applications, 151–152
    sandboxType property, 145–147
    setting type, 145
flashChat table, 255, 259
flashservices directory, 198
flat files, 57, 63

493

Index

flickr photo galleries
    building custom XML document, 332–333
    interfacing with Web service, 331
    overview, 326–330
`flush( )` method, 118–119
`FLVPlayback` component, 430
Font tag, 247
fopen function, 374
`for` loop, 52–53, 152
`for..` loop, 217, 252, 300, 332
`for..each` loop, 53, 91–92, 170, 173, 248, 262, 323, 328, 353, 422, 450
`for..in` loop, 207
form development, Flash, 99–100
`$from` variable, 350
functions
    addChild, 233, 265, 324
    addDataToObject, 121
    addItem( ), 217, 275, 376
    addItemHandler, 306
    addServer( ), 420
    addslashes( ), 133, 134, 137
    allowDomain( ), 145, 164
    anonymous, 263–266
    array_search, 175
    array_shift, 171
    auto_increment, 255
    bodyTxt TextArea, 376
    callback, 87, 141, 389
    callPaypal, 294
    clearButtonHandler, 180
    clearIndicators, 108
    closeHandler, 182
    connectHandler, 163
    disable, 182
    disableInterface, 182
    dispatchEvent, 180
    displayImage, 265
    drawCategories, 262, 263
    echo, 383
    enable, 182
    error_log, 382
    Fatal Error:, 197
    feedBody TextArea, 276
    feedHandler( ), 275
    file_get_contents, 320, 374
    fopen, 374
    fwrite( ), 374
    getCategories( ), 270, 438, 441, 444, 448–449, 451

getdate( ), 201, 206, 208, 425
getPhotosFromID( ), 272
getTimer( ), 149, 249
gzip, 425
handleServerResp( ), 286
htmlentities( ), 136
imagecreatetruecolor( ), 343
imagejpeg( ), 343
imageLoaded, 264–265, 280
imagesetpixel, 344
import, 229
include, 226, 424
init( )
    developing ActionScript, 261
    Flash, 244
    managing messages, 247
    opening browser windows, 281
    photo gallery navigation, 267
    running applications in local sandbox, 148
    unloading applications, 150
initLoop, 169, 172
IO_ERROR, 356
is_numeric( ), 132
length, 132
loadCategories( ), 261–262
loadFeeds, 276
loadHitCounter( ), 286
loadImage( ), 264, 280
loadMessages( ), 244, 247
loadMessagesHandler, 249
loginHandler, 107–108, 469–472, 483
loginMC MovieClip, 468
mail( ), 349–350
md5, 477
movieclip, 323, 339
msgTxt TextInput, 180
mt_rand( ), 283
mysql_close, 75–76, 409
mysql_connect( ), 75, 256, 435
mysql_fetch_array( ), 79, 253
mysql_num_rows( ), 252, 442, 462
mysql_pconnect, 75
mysql_query( ), 252, 254, 444
mysql_real_escape_string, 134, 136
mysql_select_db, 76
navigateToURL( ), 65–66, 281, 294
nextImage( ), 266
onResult, 207, 216
output_errors, 382

PHP, 49–50
phpinfo( ), 139
phpize, 417
populateFileList( ), 377
preg_replace( ), 278, 422
prevImage( ), 266
print, 383, 409
print_r( ), 383
removeChild, 324
removeChildAt, 150
require, 226, 424
response, 69, 143
saveCookie, 117
searchAndReplace, 206, 207
sendHandler, 102–103, 109
sendMessage, 102
sendMessageHandler, 247
sendRequest, 182
serverResponse, 70–72
set_time_limit, 156
setcookie, 115, 117
siteContainer movieclip, 352
socket_accept, 157
socket_create, 156
socket_listen, 173
socket_read, 157, 160
socket_select, 170
socket_write, 157, 173
source handler, 97
sprint( ), 331–332, 348, 425, 463
{START_FILE}, 336
startTimer, 148–149
statusMessage, 183
stopServer, 169
StoreItem movieclip, 305
strlen( ), 254
strpos, 130
substring, 183
table_name, 414
TextArea, 184
time( ), 116, 142, 252
timerHandler, 245
trigger_ error, 453
typeof, 132
ucwords, 202
unset( ), 257, 410
upperCaseWords, 205, 207
URLLoader, 275
URLRequest, 141, 265, 275, 322
varchar( ), 259

whichSandbox, 146
writeLine, 182
xmlHandler, 91
fwrite( ) function, 374

G

gallery.php file, 273
gateway property, 304
gateway url variable, 206
gateway variable, 478
gateway.php file, 198–199, 478
GD library
    gathering pixel data in Flash, 345–346
    generating image in, 343–345
    overview, 341–343
GET format, 317
GET request, 328, 343, 370, 374
$_GET['action'] variable, 273
getAlbumByGenreID method, 213
getCategories( ) function, 270, 438, 441, 444, 448–449, 451
getdate( ) function, 201, 206, 208, 425
getID method, 302
getInstance method, 224
getMessages.php file, 252
getPhotosFromID( ) function, 272
getPhotos.php file, 272
getproducts option, 307, 308
getsites value, 348
getters and setters
    defining methods, 459–461
    overview, 224–225
getTimer( ) function, 149, 249
getVideos method, 440, 450, 451
global variable, 283
globals, 105–106
gskinner, 192
GUI-enabled tools, 415
gzip function, 425

H

handleError method, 174
handler functions, 68–69, 87
handlers
    custom playback, 431
    event
        contact form, 103–105
        login module, 107–110
        sandbox, 149

495

H Index

handlers (continued)
  sockets, 162–163
  stage, 473
  mouse event, 337
  stage event, 473
`handleServerResp( )` function, 286
hardware, Apache, 412
`hash` method, 196
hashing algorithms, 111
`header( )` call, 273
`helloWorld` method, 227
`help` command, 172
helpers, debug, 399
hit counter applications, 285–286
.htaccess files, 37–39, 397
HTML data, 136
HTML tags, 247
`htmlentities( )` function, 136
httpd.conf files, 407, 413
HTTPS call, 293

I

`id` row, 259, 438
`id` variable, 368
`if` statements
  active sandbox, 148
  checking file existence, 226
  control structures, 51
  date values, 425
  developing ActionScript, 360
  developing poll application, 366
  file editor, 373
  interfacing with Web service, 331
  logical order of data, 137
  PHP cookies, 123
  `ShoppingCartItem` class, 303
  valid rows, 444
  validating ZIP codes, 132
`if/else` statements, 409
image loader, 96–97
Image tag, 247
`imagecreatetruecolor( )` function, 343
`imageDir` variable, 261
`imagejpeg( )` function, 343
`imageLoaded` function, 264–265, 280
ImageMagick library, 193

images
  generating in GD library, 343–345
  navigating in photo gallery applications, 266–270
`imagesetpixel` function, 344
`import` function, 229
importing
  classes
    in Flash, 229
    in PHP, 226
    RSS reader applications, 275
  OOP, 222
`include` function, 226, 424
`include` statement, 55
`include_once( )` statement, 56
`$incomingData` variable, 157
info.php file, 382
ini path, 382
`init( )` function
  developing ActionScript, 261
  Flash, 244
  managing messages, 247
  opening browser windows, 281
  photo gallery navigation, 267
  running applications in local sandbox, 148
  unloading applications, 150
initialization variables, 97, 244, 336
`initLoop` function, 169, 172
inline comments, 396
InnoDB storage engines, 16–18
input box, 130
`INSERT` statements, 57–58, 255, 306, 434
Install Apache HTTP Server 2.0 programs and shortcuts for: option, 6
installing
  AMFPHP, 198–199
  Apache
    UNIX, 9–12
    Windows, 4–9
  development systems, 406–408
  memcached, 416–420
  MySQL, 24–26
  MySQL library, 197–198
  PHP
    for UNIX, 33–34
    for Windows, 27, 31
  third-party libraries
    in Flash CS3, 194–195
    in PHP, 195
`instance` variable, 227
instantiation, class, 226–227

Index

I (cont.)

interacting, with users
    contact form, 101–106
    form development using Flash, 99–100
    login module in Flash, 106–111
interfacing, flickr photo galleries, 331
`IO_ERROR` function, 356
`IOError` event, 87
`is_numeric( )` function, 132
`isDrawing` variable, 337
`isset( )` method, 123
Italic tag, 247
`ITEM_CLICK` event, 259, 276, 457–458
`ItemAttributes` node, 320
`itemLength` variable, 72–73
Items node, 320

J

.`jpg` file extension, 128

L

`label` property, 275
`length` function, 132
`libevent` library, 416
`libjpeg` library, 407
libraries
    as3CoreLib, 192, 196
    custom, 403–404
    external, 192, 482
    GD
        gathering pixel data in Flash, 345–346
        generating image in, 343–345
        overview, 341–343
    ImageMagick, 193
    MySQL, 197–198
    PDF, 193
    Red5, 192
    `SimpleXML`, 278, 308, 320
    spell-check, 192
    third-party
        AMFPHP, 198–218
        commercial Flash, 192–193
        in Flash CS3, 194–196
        MySQL, 197–198
        overview, 191–192
        in PHP, 193, 195
Library classes, 230–231
line comments, 396
`$link` variable, 256, 441, 462
Linkage Identifier, 230

Linux, 416–420
List component, 275
List Item tag, 247
Listen directive, 13
listening, sockets, 154
`ListEvent` class, 275
`listItemHandler` method, 452–453, 464
`LiveHTTPHeaders`, 389
`loadbtn` method, 376
`loadCategories( )` function, 261–262
`loadData( )` method, 360
loaded data, 88–89
`loadedResultsHandler( )` method, 323
`loader` variables, 70
`loaderInfo` object, 151
`loadFeeds` function, 276
`loadFile` method, 376
`loadHitCounter( )` function, 286
`loadImage( )` function, 264, 280
loading
    cached data, 420
    cookies
        Flash, 118–122
        PHP, 114–118
    data
        in Flash, 85–87
        in PHP, 92–93
        XML in Flash, 89–92
    one-way, 88
    PHP, RSS reader applications, 275–279
    two-way, 88–89
loading processes, 88–89
`loadingMessages` variable, 248–249
`loadMessages( )` function, 244, 247
`loadMessagesHandler` function, 249
`loadPolicyFile` file, 164
`loadSites( )` method, 352
`loadThumb` method, 325, 330
`local` string, 148
`LocalConnection` class, 389
`localhost` domain, 176
`localhost` variable, 256
`local-trusted` sandbox, 145
`local-with-filesystem` sandbox, 145
`local-with-networking-sandbox` sandbox, 145
`loggedIn` variable, 109–110
`$loggedIn` variable, 477
logging
    optimizing Apache, 413
    slow MySQL queries, 414

497

Index

logic, hit counters, 285
login
    overview, 292
    user login component
        adding remoting, 478–481
        adding to player, 482–486
        `LoginWindow` class, 466–472
        overview, 465
        PHP login manager class, 476–478
        testing, 473–475
login component, 473
login manager class, 476–478
`login` method, 221, 477–478
login module
    Flash
        code skeleton, 106–107
        event handlers, 107–110
        server integration, 110–111
    form components, 106
`login` variable, 484
`LOGIN_ATTEMPT` event, 473
`loginBtn` method, 469
`loginHandler` function, 107–108, 469–472, 483
`loginMC MovieClip` function, 468
`loginRespHandler` method, 484
logins, 476
`LoginWindow` class
    centering `MovieClip`, 468
    `close` method, 468
    constructor, 466–467
    in Flash, 465
    `loginHandler` method, 469–472
    overview, 466
    `redraw` method, 467–468
    `resetHandler` method, 469
    swapping placement of `MovieClips`, 468
`LoginWindowMC` file, 482
loops. *See also individual loops by name*
    control structures, 52–54
    recursive, 160

M

`magic_quotes_gpc` property, 138–139
`mail( )` function, 349–350
mailing in PHP
    globals, 105–106
    security, 106

maintenance, application
    `ChangeLog`, 399–400
    commenting code, 395–399
    custom libraries, 403–404
    overview, 395
    version control, 401–403
make commands, 11
`makeCall( )` method, 233
manager class, 476–478
managing servers, 420–421
master client connections, 172–173
master connections, 154
master sockets, 154
`MAX_ATTEMPTS` constant, 356–357
`MaxClients` directive, 413
`MD5` class, 196
md5 function, 477
md5 hash, 141
`Member` class, 222
memcached system
    installing, 416–420
    managing servers, 420–421
    overview, 416
message buffer, 171
message node, 248
message row, 259
messages.php file, 252, 254–255
`messagesTxt`, 243
`messagesTxt TextArea` event, 246
method tables, 201, 204, 212
methods. *See also individual methods by name*
    accessibility, 169
    defined, 50
    static, 223
mixing comments, 397–398
moderation script, 260
`monitor.php` file, 348, 350
mouse event handlers, 337
mouse handler methods, 431, 458
mouse up event, 337
`MovieClip` class
    centering, 468
    `Document` class, 230
    login component, 465–466
    `StoreItem` class, 296
    swapping placement of, 468
    video player, 447
    `VideoListItem` class, 456

Index — N

`movieclip` function, 323, 339
`msgTxt` box, 180
`msgTxt TextInput` function, 180
`mt_rand( )` function, 283
multiple application version maintenance, 401–403
multiple classes, PHP, 228
MXP file, 194
MyISAM storage engines, 16–17
`myPlayBtn`, 431
`myPlaycr`, 430
MySQL
    conditions
        `AND`, 58
        `OR`, 59
        `WHERE`, 58
    library, 197–198
    line comments, 396
    logging slow queries, 414
    optimizing, 413–415
    performance, 414
    PHP
        closing connections, 75–76
        connecting to, 74–75
        determining status of MySQL, 73–74
        persistent connections, 75
        selecting databases, 76
    poll applications, 364–368
    statements
        `DELETE` statement, 58
        `INSERT` statement, 57–58, 77
        `SELECT` statement, 57
    tables, 57
    UNIX Web server
        ownership command, 25
        passwords, 27
        testing, 26
    video player applications
        building tables in, 433–434
        user tables, 476
    website, 14
    Windows Web server
        Best Support for Multilingualism option, 20
        concurrent connections, 18–19
        configuration process, 22–23
        database server commands, 24
        Dedicated MySQL Server Machine option, 16
        Detailed Configuration option, 14–15
        Developer Machine option, 16
        downloading, 14
        Enable root access from remote machines option, 22
        Enable Strict Mode option, 19
        Enable TCP/IP option, 19
        free memory, 16
        Include Bin Directory in Windows PATH option, 21
        Manual Selected Default Character Set/Collection option, 20–21
        Manual Setting option, 19
        Multifunctional Database option, 16–17
        networking options, 19–20
        new command prompt, 23–24
        Non-Transactional Database Only option, 17
        OLTP option, 18
        passwords, 26
        security options, 22
        Server Machine option, 16
        Standard Character Set option, 20
        Standard Configuration option, 15
        testing, 23–24
        Transactional Database Only option, 17
        Typical install option, 14
`mysql library` file, 195
`mysql_close` function, 75–76, 409
`mysql_connect( )` function, 75, 256, 435
`mysql_fetch_array( )` function, 79, 253
`mysql_num_rows( )` function, 252, 442, 462
`mysql_pconnect` function, 75
`mysql_query( )` function, 252, 254, 444
`mysql_query( )` method, 213
`mysql_real_escape_string` function, 134, 136
`mysql_select_db` function, 76
`myStopBtn`, 431

N

`navigateToURL( )` function, 65–66, 281, 294
navigation, photo gallery, 266–270
`net.*` package, 447
`NetConnection` class, 205, 206, 448, 463
`$newCount` variable, 285
`newMsgTxt` instance, 243
`nextImage( )` function, 266
`nextY` variable, 451–452
node values, 92–93
`nodeCount` variable, 320
`noResponse( )` method, 356
`notifyClients` method, 174
numeric values, zip codes, 132

Index

O

`Object` type, 297
`Object` variable, 72
object-oriented programming (OOP)
    classes
        building custom, 231–235
        defined, 220–221
        in Flash, 229–231
        in PHP, 225–228
    constructor, 221
    getters and setters, 224–225
    importing, 222
    overview, 219–220
    packages, 221–222
    singletons, 223–224
    static methods and properties, 223
objects, defined, 48–49. *See also individual objects by name*
`Oldfilename.php` file, 421
Omit Trace Actions, 399
one-way communication, 65–67
one-way loading, 88
`onFault` method, 207, 463
`onResult` function, 207, 216
OOP (object-oriented programming)
    classes
        building custom, 231–235
        defined, 220–221
        in Flash, 229–231
        in PHP, 225–228
    constructor, 221
    getters and setters, 224–225
    importing, 222
    overview, 219–220
    packages, 221–222
    singletons, 223–224
    static methods and properties, 223
operation parameters, 319
optimizing
    Apache, 412–413
    MySQL, 413–415
    PHP, 408–412
OR condition, 59
output buffer, 409
`output_errors` function, 382

P

Paamayim Nekudotayim, 227
packages
    crypto, 196
    custom libraries, 403
    overview, 221–222
    standard class, 194–195
Papervision3D, 192
Paragraph tag, 247
parameters
    connection, 213
    exit, 175
    operation, 319
    search, 320
    special chat, 171–172
`parent` reference, 302
passed-in data, 133, 210
password-creation command, 38–39
passwords
    PayPal, 292
    setting on UNIX, 27
    setting on Windows, 26
    storing using PHP, 141–142
PayPal cart applications
    overview, 290–291
    `POST` data, 293–294
    `sendToURL` method, 294
    setting up communication, 294–295
    signing up for PayPal Premier, 291–293
PDF Library, 193
Pear, 193
persistent connections, 75
persistent socket server, 160–161
`_person` property, 225
photo gallery application
    ActionScript, 261–266
    developing using flickr
        building custom XML document, 332–333
        interfacing with Web service, 331
        overview, 326–330
    `Document` class, 327–329
    navigation, 266–270
    overview, 260–261
    PHP for, 270–274
`PhotoItem` instance, 329

Index P

PHP
   AMFPHP
      and ActionScript 3, 198
      debug gateway, 200–201
      debugging tools, 199
      installing, 198
      service browser, 200
      testing installation, 199
   coding structure, 47, 122
   connecting to Flash, 71–73
   connecting to MySQL, 73–84
   control structures, 51–55
   cookies, 114–124
   determining status of, 64–65
   file location, 69
   functions, 49–50
   mailing, 105–106
   MySQL, 57–59
   shared object data, 140–141
   sockets, 155–161
   storing passwords, 141–142
   third-party libraries, 193, 197–198
   type checking, 56–57
   variables, 47–49, 56
   on Web servers, 27–35
   website, 93
   XML data, 92–95
php files, 176, 304, 410
php reference, 275
PHP socket server
   for chat clients, 168–171
   ending connections, 175
   excluding master server from communication, 171
   handling errors, 174–175
   master client connection, 172–173
   notifying all clients, 174
   notifying specific client, 173–174
   server monitoring, 175
   special chat parameters, 171–172
PHP User class, 478
PHPEclipse, 385
phpFile variable, 286
phpinfo file, 73–74, 197
phpinfo( ) function, 139
php.ini file, 129, 195, 197, 381, 384, 407, 426
phpize function, 417
pipe (|) character, 426
pixel data, for GD library, 345–346

planning stage, applications, 240–242
play method, 431
playback controls, 432
playback handlers, custom, 431
policy file, 164
poll applications
   building PHP and MySQL, 364–368
   developing ActionScript, 368–372
   overview, 364
PollItem class, 368, 483
PollItem instances, 370
pollItem variable, 370
pollItems array, 371
populateFileList( ) function, 377
port numbers, 156, 176
ports, 407
POST data, 67–68, 122, 292–294, 343
prebuilt video skins, 432
predefined logins, 476
prefixes, 11
prefork module, 413
preg_replace( ) function, 278, 422
prevImage( ) function, 266
print function, 383, 409
print statement, 79
print_r( ) function, 383
private properties, 225
private variables, 296, 369, 437
processors, PHP, 409
programs, scalable, 219
progress bars, 7
properties. *See also individual properties by name*
   accessibility, 169
   overview, 47
   private, 225
   static, 223
Property inspector, 230, 432
protecting
   MySQL
      setting password on UNIX, 27
      setting password on Windows, 26
   Web server content, 38–39
pseudo-code, 240–241
public class, 220
Publish Settings dialog box, 195, 399, 404
publishing SWCs, 404
push method, 153

501

Index

Q
-q option, 176
queries
    MySQL, 414
    SQL, 133–135
Quick Start options, 342
$quote variable, 133

R
random access memory (RAM), 409
random selection, dynamic banner ads, 283–284
$rawXml variable, 320, 331
real-world applications. *See also* shopping cart applications
    Amazon search application
        overview, 317
        simplifying XML response, 319–326
        using Amazon Web Service, 317–319
    developing photo gallery using flickr
        building custom XML document, 332–333
        interfacing with Web service, 331
        overview, 326–332
    drawing application
        in Flash, 336–341
        overview, 335–336
    GD library
        gathering pixel data in Flash, 345–346
        generating image in, 343–345
        overview, 341–343
    overview, 289–290, 335
    PayPal cart
        overview, 290–291
        POST data, 293–294
        sendToURL method, 294
        setting up communication, 294–295
        signing up for PayPal Premier, 291–293
    poll application
        building PHP and MySQL, 364–368
        developing ActionScript, 368–372
        overview, 364
    simple file editor, 373–379
    site monitors
        developing ActionScript for, 351–359
        developing PHP for, 347–349
        overview, 347
        using PHP to e-mail administrator, 349–351
    video player
        developing ActionScript, 360–364
        overview, 359–360
records, valid, 462–463

RecordSet class, 214
recordset method, 449
recursive loops, 160
Red5 library, 192
redraw method, 467–468, 473–474
remote socket connections, 163–164
remoting
    classes, 205–210
    errors in responses, 453–456
    video player integration
        DatabaseConnector class, 437–439
        overview, 437
        testing classes, 445–446
        Videos class, 439–445
    video player user login component, 478–481
remove method, 303
removeAll method, 216
removeChild function, 324
removeChildAt function, 150
removeOldPhotos method, 329
removeProduct button, 301
removing comments, 399
repeating code, 49–50
reporting, error, 381–385
Representational State Transfer (REST), 317
require function, 226, 424
require statement, 54–55
require_once statement, 55
resetHandler method, 469
resize event, 474
resp property, 286
resp variable, 123–124
respond( ) method, 232
Responder class, 206, 463, 479
Responder instance, 448–449, 451
response function, 69, 143
$response variable, 157
responseTxt TextInput component, 196
REST (Representational State Transfer), 317
$result variable, 252, 477
Results tab, 202
reverse domain package path, 221
Rich Internet Applications (RIA), 62
root passwords, 22
$row data, 348
$rows variable, 253, 444
RSS reader applications
    importing classes, 275
    loading PHP, 275–279
    overview, 274–275
Run dialog box, 155

Index S

S

sandboxType property, 145–147
save action, 373
saveCookie function, 117
saving data to caches, 418–419
scalable applications, 219, 242
Scope Resolution Operator, 227
SCPlugin version control manager, 402
ScrollPane component, 451–452, 461
search parameters, 320
SEARCH_TERMS keyword, 318
searchAndReplace function, 206, 207
searchHandler( ) method, 322, 327
sec variable, 150
security
    connecting PHP to MySQL, 256
    Flash Security Sandbox
        active, 147–151
        applications, 151–152
        sandboxType property, 145–147
        setting type, 145
    mailing in PHP, 106
    returning data, 143–144
    sockets, 154
    storing data
        passwords, using PHP, 141–142
        securely writing to file, 137–141
    user data
        file uploads, 128–130
        HTML data, 136
        sanitizing, 133–135
        valid input, 131–132
    Windows Web server, 22
Security class, 145
security trust, 164
Security.sandboxType property, 145
SELECT statement, 57, 366
selectedCatID property, 450
selectedItem object, 377
selectedItem property, 450
selection, random, 283–284
semicolon (;), 382
send( ) method, 247, 391
sendBtn instance name, 243
sendHandler function, 102–103, 109
sendMessage function, 102
sendMessageHandler function, 247
sendRequest function, 182
sendToURL method, 66, 294, 346
serverHandler( ) method, 234

serverMessage method, 174–175
serverResponse function, 70–72
servers
    caching with memcached
        installing, 416–420
        overview, 416
    development systems, 406–408
    handling backups
        backup management, 421–424
        file management, 421
        overview, 421
        using PHP to back up databases, 424–427
    integration, 110–111
    managing, 420–421
    optimizing
        Apache, 412–413
        MySQL, 413–415
        PHP, 408–412
    overview, 405
    running updated, 405–406
    socket
        building, 156–158
        responding to client connection, 157–158
        simple PHP-based socket server, 156–157
        testing, 158–160
    UNIX Web server
        Apache, 9–13
        installing PHP, 34–35
        MySQL, 24–26
        setting passwords on, 27
    Windows Web server
        Apache, 4–13
        installing memcached on, 418–420
        MySQL, 14–24
        PHP, 27–33
        setting passwords on, 26
service browser, 200, 205
/services directory, 202
set_time_limit function, 156
setcookie function, 115, 117
setGatewayURL method, 304
setItem method, 457–458
setters, and getters, 224–225, 459–461
setValues method, 325, 329
shared objects
    deleting, 119
    loading, 118
    remote settings, 122
    saving, 118–119
    securely writing to file, 139–141
SharedObject class, 118

503

Index

shopping cart applications
    building PHP
        overview, 306–309
        PHP code, 315–317
        `ShoppingCart` class, 304, 309–313
        `ShoppingCartItem` class, 298–306, 313
        `StoreItem` class, 313–314
        Timeline code, 314–315
    developing `ShoppingCartItem` class, 298–306
    developing `StoreItem` class, 296–298
    overview, 295–296
`ShoppingCart` class, 304, 309–313
`ShoppingCartItem` class, 298–306, 313
`SHOW_ERRORS` property, 174–175
Simple XML, 93
`SimpleSocket` class, 166–167
`SimpleXML` library, 278, 308, 320
`simplexml_load_string( )` method, 331
single quote ('), 133
singletons, 223–224
site monitors
    developing ActionScript for, 351–359
    developing PHP for, 347–349
    overview, 347
    using PHP to e-mail administrator, 349–351
`siteContainer` movieclip function, 352
`siteItem` variable, 354
`SiteMonitorItem` class, 353, 355, 357
`siteResponsedHandler( )` method, 356
`size` property, 119
skins, prebuilt video, 432
`$sock` variable, 156
`Socket` class, 162, 177
socket options, 173
socket termination method, 175
`$socket` variable, 156
`socket_accept` function, 157
`socket_create` function, 156
`socket_listen` function, 173
`socket_read` function, 157, 160
`socket_select` function, 170
`socket_write` function, 157, 173
sockets
    building Flash client
        checking text input length, 180–181
        clearing message input, 180
        event handler functions, 179
        handling status updates, 183–188

        maintaining stable interface, 181–182
        overview, 177–179
        sending initial request, 182
        sending messages to socket server, 182–183
        submit message handler, 180
        trapping key presses, 179–180
    connecting to socket server, 175–177
    connections, 154
    in Flash
        class for socket connections, 164–167
        event handlers, 162–163
        initializing socket connection, 161–162
        remote socket connections, 163–164
    implementing server, 154
    master, 154
    overview, 153
    in PHP
        building server, 156–158
        chat clients, 167–175
        CLI, 155–156
        overview, 154–156
        persistent socket server, 160–161
        testing server, 158–160
    security, 154
`$socketsChanged` variable, 169
source codes, 9–11
source files, 69
SourceForge Web site, 198
`sourceFunction` handler, 97
`Span` tag, 247
`Speak` class, 227
specialized file extensions, 38
spell-check library, 192
`sprint( )` function, 331–332, 348, 425, 463
`Sprite` class, 230
SQL queries, 133–135
`$sql` string, 213
`sqltest.php` file, 436
stage event handlers, 473
stage object, 473
standalone variables, 325
standard class package
    custom classpath, 194–195
    default classpaths, 195
`{START_FILE}` function, 336
`startDrawing( )` method, 337
`startTimer` function, 148–149
startup options, MySQL, 415

Index T

statements, 57–58. *See also individual statements by name*
static data, 85
static methods, 223
static properties, 223
`statusMessage` function, 183
`stopChecking( )` method, 356–357
`stopServer` function, 169
`storedFileData` variable, 376
`$storedPassword` variable, 111
`StoreItem` class, 296–298, 313–314
`StoreItem` method, 296
`StoreItem` movieclip function, 305
`str` variable, 183
`String` type, 297
`string` variable, 171
strings, 47, 141. *See also individual strings by name*
`strlen( )` function, 254
`strpos` function, 130
styles, for commenting code, 396–398
subdomains, 114
Submit button, 373
Submit component, 275
`substring` function, 183
SubVersion (SVN), 401
SWCs, 404
`switch` control, 54
`switch..case` statement, 179
`system( )` command, 426

T

`table_name` function, 414
tables
    checking MySQL, 414–415
    video player applications
        adding sample data to, 434–435
        building, 433–434
        user MySQL, 476
tag value, 331
`tags` variable, 328
teams, bug tracking with, 399–400
Telnet, 161
Test tab, 202
testing
    AMFPHP, with custom service, 201–205
    PHP, 31–33
    socket servers, 158–160
    UNIX Web server, 26
    video player applications

        databases, 435–437
        remoting integration classes, 445–446
        user login component, 473–475
    Windows Web server, 23–24
`test.php` file, 421
text files, loading, 85–86
`TextArea` component
    designing file editor, 373
    developing chat clients, 242
    loading remoting classes, 207
    messagesTxt, 243
    RSS readers, 275
`TextArea` function, 184
`TextBox` class, 230
`TextField` class, 233, 296, 298, 373
`TextField` instance, 263
`TextInput` component
    Flash, 242
    newMsgTxt instance, 243
    usernameTxt instance, 243
`$this` variable, 227
`$this->link` property, 438
`thumbnail` path argument, 330
`time( )` function, 116, 142, 252
timed backups, 421–422
Timeline ActionScript, 304
Timeline code, 314–315
`time_logged_in` cookie, 115
`TIMER` event, 244
timer handler, 244, 247
`Timer` object, 244
`timerHandler` function, 245
`timerTxt` textfield, 149
`title` argument, 330
title nodes, 320
`title` property, 458
`titleTxt` component, 330
tools
    debugging, AMFPHP, 199
    GUI-enabled, 415
    Zend Optimizer tool, 410–411
    Zend Studio tool, 411–412
TortoiseSVN version control manager, 402
trace alternatives, 389–391
`trace` statements, 82–84, 306, 386
tracking
    bug, 399–400
    video, 461–464

505

Index

trigger_error function, 453
trigger_error( ) method, 383, 440
true flag, 419
try..catch programming style, 182
two-way communication, 68–69
two-way loading, 88–89
txt variable, 263
type checking, 56–57
type variable, 370
typeof function, 132

U

ucwords function, 202
Underline tag, 247
UNIX Web server
    Apache
        installing, 9–12
        modifying, 13
    installing PHP, 34–35
    MySQL, 24–26
    setting passwords on, 27
unset( ) function, 257, 410
untarring files, 10
updated servers, 405–406
updateList method, 303
updateTotal method, 303
updateVideoTracking method, 463–464
uppercase method, 207
upperCaseWords function, 205, 207
url property, 151
URLLoader class, 86, 103–104, 124
URLLoader function, 275
URLRequest class, 86, 103
URLRequest function, 141, 265, 275, 322
urlRequest variable, 81
URLRequestMethod class, 67–68
URLVariables class, 67, 103, 123, 124, 286
URLVariables object, 246, 346
User class, 478
user data
    sanitizing
        HTML data, 136
        SQL queries, 133–135
    security
        file uploads, 128–130
        valid input, 131–132
user id, 139

user login component
    adding remoting, 478–481
    adding to player, 482–486
    LoginWindow class
        centering MovieClip, 468
        close method, 468
        constructor, 466–467
        loginHandler method, 469–472
        overview, 466
        redraw method, 467–468
        resetHandler method, 469
        swapping placement of MovieClips, 468
    overview, 465
    PHP login manager class, 476–478
    testing, 473–475
user MySQL tables, 476
UserCredentials class, 222
username row, 259
usernameTxt instance, 243
User.php class, 476, 478
users
    contact form, 101–106
    form development using Flash, 99–100

V

valid input
    checking for, 131–132
    ZIP codes, 132
valid records, 462–463
validation variable, 144
var_dump call, 341
varchar( ) function, 259
variables. *See also individual variables by name*
    ActionScript, 261
    debugging, 383
    PayPal, 293
    PHP
        arrays, 48
        booleans, 48
        objects, 48–49
        strings, 47
    and socket connections, 162
    and types, 225
version control
    overview, 401–403
    using custom libraries with, 403
Version Cue application, 401–402
vi command, 382

506

vi text editor, 12
video, 445
video class
    overview, 439–445
    updating, 462–463
video player applications
    advanced development
        categoryHandler method, 450
        categoryResponseHandler method, 449–450
        document class, 446–448
        getCategories method, 448–449
        getVideos method, 451
        handling errors in remoting responses, 453–456
        listItemHandler method, 452–453
        overview, 446
        VideoPlayer class, 448
        videosResponseHandler method, 451–452
    basic, 429–432
    building VideoListItem class
        defining getter and setter methods, 459–461
        mouse handler methods, 458
        overview, 456–457
        setItem method, 457–458
        VideoListItem constructor, 457
    finalizing
        adding login component, 482–486
        overview, 481
        using external library, 482
    getting started
        adding sample data to tables, 434–435
        building database and MySQL tables, 433–434
        overview, 432
        testing database, 435–437
    overview, 429
    remoting integration
        DatabaseConnector class, 437–439
        overview, 437
        testing classes, 445–446
        Videos class, 439–445
    user login component
        adding remoting, 478–481
        LoginWindow class, 465–473
        overview, 465
        PHP login manager class, 476–478
        testing, 473–475
    using Flash to develop
        developing ActionScript, 360–364
        overview, 359–360
    video tracking, 461–464

VideoListItem class
    constructor, 457
    defining getter and setter methods, 459–461
    mouse handler methods, 458
    overview, 456–457
    setItem method, 457–458
    videosResponseHandler method, 451–452
VideoListItem.as file, 456
videoMetaInfo MovieClip method, 453, 464
VideoPlayer class, 359–360, 446, 448, 453, 482
VideoPlayer.as file, 446
VideoPlayer.fla file, 482
Videos class, 441, 444
Videos.php file, 442, 463
videosResponseHandler method, 451–452
$vidSQL variable, 441
vote variable, 368

W

Web servers
    .htaccess files, 37–38
    adding Apache to, 4–13
        installing for UNIX, 9–12
        installing for Windows, 4–9
        modifying for Windows and UNIX, 13
    Apache
        determining modules installed, 40–42
        determining version, 40
        starting and stopping, 40
    custom error documents
        dynamic error documents, 43–46
        modifying Apache, 43
        overview, 42
    protecting content, 38–39
    setting up PHP on
        UNIX, 33–35
        Windows, 27–33
    UNIX
        Apache, 9–13
        installing PHP, 34–35
        MySQL, 24–26
        setting passwords on, 27
    Windows
        Apache, 4–13
        installing memcached on, 418–420
        MySQL, 14–24
        PHP, 27–33
        setting passwords on, 26

Index

Welcome Screens, 7–8
`WHERE` clause, 396
`WHERE` condition, 58
`whichSandbox` function, 146
`while` loop
    AMFPHP services, 213
    building PHP, 308
    building XML from database, 95
    chat properties, 170
    connecting PHP, 78–79
    overview, 52
    and persistent socket servers, 160
    photo gallery application, 272
    valid rows, 252, 444
window targets for links, 66
windows, browser, 281–282
Windows Options page, 20
Windows Web server
    Apache
        installing, 4–9
        modifying, 13
    installing memcached on, 418–420
    MySQL
        downloading, 14
        installation, 14–23
        testing, 23–24
    PHP
        installation, 27–31
        testing, 31–33
    setting passwords on, 26
`writeLine` function, 182

X

$x variable, 344
XML
    comments in, 397
    custom documents, flickr photo galleries, 332–333
    loading data in Flash, 89–92
    loading data in PHP
        Dom XML, 92–93
        Simple XML, 93
    sending data in PHP
        dynamic XML from database, 94–95
        printing dynamic XML, 93–94
    simplifying response in Amazon search applications, 319–326
`xml` attribute, 366
XML data, 301
`xml` document, 307
XML object, 328
`$xmlData` variable, 253
`xmlHandler` function, 91

Y

$y variable, 344

Z

Zend Optimizer tool, 410–411
Zend Platform toolkit, 406
Zend Studio tool, 385, 411–412
ZIP codes, 132